MW00804215

Sedum

CULTIVATED STONECROPS

Sedum

CULTIVATED STONECROPS

Ray Stephenson

Timber Press
Portland, Oregon

To all who have been fascinated by the humble stonecrop

Library of Congress Cataloging-in-Publication Data

Stephenson, Ray.
    Sedum : cultivated stonecrops / Ray Stephenson.
        p.   cm.
    Includes bibliographical references (p.   ) and index.
    ISBN 0-88192-238-2
    1. Sedum. I. Title.
SB413.S43S74 1994
635.9'3338—dc20   93-683
                                                                        CIP

Copyright © 1994 by Timber Press, Inc.
All rights reserved.

Reprinted 1999, 2002

Printed through Colorcraft Ltd, Hong Kong

TIMBER PRESS, Inc.
The Haseltine Building
133 S.W. Second Avenue, Suite 450
Portland, Oregon 97204-3527, U.S.A.

Contents

Foreword, 9

Preface, 11

Special Thanks To, 13

PART ONE

Chapter 1   Uses of Stonecrops, 17
    Rock Gardens, Raised Beds, and Scree Gardens, 17
    Ground Cover, Beds, and Borders, 20
    Pots, Tubs, and Containers, 21
    Courtyards and City Gardens, 24
    House Plants and Hanging Baskets, 24
    Other Uses of Stonecrops, 25
    Historical Uses, 25

Chapter 2   Growing Stonecrops, 27
    Temperatures, 27
    Water, 30
    Composts, 31
    Propagation, 32
    Pests, 34

Chapter 3   Morphology and Distribution, 38
    Sepals, 38
    Petals, 39
    Stamens, 40
    Carpels, 41

Nectaries, 41

Pedicels, 42

Inflorescences, 42

Stems, 44

Leaves, 45

Roots, 48

Cytology, 48

Distribution, 52

Chapter 4   Crassulaceae, 55

Characteristics, 55

Subfamilies and Genera, 56

Problems of Status, 74

Natural Groups of Stonecrops, 77

PART TWO

How to Use Part Two, 87

Chapter 5   European Species of Subgenus *Sedum*, 92

Yellow-flowered Kyphocarpic Species, 93

Kyphocarpic Species Without Yellow Flowers, 103

Yellow-flowered Orthocarpic Species, 115

Orthocarpic Species Without Yellow Flowers, 124

Chapter 6   Far Eastern Species of Subgenus *Sedum*, 146

Aizoon Group, 146

Species with Fibrous Roots, 157

Chapter 7   Eurasian Oddities of Subgenus *Sedum*
              and Related *Rosularia*, 174

Meterostachys Group, 174

Mucizonia Group, 175

Orostachys Group, 176

Prometheum Group, 183

Pseudosedum Group, 184

Sinocrassula Group, 184

Rosularia Species, 186

Chapter 8   African Species of Subgenus *Sedum*, 188
    Macronesian Island Species, 189
    Mainland Species, 192

Chapter 9   North American Species of Subgenus *Sedum*, 194

Chapter 10   Latin American Species of Subgenus *Sedum*, 213
    Pachysedum Group, 213
    Mexican Woody Species, 233
    Mexican Nonwoody Species, 244
    South American Species, 264

Chapter 11   Subgenus *Hylotelephium*, 266
    Hylotelephium Group, 267
    Sieboldii Group, 279
    Populisedum Group, 281

Chapter 12   Subgenus *Rhodiola*, 288
    Rhodiola Group, 289
    Chamaerhodiola Group, 295
    Clementsia Group, 297
    Crassipedes Group, 298
    Primuloida Group, 299
    Hobsonia Group, 301

Appendix 1   *Sedum* Species Not in Cultivation, 303
Appendix 2   Select Lists of Sedums, 307
Appendix 3   I.S.I. Distributions, 310
Appendix 4   Useful Addresses, 312
Glossary, 314
Bibliography, 320
Index, 326

Color plates follow page 224

Foreword

This is another book in the steady flow of authoritative works being produced by British National Plant Collection Holders; it has been said that in
time each Collection Holder will become the recognized expert on a genus,
and this is now being realized.

This book attempts to bring up-to-date, as much as is possible, the
present trends in the nomenclature of *Sedum*, a very complex genus, and
builds on the works of Ron Evans (1983), Harald Fröderström (1930), and
Lloyd Praeger (1921). It is inevitable that people will debate forever the
validity of plant names in the present volume. More than anything Ray
Stephenson is putting pen to paper and having the courage of his convic-
tions.

This volume gives us an insight into the wealth of plants that have been
introduced into cultivation from various parts of the world and the influence that growers and enthusiasts have had in selecting forms for gardens.
The plant names and descriptions are adequately supplemented by a large
number of color plates and black-and-white illustrations, which will be
very useful to the reader.

To help the reader, should he or she become infatuated with the stonecrops, this book provides adequate information on the cultivation of the
plants and Ray, who at the last count had more than 800 different stonecrops, is the right man to tell us how to grow them. A National Collection
Holder, Ray Stephenson is also chairman of the specialist Sedum Society.
Readers are bound to be infected by his enthusiasm, which is evidenced by
his immense fund of knowledge and expertise.

G. A. Pattison DIPL. HORT. KEW, M.I. HORT.
Council for the Conservation of Plants and Gardens
The Pines, Wisley Garden
Woking, Surrey, England

Preface

I acquired my first sedum as a small child and have been fascinated by succulent plants ever since. In more recent years, the seemingly infinite variety of stonecrops has captivated my interest and given me immeasurable pleasure. I have spent many hours poring over Latin descriptions in esoteric publications, trying to verify plants, wishing for an easier, more reliable way to ensure that the plants in my collection are correctly identified. Ron Evans's publication, titled *Handbook of Cultivated Sedums* (1983), and the lengthy discussions I held with him, converted me into a real sedophile.

Formal descriptions and photographs of dried, pressed herbarium specimens are no substitute for a realistic image of a growing plant. I have always felt that photographs are the best aid to identification. I liken the situation to reading descriptions of the faces of 600 people, and then, from a few brief jottings, attempting to identify each person in turn. The ginger-bearded people, for instance, would certainly be easily separated from the main group, but differentiating the dozen or so in this group would be difficult—especially if only 2 of the 12 ginger-bearded people were present. Often gardeners have several similar-looking specimens and are unsure whether they have several forms of one species, or several similar-looking, distantly related plants. If gardeners are interested enough to inquire, they may be lucky to find relevant literature. If no drawings or photographs depicting the plants in question can be located, the text may leave much to be desired.

Much of a plant's formal description repeats features common to all close relatives, so it is often difficult and frustrating for enthusiasts to pinpoint the important features that distinguish a species. Good formal descriptions often conclude by pointing out differences between the plant in question and closely related species. Unfortunately, the lonely *Sedum* collector may have only a single plant and nothing to compare. It would be pointless to tell someone that Charolais are taller than Dexters if that person has never seen a Dexter or does not even realize that a Dexter is a breed of cattle. Yet a photograph of two animals side-by-side, properly captioned, would say all that was necessary to clarify the distinction. Lloyd Praeger (1921, 1) wrote,

> It is doubtful if any genus of plants which is widely cultivated is in such a confused state in our gardens and horticultural books as is the genus *Sedum*. Some of the species, it is true, are variable and in some of their forms not at once recognizable by the uninitiated but the majority are stable and distinct plants recognizable at a glance.

Praeger's great work, *Account of the Genus* Sedum *as Found in Cultivation* (1921), is a monument to his talent and enthusiasm. It is unfortunately almost impossible to acquire, even through the library services.

Ronald Lewis Evans in 1983 tried to update Praeger's work. I have a copy of Evans's *Handbook of Cultivated Sedums*, which has worn out through constant use. Unfortunately, this book, too, is now out of print. I had considered trying to update Evans's fine work, but so much research has been carried out in the 1980s, I was persuaded this would be like trying to uncook and remix an already delicious cake.

Since Praeger's time, the standard of labeling has improved only slightly, so the aim of the present book is to bridge the gap between scientific descriptions scattered in countless esoteric journals and available only in specialist libraries, and the general garden encyclopedia. Such encyclopedias often fleetingly mention an odd stonecrop and occasionally wrongly identify species, perpetuating mythical names and confusion. Most general nurseries use incorrect names for *Sedum* species, and even well-meaning nursery operators do so, pointing out that no reference book is available to help them differentiate their stonecrops. The present publication should help to overcome most difficulties heretofore encountered by the serious *Sedum* enthusiast or conscientious nursery manager. This is my earnest hope. As new species are steadily entering cultivation, a book reviewing a plant genus can never be definitive, yet within, I have aimed to make the identification of over 400 stonecrops in cultivation as reliable as possible.

I hope that the reader will gain a great deal of pleasure from merely browsing through the pages of this volume, and that the information therein will prove invaluable as a guide to positively verify plants already familiar to the reader, to identify unknown species, to define the acceptable variation within a particular species, to select the appropriate species for a particular location, and to successfully cultivate sedums.

Special Thanks To

Steve Almand, Francesco Baldi, Willy Bellotte, Yves Bernard, John Briscoe, Jenny Burgess, Arthur Byrne, Dick Cavender, Micki Crozier, Joyce Descloux, Mavis Doyle O.B.E., J. Dupin, Rene Echard, Pascal Femenia, Joyce Hoekstra, Pearl Holland, David Jackson, Rob Larkin, Henri Lieutier, James Low, Eric Marsh, Rachel Marsh-Sachs, Jean Metzger, Roy Mottram, Yuichiro and Keiko Ochi, Václav Pleštil, Keith Powell, Helmut Regnat, Gordon Rowley, Sarah Sage, Ed Skrocki, Lawrie Springate, James Totty, Val and Jim Tuton, Daan Vergunst, Colin Walker, Molly Walker, Paul Whicher, C. H. Winton, Ben Zonneveld, and all those who shared their plants with me over the many years. Without Ron Evans sparking the latent fervor, or the publication of scientific works by real experts—Charles Uhl and Henk 't Hart, in particular—such a volume would not have been possible.

Most thanks must go to my wife, Joyce, who has not only encouraged me throughout, but has been neglected for more than four years in the book's preparation, and been driven thousands of miles for many years in the hopes of photographing *Sedum* species in habitat.

Part One

CHAPTER 1

Uses of Stonecrops

The genus *Sedum* is much neglected by general gardening books but always popular with gardeners who realize plants do not have to be ostentatious, expensive, or difficult to grow to be charming. For very little capital outlay, the gardener acquires a tremendous return from a meager investment. Few gardens have no stonecrops, and few alpine specialists deny the versatility of the genus.

ROCK GARDENS, RAISED BEDS, AND SCREE GARDENS

Gardeners have always realized that the humble stonecrops are attractive and useful plants for rock gardens, raised beds, and scree gardens. Because of their succulent nature, sedums are renowned for their ability to grow in the driest part of the garden, coping with summer drought when less drought-resistant plants are drooping. Because stonecrops are cosmopolitan plants, choosing the most suitable species for a site is very important. Wrong selections of stonecrops have given the genus a bad name. Some species, for example, make ideal rapid and colorful ground-cover plants, but they grow too rapidly to be introduced into a rock garden, raised bed, or scree. A species originating in areas of barren soil, little nutriment, and little warmth could find a rock garden with rich pockets of soil, ample rain, and pleasant sunshine nothing short of paradise. These less extreme conditions often mean species become abnormally fast growing. They quickly smother neighboring plants as if in a race to occupy much of the bed or garden.

There are literally hundreds of choice sedums that would enhance a rock garden, raised bed, or scree. The carpet or mound of tightly packed, succulent leaves can be a focal point throughout the year, and flowers are often produced in such profusion that pockets of long-lasting color add interest to a garden feature over the full growing season. Planned carefully, a rock garden, raised bed, or scree could have *Sedum* species in flower from March to November. Few sedums flower in early spring; many flower in summer; but they are often most useful to gardeners who want color at the end of the year. Very late flowering species produce masses of color in October, when most other genera are spent, and an Indian summer often means stonecrops can still be in flower in November. Nectar-feeding insects find the late flowerers addictive. In addition to attracting beautiful butterflies, sedums attract hoverflies, which are very beneficial as they feed on aphids trying to find a spot to overwinter. Hoverflies cannot resist flat umbels, which are produced in profusion by many of the autumn-flowering stonecrops. Just about every foliage color and texture can be found in *Sedum*, and, although flower colors of white, pink, purple, and yellow predominate, blue, cream, orange, and green can be acquired.

Stonecrops are found in most professionally designed rock gardens, as garden designers try more than ever to introduce different levels to contour an area. Lots of books describe the construction of a rock garden, so I do not intend to be repetitious, but in the many years I have grown *Sedum*, I have accumulated a number of tips and ideas that I would like to pass on.

A very simple way of adding a feature to a garden incorporates both a rock garden and a scree garden with a minimum of effort (Fig. 1.1).

1. Arrange earth in the shape of a cuesta (escarpment) with a scarp face and a less steep dip slope. The orientation of the feature needs a great deal of thought: a north-facing scarp face provides a cozy niche for shade-loving, high-latitude or high-altitude species, and a south-facing dip slope would be particularly sunny and therefore ideal for low-latitude species. (Southern Hemisphere readers need to reverse these directions.) An east-west alignment provides two environments for species of different forms.

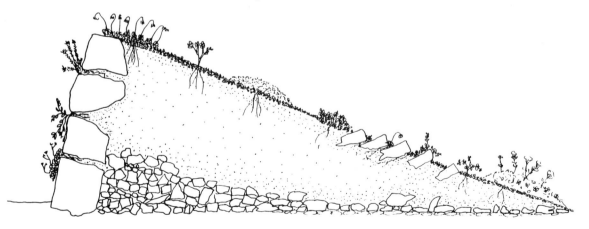

Figure 1.1. A scree-covered cuesta is ideal for displaying sedums and can be incorporated in any garden with a minimum of effort.

2. Bank the scarp face with natural stone or any type of building block, leaving narrow gaps where plants can gain a foothold.
3. Cover the dip slope with angular scree. Avoid pea gravel or river-washed gravel as they are too round and will retain water.
4. Plant with stonecrops.

Raised beds in tiers give height to an otherwise flat garden, and *Sedum* species are perfect occupants of such for two reasons: uplifted beds drain quickly, an important factor in growing stonecrops, and the full beauty of low-growing plants can be best appreciated if the plants are elevated towards the eyes. Thus to create height in a garden and at the same time improve drainage, raised beds are the answer. Raised beds also save a lot of stooping; carefully planned, they can be a boon to elderly or disabled gardeners.

There are many ways to construct a raised bed. Any building material could be used to construct a retaining wall. Treated wooden palings stapled to wire are an inexpensive method of containing a terrace. To ensure good drainage, use rubble for the foundation and sharp gravel for a top dressing. Try to give the bed at least a slight slope to avoid wet pockets.

Sedums are ideal plants for the busy person who would like to transform a piece of land into an attractive landscape feature with a minimum of effort and very low maintenance requirements. One way to do this is to plant a scree garden. A scree garden is an area of gravel or pebbles on which creeping plants grow. The idea behind covering the slope with rock fragments is to allow only a particular kind of alpine plant to grow and at the same time to deter indigenous annual weeds from gaining a foothold. The gravel cuts down on the amount of time needed to maintain an area. Scree gardens are easy to make and once constructed require hardly any maintenance. In fact, the scree garden could be called the one-hour-a-year scree garden.

1. Remove the largest weeds from an area of land and cover the ground with black polyethylene film or a similar material. Lack of light will kill the most troublesome weeds. I once covered a lawn in this way and waited six months to be sure that all the grass was dead.
2. Cover the film with stones to hold it down until gravel can be obtained. Larger stones placed naturally on this artificial scree will add a little interest until it is time to plant, and retaining a group of rocks as a permanent feature is advisable. I choose drab, dark gray whinstone (dolerite) gravel because it is cheap in my area and I prefer a neutral background. It is merely a matter of taste, however; others prefer a pleasant pink granite or dark red andesite. Keep in

mind that light marble chips or white quartz may detract attention
from the plants.

3. If the scree is level, dig a small ditch around it to aid drainage and
   to act as a moat. Make sure the scree is not dish-shaped, as water
   will collect in it, and this is the opposite of what is intended.

4. Plant narrow conifers beyond the moat, choosing trees that will not
   outgrow their welcome. These trees must not overhang the scree, as
   dripping water could damage plants. The soil in my area is heavy
   boulder-clay, so I use tall, narrow conifers to lift water year-round.
   In drier areas it may not be necessary to include conifers in the plan.

5. When all unwanted growth under the polyethylene film is dead, it
   is time to plant. If you do not hurry this stage, life will be much easier later. Dig small holes here and there through the scree and polyethylene film with a sharp trowel. Try not to tear a big hole in the
   plastic film, otherwise weeds may get a foothold below it. Each
   hole should be big enough to take a small pot with an overflowing
   Sedum. Propagations may be removed from their pots prior to
   planting.

6. Select plants carefully. Slow-growing sedums, which take years to
   cover the scree area, are desirable as rampant species get out of control. Do not choose *Sedum album*, *S. spurium*, or other rapid-spread-
   ing species that will smother choicer plants. Include some ever-
   greens for year-round color and both spring-blooming as well as fall-
   blooming plants.

7. Rake the scree twice in summer to obliterate any annual weeds that
   root in the gravel. Otherwise this garden requires no attention, can
   give you tremendous pleasure, and will receive many admiring
   looks.

GROUND COVER, BEDS, AND BORDERS

The maintenance of grass lawns can be very time consuming. A few weeds
or bare patches in a lawn can spoil the overall effect, and, if a grass lawn is
unattended for several weeks, it can soon acquire a neglected appearance.
In dry spells, lawns suffer unless irrigated, but continuous use of irrigation
is expensive, can be considered antisocial, and in some areas is illegal. Beds
of *Sedum* species are less demanding than grass lawns as they never need
mowing. Dense growth tends to smother potential weeds, and dry summers
actually enhance the beauty of such a bed, as underwatering emphasizes
the rich hues of the succulent leaves. On the other hand, a bed of stonecrops is no substitute for a playing field; ball games would ruin the plants,
but paving stones sensibly placed to form paths and islands would mean

that the area could be utilized. A bed of stonecrops can be a place of beauty without being too demanding.

Low-growing, quickly spreading, colorful *Sedum* species are plentiful and can be highly contrasting. Some gardeners prefer to use only one species of *Sedum*, as intermingled stonecrops may not portray the uniformity intended. Paving, however, can act as a division between species and create areas in which contrasting stonecrops can be kept in separate beds. Elizabethan herb gardens were geometrically divided by a pattern of pathways, and each shape created by the network was used to grow a single herb. Modern variations on this theme tend to dispense with the labor-intensive box hedging, which was used to edge pathways and growing areas in an Elizabethan garden, and instead use creative paving of different colors, patterns, and textures to divide an area into beds. Into each of these beds, low-spreading species of high contrast can be cultivated with dazzling effect.

Herbaceous stonecrops are rather old-fashioned cottage garden plants. The tallest *Sedum* species grow to about a meter (just over a yard) in height and spread about the same distance. In a world where horticulturists compete to produce new, bigger, better, more colorful varieties, more gardeners are realizing that traditional varieties have a subtlety often missing in modern cultivars. In addition, traditional forms tend to be more hardy, more disease resistant, less attractive to pests, and they require less fuss. Tall, herbaceous *Sedum* species look magnificent in a mixed border. Deep purple Foliage can appear almost black. More commonly, glaucous-blue hues are a fundamental ingredient of formal parks and gardens. *Sedum* species exist in all hues from light green to red to almost black. They also are available in sizes from a meter tall to ground-hugging, mossy species. Throughout the descriptions which follow in this volume, I have indicated those herbs that are suitable for the back or front of a border.

In addition to the species of *Sedum*, several worthwhile cultivars and hybrids are highly attractive in borders. Again, it is the late flowerers that deserve special mention. Large umbels of white, pink, and purple are most useful in a garden in late autumn when many other herbs are very much past their best.

POTS, TUBS, AND CONTAINERS

Since the Second World War in particular, interest in cultivating tropical succulents in temperate areas has developed rapidly. Few succulent collections have no cacti or no *Sedum* species. Lovers of succulent plants value the wide range of forms of Mexican stonecrops in particular. Many of these species are easy to cultivate and require little attention once they have been placed in a container. As tropical plants, they need greenhouse cultivation in winter months, but actually grow much better outdoors in summer. They are often grown throughout the year in greenhouses, but subtle foliage shades and compact, authentic growth are more likely to be achieved from natural action of the elements.

A few tropical *Sedum* species are a real challenge to cultivate successfully. Often succulent specialists are only interested in growing plants that demonstrate the specialist's expertise. Species considered easy to cultivate are discarded in favor of those that set a challenge. I have grown cacti and succulents for as long as I remember, and several *Sedum* species have proved far more difficult to grow successfully than succulents of other families.

Alpine stonecrops, too, need special horticulture and are usually grown in containers. Specialists keep specimens in an alpine house, which is usually unheated in winter. Rain is kept from specimens, as the drying effect of lowland winds is not as efficient as that of high mountain areas where humidity is very low. Alpines are generally watered very carefully and perhaps not at all during long cold periods. Because alpines must be kept cool in summer, they are best cultivated in pots, which can be moved easily to a more favorable site whenever necessary. Without an alpine house or greenhouse, it is still possible to grow alpine stonecrops with great success. Much pleasure can be achieved from these delightful plants by utilizing pots, tubs, and containers.

Never plant stonecrops in containers without adequate drainage holes. If the container is more than 30 cm (12 in) deep, allow air to pass underneath it (Fig. 1.2a); set it on bricks or stones to allow the drainage holes to function efficiently. It is best to fill the bottom third of a deep container with rubble and to use a top dressing of coarse grit. Sharp grit aids drainage near the surface and prevents plants from rotting in wet weather. Taller species should be placed near the back of a container. Around the edge, plant species likely to hang over and, if possible, place rocks in the container to create a miniature alpine scene.

Miniature stonecrops, in particular, look their best when grown in containers. In England it has become very fashionable to grow them in stone troughs in which farm animals once fed, but old glazed sinks and mock stone containers are much cheaper and just as effective. I prefer natural stone sinks or troughs, although they are expensive, heavy, and difficult to make. Imitation stone troughs are very easy and fun to make (Plate 1). Mix one part cement, two parts sand, and three parts peat with a little water. Mold the stiff, mudlike mixture around a suitable shape. A wooden fruit box is ideal for this purpose as it can remain as the skeleton of the structure. The mixture can also be molded around plastic bowls or shaped into large boulders in which ready-made pockets can be formed for planting sedums. Allow the wet mixture to dry at least one full week before moving it. When dry, the material is relatively light, porous, and fairly frost-proof. If the finished container is too cement-colored, paint it with liquid manure or milk to encourage bacteria and moss to grow on it, making the trough more natural-looking. Finished examples are almost impossible to distinguish from the real thing.

The most effective way of planting a stone trough or similar vessel is to recreate a miniature alpine scene with the help of rocks (Fig. 1.2b). *Sedum* species cluster and form compact pillows of succulent vegetation, which tumble over a container's edges breaking up the straight lines of the container and making it look more natural. Half barrels, window boxes, and plastic bowls can be used in the same way. Wooden containers allow plants to grow through the walls (e.g., through a knot in the wood), which adds to the interest and breaks up the starkness of the container (Fig. 1.2c). Additional perforations may be planted with decumbent species.

Terra-cotta parsley pots or strawberry towers are perforated cylindrical containers that can be planted to good effect (Fig. 1.2d). They are ideal to display stonecrops, but may not withstand frosts unless they have a salt glaze. Victorian chimney pots often have useful perforations and are becoming highly prized containers for growing stonecrops; they are inter-

Figure 1.2 Stonecrops are suitable for all types of containers: (a) a deep container partly filled with rubble and set on stones or bricks to improve drainage; (b) a sink covered with colored concrete; (c) a half barrel; (d) a perforated terra-cotta tower pot; and e) an ornate Victorian chimney.

esting garden features even before they have been planted (Fig. 1.2e). Old wheelbarrows, carts, and archaic farm equipment are all acceptable hosts for the humble stonecrops. In general, shallow containers are better for *Sedum* species as the plants have a better chance of drying out more quickly.

Stonecrops make excellent companion plants for potted shrubs (Plate 1). Even rapid-growing species can be suitably contained in this way. There are literally hundreds of hardy evergreen *Sedum* species that would enhance the look of any container.

COURTYARDS AND CITY GARDENS

As most *Sedum* species are perfectly happy in containers, they are ideal plants for those individuals who have tiny gardens, roof gardens, or no garden at all. Planted between paving slabs or cobblestones, sedums can transform a drab area into a warmer, friendlier environment. Within this volume I make special note of stonecrops particularly adept at growing on walls, on a roof, or in a spot where there is little or no soil. Once containers have been selected, species can be chosen that are tolerant of shade, or of hot, baking, sunny conditions, or of infrequent watering. Fortunately, most sedums are highly tolerant of neglect.

For those who work away from home and dread the thought of returning to an overgrown garden, or for those who take frequent vacations, stonecrops could be the answer. If sedums are contained in pots, they could literally be left unattended for years without any ill effect. Indeed, the only change would be for the better as the plants mature. The appearance of a patio can be transformed by using planted containers, and maintenance is minimal. Wall-mounted planters need to be watered frequently if planted with mesophitic (thin-leaved) plants, but those planted with xerophitic, succulent plants need little fuss. Bracketed onto walls, these containers can be made of redwood, ceramic, or plastic. Window boxes, too, are ideal for courtyards and city gardens.

HOUSE PLANTS AND HANGING BASKETS

Many sedums make excellent house plants for the windowsill, indoor rock garden, porch, or conservatory. Mexican species are excellent for this purpose as they relish high temperatures in summer and withstand low winter temperatures, as long as they are kept dry. Some *Sedum* species enjoy cooler north-facing windowsills, but few would be happy in dull rooms away from a good light source. With artificial lighting, it is possible, especially in very cold areas, to grow *Sedum* species successfully.

A large area is not essential for an indoor rock garden. Miniature gardens can be created in a container such as a large plastic bowl. Often these miniature gardens are called bowl gardens. Several *Sedum* species both tender and hardy have a tumbling nature, and throughout the descriptions in this volume I point out which would be ideal for hanging baskets.

OTHER USES OF STONECROPS

In parks and gardens where plants are used to create pictures, *Sedum, Sempervivum*, and *Echeveria* are the most important components (Plate 2). Very low growing, highly colored stonecrops are ideal for floral clocks and other forms of floral art. In recent years I have noticed an increasing number of three-dimensional floral models at exhibitions and horticultural shows. By growing miniature sedums on sheets of rockwool, almost any construction can appear as though it is made entirely of living plants.

At the National Garden Festival, Gateshead, England, in 1990, a model of Durham Cathedral was encrusted with *Sedum dasyphyllum*; the contrasting foliage color of *S. spathulifolium* 'Cape Blanco' and *S. ×rubrotinctum* picked out architectural detail. Fish and other sea creatures were modeled with chicken wire, stuffed with sphagnum, and then covered with *Sedum* plants. These were suspended above blue beds of *Lobelia* cultivars, which represented water, creating the illusion of fish leaping from the sea. The scaly texture of the fish was well represented by *S. spathulifolium* var. *purpureum*.

Few *Sedum* species make good cut blooms, but several of the herbaceous species make very long-lasting decorations. Only *S. telephium* 'Autumn Joy' is dried and dyed or painted to make dried-flower arrangements. The large flat umbels are an important ingredient of floral art on both sides of the Atlantic. Posies and small decorative wreaths for hanging on doors are made in some European countries from *S. acre*. The cut stems, although very short, are long lasting, and flowers open progressively over several weeks.

HISTORICAL USES

Long before people grew plants merely for the pleasure of watching them grow, sedums were planted for special reasons. Early Homo sapiens must have been surprised to see sedums refusing to wither when other herbs wilted within hours of being picked. In medieval England, the orpine or livelong (*Sedum telephium*) was picked on Midsummer Day and hung from cottage rafters where it continued to grow. Also known as midsummer men, the orpine was thought to keep away distemper as long as it remained green until Christmas. So tenacious of life is *S. telephium* that the chance of keeping a sprig green under shady rafters was very good. The name orpine, which refers to gold, cannot refer to the flower color but rather to the longevity which the plants shared with this inert, precious metal.

Sedums have long been included in herbalists' lists of cures. The leaves have been used externally to bring relief to wounds, and even before the Middle Ages they were taken internally as emetics or vermifuges. Some individuals suggest that the name *Sedum* is from the Latin *sedeo* (sit), for the plants appear legless as they perch on rocks, but I prefer the suggestion that the verb *sedo* (to calm or check) is the origin of the genus name.

Sedum acre, the biting stonecrop, also known as pricket or iacke-of-the-butterie, was known by the great sixteenth-century herbalist John Gerard as wall-pepper, though wall-ginger was almost as common a name. This plant is the most frequently encountered *Sedum* species said to be an important cure. Generations of countrywomen in England knew it as welcome-home-husband-though-never-so-drunk, but I cannot endorse these claimed powers. Even as early as Anglo-Saxon times it was used to treat gout, "foot-adle," and numerous other ailments. Nicholas Culpepper said that it had been used as an abortifacient, a cure for scurvy, a fomentation, an emetic, and a purgative, and was prescribed in small doses by homeopaths for anal fistulas and hemorrhoids. He even recommended it to cure venereal disease. William Curtis said:

> According to the account which some medical writers give of this plant, it appears to possess considerable virtues; while for others, from the durability of its acrimony and the violence of its operation, have thought it scarce safe to be administered. Applied to the skin, it excoriates and ulcerates it (Hulme 1902, 144).

Carl Linnaeus recommended it for scurvy and dropsy.

Sedum anglicum, known in the sixteenth and seventeenth centuries as prick-madam, like *S. album*, was used to stop internal and external bleeding. It was recommended also for fevers, cankers, fretting sores, and scorbutic cases.

The roseroot (*Sedum rosea*) was so named because of the odor given by the broken, dried roots, which were used as an additive to ointments. Roseroot contains potent alkaloids that are used even today to treat diseased eyes.

It is suggested that *Sedum reflexum* (*S. rupestre* not *S. forsterianum*) was introduced from Flanders to Britain as a salad crop. It was said to have a fine relish, pleasant taste, and to be a good treatment for heartburn (indigestion). No other leaves are said to be succulent both botanically and gastronomically.

Native Americans, ancient Romans, Russian peoples, and Japanese believed sedums had special powers or qualities. They grew the plants for their malic acid or planted them above the doorways of their dwellings to keep away lightning or evil. Today few people grow sedums for these reasons. Modern gardeners grow sedums for the pleasure of their succulent forms and for the dazzling displays of their starlike flowers.

CHAPTER 2

Growing Stonecrops

Knowing where a species originated is a good step towards realizing any plant's horticultural requirements. Comparing the latitude of the plant's natural habitat with that of its future site will give an indication of the plant's potential hardiness, and comparing the natural habitat's distance from the sea with the intended site's distance from the sea will give some indication of the extremes the species is likely to tolerate. Recognizing that altitudinal differences between the original habitat and the potential site means that plants require special attention will improve chances of successful growth. Few *Sedum* species originate from areas of high rainfall, but those that do, grow in particularly well-drained sites. Seasonal distribution of rainfall of the habitat will indicate whether the species will need some protection in its new home.

If a stonecrop originates from a rocky, exposed site, it needs to be given perfect drainage. Porous terra-cotta pots are ideal for sedums from arid areas. Species from forest glades will perform better in a rich, damp, partly shaded border. Shoreline annuals require sandy or gravel areas, and herbaceous species from alluvial lowlands require a rich loam. Several species appear to favor a particular rock type in habitat, so it is often an aid to cultivation if acid volcanic chips or alkaline calcareous gravel is used for top dressing, depending on the species.

TEMPERATURES

Most sedums are tolerant of a large diurnal temperature range; in fact, this is often preferable to a small diurnal temperature range. Most *Sedum* species are Crassulacean Acidic Metabolism (CAM) plants. CAM plants have evolved a special way of avoiding transpiration (the equivalent of perspiration in the plant world). Non-CAM plants, which breathe through their stomata during the day, use the energy of the sun to convert absorbed carbon dioxide into sugars in the process known as photosynthesis. They therefore suffer tremendous water loss during the heat of day, or if grown on windward slopes and in other areas of high evaporation.

CAM plants avoid this water loss through a very specialized form of photosynthesis in which their fewer stomata open at night to take in carbon dioxide. Keeping stomata closed during the day cuts down transpiration and allows plants to survive arid conditions. The carbon dioxide they take in at night is stored overnight in the form of malic acid, a substance well-known to the amateur winemaker, and one which makes the plant bitter-tasting in the morning. (Roman apothecaries realized that *Sedum acre* tasted very bitter if picked in the morning but not as bitter if picked in the evening.) The next day, CAM plants use light energy to convert malic acid to sugar. The trigger to complete this process of photosynthesis is not light but a marked temperature change. Therefore *Sedum* species and other CAM plants require a marked difference between day and night temperatures to breathe successfully. Because this odd kind of photosynthesis was first noticed in the Crassula family, it is known by the acronym CAM.

Cacti and succulent collectors in areas of England with bitter winters heat their greenhouses by night when frosts are most likely, but conserve energy by switching heat off during the day. Plant deaths are often erroneously blamed on frosts when, in fact, they are the result of suffocation. CAM plants will not survive for weeks on end where the temperature range is only a few degrees.

A freak series of events several years ago resulted in the failure of my greenhouse heating system on the coldest night of the year. The temperature at dawn was −12°C (14°F), and all my tender Mexican sedums were frozen solid. Although outside temperatures remained below freezing all day, I managed to raise the temperature in the greenhouse to 10°C (50°F). Only one species perished—*Sedum allantoides*. Others showed no signs of distress.

Stonecrops from the tropics endure occasional frosts and sometimes snow because they tend to be high-altitude plants. As long as they are dry and dormant they will survive occasional cold conditions in cultivation.

Often sedums scorch in a greenhouse even though temperatures are much lower than those endured in habitat. These species invariably grow in windy, exposed sites, so lack of ventilation in a greenhouse can cause surprising damage. Alpine species are least likely to survive in an unventilated greenhouse of hot, still air.

It is wrong to think that an Arctic *Sedum* species would grow much better on the Mediterranean coast where the climate is much less extreme. On the contrary, the plant would soon perish. High-latitude plants are perhaps more difficult to cultivate in low latitudes than low-latitude plants are to grow in high latitudes. Keeping Arctic species cool in hot summers is no easy task, and if such plants do not experience long hours of daylight in summer, they refuse to flower.

The following points help summarize the cultivation requirements of *Sedum* as far as temperatures and day/night fluctuations are concerned:

1. High-altitude plants need special attention when grown at low altitudes.
   - Avoid hot, direct sunlight, especially through glass.
   - Avoid stagnant, damp conditions.
   - Avoid waterlogged composts.
2. Low-altitude plants or those from maritime climates need special attention when grown inland or at high altitudes.
   - Avoid frost.
   - Avoid long dry periods.
3. High-latitude plants need special attention when grown nearer the tropics.
   - Avoid strong spring sunlight through glass.
   - Avoid high summer temperatures by providing shade and air circulation.
   - Avoid insufficient day/night fluctuations. In midwinter, decrease the number of hours plants are exposed to daylight by covering them with black perforated plastic sheeting in late afternoon and do not uncover until late morning; repeat daily for several weeks. In summer, increase the number of daylight hours by giving plants artificial light in early morning and late evening for two weeks either side of midsummer.
   - Avoid etiolated plant growth in areas without a marked winter (i.e., where temperatures do not fall below 6°C/43°F for a period of weeks) by placing plants in a dark, dry, cool cellar or garage for a period of weeks over midwinter.
4. Low-latitude plants need special attention when grown in areas nearer the poles.
   - Avoid weak light in winter by using grolamps or other artificial lighting.
   - Avoid frost, especially if plants are given small quantities of water.
   - Avoid watering in winter months.
   - Avoid drying out composts completely in hot summer conditions behind glass, especially if the plants are in ceramic containers.
   - Avoid artificial growing conditions by setting plants outside in summer for a few weeks.

WATER

The majority of *Sedum* species will survive if not watered for a month, though I would not recommend this during the growing season, and severed stems of succulent species can root after many months of storage. I once found a 14-month-old cutting in my garage, which I had inadvertently failed to unpack; not only was it alive, it was attempting to root and grow. Obviously, the cool garage helped increase the longevity of this tenacious specimen. In general, sedums are more likely to be harmed by overwatering than by underwatering. A good watering once a week in the growing season is ideal in most areas.

The habitat of a species is a general guide to its watering requirements. The following generalizations apply to the broad geographic areas in which sedums are grouped in this volume.

1. Species centered around the Mediterranean enjoy hot, dry summers and warm, wet winters. They can go for long periods in summer with no rain at all, but may rot if they are grown outdoors in places like Japan or Florida that experience much summer rain. Some Mediterranean species have evolved to grow in winter only to bridge summer drought. They are winter-growing annuals or perennials which disintegrate in the middle of the year. In areas of high summer rainfall, give Mediterranean species some overhead protection, and in areas of high summer humidity, keep plants well ventilated. Protect these stonecrops against winter snow.

2. Species from Central or Northern Europe cope with a lot of rainfall as long as they are well drained; however, they suffer if heavy rains occur when temperatures are over 25°C (77°F). Thus, in areas of monsoon or tropical storms, give plants some shade and shelter.

3. Himalayan species could be from areas of high rainfall, but all grow in sites of perfect drainage and drying winds. They do not tolerate high summer temperatures but need regular water in spring. They appreciate a drier end to the summer and are dormant in winter. Thus, give these species some protection against rain from the longest day of the year until winter begins, and protect plants in areas of very heavy winter rains. No protection is needed against dry winter snow, but in areas where thaw is followed by frost many times during winter months, protection is necessary.

4. Most Oriental species experience high summer rainfall but grow in spots with perfect drainage. When growing these species in areas where summer droughts are experienced, it is important to irrigate plants.

5. Rocky Mountain species withstand a lot of summer rain, but the more southerly Western Cordilleran species will be less tolerant. Northerly species should be irrigated in summer.

6. Appalachian and Ozark species require watering in summer droughts, and plants should be partially shaded.

7. Mexican species come from a multitude of natural regions but generally need no water at all in winter in areas where temperatures fall below 10°C (50°F) for several consecutive months. Where temperatures do not fall below 10°C (50°F), water Mexican species lightly, perhaps once a month. Avoid winter wet; if grown outdoors in a hot climate, however, winter wet does not seem to have too adverse an effect. In summer, water indoor plants well once a week; if grown outdoors, avoid heavy or frequent rains.

COMPOSTS

Stonecrops grow in almost any medium, sometimes prefering no soil. Often a species migrates from a rich niche in which it was planted and grows to perfection on an adjacent concrete pavement, leaving behind the original plant to perish. If little nutriment exists in a particular spot, a stonecrop will not remain sedentary, but may vacate the site by spreading elsewhere. If a plant is contained in a pot, a low-nitrogen, slow-release fertilizer can help produce strong, sturdy specimens, but use fertilizer very sparingly as plants can become overlush and uncharacteristic. Fertilizers can be applied in solution or in granular form as part of the compost. Application of trace elements via watering promotes strong growth.

Some stonecrops are said to be lovers of lime because they have been observed in the wild festooning limestone crags. I do not believe that such stonecrops necessarily love lime; they tolerate it and only grow on it because other plants can not. *Sedum* species prosper where there is little competition from other genera. Sedums can be lithophytic, but they are more likely to grow on thin layers of soil or in tiny pockets of soil or rock detritus where drainage is rapid.

To be honest, I have yet to find a potting material in which stonecrops refuse to grow. The most important factor for strong, lasting growth is very porous compost. This can be achieved by adding sharp grit, gravel, or an inert material like rockwool (expanded mica), vermiculate (expanded igneous rock), or crocks to the soil. Quartz grit and volcanic gravel are very heavy and could strain benches packed with pots, but they have the advantage of anchoring pots down during high winds. Rockwool and vermiculate are very light materials that make transporting pots very easy.

I do not recommend peat-based composts. Although sedums would thrive in such a compost, so would all their major enemies. A loam-based compost, however, appears not to harbor pests, especially if topped with a layer of coarse gravel. To a measure of proprietory loam-based compost, I add one-third measure of 2 mm (0.08 in) quartz grit (the kind that is sold to chicken farmers for their chicks), a small quantity of powdered pesticide, and a small quantity of powdered low-nitrogen fertilizer. I cover the surface with at least 10 mm (0.4 in) of larger, sharp flint (the kind that is sold to chicken farmers for their hens). I recommend growers use the cheapest crushed stone available in their area, as long as it is not such a garish color that it detracts from the plants. Dolerite, granite, and andesite as top dressings look very tasteful and create a somewhat acid compost. Dolomite and limestone, which can be too white, create an alkaline compost. I use a top dressing of gray calcareous gravel for plants originating in a limestone area. They would probably grow as well in a more acid compost but might lose regional characteristics, which I wish to preserve.

To grow sedums in an open garden where the soil is glutinous, add gravel as the ground is prepared for planting. An additional top layer of gravel will improve drainage, deter annual weeds, and add to the beauty of the area. Create contours wherever possible in badly drained sites, clay soils, or areas of heavy rain, and plant stonecrops on the higher levels.

PROPAGATION

Few plants are easier to propagate than sedums, many of which will grow from a single leaf if it is removed with care. The general rule is this: the more succulent the leaf, the more likely it is to root and generate a new plant. For the majority of *Sedum* species, if pieces were merely ripped off the parent and rammed into any growing medium, some propagations would be successful.

To be even more successful, choose healthy, sterile stems (without flowers or buds) and strip them of their lower leaves. When inserted into a porous, sandy or gritty compost, these stems quickly form roots. Avoid keeping cuttings in full sun. Put them in a position where birds, cats, or rodents will not disturb plants and labels. Water the cuttings after a week or so. Unlike mesophytes that relish a watering-in process, *Sedum* cuttings are likely to rot if watered immediately. By waiting at least three days so that tissue damage has had time to callus, rot is unlikely and small rootlets are likely to have formed to make use of the delayed moisture. Finally, do not take cuttings of biennials or annuals after the longest day of the year. An almost foolproof method of propagating vegetatively follows:

1. Half fill a seed tray (flat) with a mixture of equal parts of loamy compost and fine gravel. Add some powdered pesticide to the mixture

and cover it with 10 mm (0.4 in) of coarser gravel. If a deeper container is used, line the bottom with stones to aid drainage.

2. Push cuttings through the top layer of gravel, which supports them and prevents rotting. Any stems removed from perennial sedums can be used for propagation, but *Rhodiola* species will generally not propagate using this method.

3. Label each row carefully. An extra, smaller label pushed fully into the compost is good insurance if the main label is lost. Do not propagate similar species side by side if their identity is to be preserved.

4. Place the seed tray outdoors or under a bench in the greenhouse in a well-ventilated position away from direct light.

5. Drench the cuttings with a fine mist each week. After three weeks, the plantlets should have rooted and started to grow.

6. Move the tray to a brighter, airy position, but again protect the cuttings from birds and other creatures who may use the tray for other purposes. Continue the weekly drenchings. If the cuttings are started in spring, the plants will be ready to move into pots, to the rockery, or wherever in an additional three weeks (a total of six weeks). The further into the year, the less vigorous the plantlets become and the greater the percentage of failure.

Herbaceous species are much more difficult to propagate because often the rootstock must be split. This procedure is best done in spring. Parent plants need to be lifted and divided, using a sharp knife to cut between the stems through the rootstock. It is prudent to thoroughly dry the split rootstocks before attempting to plant them. Choose bits with both roots and shoots. Dust injured tissue with a fungicide and leave the rootstocks in a cool place, out of direct sunlight, to allow the wounds to callus before replanting. Plants of *Aizoon* group and subgenus *Hylotelephium* grow from stem cuttings, but subgenus *Rhodiola* species are notoriously difficult to propagate by any method. Cuttings of the latter must comprise more than just bits of stem or caudex which dry out completely and most times refuse to root. If a piece of caudex with roots and buds can be removed cleanly from the main plant, there is every chance of success. Very large plants of subgenus *Rhodiola* can be split easily, but it is exceptionally difficult to propagate such species in bulk.

Few people attempt to grow sedums from seed since it is much easier to grow them from cuttings. Seed is tiny and difficult to handle; it loses viability quickly (although I have sown seed over five years old with some success). Seed trays must never become waterlogged or be allowed to grow algae. A good surface of sharp grit helps to avoid algae growth. Biennial and annual species must be grown from seed, however. I have had the greatest success by growing these species in fall and overwintering them in a frost-free but cool environment. Seed is best stored in paper rather than in polyethylene packets. I usually store complete inflorescences as the seed is difficult to differentiate from desiccated carpel and petal fragments. Seeds from species that are liable to freeze completely in winter in their native habitat are best stored in the freezer compartment of the refrigerator. Some high alpine species require this treatment to trigger germination.

PESTS

Fortunately sedums are almost always free from pests and diseases. There are no diseases associated with the genus *Sedum*, but damp summers bring fungal infections to some members of subgenus *Hylotelephium*. All in all, sedums are remarkably trouble-free. Introducing predators to control pests became big business in Europe in the early 1990s. Unfortunately, the predators are not very hardy and must be given very controlled conditions to function as intended.

Aphids (Adelgidae)

Aphids, especially blackfly, attack new growth in spring and summer. Often the black clusters of insects are more unsightly than the damage they create. Adelgid colonies are easily eradicated with insecticide, but beware, for many sprays are not suitable for sedums. If instructions for using the spray are brief, or if it is unclear whether the chemical is suitable for flowering currants (close relatives of the Crassulaceae, the family to which *Sedum* species belong), it is best to avoid that particular spray. As a general rule, contact killing or systemic insecticides unsuitable for blackcurrant or any member of the currant family are also unsuitable for *Sedum* species. Such insecticides burn leaves and, although they do not often wipe out plants completely, can leave them scarred.

Dusts are less damaging than sprays but ugly. Soap-and-water spray is very effective, but needs to be applied repeatedly. To avoid the harmful side effects of insecticides, a tea made from several common herbs is a natural insecticide. It is made by infusing chopped green leaves. Garlic (*Allium ursinum* or *A. sativum*) works, but its smell lingers. Tansy (*Tanacetum vulgare*) tea removes greenfly very effectively and does not smell unpleasant. *Aphiodoletes* are predatory midges that attack aphids, but they are more effective in a greenhouse. In the United States it is popular to buy large quantities of ladybugs (ladybirds) to decimate aphid colonies. Ecologically this practice has much to offer, but it should be remembered that in times of need, when ladybugs outnumber aphids, the delightful red beetles distribute greenfly for the purpose of milking them and encouraging their procreation. Sticky deposits produced by aphids are unsightly, but a light pressure spray not only rids the plants of pests but washes away the mess they have made.

Mealy Bugs (*Planococcus* and *Rhizeocus* Species)

In the greenhouse, in particular, mealy bug colonies, once established, can ruin fine plants and become almost impossible to eradicate completely. Sticky nectarlike daubs soon become infested with black mold, which often growers do not associate with mealy bugs as they have not seen the culprits. Mealy bugs inhabit the roots of potted plants and climb up the stems as the sun rises. Small woolly spots adhering to the roots or leaf axils of plants are a telltale sign of infestation.

When repotting plants, adding a powdered insecticide to the compost may alleviate the problem, especially in the short term. Chemicals dangerous to sedums are harmless if poured into the soil, avoiding the plants themselves. This treatment may be necessary if the infestation is advanced; however, it is often better to take cuttings and start plants again rather than to try to regenerate an ailing one.

Sciara Flies *(Lycoriella auripila)*

Sciara (sciarid) or mushroom flies are true flies that lay their eggs in peaty compost. The small black flies are harmless, but the threadlike, semitransparent worms (their larvae) burrow in fleshy roots and stems (Fig. 2.1). Adding powdered insecticide to the soil of potted plants deters adults from alighting, as does a top layer of gravel, but is best to avoid using peaty compost, which attracts adult flies.

Thrips *(*Thysanopterae)

In recent years, two voracious insects have caused great concern. In the United States, the Western flower thrip (*Frankliniella occidentalis*) has ruined

Figure 2.1. Two sciara larvae inhabiting a rotted caudex of subgenus *Rhodiola*. Like hyena, sciara are invariably found scavenging, although they may not necessarily be the killers.

many blooming plants. It is tiny and narrow like a storm fly or harvest fly, but is ginger colored and runs very quickly. Although it attacks *Sedum*, causing plants to be contorted or to produce freak growth, it does not create major damage. *Amblyseius cucumeris* and *A. barkeri* are predatory mites that attack Western flower thrips. In Europe the pest is still rare but perhaps more to be feared by growers of plants with large blooms. The much larger vine weevil has wreaked havoc in Europe.

Vine Weevils (*Otiorhynchus sulcatus*)

Vine weevils devastate mature plants of subgenera *Rhodiola* and *Hylotelephium*, and plants of *Aizoon* group. All beetles are female and feed on the edges of the newest, most-succulent leaves as soon as day ends (Fig. 2.2). Their grub which are fat and white with a darker head grow to 2 cm (0.8 in) long and hollow out a plant from below the ground (Fig. 2.3). The collapsing rootstock and stems appear as if they are full of snuff. No chemical is strong enough to kill adult insects without killing the plants also, and soil poisons, which could irritate the grub, are illegal in many countries.

Figure 2.2 *Otiorhynchus salcatus* (vine weevil) is the greatest enemy of Sedum species.

The counterattack against this pest must be two-pronged. The first tactic requires vigilance. To locate the vine weevil, shine a flashlight on plants at midnight when the beetles come out to feed. They are large and slow-moving but impossible to spot if they drop to the soil, so growers place white sheets around the base of any plant suspected of being infested before they shake the branches in the middle of the night. Only by being vigilant over a long period can the enemy be kept at bay.

The second tactic involves destroying the host plants. Currant bushes, lily of the valley, ericaceous plants, and cyclamen are known hosts, but any tuberous or fleshy-rooted plant can harbor this pest. By digging a little around plants, grubs in various stages of development may be found. Although adult vine weevils can fly, they rarely do so. However, they travel

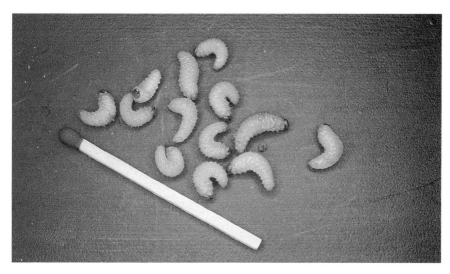

Figure 2.3. Vine weevil larvae devastate succulent rootstocks.

considerable distances, so the host plant may be in a neighbor's garden. Vine weevils have been distributed widely from Dutch nurseries in rootstocks of rhododendron, and successive mild winters have not reduced their numbers. This pest has few natural enemies, and a single adult can clone 1500 offspring in one season.

Adult vine weevils nibble edges of newer succulent leaves and return each evening to their favorite eating places. Bacteria infected *Heterorhabditis* nematodes are dual-purpose predators that carry disease to larvae of both vine weevil and sciara fly.

Other Pests

Wood lice often nibble roots of *Sedum* plants, especially at night, but cures are often more harmful than the pest. Ants can transport mealy bugs to *Sedum* plants where they will breed. The ants return periodically to "milk" their livestock. Occasionally, caterpillars stray onto herbaceous specimens. Slugs and snails, too, enjoy a succulent nibble, but with frequent inspections of plants, these pests are easily destroyed before they become too troublesome.

CHAPTER 3

Morphology and Distribution

To identify sedums with any degree of accuracy, it is important to be familiar with the parts of a plant, especially the flower (Fig. 3.1).

SEPALS

Sepals are the leaflike bracts that partly enclose the flower. Collectively the sepals are often referred to as the *calyx*. Sometimes the calyx is a definite tube, but *Sedum* species invariably have well-defined sepals. Their shape and fusion are best observed at the end of the bud stage, just as the flower first opens.

Sepals are an important aid to positive identification of plants. Some species have particularly large sepals, while other species that are vegetatively very similar may have hardly any sepals. For example, although *Sedum obtusatum* and *S. oregonense* are distinct cytologically, for many gardeners the most reliable way to differentiate the two species is on the basis of sepal

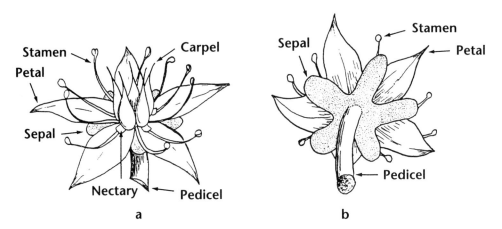

Figure 3.1. Parts of a *Sedum* flower: (a) side view of flower; (b) bottom view.

size: sepals of the former are large in relation to petals, while those of the latter are meager (Fig. 3.2a, b). Sepals may be free or united at the base (Fig. 3.2c, d). Completely free sepals are an unusual feature and therefore are excellent proof of identification for certain species. Some stonecrops have uneven sepals on each flower that are very acute (pointed) or obtuse (blunt) at the apex; other species have equal-sized sepals. Variation does not occur only at the apex, for sepals can be long and narrow (linear) or perhaps triangular (deltoid). They can be appressed to (lying against) the petals, remain upright as the petals spread, or be patent (sticking out at right angles to the closed petals).

The number of sepals per flower always equals the numbers of petals. Sometimes sepals have the same covering as leaves; they may be pruinose, hirsute, glaucous, glandular-papillose, or glabrous.

PETALS

Viewed together, petals are often called the *corolla*. Apart from differences in their shape and color, which are good indicators of a plant's identity, petals have mucronate (apiculate or sharply tipped) or obtuse apices (Fig. 3.3a, b, c). They can be heavily keeled (carinate) or relatively flat. Sometimes they are hooded and hollowed, like a cape (Fig. 3.3d). Important factors to the

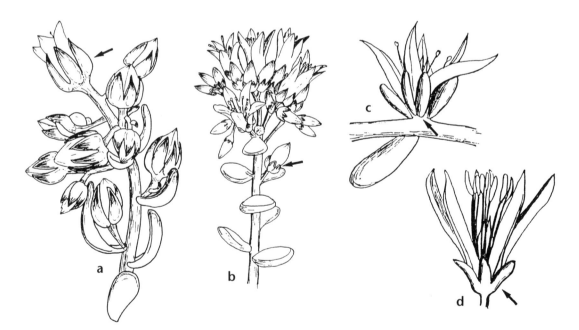

Figure 3.2. Size of sepals in relation to petals and degree of sepal fusion are important aids to positive identification of plants: (a) sepals of *Sedum obtusatum* are large in relation to petals, while (b) sepals of *S. oregonense* are meager; (c) *S. fusiforme* has free sepals, while (d) *S. sediforme* has united sepals.

taxonomist are the degree of petal connation (fusion) and whether the petals are horizontally spreading (patent) from the base or upright at the base. Spreading petals form a star, so they are said to be stellate. Typical *Sedum* species have stellate petals but there are a number of anomalies (Fig. 3.3e).

Upright (erect) petals are not usually associated with *Sedum*, but several borderline species with upright petals have been placed in the genus. Sometimes petals are erect in the lower portion only, rarely for most of their length, or even more rarely for their full length. Erect petals are so unusual, they are an excellent indicator of identity. It is unusual for petals not to be entire (having a smooth, unbroken margin); eroded (uneven, fringed, or toothed) petals are encountered only rarely.

General florae describe *Sedum* as having five petals; sometimes such volumes add "rarely four or six." Anyone who has grown sedums knows that some species are fairly constant as to the number of petals per flower but this can be four, five, six, seven, or eight. Often a species shows contempt for taxonomists by displaying everything from 3-partite to 11-partite flowers on the same inflorescence.

Petals can be incurved or recurved. They are commonly glabrous, though rarely hirsute. In certain annuals they are ephemeral (small, unimportant, and short-lived), and many have ultra-violet markings to attract insects, but petals are never longer than 2 cm (0.8 in).

STAMENS

Sedum species generally have twice as many stamens (male parts) as other flower parts. Together, stamens are often called the *androecium*. Because *Sedum* stamens are produced in two whorls—an inner whorl fixed to the petals and an outer whorl fixed between the petals—plants are said to be

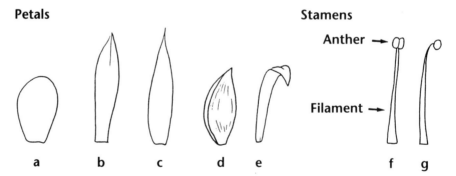

Figure 3.3. Shapes and relative sizes of petals and stamens are important details that help discriminate species: (a) *Sedum brevifolium* has relatively wide, obtuse petals; (b) *S. sediforme* has linear-spathulate petals with acute apices; (c) *S. kamtschaticum* has lanceolate petals with apiculate or spine-tipped mucrones; (d) *S. glabrum* has hooded petals; and (e) *S. craigii* has petals that spread only at tips; all *Sedum* species have (f) basifixed anthers, except (g) *S. hobsonii*, which has dorsifixed anthers.

obdiplostemonous. The points at which each whorl contact the petals are important for identification. Epipetalous stamens (i.e., the inner whorl) are sometimes inserted at the base of the petals, or, in other species, fused some distance from the base; alternipetalous stamens (i.e., the outer whorl) are sometimes fused between the petals or, in other species, are completely free of the petals.

Haplostemonous flowers in *Sedum* are exceptions to the rule; because they have a suppressed outer whorl of stamens (i.e., only one whorl of stamens inserted into the petals), they are therefore an excellent pointer to identification. Even rarer among the stonecrops are diplostemonous flowers, which have two whorls of stamens, the outer whorl opposite the sepals and the inner whorl opposite the petals. An example of a diplostemonous stonecrop is *Sedum heterodontum*; it has an oppositipetalous outer whorl of stamens and an alternipetalous inner whorl.

A stamen is made up of a filament and an anther. A stamen is said to be short if it is shorter than the petals, and long if it is longer than the petals. Such a relation is a further aid to identification. As a rule, the anther, which produces the pollen, is two-lobed, and all stonecrops except one are basifixed (i.e., joined by the base) (Fig. 3.3f, g). *Sedum hobsonii* alone has dorsifixed anthers (i.e., the filament enters the back of the anther).

CARPELS

Collectively, carpels are referred to as the *gynoecium, ovaries,* or *pistils*. They are the female parts of the flower. *Sedum* carpels are beaked, and the seeds are produced below the beak or style, inside the follicle (pistil cell). When a carpel is ripe, it splits vertically, and the seeds, which are very small, spill out or are blown away.

Carpel behavior has always been of prime importance in grouping *Sedum* species. Two distinct categories are possible (Fig. 3.4). The carpels of kyphocarpic flowers show gibbosity (bulging) on the ventral (inner) side; this inner wall grows, causing the carpels to arch outward (Fig. 3.4b) until the flower in fruit has its carpels spread out like a star (patent or stellate fruit, Fig. 3.4c). On the other hand, orthocarpic flowers have carpels that remain upright throughout; that is, when the carpels dehisce (burst open to reveal seeds), they are still fairly upright (Fig. 3.4e).

Species of subgenus *Hylotelephium* and *Orostachys* group of subgenus *Sedum* have stipitate carpels (Fig. 3.4f–h).

NECTARIES

Nectary glands (usually shortened to nectaries), known as *hypogynous scales* or *squamae*, are usually found at the base of carpels (Fig. 3.1). Sometimes they are absent. To see a nectary, often it is necessary to remove a petal, so a magnifying glass is useful. These nectaries can be brightly colored. Their absence, presence, shape, and color are good aids to identification.

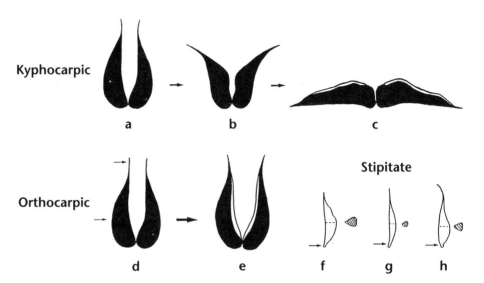

Figure 3.4. Carpel shape and development: (a–c) in kyphocarpic species, the inner wall of each carpel swells, causing the carpels to arch outward and spread out flat when the flower is in fruit, but (d, e) in orthocarpic species, the carpels remain upright even after they burst open to reveal seed; (f–h) stipitate carpels, such as those in (f) *Sedum ewersii*, (g) *S. populifolium*, and (h) *S. erubescens*, are constricted near the base.

PEDICELS

Pedicels are stalks on which flowers are carried. Some *Sedum* species have particularly long pedicels, while other species lack pedicels (i.e., flowers appear from the main stem or branch). Flowers are said to be sessile when pedicels are absent, and pedicellate when pedicels are present. Subsessile describes pedicels that are very short.

INFLORESCENCES

The first sedums to be described by botanists had terminal flowers. As a result, many older books or florae of the Old World suggest that sedums only have terminal inflorescences. This is not true, however, as many New World sedums have lateral flowers. Most stonecrop inflorescences have bracts that are invariably leaflike, although these bracts are usually much smaller than the leaves. Where they differ considerably in shape, rather than in size, from the leaves, the difference can help identification.

The basic flower form in the genus is a dichasial cyme, which, in its simplest form, is an inflorescence that terminates a stem (Fig. 3.5a). Any further growth is by lateral branches, which may end in further flowers but are in opposite (or almost opposite) pairs. Five other main types of inflorescences can be distinguished in *Sedum*: (1) a reduced cyme that produces a single or several flowers, such as *S. pachyclados* (Fig. 3.5b); (2) a single erect stem (peduncle) that carries a large number of terminal subsidiary axes resulting in a cyme (Fig. 3.5c) or a corymb (Fig. 3.5d), as in most species of subgenera *Hylotelephium* and *Rhodiola*; (3) two or three scorpioid branches, as in *S. aizoon* (Fig. 3.5e); (4) a spike or elongated inflorescence shaped like a cylinder or a cone with flowers arranged in racemes, cymes, monochasiums, or dichasiums, of which *S. rhodanthum* is an example (Fig. 3.5f); and (5) a lateral inflorescence as in *S. pachyphyllum* (Fig. 3.5g).

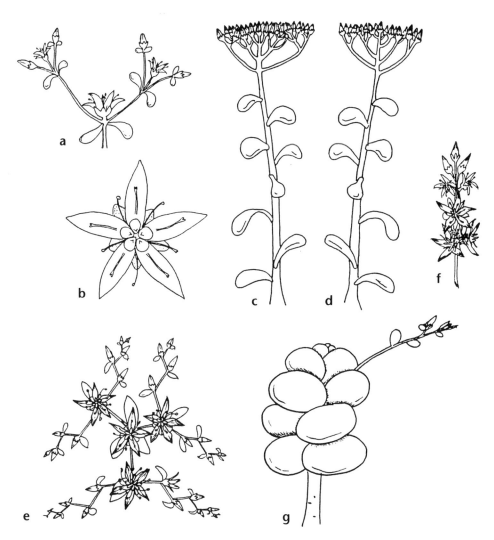

Figure 3.5. The basic inflorescence in the genus *Sedum* is (a) a dichasial cyme. Development or reduction of a dichasial cyme has resulted in six inflorescence types: (b) a single flower; (c) a cyme; (d) a corymb; (e) scorpioid branches; (f) a spike; and (g) a lateral inflorescence.

STEMS

Sedums can be annual, biennial, triennial, perennial, or herbaceous. Therefore, the lifespan of a single specimen can range from weeks to many years. Some annuals are desert-margin ephemerals. They grow briefly after a heavy downpour, rise rapidly, and expend little energy to produce leaves, which will soon be dead. Instead, these plants expend their energy only to produce flowers quickly. The flowers are fertilized by insects, and in a matter of weeks, seed is scattered, but this seed only germinates after a cloudburst, which might not occur for several months or years. Such ephemerals are not good garden plants; they tend to be spindly and weak, and flowers are short-lived. Perhaps the only species of horticultural note is *Sedum caeruleum*; it is unique in Crassulaceae because of its cascades of azure flowers.

Several other annual sedums are perpetuated in cultivation. In the past, far too much emphasis was placed on the annual nature of a stonecrop when classifying or grouping species. Many species of *Sedum* will act as annuals in very adverse conditions and rely upon seed to perpetuate themselves. In times of intense drought, perennial species do not produce sterile shoots, but instead only produce inflorescences. Thus, in this instance, these perennials act as annuals (Fig. 3.6).

On the contrary, species that are annual in the wild (e.g., *Sedum drymarioides*) can be persuaded to act as perennial in cultivation. The North American species *S. pulchellum* can be annual or biennial; it also can perpetuate itself for many years by sideshoots, but these are only formed if the conditions are just right.

Some species of *Sedum* produce two distinct kinds of growth. Starting as a series of rosettes in the first season, these growths elongate in the second season to form inflorescences. Monocarpic rosettes could render the species biennial. In some cases, new rosettes form at the base of the spent inflorescences, making the plants perennial.

Herbaceous species die back to underground or partly underground rootstocks in the cold season. In this case, sterile shoots (those without flowers) are less common, as the main purpose of each annual stem is to produce seed.

Sedum stems are almost invariably round in section. The exceptions to this rule are noted and can therefore be a reliable aid to positive identification. Plants that are erect in the wild can be decumbent in cultivation if grown in clay pots, and stems that are usually short in habitat can be etiolated if grown in too much shade. *Sedum* stems are generally smooth, but those with hair or those shaggy with dead leaves that refuse to fall are good pointers to identification. Several Mexican tree stonecrops have peeling, paperlike bark; other species have scabrid (rough) or textured stems. As an aid to positively identifying a plant, these features have been noted throughout the descriptions.

Figure 3.6. A very underwatered specimen of the perennial species *Sedum oreganum* is acting as an annual and has put all its energy into making seed.

The height of a plant (which is often equivalent to the length of the stem) is given in this volume based on plants in cultivation in Mid Northumberland, England. All plants in my collection have been carefully checked with their original descriptions, wherever possible, to verify identification. If an obvious discrepancy between the length of stems in habitat and those in cultivation arises, this is noted.

Stems of stonecrops can be erect (upright) or arched, creeping or procumbent. Occasionally, stonecrops cascade or tumble downward (decumbent) over rocks or hang (pendulous) from cliffs or other vegetation. Stems are rarely full of twists and turns (tortuous). Especially in the New World, species have no stem at all.

LEAVES

Attempting to give a general description of *Sedum* leaves is virtually impossible, as almost every shape, hue, and texture exists. Leaves, although variable within a species and even on a single plant, are still a very good aid to identification. Variation of leaf size, shape, or pattern is noted in the descriptions. Generally, an average, mature typical leaf was chosen as the model for each sketch.

A section of a leaf is an indication of how succulent a particular plant is. If the section is round, the leaf is said to be terete. The arrangement of leaves on the stem is a relatively constant feature of a species and can therefore be a reliable guide to identification. Scattered (alternate) leaves are the most common arrangement (Fig. 3.7a), but often leaves are opposite-decussate (Fig. 3.7b), which means that each pair of leaves is at right angles to its neighbors. Leaves often occur in whorls (verticillate, grouped on the same plane) (Fig. 3.7c); if the leaves are in groups of three, they are said to be ternate. Rosettes (leaves arranged like the petals of a rose) (Fig. 3.7d) are commonly found on North American species of *Sedum* but rarely found on European species. The latter commonly have tufted leaves (bunched closely together) in winter, which then spread as the stems elongate in spring. If leaves overlap and appear pressed to the stem, they are said to be imbricate (Fig. 3.7e).

Some sedums have a spur at the base of the leaf, a feature which often helps separate similar species (Fig. 3.8a). A leaf is said to be entire if it is without indentation of any sort. In the descriptions that follow, each leaf is clearly depicted in the sketches and/or figures, so there is no need to complicate matters by outlining the botanical terms for the numerous shapes and forms. Attachment of a leaf to a stem or inflorescence is an important

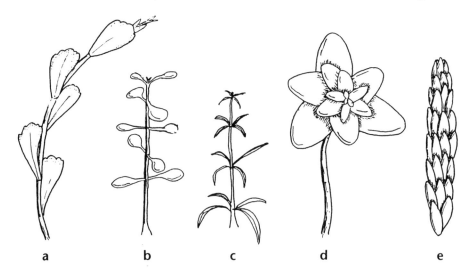

a   b   c   d   e

Figure 3.7. Leaf arrangement: (a) alternate (scattered), ascending (upward pointing) leaves on an arching, erect stem; (b) opposite-decussate leaves—which in this case are patent (outspreading) on an erect stem; (c) deflexed (pointing down), verticillate leaves in whorls of four; (d) leaves clustered into a terminal rosette on a somewhat tortuous stem; and (e) crowded, imbricate leaves (appearing appressed to the stem).

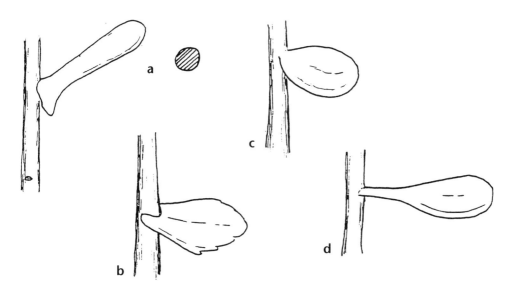

Figure 3.8. Leaf attachment: (a) terete leaf with spur; (b) sessile, amplexicaul leaf; (c) ovate, sessile leaf; and (d) petiolate, spathulate leaf.

feature (Fig. 3.8b, c, d). Sessile (not stalked), amplexicaul (stem-clasping) leaves can distinguish a stonecrop from closely related species that may have petiolate (stalked), spathulate (spoon-shaped) leaves, or ovate (egg-shaped), sessile leaves.

In some species, dried, dead leaves fall to the ground leaving long bare stems (Fig. 3.9a); in other species, the dead leaves hang on the stem, making it shaggy (Fig. 3.9b). North American species in particular can be stemless with leaves clustering in rosettes (Fig. 3.9c).

The color of leaves is fairly constant in some species of *Sedum*, but in oth-

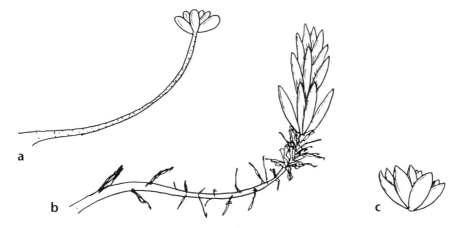

Figure 3.9. Adhesion of leaves: (a) bare stem with leaf scars terminating in a rosette of terete leaves; (b) procumbent stem, shaggy with persistent dead leaves; and (c) stemless rosette.

ers, intense sunlight can change the hue from light green to deep purple in a few weeks. A leaf may have no covering, in which case it is said to be glabrous (naked); or it may be glaucous (having the bloom of a plum or cabbage), pruinose (covered with a white powdery substance), or even hirsute (hairy). Occasionally leaves are papillose (with tiny nipplelike protruberances) or scabrid (rough, scurfy).

The leaves on the lower part of a stem usually fall off; the scar that remains is, in some species, very pronounced. Careful examination of *Sedum* leaves alone is not infallible proof of identification, but, when considered with details of arrangement and flower color, can lead to positive identification.

ROOTS

Roots of *Sedum* species can be fibrous, woody, rhizomatose, or caudiciform (having rhizomes or a caudex) and are a fairly reliable guide to the subgenus or group to which a particular plant belongs. Rhizomes of subgenus *Rhodiola* are massive (i.e., have a caudex that is partly above ground) or slender, and have scalelike leaves (Fig. 3.10a, b), but rhizomes of subgenus *Hylotelephium* often are carrotlike and never have scalelike leaves (Fig. 3.10c, d), and plants of subgenus *Sedum* generally have only fibrous roots (Fig. 3.10e–g). One group of subgenus *Hylotelephium* produces roots very similar to the woody rootstocks of *Aizoon* group (Fig. 3.10d, e), and several closely related North American species of subgenus *Sedum*, which look very similar above ground, are more easily identified by their contrasting fibrous and fleshy root systems (Fig. 3.10f, g).

CYTOLOGY

Species, especially those at the end of an evolutionary chain or those that inhabit rapidly changing environments, are far from being fixed. Mexican sedums in particular are relatively recent species, still very much evolving. Uhl (1961, 376) summarizes the reasons for the unstable nature of species.

> Typically the Crassulaceae are denizens of cliffs and rocks. Such habitats usually are discontinuous and, in terms of geologic time, rapidly changing. Populations must fluctuate greatly in size and degree of isolation as the area of suitable habitat changes with climate and erosion. Such conditions are generally considered to be conducive to rapid evolution.

Species do change. They often wholly or partly evolve into new species. This process of speciation is not fully understood, but is a fascinating key element in understanding evolution.

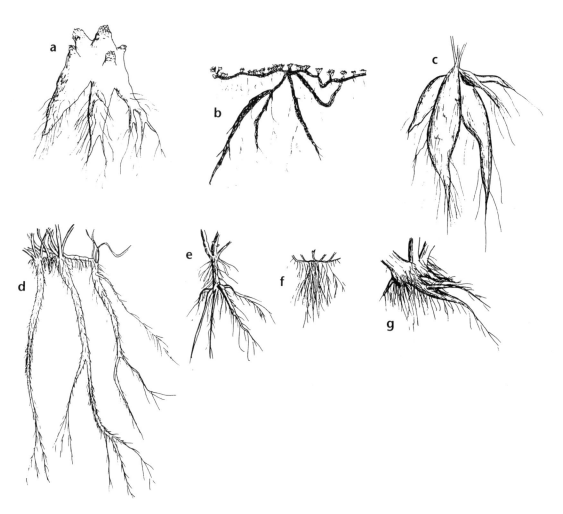

Figure 3.10. Root systems: (a) the massive rhizome of *Sedum bupleuroides* and (b) the tangled, slender rhizomes of *S. trollii* are characteristic of the subgenus *Rhodiola*, while (c) the fleshy, carrotlike rhizome of *S. spectabile* and (d) the woody rootstock of *S. ewersii* are characteristic of the subgenus *Hylotelephium*, although (e) *S. kamtschaticum* of the subgenus *Sedum* group *Aizoon* also has a woody rootstock; (f) *S. anglicum*, like most species of subgenus *Sedum*, has fibrous roots and (g) *S. glabrum*, a Mexican species of the subgenus *Sedum*, has an anomalous well-developed rootstock.

Speciation raises practical difficulties. If an isolated clone of a particular species is showing signs of evolving into a new species, what do we call the new form? Normally such a form is referred to as a subspecies. If the subspecies can no longer breed with the species, then it can be assumed that the subspecies has acquired new status and is a species in its own right. Often new species or subspecies are erected tentatively, as they appear unstable, and scientists are unsure how to name the new taxon. Assume, for example, that three named species exist; for simplicity, let them be A, B, and C. If species A interbreeds with species B where their habitats overlap, and species B interbreeds with species C where their habitats overlap, there is good reason to unite all three species under the oldest of the three names. Species A and C may not interbreed in nature because they do not have overlapping habitats; but if interbreeding cannot be induced in the laboratory, then the situation is very difficult to assess. Species A and C cannot be the same species as they are incapable of interbreeding, yet each interbreeds with a common species B.

Cytology is the science of microscopic anatomy, physiology, and biochemistry of the cell. Robert Hooke, as early as 1665, named the cell, and by 1885 Rudolf Virchow recognized that cells arise only from pre-existing cells. In 1888 Wilhelm von Waldeyer suggested the name *chromosome* for threadlike or rodlike bodies in the nucleus of a cell. Six years earlier Walter Flemming observed the process of cell division.

An important aid to the plant scientist when assessing the relationship between geographical races is this study of plant cells. Studying cells of a particular species as they divide sheds light on a clone's relationship with other plants. If cells behave in very similar ways, a close relationship is suggested. Cells behaving in very different ways have highlighted examples of convergent evolution where two vegetatively similar species are not related.

There are two types of cell division: mitosis and meiosis. Mitosis takes place during an organism's ordinary growth and is best observed at points on a plant where rapid growth is taking place. Meiosis is more complicated and is the source of much intrigue; it is sometimes referred to as "the dance of the chromosomes." To observe meiosis, pollen grains (or anthers) and carpels—the tissue in which gametes contribute to inheritance—are squashed, dyed, and studied under a microscope.

Gametes are generic material found on chromosomes. The structure of the chromosomes is stained so that the gametes can be observed more easily. During meiosis, chromosomes replicate once but the nucleus divides twice. As sexual reproduction doubles the chromosome number, meiosis halves it back to the original (i.e., haploid) stage. Occasionally meiosis fails to occur and a cell retains double the number of chromosomes; living organisms with double the number of chromosomes are said to be diploid. Many plants and animals have diploid chromosomes. Diploid chromosomes, in turn, can be doubled so a cell has four times the usual number of chromosomes; in this instance, an organism is said to be tetraploid.

If a squash is taken from unopened flower buds, it is usually stained with a black dye and an n count (the number of chromosomes) will be obtained. If a squash from the root tips or a cut from the meristem (growing tip) is used, reddish dyes enable a $2n$ count to be obtained. Leaves, except for growing tips, are poor sources of reliable counts as the water content is so high and the cells divide when they are very small.

In many cases, the difference in n (or $2n$) numbers between *Sedum* species prevents gene interchange and is an important criterion for differentiating species. If similar plants are incapable of sexual reproduction, they are considered different species. Unfortunately, it is not as simple as this. There are examples of species with several vegetatively contrasting subspecies that are cytologically stable (i.e., they have the same chromosome count). On the other hand, heteroploidy (the existence of different levels of ploidy) is not uncommon in sedums where plants of a single species grow alongside each other. Where several Mexican sedums are obviously evolving rapidly, many levels of ploidy can be observed from plants growing on a single hillside.

Aneuploidy, the gain or loss of a chromosome, is serious in humans (resulting, for example, in Down Syndrome), but not in plants. A species of *Sedum* often has several levels of ploidy. Thus, as a result of aneuploidy, a species may exist with $n = 7$ and $n = 8$.

Where aneuploidy has occured repeatedly, a species may have several levels of ploidy. This state is known as polyploidy. Perhaps the number of chromosomes has doubled again and again. Sometimes aneuploidy and polyploidy occur in the same species so that, as a result of chromosome doubling, chromosome counts of $n = 8, 16, 32$, and 64 are found plus, as a result of aneuploidy, $n = 31$. Often it is difficult for scientists to ascertain the basic chromosome numbers with existing evidence, or frequently they miscount chromosomes, especially when the chromosomes are particularly small.

> Morphological variation within the species is not always closely correlated with the differences in chromosome number. The frequency of such incipient species suggests rapid evolution . . . [and] some genera are extremely diverse cytologically with no one basic or ancestral number [x number] evident (Uhl 1961, 377).

Hybrid plants are rare with the genus *Sedum* but generally those determined to be of hybrid origin show great irregularity at meiosis and are normally sterile. Mexican species of *Pachysedum* group, in sharp contrast, are often capable of hybridizing with other species. In this case, outbreeding results in fertile hybrids with hybrid vigor. Species of *Pachysedum* group have an amazing propensity to hybridize with *Echeveria* and other genera. Intergeneric hybrids have been located in the wild and in cultivation. *Sedeveria* crosses (i.e., *Sedum* × *Echeveria*) are very common in cultivation and are invariably of unknown origin.

Hybridization followed by polyploidy has been important in the evolution of flowering plants. Some Mexican stonecrops have exceptionally high chromosome counts. Because of the small size of these chromosomes, it was first thought that these high counts were a result of fragmentation of the chromosomes. Evidence indicates that this is not so and that these plants are true polyploids at the end of a very long evolutionary chain. They have more chromosomes than any other living thing on planet Earth.

> In the genus *Sedum* every gametic chromosome number from 4 to 38 is known, as well as many higher numbers. . . . However this genus is considered the ancestral one for the family, and it serves as a repository for many short evolutionary lines that do not fit elsewhere (Uhl 1961, 376).

DISTRIBUTION

Generally speaking, *Sedum* species are Northern Hemisphere plants that occupy areas of rapid drainage where there is little competition from other vegetation (Fig. 3.11). Few Northern Hemisphere ranges of new fold mountains do not have at least one species of *Sedum*. Several species are circumpolar, such as tundra species growing north of the Arctic Circle. In very high latitudes, sedums tend to be associated with rocky or sandy coastal fringes. Towards the tropics, more species are alpine (i.e., they grow above the tree line), but even here, many species are still found at low altitudes and at sea fringes.

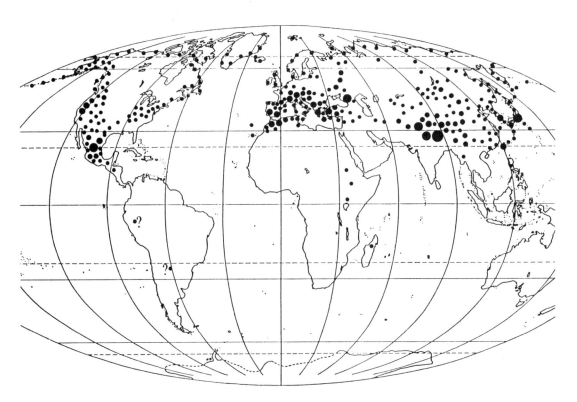

Figure 3.11. World distribution of stonecrops.

Three remarkably contrasting areas have a particularly rich *Sedum* population. The Mediterranean Sea margins and islands, plus its adjacent new fold mountain ranges—especially Sierra Nevada, Pyrenees, Central Massif, Alps, Apennines, Dinaric Alps, Balkan Uplands, and the Atlas ranges—are home to over 100 species and as many more varieties and regional forms. Much of this zone has a dry summer. The shores of the Mediterranean have a marked summer drought, and species have adapted in contrasting ways to withstand this. A number of annuals (e.g., *Sedum caespitosum*) are winter growers; by late spring they have flowered, cast seed to the wind, and died. Others, such as *S. amplexicaule*, become completely dormant in summer when plants die down to propagules. *Sedum sediforme*, which is found throughout this zone, is the most succulent of any of the Eurasian species. Its thick, leathery, often glaucous leaves help to conserve moisture, and by the end of summer, only a tuft of leaves may be left at stem tips. *Sedum tuberiferum* has tuberous propagules which store moisture below ground level to bridge the drought period.

The Himalayan Mountains are rich in *Sedum* species. This series of mountain chains and associated ranges is home to most species of subgenus *Rhodiola*, usually at very high altitudes. Adjacent southwestern China has a rich *Sedum* flora of subgenus *Hylotelephium*, subgenus *Sedum* groups *Aizoon* and *Orostachys*, and *Sedum* sensu stricto. These species spill over into Central Asia and the volcanic islands of the Pacific fringe including Japan. Hokkaido, the most northerly of the four main Japanese islands, has bitter winters, but several *Sedum* species grow within the spray of the ocean. Kyushu, the most southerly of the main Japanese islands, has such a short winter that two rice crops can be grown each year, yet several species inhabit alpine regions. Lowland species from Kyushu will need winter protection in areas of higher latitude and in continental interiors.

In all, perhaps as many as 200 species of *Sedum* sensu lato from the Far East area have been registered and are recognized as distinct. Very high altitude members of subgenus *Rhodiola* usually have a large rootstock, but in contrast, many Far Eastern species of subgenus *Sedum* are not particularly succulent, growing in areas experiencing heavy summer monsoons. Several species (e.g., *S. rosulatobulbosum*) are associated with wet places, though sites have perfect drainage.

Mexico is the third area with a rich *Sedum* flora. Consisting of three fold ranges with an intermontane plateau, and a relatively new volcanic upland zone, Mexico has about 100 species, some of which spill over into the United States. Some species (e.g., *S. frutescens*) grow on lava fields where they have developed massive stems to store moisture, and papery bark and small, deciduous leaves to restrict transpiration. Other species prefer damp, shady canyon walls in areas of higher rainfall where they tend to grow downwards. Because of its semidesert nature, Mexico is perhaps the richest country in the world for xerophitic and succulent plants. Several Mexican species (e.g., *S. moranense*) are hardy in temperate countries, for they grow at very high altitudes and can withstand frost and ice. In wetter regions of Mexico, several *Sedum* species are epiphytic, growing on trees, agave, or cacti. Generally, Mexican stonecrops are associated with sloping, well-drained land where competition from other plants is limited.

In addition to these three areas rich in *Sedum* species, North America has over 30 endemic species, mostly from the Western Cordillera, but several are from the Eastern Cordillera and associated plateaux. Europe has several widespread species north of the Alps. The Middle East has a few endemic ephemerals, and East Africa to just below the equator has a handful of true *Sedum* species. Several species are endemic to the Atlantic islands of the Macronesian group. I have also included a doubtful South American species, which geographically is so disjunct that it should be assigned to another genus.

Wherever colonies were set up in the temperate Southern Hemisphere, sedums seem to have been established. From Tierra del Fuego to New Zealand, stonecrops have escaped and intermingled with native flora. Unlike the weed *Carpobrotus*, the South African Hottentot fig that brightens up beaches and coastal cliffs throughout the warm temperate zone, I have never heard of sedums smothering and endangering indigenous species.

CHAPTER 4

Crassulaceae

Flowering plants with seeds enclosed in an ovary are known as angiosperms. Angiosperms are divided into dicotyledons and monocotyledons, distinguished by, among other features, the number of cotyledons or seed leaves in the embryo. Just after germination, seedlings take on one of two distinct forms: some seedlings form two seed lobes, from the center of which true leaves and stem emerge; cabbage, cactus, and stonecrops are examples of dicotyledons. Other seedlings have an embryo that forms one grasslike seed lobe; *Aloe*, onion, and maize are examples of monocotyledons (Fig. 4.1).

Within the dicotyledons is Crassulaceae (*Crassula* family). All stonecrops as well as crassulas and other genera belong to this family.

CHARACTERISTICS

Plants within Crassulaceae are characterized by the following:

A SUPERIOR OVARY (Fig. 4.1). Seeds must be produced above the line formed by the petals emerging, rather than below the line of emergence. Subgenus *Rhodiola* infringes this rule somewhat: its ovary is sunken and therefore partly below the line of petals.

ACTINOMORPHIC FLOWERS (Fig. 4.1). Petals must radiate out from the center of the flower like rays of the sun. They are symmetric with relation to many diameters.

ISOMEROUS FLOWERS (Fig. 4.1). Flower parts must occur in equal numbers; that is, the number of sepals equals the number of petals, equals the number of stamens, equals the number of carpels. A 4-partite member of Crassulaceae has four sepals, four petals, four stamens, and four carpels. Often however, especially in *Sedum*, flowers have two whorls of stamens. Thus a 5-partite member of Crassulaceae could have five sepals, five petals, ten stamens, and five carpels.

COMPOUND CARPELS (pistil-cell, seed-lobe, or fruit) are common to other families, but the carpels of plants in Crassulaceae each form a cell that splits vertically after drying and sheds dustlike seed (Fig. 4.1). The fruit is never fleshy.

SUCCULENCE. Crassulaceae species are water-storing, drought-resistant (xerophitic) plants with fleshy leaves, stems, or rootstocks (caudex or rhizome). The degree of succulence varies from species to species. As an exception to drought resistance, a fleshy aquatic *Crassula* species has become a nuisance by blocking up waterways. Generally these plants inhabit areas of rapid drainage, low rainfall, or both.

SUBFAMILIES AND GENERA

Sorting the Crassulaceae into easily defined subfamilies and genera has probably caused more disagreement among taxonomists than sorting any other plant family. Some taxonomists lump hundreds of species under one genetic umbrella, while others emphasize minute floral detail and end up with scores of genera. Horticulturists are often puzzled and exhausted by botanists' changing ideas of nomenclature. Most taxonomists accept the

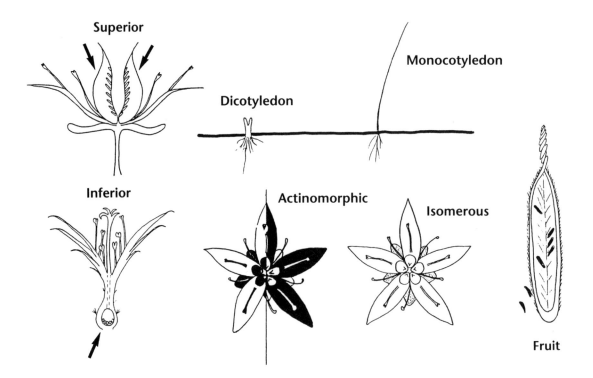

Figure 4.1. Crassulaceae plants have dicotyledonous seedlings. Flowers have a superior ovary and are actinomorphic and isomerous. Fruits (carpels) split vertically to release dust-like seed.

six subfamilies used by Berger (1930)—Cotyledonoideae, Crassuloideae, Echeverioideae, Kalanchoideae, Sedoideae, and Sempervivoideae—but there is much disagreement over the placement of certain genera (Fig. 4.2).

Isolating the Crassuloideae from other subfamilies is very straightforward. Its members have a single whorl of stamens and are Southern Hemisphere plants, centered in Africa (Fig. 4.3a). All other subfamilies have two

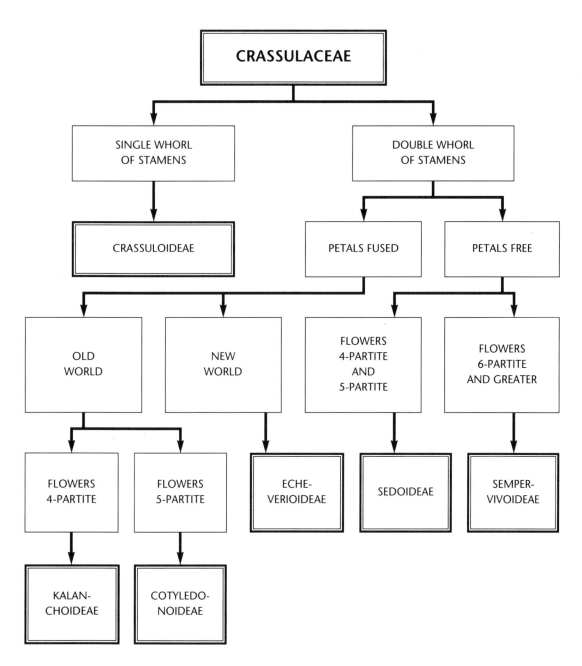

Figure 4.2. Berger's taxonomy of the six subfamilies of Crassulaceae.

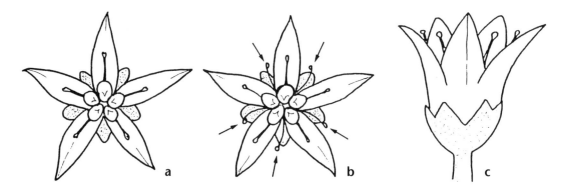

Figure 4.3. Crassulaceae plants producing flowers (a) with a single whorl of stamens are placed in subfamily Crassuloideae, while flowers (b) with a double whorl of stamens are associated with all other subfamilies. The five subfamilies whose flowers have a double whorl of stamens can be further divided into two groups based on petal fusion: (b) Sedoideae and Sempervivoideae have free petals; (c) Cotyledonoideae, Echeverioideae, and Kalanchoideae have petals united into a tube.

whorls of stamens, though several anomalies such as *Sinocrassula* group from China and a few *Sedum* species from both the Old and New Worlds have apparently, through evolution, discarded a whorl of stamens (Fig. 4.3b).

Once Berger (1930) removed Crassuloideae from Crassulaceae, his definitions to delimit the remaining subfamilies were equally precise. Plants newly discovered since Berger's publication do not fit neatly into his strictly defined compartments. Therefore, other botanists have expanded his definitions to accomodate new species that appear to bridge boundaries between the strictly defined subfamilies. The result is that the Crassulaceae can be broken into manageable-sized groups but, as a consequence, the new, less strictly defined subfamilies have indistinct boundaries and several genera have been transferred from one subfamily to another.

Fusion of petals has long been considered an important factor when delimiting subfamilies. Long before Berger erected his six subfamilies, Linnaeus in *Genera Plantarum* (1737) used petal fusion as a feature to separate *Cotyledon* from the genera which today make up Sedoideae and Sempervivoideae. "Schönland, again using fusion of petals as a prime consideration, went a great way towards establishing relationships within Crassulaceae" (qtd. in Fröderström 1930). Berger (1930) considered all members of Crassulaceae with petals unattached to each other at the base (free) to be members of subfamilies Sedoideae and Sempervivoideae (Fig. 4.3b), and all those with petals united at the base to form a flower tube to be members of subfamilies Cotyledonoideae, Echeverioideae, or Kalanchoideae (Fig. 4.3c).

As early as 1828, De Candolle erected the genus *Echeveria* for all New World *Cotyledon* species, leaving only Old World species in *Cotyledon*. More taxonomists began to realize that geographical location was as important as physical appearance when systematizing subfamilies or genera. For the same reasons, New World Rocky Mountain goat, *Oreamnos americanus*, despite its similarities to Old World chamois, *Rupicapra rupicapra*, is placed in a different genus. Berger's commonly accepted groupings of Crassulaceae with two whorls of stamens and petals united into a tube comprise the following:

Old World subfamilies and their genera
    Kalanchoideae
        Kalanchoe Adanson
    Cotyledonoideae
        Adromischus Lemaire
        Chiastophyllum Berger
        Cotyledon Linnaeus
        Mucizonia Battandier & Trabut
        Pistorinia De Candolle
        Tylecodon Toelken
        Umbilicus De Candolle

New World subfamily and its genera
    Echeverioideae
        Dudleya Britton & Rose
        Echeveria De Candolle
        Graptopetalum Rose
        Pachyphytum Link, Klotzsch & Otto
        Tacitus Moran
        Thompsonella Britton & Rose

Many taxonomists are unhappy about the status quo, as recent investigation shows very closely related species have not only been placed in different genera, but sometimes in different subfamilies.

Crassuloideae

Crassula is the only genus within the subfamily Crassuloideae that is generally accepted by modern taxonomists. Even *Tillaea* with its 3-partite to 5-partite flowers, and only two seeds per carpel, appears more frequently as *Crassula* in modern texts (Fig. 4.4). *Dinacria, Kalosanthes, Pagella, Rhopalota, Rochea,* and *Vauanthes* have all been assimilated into *Crassula*. A single whorl of stamens and usually opposite leaves are the characteristic features of this subfamily.

Once Crassuloideae has been removed from the family Crassulaceae, traditionally the remaining subfamilies are grouped according to fusion of the

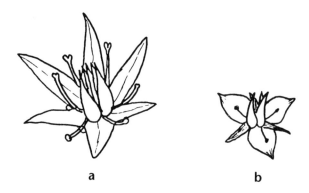

Figure 4.4. (a) The flower of *Crassula grisea* is large for *Crassula* and measures 1 cm (0.4 in) across; (b) the flower of *Tillaea muscosa*, a minute member of *Crassuloideae* with only two seeds per carpel, measures 3 mm (0.1 in) across. *Tillaea* flowers are tiny and often only 3-partite.

petals and their continent of origin. Sempervivoideae and Sedoideae have free petals; Kalanchoideae, Cotyledonoideae, and Echeverioideae have fused petals, or at least petals that are upright at the base (Fig. 4.3).

Kalanchoideae

Modern taxonomists only recognize one genus in the subfamily Kalanchoideae, namely, *Kalanchoe*. Today, it is generally accepted that *Bryophyllum* and *Kitchingia* have been assimilated into *Kalanchoe*. All *Kalanchoe* species are Old World members of the Crassulaceae producing 4-partite flowers with distinct tubes formed by fusion of petals. *Kalanchoe* flowers have four sepals, four petals, eight stamens, and four carpels (Fig. 4.5).

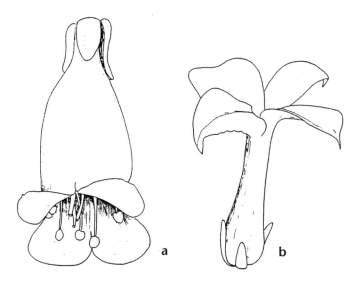

Figure 4.5. Kalanchoideae 4-partite flowers have distinct tubes formed by petal fusion: (a) *Kalanchoe porohydrocalyx* has petals 2.5 cm (1 in) long; (b) *Kalanchoe* sp. CB178 has contrasting upright, slightly shorter flowers.

Cotyledonoideae

Cotyledonoideae members also have tubed flowers and comprise Old World genera *Adromischus, Chiastophyllum, Cotyledon, Mucizonia, Pistorinia, Tylecodon,* and *Umbilicus* (Fig. 4.6). In older books, these genera are all included with *Cotyledon*. By and large, plants of Cotyledonoideae produce 5-partite flowers. Cytologically, South African *Adromischus, Cotyledon,* and *Tylecodon* cannot be distinguished from each other, but tenuous and subtle vegetative differences make identification relatively easy for the majority of species (Fig. 4.7). *Tylecodon* species are pachycaul and lose their leaves as they flower. *Adromischus* and *Cotyledon* retain their leaves and the former has somewhat erect flowers.

Umbilicus (pennywort) is composed of relatively hardy European species, though they are not as hardy as the monotypic *Chiastophyllum oppositifolium* from the former Soviet Union, which is a popular rock garden plant with nodding yellow flowers. Cytological study has shown that these two temperate genera plus *Mucizonia* and *Pistorinia* seem to be only very distantly related to the three African genera. Recent opinion is that *Umbilicus, Chiastophyllum, Mucizonia,* and *Pistorinia* may all have evolved from *Sedum*

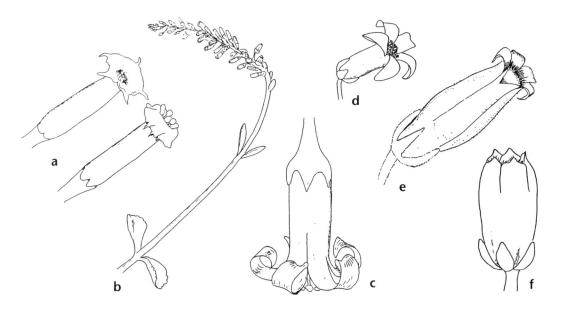

Figure 4.6. Plants of the subfamily Cotyledonoideae have tubed, 5-partite flowers: (a) two stages in the development of the upright, tubular, 2.6-cm (1-in) long flowers of *Adromischus roaneanus*; (b) *Chiastophyllum oppositifolium* has nodding heads of yellow, tubed flowers about 1.4 cm (0.6 in) long; (c) *Cotyledon decussata* has nodding, red 5-partite flowers 3.7 cm (1.5 in) long; (d) *Tylecodon shafferiana* has flowers 1.9 cm (0.8 in) long; (e) *Tylecodon grandiflora* boasts the largest of Crassulaceae flowers—6 cm (2 in) long; (f) flowers of *Umbilicus rupestris*, the common navelwort or pennywort, are 1.8 cm (0.7 in) long.

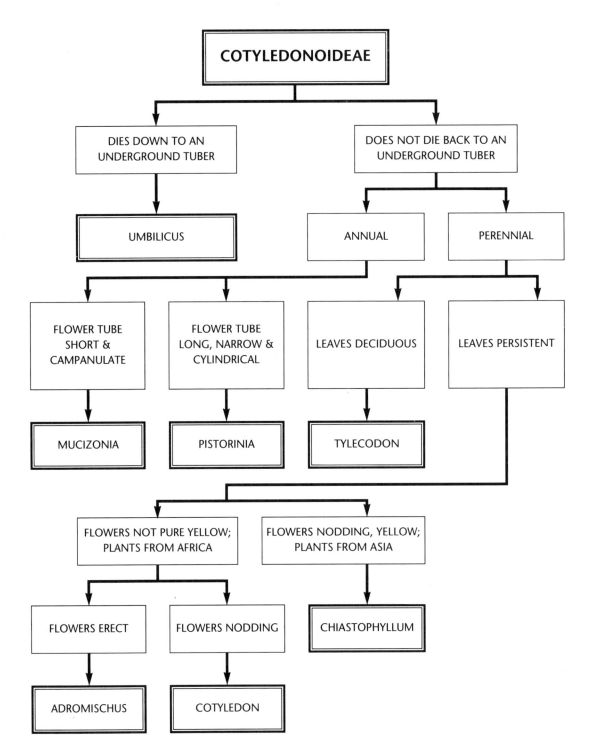

Figure 4.7. Divisions within the subfamily Cotyledonoideae.

and should perhaps be disassociated with South African genera of Cotyledonoideae.

Tubed, 5-partite flowers are still the best means by which gardeners can identify members of the subfamily Cotyledonoideae.

Echeverioideae

The subfamily Echeverioideae includes New World genera *Dudleya*, *Echeveria*, *Graptopetalum*, *Pachyphytum*, *Tacitus*, and *Thompsonella*. Although the boundaries of these genera have been redefined to include or exclude newly discovered species, gardeners, by studying the flowers of Echeverioideae, can identify each of the genera without too much difficulty (Fig. 4.8). Other recently discovered species of Echeverioideae are difficult to assign with confidence to any genus, as they appear to bridge gaps between existing genera. These species, called "gap-bridgers," have endured many name changes as taxonomists try to group closely related species. Most gap-bridgers have been assigned to very small new genera, which have been established to keep apart larger, older, generally accepted genera. Several have suffered many name changes and have been moved from one subfamily to another by a succession of taxonomists. *Villadia* and *Lenophyllum*, for example, were placed in the subfamily Echeverioideae by Berger, but now are considered better accommodated in the subfamily Sedoideae.

Graptopetalum species were considered by Berger to be a group within *Sedum*, but now are placed alongside *Echeveria*. Their flowers show mottled petals, a major feature of this genus, though the degree of reddish dappling is variable (Fig. 4.9a–e). Petals are erect at the base and then spreading; they never become wider in the middle but gradually taper upwards. Although they are somewhat united, the degree of fusion is not a good guide to identification. Despite the placement of *Graptopetalum* in Echeverioideae, its petals are relatively free. One whorl of stamens arches back through the petals as flowers mature (Fig. 4.9e), and inflorescences are frequently very angular.

Pachyphytum flowers have a pair of lobes where the epipetalous stamens are inserted, a feature that alone differentiates this genus from *Echeveria* (Fig. 4.9f, g). Petals are very fleshy and often bicolored. Inflorescences are usually erect with flowers on one side.

Tacitus is a monotypic genus that has made a remarkable impact on the succulent trade since its introduction in the 1980s. It has since been assigned to *Graptopetalum*, although its large, plain, stellate petals are deep red and have lips that enclose the carpels (Fig. 4.9h). In addition to these differences, its alternipetalous stamens do not act like those of *Graptopetalum*, so I believe *Tacitus* is best kept as a separate genus. Like all species in the subfamily Crassulaceae, *Tacitus*, too, can produce anomalous 3-partite flowers (Fig. 4.9i).

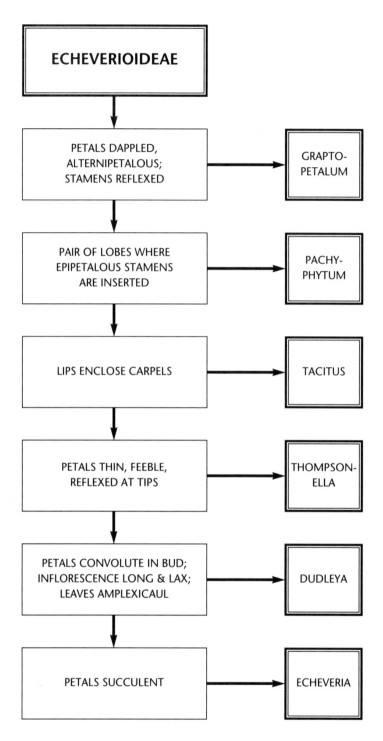

Figure 4.8. Divisions within the subfamily Echeverioideae.

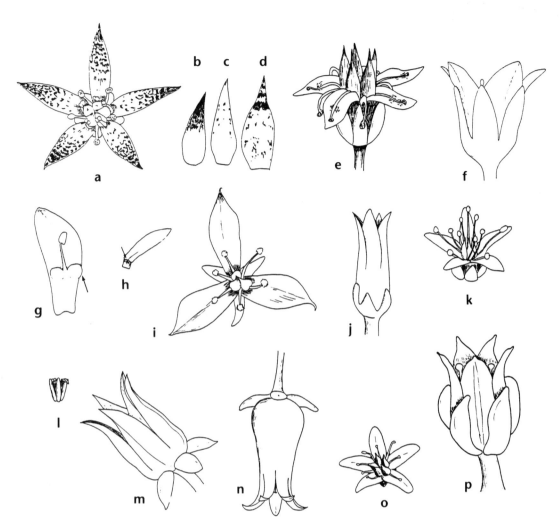

Figure 4.9. Floral differences displayed by species of the subfamily Echeverioideae. *Grapto-petalum* flowers are distinctly dappled; (a) *G. saxifragoides* petals, only 1.6 cm (0.6 in) long; (b) *G. filiferum*; (c) *G. pachyphyllum*; (d) *G. pentandrum*; and (e) *G. paraguayense*, typical of the genus, displays one whorl of stamens reflexed between petals as the flower ages; (f) *Pachyphytum hookeri* flower is typical of the genus, whose flowers (g) are identical to those of *Echeveria* except for a pair of lobes in which a stamen is inserted on a petal, which in this instance is 1.6 cm (0.6 in) long; *Tacitus bellus* (h) has lips enclosing the carpels and (i) can produce anomalous 3-partite flowers; (j) *Dudleya caespitosa* flower is typical of the genus with upright 1.6 cm (0.6 in) petals that are convolute in bud and united to a tube, but in contrast, (k) *D. edulis* has very sedumlike flowers, except 0.7 cm (0.3 in) petals are united for a short way and are upright at the base; (l) *Thompsonella minutiflora* has very thin, upright petals that turn out at the tips and waisted carpels; *Echeveria* includes a wide range of flowers; (m) the flower of *E. sedoides* is large, upright, and 3.1 cm (1.2 in) long, about the same length as (n) the flower of *E. lilacina*, which hangs; (o) *E. carnicolor* has smaller petals, 1.5 cm (0.6 in) long; and (p) *E. affinis* has deep red petals 1.4 cm (0.6 in) long; here. *E. carnicolor* has the most stellate flowers and the least fusion of petals, and *E. lilacina* has petals united for most of their length.

Before cytological evidence was available, *Dudleya* and *Echeveria* were difficult to differentiate. The former is a natural group of species, each with 17 pairs of small chromosomes, and appears to have evolved on a different tectonic plate from *Echeveria* (Uhl, 1992). The layperson can confidently differentiate between the vegetatively very similar *Dudleya* and *Echeveria* when species are in flower. *Dudleya* flowers are convolute in bud (Fig. 4.10a, b, c); that is, each petal is half-wrapped around its neighbor. *Echeveria* flowers are not convolute in bud (Fig. 4.10d, e, f). Inflorescences of *Dudleya* and *Echeveria* are highly contrasting: the latter are usually upright and relatively compact, while the former are very long, lax, and often decumbent.

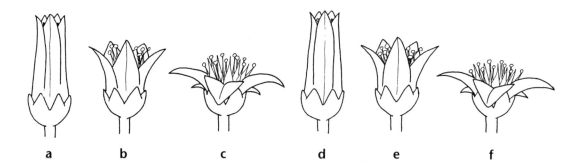

a   b   c   d   e   f

Figure 4.10. Differentiating between *Echeveria* and *Dudleya* flowers: (a, b, c) *Dudleya* flowers have a similar range of form and fusion but are convolute in bud. By the time stellate *Stylophyllum* group flowers (f) are open, it is too late to check whether petals were convolute or not. (d, e, f) *Echeveria* flowers have fleshy petals that are somewhat upright and usually united to each other. They range in form from tubular flowers with upright petals to quite patent, stellate petals forming star-shaped flowers.

Stylophyllum has had a checkered history. Some species were originally described as belonging to *Sedum*, but cytological work of the 1980s has shown *Stylophyllum* to be part of *Dudleya* rather than part of *Sedum*. *Dudleya* and *Stylophyllum* were considered distinct because the former has upright petals and the latter has spreading petals (Fig. 4.9j, k), but in more recent years, intermediate forms have been discovered, thus uniting the two. It is more difficult to check that *Stylophyllum* flowers have convolute petals (Fig. 4.10c) because of their stellate nature, but the feature is easily checked while the buds are still closed or just opening.

Thompsonella comprises several species closely related to *Echeveria* but with minor floral differences. *Thompsonella* flowers are small and feeble; they have very thin, upright petals that spread and reflex at the tips (Fig. 4.9l). These features distinguish this small genus from *Echeveria*, but the differences are meager and species within also have much affinity to *Villadia*.

Echeveria flowers are far more difficult to define than those of the other genera of Echeverioideae—they encompass all forms that have not already been removed from the subfamily. Petals are very thick and succulent, particularly near the base. They do not possess lobes or lips (as do *Pachyphytum* and *Tacitus,* respectively); they are not dappled or convolute in bud (as are *Graptopetalum* and *Dudleya,* respectively), and the alternipetalous stamens do not reflex between the petals (as do *Graptopetalum*). Despite the wide range of flower forms (Fig. 4.9m, n, o, p) and inflorescence arrangements within *Echeveria,* all flowers in this genus have succulent petals, which may be united into a tube or which may have thick, upright bases.

Genera of Echeverioideae show remarkable cytological diversity. Uhl, in particular, has shown that the Echeverioideae may be more closely related to *Sedum* than to Old World Cotyledonoideae. Too much emphasis has been placed on petal fusion in the past. It is now realized that Echeverioideae may well have evolved from *Sedum* with free petals rather than from any ancestors with fused petals. Uhl (1963, 80), discussing the flowers of Crassulaceae, wrote:

> All the other floral types [other than *Sedum* with free petals and two whorls of stamens] could have been derived from the *Sedum* type, most of them in one step, by fusion or loss of floral parts or by change in the number of parts in each whorl. The characters, plus the geographical distribution, have served to distinguish the six subfamilies [of Berger]. Howevever, it has become clear that similar floral characters have evolved independently, some of them many times, in groups that are not closely related.

As late as 1991, Jorge Meyrán, in "The Generic Classification of the Mexican Crassulaceae," used lateral inflorescences of Echeverioideae to differentiate from Sedoideae, but species of the genus *Sedum* group *Pachysedum* have lateral inflorescences. Perhaps in the near future a bold taxonomist will erect *Pachysedum* as a genus, remove it from Sedioideae, and place it in Echeverioideae. Or perhaps Kuntze's proposal of uniting all Crassulaceae into one genus (*Sedum*) may gain more support. A monograph on the expanded genus *Sedum* would indeed be mighty.

Sempervivoideae

Sempervivoideae members have free petals and are very difficult to separate from the subfamily Sedoideae. At one time, the number of petals was considered the prime indicator. Athough it is true that Sempervivoideae species generally produce more petals than Sedoideae species, actually drawing a line to separate the two subfamilies is impossible or, if done, completely unreliable. In 1737 Linnaeus wrote (qtd. in Fröderström 1930, 5), "*Cotyledon* [which at the time included *Echeveria*], *Sempervivum* and *Rhodiola* are so closely related to *Sedum* that they should either be grouped together as one genus or divided . . . if ever the limits can be fixed." Fröderström (1930, 7) added that "these difficulties have not been lessened . . . but have become more accentuated by the discovery of a great many intermediary forms . . . especially in the Chinese and Mexican flora." Because of the larger number of flower parts, Sempervivoideae plants tend to form a central cavity between their carpels. This alone is the only reliable feature to help differentiate plants of this subfamily from those of Sedoideae.

There is no precise way of circumscribing Sedoideae: it is the subfamily left after the other five subfamilies have been removed. Free petals and stellate flowers are the best indicators to distinguish Sempervivoideae from Cotyledonoideae, Echeverioideae, and Kalanchoideae. High numbers of flower parts is the best indicator to distinguish Sempervivoideae from Sedoideae, but a growing number of species transgress.

In general, Sempervivoideae flower parts occur in whorls of 6 or more (Fig. 4.11). They are Old World plants from Eurasia and North Africa. The work of Pilon-Smits on CAM (1992) supports the hypothesis that Sempervivoideae species have evolved from *Sedum*. The following guidelines outline the characteristics of the rather badly defined genera within the subfamily Sempervivoideae:

Aeonium **Webb & Berthelot**. Flowers are 6-partite to 12-partite, with more or less quadrate, spathulate, obcordate, or rarely absent nectary glands (Fig 4.11a). Plants are tender, with a basic chromosome count of $x = 18$.

Aichryson **Webb & Berthelot**. Flowers are 6-partite to 12-partite, with two-horned or digitate nectaries (Fig. 4.11b). Plants are tender, with a basic chromosome count of $x = 15$.

Greenovia **Webb & Berthelot**. Flowers are 20-partite to 32-partite, without nectaries (Fig. 4.11c). Plants are tender, with a basic chromosome count of $x = 18$.

Jovibarba **Opiz**. Flowers are 6-partite to 7-partite, with erect and fringed petals (not entire) and quadrate nectaries (Fig. 4.11d). Plants are hardy, with a chromosome count of $n = 19$.

Monanthes **Haworth**. Flowers are 6-partite to 9-partite, with huge, in relation to the size of the flower, nectary glands of two emarginate lobes on a short stalk or with fan-shaped nectaries (Fig. 4.11e). Plants are tender, with a basic chromosome count of $x = 18$.

Sempervivum **L**. Flowers are 8-partite to 16-partite, with quadrate nectaries (Fig. 4.11f). Plants are hardy, with chromosome counts of $n = 16, 17, 18, 19, 20, 21, 32$, and 37.

All genera of Sempervivoideae are at best only arbitrary groupings (Fig. 4.12). I have observed 5-partite *Monanthes* species and 11-partite *Sedum* species, and I am aquainted with several *Sempervivum* species that could not be considered hardy. Sempervivoideae produces monocarpic inflorescences (except for some species of *Monanthes*), or at least the rosette or branch carrying the inflorescence dies after flowering. A monocarpic inflorescence is a good pointer to differentiate the two subfamilies Sedoideae and Sempervivoideae, but not a firm rule. Huge nectary glands of *Monanthes* are fairly unique in the Old World Crassulaceae, but the genus has often been considered closer to *Sedum* than to *Sempervivum*.

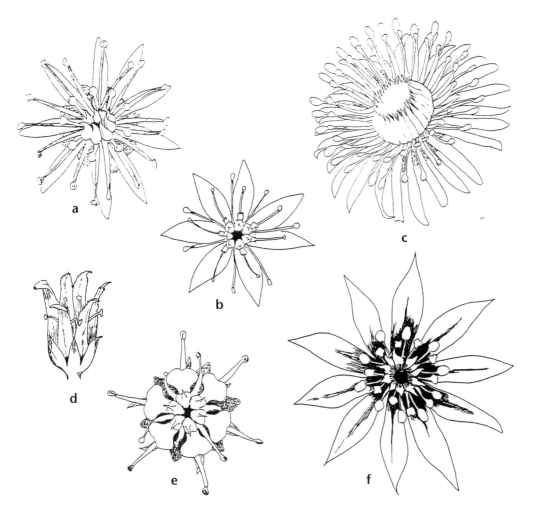

Figure 4.11. Subfamily Sempervivoideae flowers: (a) *Aeonium tabuliforme* flowers are 1.4 cm (0.6 in) across: (b) *Aichryson punctatum* has fingerlike protruberences at the ends of its nectaries and its flowers are small, measuring only 0.9 cm (0.4 in) across; (c) *Greenovia aurea*, which has the highest number of floral parts of any member of Crassulaceae, has a flower that measures nearly 3 cm (1 in) across; (d) *Jovibarba hirta* has upright, eroded petals 1.4 cm (0.6 in) long which distinguish this genus from *Sempervivum*; (e) *Monanthes muralis* has huge nectary glands, narrow and reflexed petals that can just be seen behind long stamens, and tiny flowers measuring 0.5 cm (0.2 in) across; (f) like all flowers of this subfamily, *Sempervivum tectorum*, here measuring 2.8 cm (1.1 in) across, has a cavity in the center of the carpels.

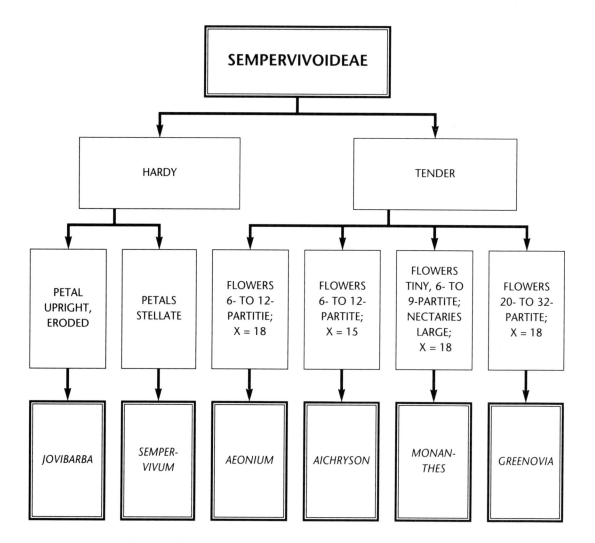

Figure 4.12. Divisions of subfamily Sempervivoideae.

Sedoideae

Not only are the boundaries between the genera of Sedoideae easily bridged, but boundaries between them and genera in the Sempervivoideae and Echeverioideae are also fogged. As a result, plants that appear in this volume as *Sedum* species may well appear somewhere else as *Rosularia* or *Villadia*. The reader must come to his or her own conclusions. Uhl (1961, 1963, 1970, 1976) has shown beyond much doubt that *Echeveria* species are closely related to certain North American *Sedum* species and often hybridize freely with them. He believes *Sedum* species were probably ancestors of *Echeveria* species, but now the two genera appear in different subfamilies because taxonomists in the past placed too much emphasis on the connation and fusion of petals. Despite Uhl's conclusion and the seemingly artificial boundaries between genera and subfamilies, other taxonomists are carving up *Sedum* into dozens of smaller genera.

Leaving aside present disputes, the genera listed below have been included in the genus *Sedum* in whole or in part at some time in their taxonomic history (Fig. 4.13). *Mucizonia*, *Rosularia*, and *Villadia* are obviously very

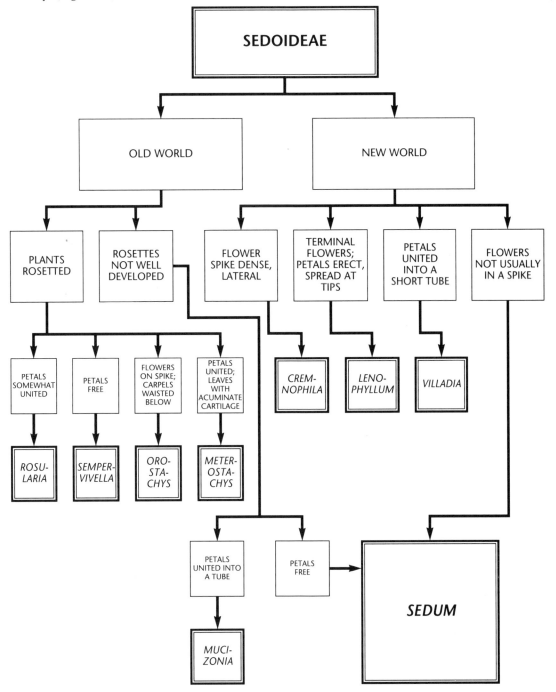

Figure 4.13. Divisions of subfamily Sedoideae.

closely related to *Sedum* but have petals that are fused to some extent. As a result, they contradict the definition of the subfamily and therefore may be found listed elsewhere under Echeverioideae or Cotyledonoideae. Recent scientific work seems to suggest that *Umbilicus* and *Chiastophyllum* are also better placed within the subfamily Sedoideae. Sedoideae genera grow in both the Old and New Worlds, mostly north of the equator.

The following guidelines outline the proposed genera of the Sedoideae (Fig. 4.14):

Cremnophila Rose. Originally comprised a single Mexican species midway between *Echeveria* and *Sedum*, which is described within this publication as *Sedum cremnophila*. More recently Moran (1978) removed a near relative from *Echeveria* and expanded and redefined *Cremnophila* to act as a buffer between the large genera of *Echeveria* and *Sedum*.

Lenophyllum Rose. These North American plants are close to *Sedum* and

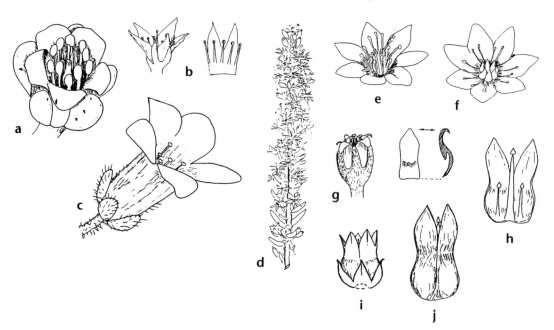

Figure 4.14. Subfamily Sedoideae flowers: (a) this *Lenophyllum guttatum* flower measures 0.8 cm (0.3 in) across; (b) *Sedum leveillianum* (syn. *Meterostachys sikokianus*) flowers have two whorls of stamens on petals 0.6 cm (0.2 in) long; (c) *Sedum mucizonia* (syn. *Mucizonia hispida*) flowers have united petals forming a floral tube 0.9 cm (0.4 in) long; (d) *Sedum chanetii* (syn. *Orostachys chanetii*) flowers closely resemble those of subgenus *Hylotelephium*, except for their spike arrangement (the inflorescence measures 20 cm, or 8 in); (e) *Rosularia alpestris*, a form from Zozila, Turkey, has relatively stellate flowers 2 cm (0.8 in) across. (f) *Sempervivella alba* (syn. *Rosularia sedoides*, *Sedum sedoides*) has slightly cupped flowers almost 2 cm (0.8 in) across; (g) *Sedum indicum* var. *densirosulatum* (syn. *Sinocrassula densirosulatum*) has a single whorl of stamens and its petals, only 0.7 cm (0.3 in) long, have an unusual vertical section; *Villadia ramosissima* (h) inside petals with three stamens (i) flower measuring 0.8 cm (0.3 in) long, and (j) two petals with sepals removed to show degree of fusion.

Echeveria. Their diagnostic features are terminal inflorescences and erect petals that spread only at the very tips (Fig. 4.14a). *Lenophyllum* leaves are opposite. This combination of features separates a handful of species from *Sedum*.

Meterostachys Nakai. The genus *Meterostachys* contains only a single Japanese species which is similar to plants of *Orostachys* group and other *Sedum* species. Petals of this species are somewhat fused, a feature that is generally accepted today in several North American *Sedum* species which were once considered to belong to the genus *Gormania* (Fig. 4.14b). *Meterostachys* is considered a group within subgenus *Sedum* in this volume.

Mucizonia (De Candolle) Battandier & Trabut. This sedumlike plant or group of very closely related species comes from the Mediterranean. The flower tube is distinct, with petals united for more than half their length (Fig. 4.14c). There have been a number of attempts to include this group with *Sedum*, a placement I have followed in this volume.

Orostachys Fischer. This group comprises a dozen or more Asian species that are often included with *Sedum*, as individual flowers are very similar to those of subgenus *Hylotelephium*. Literally hundreds of flowers are carried on a terminal, monocarpic spike (Fig. 4.14d). Because of this spike arrangement, *Orostachys* is sometimes removed from *Sedum*, but in this volume, it is treated as a group within *Sedum*.

Rosularia (De Candolle) Stapf. In a recent monograph on this genus, Eggli (1988) poached several plants long considered to be *Sedum*. He included *S. hirsutum*, which in its North African forms is very difficult to separate from *S. dasyphyllum*, which in turn is linked with *S. brevifolium* and *S. album*. Inadvertently Eggli made a very good case for uniting *Sedum* and *Rosularia*. The differentiating characteristics of *Rosularia* are, apparently, (1) leaves never terete but always united into rosettes and (2) mostly funnel-shaped flowers with the petals somewhat united. Unfortunately, several species of *Rosularia* have stellate petals (Fig. 4.14e). As a general guide, few Old World sedums are made up of rosettes. *Rosularia* is considered beyond the scope of this volume except for a single species that is usually labelled *Sedum adenotrichum*.

Sedum L. This genus contains all the species left after the more easily defined genera are removed. Flowers usually have free petals (Fig. 3.1).

Sempervivella Stapf. This genus is often included with *Rosularia* or *Sedum*. Plants produce rosulate bodies like those of *Rosularia*, but have large *Sedum*-like flowers (Fig. 4.14f). *Sempervivella* is considered beyond the scope of this volume.

Sinocrassula Berger. I have included *Sinocrassula* within *Sedum* despite its single whorl of stamens (Fig. 4.14g).

Villadia Haworth (Fig. 4.14h, i, j). This New World genus now includes all the species once considered to be *Altamiranoa*. *Villadia* originally included only species with cupped flowers and united petals. *Altamiranoa* was composed of species with stellate flowers and vaguely united petals. Baehni united the two genera in 1937; and Clausen, agreeing with Baehni, transferred to *Villadia* a species of *Sedum* he had himself described. Jacobsen (1960), in a tidying-up exercise, transferred the remaining *Altimiranoa* to *Villadia*, but several species would perhaps be more sensibly placed in *Sedum*. At the time this volume is being written, Moran and Uhl are preparing a reappraisal of genus *Villadia*.

PROBLEMS OF STATUS

If seeds removed from a single carpel of a *Sedum* species are germinated, individual plants will take on different forms if they are grown in different materials; receive varying amounts of water, sunshine, and nutriments; or are subject to differing temperatures. Therefore, it is possible for identical clones to have a wide variety of appearances. If grown in full sun with restricted water or rapid drainage, plants tend to be compact and turn rich colors; but grown in shade, they can become etiolated (leggy) and pallid. Upon observing identical clones in contrasting situations, observers could erroneously believe that they were seeing several distinct species. When clones of a single species are collected from contrasting sites and brought together in a collection, within a season they could become indistinguishable.

On the contrary, when a particular *Sedum* species grows in a number of distinct zones—for example, limestone cliffs, sandy beach fringes, rocky river margins, or over a vast area—it is possible that plants could take on distinct forms. In other words, if pieces of each were collected from contrasting sites, grown side-by-side, and given identical treatment, they would still remain distinct enough to be differentiated even after many seasons. In a particular colony, say that of the limestone cliff area, offspring would inherit features from the parents most adept at surviving and flowering in such an environment.

Over countless generations, some traits may be emphasized and others made less important or distinct. As a result, overly keen taxonomists might erect new species names for regional forms of one species. Over zealous collectors, wishing to name all their plants, often expect that each form of a plant in cultivation has been individually named. Where only a few forms of a species occur, it is possible that suitable names, such as *Sedum makinoi* "minor form" are in common use. Cultivar names are often used to differentiate true wild forms, as *S. album* 'Coral Carpet', a low-growing Iberian form of *S. album* that blushes red throughout the summer.

In many cases, however, the forms encountered within a species are so numerous, despite their constant nature, that the only epithet of value is the one that identifies its habitat (e.g., *Sedum kamtschaticum* "from Fuji Yama"). In my personal reference collection, I have over 40 regional forms of *S. album*, each quite distinct; but even as a mere sample of the range of the species, the variations are impossible to subgroup. Attempts to place the pink-flowered forms, the large-leafed forms, the tiny ground-huggers, the deep red types, the forms with tall, many-flowered inflorescences, and so on into subsets have proved futile. Species, such as *S. album*, which have a vast natural range and have adapted to a multitude of climates, altitudes, and terrains, are said to be polymorphic. This does not deter the earnest taxonomist from attempting to erect subspecies, varieties, subvarieties, and forms. Plants of the same species should be able to interbreed, producing a range of offspring—some resembling each parent and perhaps some intermediates.

Sedum species tend to colonize new fold mountain ranges (Tertiary chains). Over time, colonies of plants can become disjunct, each occupying a separate range and developing independently into distinct yet sexually compatible groups. For example, if a certain *Sedum* species inhabits a particular altitude, it is possible for two colonies to be close enough for cross-fertilization by insects (Fig. 4.15a). After centuries of uplift and erosion of the sedimentary beds, these colonies could be disjunct and therefore develop separately (Fig. 4.15b). A cooling in general climate could cause two close colonies to migrate downhill with similar results. Taxonomist may feel that two such colonies of plants are distinct enough to warrant splitting the species into two subspecies or to warrent erecting a new variety.

A species often shows some variation throughout its range but if one disjunct colony shows extreme features, it can therefore be considered a variety (Fig. 4.15c). The terms "variety" and "subspecies" are not used consis-

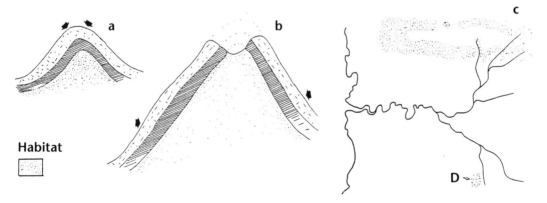

Figure 4.15. Close colonies of plants can develop into distinct groups: (a) two colonies of a species growing at the same altitude may interbreed due to cross-fertilization by insects; (b) as the sedimentary bed erodes or shifts, two disjunct clones could develop into distinct species; (c) if one colony (D) becomes so disjunct, it may evolve into a subspecies with certain of its features emphasized or greatly reduced.

tently by taxonomists. To give an example: a disjunct colony of *Sedum jaliscanum* (which unfortunately is not in cultivation) was discovered by Clausen and named *S. jaliscanum* subsp. *angustifolium*. Therefore, the already-known *S. jaliscanum* had to be called *S. jaliscanum* subsp. *jaliscanum*. In another case, Praeger (1921, 96–97) considered a particular plant with flowers identical to *S. ewersii* to be a distinct variety because it was very much the miniature of the species. He therefore erected *S. ewersii* var. *homophyllum*. Perhaps with more diligent exploration of the wild in years to come, it may become apparent that this variety is only one of a long string of forms connecting the two extremes of the species and therefore of no real status. If this is the case, taxonomists may reduce all the forms to one polymorphic species. Gardeners would be unhappy to have two plants of contrasting natures with the same name and would probably keep the old names, despite the existence of intermediate forms.

If, however, two plants were found to be distinct species due to their sexual incompatability, rather than reducing the status of the variety, it could be elevated. Cytological work is being carried out in universities throughout the world and much weight is now placed on the importance of chromosome counts to distinguish species. If two plants in question are found to have unrelated chromosome counts, the variety could be elevated to a subspecies or even proposed as an entirely new species. An example is the relationship of *Sedum praealtum* and *S. dendroideum*, which have always been considered closely related, if not one and the same species, yet they have unrelated chromosome counts. This feature helps to distinguish them as separate species.

When small, isolated groups of plants encounter new ecological pressure, the resulting favorable mutations can spread quickly. *Sedum* species grow in areas of rapid change such as denudated upland, shifting scree, scarp face, and sand dunes. As marginals, disjunct populations must fluctuate not only in size but in degree of isolation. Uhl (1961, 376) reported, "Such conditions are generally considered to be conducive to rapid evolution." *Sedum* species are prone to polyploidy; that is, they have evolved to have more than twice the number of chromosomes. Through natural selection, they adapt rapidly to changing conditions, and because they have large numbers of chromosomes, their offspring are diverse. Moreover, *Sedum* chromosomes are subject to structural changes, so plants within the same species exist with different levels of ploidy and dysploidy (unrelated chromosome counts).

Most species of *Sedum* have a high degree of reproductive isolation. An exception is subgenus *Hylotelephium*, whose species are geographically isolated. *Sedum* species have a built-in sexual barrier for one of the following reasons: their flowering seasons do not overlap; their flowers are pollinated by different insects; their chromosome counts are incompatible; and species grow hundreds of miles apart.

A few wild hybrid sedums exist. Most of these are sterile, but several Mexican *Sedum* species have successfully crossed with members of other genera. Plants of *Pachysedum* group are more able to cross with other genera than with *Sedum*. On the whole, sedums of different species are unlikely to hybridize in the wild, and the very rare hybrids that are produced are usually sterile. Subgenus *Hylotelephium* plants and Mexican species are very promiscuous in cultivation, but in the wild, such forms have geographical rather than genetic barriers.

NATURAL GROUPS OF STONECROPS

Sedum sensu lato could contain as many as a thousand species and subspecies. To make such a cosmopolitan genus more manageable, taxonomists have grouped closely related plants into subgenera, groups, sections, or series. At times, some of these assemblages have been considered beyond the bounds of the genus *Sedum* and have been given generic status, only to be returned to *Sedum* at a later date. One school of thought would fragment *Sedum* into dozens of tiny genera, while another would prefer to consider natural groups within the vast range of the genus *Sedum*. The position taken in the present volume is that the genus *Sedum* in cultivation can be divided into 28 natural groupings consisting of three subgenera—*Hylotelephium*, *Rhodiola*, and *Sedum*—which in turn are subdivided. Subgenus *Hylotelephium* is divided into 3 groups: *Hylotelephium*, *Sieboldii*, and *Populisedum*. Subgenus *Rhodiola* is divided into 6 groups: *Chamaerhodiola*, *Clementsia*, *Crassipedes*, *Hobsonia*, *Primuloida*, and *Rhodiola*. Subgenus *Sedum* is divided into 19 groups: African species, *Aizoon* group, European yellow-flowered kyphocarpic species, European kyphocarpic species without yellow flowers, European yellow-flowered orthocarpic species, European orthocarpic species without yellow flowers, Far Eastern species with fibrous roots, Macronesian Island species, *Meterostachys* group, Mexican nonwoody species, Mexican woody species, *Mucizonia* group, North American species, *Orostachys* group, *Pachysedum* group, *Prometheum* group, *Pseudosedum* group, *Sinocrassula* group, and South American species.

No one feature is reliable to divide *Sedum* into natural groups, but combinations of the following nine features make separation of most of them relatively straightforward:

1. The propensity to form well-developed rootstocks.
2. Whether scaly leaves are produced on the rootstock, or at the stem bases, or not at all.

3. Whether leaves form basal rosettes.
4. Whether the plant is herbaceous with annual flowering stems dying back each season.
5. Whether the outline of flowers is an elongated cone.
6. Whether petals are free to the base.
7. Whether carpels are free and stipitate.
8. Whether fruits are kyphocarpic.
9. Whether flowers are haplostemonous.

ROOTSTOCKS. Species in subgenera *Hylotelephium* and *Rhodiola* have well-developed rootstocks. So do *Aizoon*, *Meterostachys,* and *Pseudosedum*, groups of subenus *Sedum* and some *Rosularia* species. By itself this is not always a reliable means of identification, for some species within subgenera *Hylotelephium* and *Rhodiola* have little more than slightly thickened or somewhat woody rootstocks. Only a few species of subgenus *Sedum* develop succulent rootstocks, and in the main these tend to be of North American origin, except for all species of *Aizoon* group which possess a woody rootstock.

SCALY LEAVES. Scaly leaves are produced on the roots of all species in subgenus *Rhodiola* and on the stem bases of all species of *Pseudosedum* group. They protect overwintering buds. Scaly leaves are never found in any of the other groups.

ROSETTES. Species of *Orostachys*, *Prometheum,* and *Sinocrassula* groups, and the genus *Rosularia*, always have basal rosettes, but most other groups tend to produce rosettelike growth at times, especially for overwintering.

HERBACEOUS STEMS. All species of subgenera *Hylotelephium* and *Rhodiola* and *Pseudosedum* group have annual stems but some have basal, overwintering rosettes. Most species of subgenus *Rhodiola* are herbaceous but several keep rosettes of leaves throughout the year. Species of subgenus *Sedum* are not usually herbaceous, but the majority of species of *Aizoon* group are herbaceous and so are a few North American species.

FLOWER SPIKE. Species of *Orostachys* group in particular have a very dense, elongated inflorescence, which is conical or long-oblong. Subgenera *Rhodiola* and *Sedum* species are never as extreme, but occasionally approach this. *Rosularia* species sometimes produce inflorescences which are pyramidal in outline. Inflorescences produced by the other groups are mostly fan-shaped in outline.

PETAL FUSION. Petal connation has always been an important distinguishing feature. Subgenera *Hylotelephium* and *Rhodiola* and species of *Aizoon* and *Sinocrassula* groups always have petals free to the base. Species of *Mucizonia* group have a very well-developed tube as the petals are fused in the lower half or more. Petals of *Meterostachys* group are fused in the lower third. *Orostachys, Prometheum,* and *Pseudosedum* groups and *Rosularia* species show some degree of fusion of the lower portions of the petals, but other species with partially fused petals are best placed in the subgenus *Sedum*.

STIPITATE CARPELS. Carpels of subgenus *Hylotelephium* and *Orostachys* group are indistinguishable. They are always free, upright, and are stalked or waisted at the base (stipitate or attenuate). All other groups have carpels that are not waisted at the base, and they usually have some degree of fusion.

KYPHOCARPIC OR ORTHOCARPIC FLOWERS. Species of *Aizoon* and *Pseudosedum* groups always have kyphocarpic flowers. Some subgenus *Sedum* species have kyphocarpic flowers. The other groups and subgenera always have orthocarpic flowers.

HAPLOSTEMONOUS FLOWERS. Species of *Sinocrassula* group are haplostemonous. Occasionally this feature is found in other groups of subgenus *Sedum*.

The list below summarizes these nine important features, where A = Always; M = Mostly; S = Sometimes; X = Never; and the numbers correspond to the list of features on pages 77 and 78.

	1	2	3	4	5	6	7	8	9
Aizoon	A	X	S	M	X	A	X	A	X
Hylotelephium	A	X	S	M	X	A	A	X	X
Meterostachys	A	X	S	X	X	X	X	X	X
Mucizonia	X	X	S	X	X	X	X	X	X
Orostachys	X	X	A	X	A	S	A	X	S
Prometheum	X	X	A	X	X	A	X	X	X
Pseudosedum	A	A	S	A	X	X	X	A	X
Rhodiola	A	A	S	M	S	A	X	X	X
Rosularia	S	X	A	X	S	S	X	X	X
Sedum	S	X	S	S	S	M	X	S	S
Sinocrassula	X	X	A	X	X	A	X	X	A

Each of the 11 natural units listed above have been considered at some time to be beyond the scope of the genus *Sedum* senso stricto, except for the subgenus *Sedum*. Today in some literature, several of these groupings have full generic status. I propose to consider all 11 as part of the genus *Sedum*, with the exception of the genus *Rosularia*, which is considered beyond the scope of this book except for a single borderline species that has at various times been considered a species of the genus *Sedum*.

The 10 groups and subgenera of the genus *Sedum*, which are distinct from each other, are briefly described in the following pages, in addition to *Rosularia*, which is considered a separate genus. Figure 4.16 shows the subdivisions of the genus *Sedum* used in this volume.

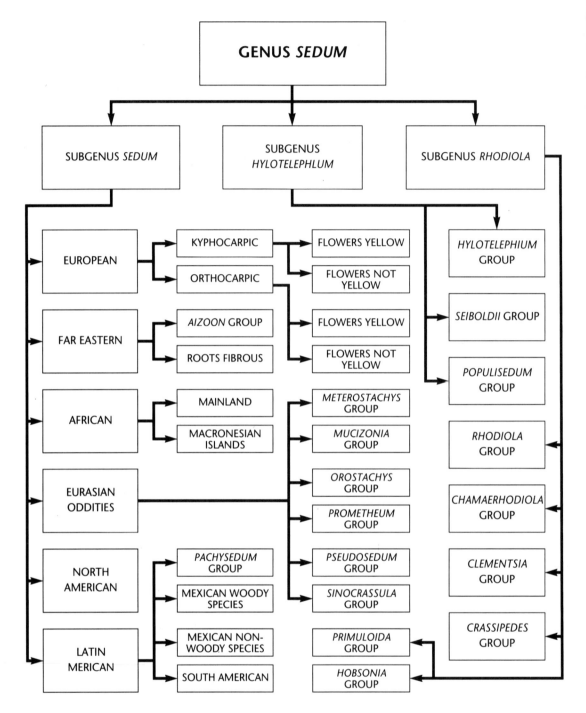

Figure 4.16. The breakdown of subgenera and groups of *Sedum* as used in this volume.

Aizoon group

syn. *Aizoon* Koch ex Schönland, genus *Aizopsis* Grulich

Species of *Aizoon* group are mostly herbaceous plants rising from woody rootstocks. They have wide, always flat leaves, and always kyphocarpic flowers with free yellow petals. All but two species are Far Eastern. The disjunct pair are from the Ural Mountains and Eastern Ukraine. The basic chromosome number for *Aizoon* group is $x = 16$.

Subgenus *Hylotelephium*

syn. *Hylotelephium* Ohba, *Telephium* Hill, section *Telephium* Gray

All species of this subgenus are herbaceous plants that rise from fleshy or woody rootstocks. The leaves are mostly wide and flat, and the flowers are always orthocarpic with each carpel free and stipitate or attenuate. Species of the subgenus *Hylotelephium* never have truly yellow flowers, and the seeds are somewhat winged. Species are Eurasian in origin with one exception—the North American species *Sedum telephoides*—and the basic chromosome number of species for the subgenus is $x = 12$.

Meterostachys group

syn. *Meterostachys* Hamet, considered a separate genus by Nakai

The single species of this group was described at first in the genus *Cotyledon*, then as a monotypic genus *Meterostachys* and later moved to the genus *Sedum* by Hamet. It is a rosetted plant on a fleshy rootstock, which elongates and develops branches, from southern Japan. The flowers have distinct tubes. The basic chromosome number is $x = 16$.

Mucizonia group

syn. *Mucizonia* Hamet, considered a separate genus by Lamark

This group comprises several closely related species in Iberia and North Africa with distinctly connate petals and bristlelike hairs. Work by 't Hart and Van den Berg (1982) shows that one species can be successfully crossed with *Sedum hispanicum* and is closely related to *S. dasyphyllum*. $x = 9, 10, 11$.

Orostachys group

syn. *Orostachys* (De Candolle) Fröderström, genus *Orostachys* Fischer

This group consists of monocarpic, rosetted plants of annual duration, or stoloniferous perennials. The flower spikes are dense pyramids or long-cylindrical in outline. The carpels are exactly the same as those of the subgenus *Hylotelephium* (stipitate), but the petals can be somewhat fused basally. Species are found from Japan to the Urals, and the basic chromosome number is $x = 12$.

Prometheum group

syn. *Prometheum* Berger, genus *Prometheum* Ohba, *Pseudorosularia* Gurgenidze

This group comprises two biennial species from the Caucasus with densely hairy, monocarpic rosettes. Even the flowers are hairy. $x = 6, 7$.

Pseudosedum group

syn. *Pseudosedum* of *Umbilicus* Boissier, genus *Pseudosedum* (Boissier) Berger

This group comprises 10 species of Himalayan plants closely related to the subgenus *Rhodiola*, each with fleshy rootstocks, and scaly leaves on the bases of annual flowering stems. Unlike flowers of the subgenus *Rhodiola*, flowers in this group are kyphocarpic with petals connate at the base.

Subgenus *Rhodiola*

syn. section *Rhodiola* Scopoli, subgenus *Rhodiolae* (L.) Ohba

Annual flowering stems rise from between scaly leaves on a fleshy rootstock—except for one group of species within subgenus *Rhodiola* that has perennial rosettes on the roots. Flowers are often single sex, and although this feature is unique to the subgenus *Rhodiola*, some species have flowers that are bisexual like the other subgenera of *Sedum*. Ohba (1978) says that when a species of subgenus *Rhodiola* is grown from seed, seedlings behave differently from those of the other subspecies. After the cotyledons are produced, all upward growth of the main stem ceases, and the understem thickens. Eggli (1988) showed *Rosularia* often behaves similarly. When a species of subgenus *Rhodiola* grows from seed, like all dicotyledonous plants, a short stem is produced, topped with a pair of primary leaves. From between these primary leaves or cotyledons, the main stem never develops any further, but instead, the primary understem thickens considerably before several annual stems form between the cotyledons. With species of other *Sedum* subgenera, the main stem continues to rise from between the cotyledons. A second characteristic unique to subgenus *Rhodiola* is the existence of root-leaves, which often have very wide bases, a petiole, and then wider apices. The basic chromosome number could be $x = 6$.

Rosularia Stapf

including *Sempervivella* Stapf but not *Afrovivella* Berger

This genus is notoriously difficult to circumscribe, but generally consists of plants with low rosettes of leaves that are never perfectly terete, rising from small fleshy rootstocks. Inflorescences are sometimes a lax pyramid in outline. The flowers range from saucer-shaped to funnel-shaped with petals somewhat united. The fruit is orthocarpic without lips along the line of dehiscence. Several basic chromosome counts exist: $x = 7, 8, 9$, and 10, with many levels of ploidy. Several species of *Sedum* have been reclassified as

Rosularia, but such moves have not always been widely accepted. Only one species of *Rosularia* is included in this volume as it is best known as a *Sedum* species.

Subgenus *Sedum* Clausen ≈ section *Seda Genuina* Koch

This subgenus includes everything that has not already been removed. Some species of subgenus *Sedum* have unusual features, such as rootstocks. Some are herbaceous, or have inflorescences that are elongated or conical in outline; others have apparently lost a whorl of stamens, but these anomalous features are never combined. North American members of subgenus *Sedum* are invariably rosetted, and two major groups of European members of subgenus *Sedum* are kyphocarpic, but generally each species shares the majority of features with the others (i.e., no scaly leaves; no developed rootstocks—only fibrous roots on annual, biennial, or perennial plants; an inflorescence that is not a congested, elongated spike; petals free to the base, or just about so; and carpels not waisted at the base). Subgenus *Sedum* species are found almost across the full range of the other subgenera.

Sinocrassula group
Sinocrassula Berger, considered a separate genus by Berger

This group comprises a single, very variable species, or several closely related haplostemonous, rosetted species from south and west China, each with terminal inflorescences. $n = 33$.

Part Two

How to Use Part Two

In this volume, the genus *Sedum* has been divided into three subgenera: *Sedum, Hylotelephium* and *Rhodiola*, (see chapter 4 for the differences between these subgenera). These subgenera have been further divided into 28 groups of geographically and taxonomically related species. Chapters 5 to 10 describe species of subgenus *Sedum* in cultivation; chapters 11 and 12 describe species of subgenera *Hylotelephium* and *Rhodiola* respectively. At the beginning of each chapter and in the introduction to each group of *Sedum* species, the entity is defined and the features pertaining to all species that follow are highlighted. It is important that the reader becomes acquainted with stonecrops in their groups and not merely with a species in isolation.

Within each chapter or subchapter the species descriptions are arranged alphabetically. On the rare occasion when species of a controversial nature are discussed together, the arrangement is noted in the list of species at the beginning of each chapter or subchapter.

Chapter 5 describes European species in four groups:
   Yellow-flowered kyphocarpic species (*Sedum acre* group)
   Kyphocarpic species without yellow flowers
   Yellow-flowered orthocarpic species (*Rupestria* group)
   Orthocarpic species without yellow flowers
Chapter 6 describes Far Eastern species in two groups:
   Aizoon group (with woody rootstocks)
   Species with fibrous roots
Chapter 7 describes six groups of plants anomalous in *Sedum* in a particular respect, plus one species of the genus *Rosularia* (sometimes considered a member of *Sedum* but excluded from the genus in this book):
   Meterostachys group

Mucizonia group

Orostachys group

Prometheum group

Pseudosedum group

Sinocrassula group

A single *Rosularia* species

Chapter 8 describes African species in two groups:

Macronesian Islands species

Mainland species

Chapter 9 describes North American species.

Chapter 10 describes Latin American species in four groups, the first three comprising Central American species centered in Mexico:

Pachysedum group (woody species with lateral inflorescences)

Mexican woody species with terminal inflorescences

Mexican nonwoody species

South American species

Chapter 11 describes species of the subgenus *Hylotelephium* in three groups:

Hylotelephium group (upright, typical species with well-developed rootstocks)

Sieboldii group (species with decumbent stems and well-developed rootstocks)

Populisedum group (species that lack well-developed fleshy rootstocks)

Chapter 12 describes species of the subgenus *Rhodiola* in six groups:

Rhodiola group (species with dioecious flowers)

Chamaerhodiola group (species with dioecious flowers and a tangle of persistent stems)

Clementsia group (species with hermaphrodite flowers clustered on a racemous spike)

Crassipedes group (species with hermaphrodite flowers in cymes or corymbs)

Primuloida group (species with hermaphrodite flowers on simple inflorescences, and with narrow, creeping rhizomes)

Hobsonia group (the only *Sedum* species with dorsifixed anthers)

DESCRIPTIONS

Each description includes six elements: plant name, general description, habitat, main points of distinction, variation, and horticulture.

Plant Names

The name of each species is followed by the name of the person first responsible for the binomial. Where the name has undergone some change, the name of the person first describing the plant is followed by the name of the person responsible for the present combination.

Synonyms are only listed where outdated names are still encountered. Some species have undergone so many name changes, and others comprise so many regional variations, each at one time considered a separate species, that pages could be filled with synonyms. On very rare occasions two botanists have used the same name for different plants. The first plant to receive that name retains it, but the name of the second plant must be altered to eradicate confusion. Sometimes publication of such synonyms causes unrelated plants to be confused.

Where common names are known, they are included, but in many instances such names refer to more than one species. Japanese names, too, are given where known.

General Description

Each description indicates the eventual size and spread of the species, its general appearance, how likely it is to be encountered, and to which other species it is similar. The description with the photograph, the main points of distinction, and the drawings will enable the reader to correctly distinguish that species.

Taken in isolation, no single feature of a plant can lead to positive identification, except perhaps in a very rare case (e.g., blue flowers are unique to *Sedum caeruleum*). Furthermore, correctly named plants in cultivation may look rather different from the accompanying photographs because plants change with the seasons. If a named plant in a garden or collection appears very different from the photograph, check the details of the distinguishing features to ensure it is correctly named.

It may be necessary to observe a plant over a whole season to positively verify all the features that make it a distinct species. Many sedums are incorrectly named in cultivation, and common mistakes are noted in the text.

Habitat

Some species are very widespread, others are only found on a particular rock, in a certain aspect, on a single hill. Altitude and sympatric vegetation are given where known.

Main Points of Distinction

General descriptions of *Sedum* species often leave the reader in a state of confusion. In fact, general descriptions of 40 European species could be almost identical. It is always easier to identify species in habitat where at most perhaps 8 species coexist, rather than in cultivation where there are over 200 common species and countless regional forms. To aid identification in this volume, major botanical features common to all species in the group are highlighted at the beginning of each chapter or section; they are not repeated in the individual descriptions. The photographs and plates will enable readers to pinpoint a section or chapter in which a plant with a particular nature is found.

By checking features highlighted at the beginning of a section, it may be immediately apparent that the plant in question is a member of that group. To check all the relevant features, specimens may need to be studied over a period of time. Unfamiliar terms are explained in the glossary. It is best to check the near relatives of the stonecrop in question to be sure the plant has been correctly identified. Chromosome numbers are given when known. They are primarily of academic interest and sometimes support the viability of a species as a unique entity.

Variation

Most formal species descriptions tend to be of a particular plant from a definite location, which was studied by the botanist first describing it. The same plant will most probably have been placed in a herbarium for reference. Other plants of the same species can deviate enormously from this holotype description, not only as a result of cultivation in contrasting situations, but perhaps due to the species' inherent variability. Species that exist in a multitude of forms are known as polymorphic species. Sometimes chromosome counts are given in this section to emphasize that variations are cytological as well as morphological.

Some species are fairly constant in cultivation because all plants have been propagated from from a particular wild collection. The International Succulent Institute (I.S.I.), for example, often finances and organizes expeditions to remote areas where small quantities of plant material are collected for study and propagation. Such propagations often result in certain species becoming remarkably popular in cultivation. As no new collections from such remote sites are likely, these species, in cultivation at least, are unlikely to show any variation.

Other species, however, show considerable variation. Common European stonecrops, for example, grow over a vast range and in a multitude of settings. Their extreme forms are so different that it is often difficult to imagine they are one and the same species without observing the forms simultaneously along with a range of intermediate forms. Regional forms and cultivars are often appealing because of their unique qualities, and some have become more common in cultivation than the type species.

Horticulture

This section of the description identifies various uses of species: as potted houseplants; in rock gardens, herbaceous borders, hanging baskets, windowboxes, or outdoor containers; if fast and dense enough for ground cover; and if possible to grow on dry stone walls or difficult spots. The section also highlights the peculiarities of a plant in cultivation: its ability to withstand extremes, its likes and dislikes, the best way to propagate it, if different from the group as a whole, and its importance to horticulture.

CHAPTER 5

European Species of Subgenus Sedum

Sedum species are found growing naturally in all European countries. They range from ephemeral, seashore annuals to true alpines. With few exceptions, they are associated with dry spots. These dry spots are the result of low rainfall, permeability of the bedrock, scree surface, or precipitous slope. *Sedum* species in Europe do not compete very well with mesophytes, but as marginals they have little competition. A few of the taller species grow on grassy banks or on sand dunes with marram, but generally they are lithophytes, preferring to grow in a fault in a rock face or to tumble across mountain scree.

However one tries to define "European *Sedum*," there will be species which could arguably be placed in other chapters. The Mediterranean margin appears to be an area with a high density of *Sedum* species, and to the south, the Sahara is a broad barrier between these species and the handful of East African species. If sedums are indigenous to Europe as well as to North African Mediterranean margins, they are included in this chapter. I tentatively leave out *S. multiceps*, which only grows naturally in North Africa, but is probably closely related to, if not part of, the *S. acre* group. A few species are endemic to the Macronesian Islands (Canaries and Madeirans), and one of these, *S. farinosum*, is probably closely related to the *S. anglicum* complex, but these species are included with other African species in chapter 8. Several species are centered in the Caucasus or Asian Turkey and have spread into the Middle East, but as they are close relatives of true European species, they are included in this chapter. The number of species is reduced considerably east of Turkey, until a different group is encountered in the Far East.

Dividing European *Sedum* into manageable sections has caused a great deal of debate among botanists. There is no clear way of alloting *Sedum* species to clearly defined compartments without some species appearing to bridge these artificially prescribed sections. The most reliable means of grouping closely related species is by the nature of the carpels. Harald Fröderström (1930, 1931, 1932, 1933, 1935) emphasized that the kyphocarpic flower type was absent from the genuine African florae, but present in Asiatic, European, and North American sedums. He suggested that this was a primitive feature, and that those species with orthocarpic flowers were more advanced. He did point out that several species appeared intermediate: *S. melanantherum* appears to have been associated with *S. album*, which has orthocarpic flowers, and now with *S. anglicum*, which has vaguely kyphocarpic flowers.

Nevertheless, with kyphocarpic versus orthocarpic, plus the presence or absence of yellow enzymes, European *Sedum* species can be roughly divided into four sections, each comprising similar, closely related species:

1. Kyphocarpic *Sedum* species with yellow or yellowish flowers are the true *Sedum* species. They are almost always considered an entity and referred to as the *S. acre* group by 't Hart (1978).

2. Kyphocarpic *Sedum* species with white, pink, or purple flowers form a heterogeneous group consisting of annuals, perennials, and a number of species that act in either way as a response to seasonal conditions.

3. Orthocarpic *Sedum* species with yellow or yellowish flowers form a group that has always been considered an entity and often called *S. rupestre* group. Berger (1930) referred to it as the series *Rupestria*, and Grulich (1984), erected a separate genus, *Petrosedum*, to accommodate the group. *Sedum ochroleucum* has almost white flowers so may cause some confusion with regard to identification. All species in this group are perennial but two die down and rest in summer.

4. Orthocarpic *Sedum* species with white, pink, purple, red, or, in one instance, sky-blue flowers, form a heterogeneous, but easily recognized group containing annuals, biennials, and perennials.

YELLOW-FLOWERED KYPHOCARPIC SPECIES

This group, which has been called the *Sedum acre* group, consists of the following species in cultivation:

Sedum acre L.
Sedum alpestre Villar
Sedum annuum L.
Sedum apoleipon 't Hart
Sedum borissovae Balkovsky
Sedum grisebachii Boissier
Sedum laconicum Boissier
Sedum litoreum Gussone
Sedum sexangulare L.
Sedum tuberiferum Stojanov & Stefanov
Sedum ursi 't Hart
Sedum urvillei De Candolle

The *Sedum acre* group has been treated inconsistently by taxonomists. Berger (1930) placed the species with parallel-sided leaves in his section *Mitia*, the annual species in section *Epeteium* of quite a separate series, and the remaining species were assigned to the series *Acria*, if the leaves were broad-based, or to *Alpestria*, if the leaves were broadest in the middle or above. Berger also included a couple of North American *Sedum* species with yellow flowers. Fröderström (1930, 1931, 1932, 1933, 1935) excluded New World species and united all the members of the then-known *S. acre* group, except *S. litoreum*, which he classified elsewhere. I intend to follow 't Hart's (1978) delimitations of this group, as his work is the most recent and reflects the result of many years of study, both cytological and in the field: therefore, I include *S. litoreum* in this group.

Plants of this group

- Have kyphocarpic 5-partite flowers with yellow or yellowish mucronate petals.
- Have densely imbricate, alternate, obtuse, or subacute leaves.
- Have spurred leaves.
- Are small herbs; the perennials have very simple terminal inflorescences, while the annuals have taller more-branched inflorescences.
- Have inflorescences with bracts.
- Have very wide lips on the carpels (except for *S. litoreum*, which has narrow ones).

Figure 5.1 shows leaf shapes of European kyphocarpic yellow-flowered species.

The following is not a formal key, but a guide to identifying species within this group:

Leaves widest in the lower quarter, sepals free: *S. acre*

Leaves widest in the lower quarter, sepals united: *S. urvillei*

Leaves with hyaline papillae, turning red: *S. grisebachii*

Leaves with hyaline papillae, remaining gray-green: *S. laconicum*

Leaves parallel-sided, arranged in six spirals: *S. sexangulare*

Propagules tuberous, subterranean: *S. tuberiferum*

Leaves oblong, glaucous, grayish blue-green, with spurs broad truncate and flowers small with light yellow petals: *S. borissovae*

Leaves narrow, glaucous, gray-green, lower stems shaggy with dead leaves, large flowers of light green-yellow: *S. apoleipon*

Glabrous leaves widest in upper half, perennial: *S. alpestre*

Glabrous leaves widest in upper half, annual lowland species: *S. litoreum*

Annual alpine, petals much longer than the sepals: *S. annuum*

Turkish plant resembling *S. laconicum* without hyaline papillae: *S. ursi*

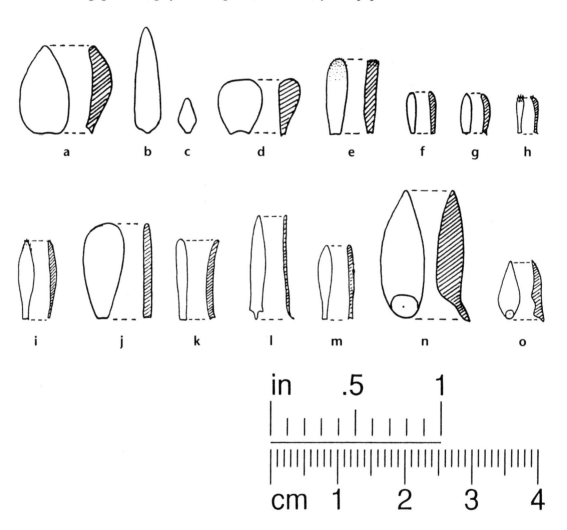

Figure 5.1. Leaf shapes of yellow-flowered kyphocarpic species from Europe: (a) *Sedum acre;* (b) *S. acre* subsp. *majus;* (c) *S. acre* 'Minus'; (d) *S. alpestre;* (e) *S. annuum;* (f) *S. apoleipon;* (g) *S. borissovae;* (h) *S. grisebachii;* (i) *S. laconicum;* (j) *S. litoreum;* (k) *S. sexangulare;* (l) *S. tuberiferum;* (m) *S. ursi;* (n, o) *S. urvillei.*

SEDUM ACRE L.

PLATE 3

SYNONYMS: *S. krajinae* Domin, *S. neglectum* Tenore,
S. zlatiborense Domin

COMMON NAMES: Biting stonecrop, wall-pepper,
welcome-home-husband-though-never-so-drunk

The acrid taste of *Sedum acre* in the morning has encouraged its use as a purgative, vermifuge, or emetic since Roman times or before. In fact there is a good correlation between sites of *S. acre* in the British Isles and medieval monasteries. This is because the species was cultivated for its medicinal qualities. In addition to being a common escape, *S. acre* is very common in cultivation and is available in numerous forms. The carpets of bright yellow flowers on a gravel drive or pillows of bright foliage on stone walls are a joy to behold. Although it is generally a vigorous species, it is not difficult to control.

Yellow flowers of nearly 2 cm (0.8 in) diameter are large for the 10-cm (4-in) high plant and are produced on very short inflorescences of a few simple branches. When the floriferous shoots die, several others rise from each base, some of which will become next year's inflorescences. The leaves are short, broad-based with an obtuse, short, broadly triangular spur, and paper-like, dead leaves persist on lower stems.

HABITAT. *Sedum acre* is exceptionally widespread in Europe and introduced to such distant places as Greenland, Tierra del Fuego, and New Zealand. Found in just about every country in Europe, except some of the Mediterranean islands, it also grows naturally in North Africa from Libya westwards. The further north the habitat, the more likely plants grow near sea level. In its southern extremes this species is associated with mountainous areas.

MAIN POINTS OF DISTINCTION. This species could be confused with *Sedum urvillei*, which has leaves with large, broad, truncate spurs, smaller flowers, and no creeping sterile shoots, or with *S. sexangulare*, which has terete, linear leaves. The broad bases of the leaves of *S. acre* are a good pointer to identification (Fig. 5.1a, b, c), as are the carpels which soon turn yellowish brown. Sepals are free and spurred, a feature that is the best aid to positive identification as *S. acre* is the only yellow-flowered European *Sedum* species with free sepals.

VARIATION. Literally dozens of names have been erected in the past for regional variations of *Sedum acre*, but few have credence. Large forms of *S. acre* collected in southern Spain are very similar to *S. acre* subsp. *majus* (Masters) Clausen (syn. "*S. maweanum* hort."), a particularly robust form from Morocco. 't Hart (1978) has shown that part of the variability of this species is correlated with differences in chromosome numbers. The most southern forms are diploid ($2n = 40$) and are usually referred to by the name *S. acre* subsp. *neglectum* (Tenore) Rouy & Camus. They are isolated from other levels of ploidy, and like the Moroccan form, the southern forms are bolder, more upright, and have less-rounded and more-triangular yellow-green leaves than the northern forms. The name *S. acre* var. *krajinae* (Domin) Ját. is applied to a bold Slovakian form sometimes encountered in cultivation. Small, north European tetraploids ($2n = 80$) are the most common plants encountered in cultivation. Apart from these two cytologically distinct forms, intermediate forms, regional variations, and distinct cultivars are frequently grown. The following horticultural variations are valuable garden plants:

Sedum acre 'Aureum' is a larger variegated form that has leaves with a silvery tint for most of the year. The golden variegation is apparent in spring.

Sedum acre 'Cristatum' has barren fasciated shoots. It is slow growing; plants frequently revert, and they do not enjoy wet winters.

Sedum acre 'Elegans' is a small variegated form, which on occasion reverts to 'Minus'. The stems, congested with leaves, look monstrous, and the creamy variegation is lost by late summer.

Sedum acre 'Minus' is a very tiny form, probably a regional variation, which has small, exceptionally imbricate leaves (Fig. 5.1c) not dissimilar vegetatively to the Mexican *S. muscoideum*.

Sedum acre var. *sopianae* (S. Priszter) R. Soo, which is usually available with the label "*S. neglectum* subsp. *sopianae*," is a Hungarian form recently introduced into cultivation. The spiralled leaves are reminiscent of *S. sexangulare*, except they are much wider and more broad-based. In addition, sepals are free.

't Hart (1991) records *x* = 20, and polyploids with 2*n* = 100 and 120. Gardeners may wish to retain names that pinpoint regional forms despite existence of a whole range of variations in the wild. 'Yellow Queen', for example, is merely a typical diploid form probably collected in Spain; Dutch nurseries in the 1970s, realizing this plant was contrasting to the typical Dutch tetraploids, erected this cultivar name.

HORTICULTURE. The Moroccan form is an ideal specimen for the alpine house for it is slow growing and succumbs to winter wet. *Sedum acre* subsp. *neglectum* (i.e., the diploid form) and the variegated forms are more likely to fail in a very severe winter than are the tetraploids. As a bright edge to a border, as a carpet growing on a stone or slate roof, or as a hummock festooning a stone wall, all forms of *S. acre* are a treasure. Try mixing clones for effect.

SEDUM ALPESTRE Villar

Sedum alpestre is a very uncommon true alpine that is difficult to perpetuate in cultivation (Fig. 5.2). It is a low-growing perennial with pale yellow or green-yellow flowers, often streaked with red, on compact inflorescences.

HABITAT. Very disjunct colonies in the alpine zones of central and southern Europe are the home of this species—from the Pyrenees to the Carpathian Mountains always above 1500 m (4900 ft).

MAIN POINTS OF DISTINCTION. Tiny, oblong, tightly packed leaves are usually green flushed with red (Fig. 5.1d). Inflorescences carry only a few flowers, each having blunt, wide petals with wavy edges, and red carpels with tiny

Figure 5.2. *Sedum alpestre* plant measuring 2 cm (0.8 in) across.

beaks. Very short stamens and sepals nearly as long as petals are useful identification points. Plants look similar to *Sedum atratum*, which has white flowers and no sterile shoots so is always annual.

Sedum annuum could also be easily confused with *S. alpestre*, especially if it perenniates, which it sometimes does. *Sedum annuum* has distinctly lanceolate petals with very acute tips and is a much more open plant than *S. alpestre*. In addition, the perenniating forms of *S. annuum* have more-linear, pea-green leaves with distinct apices.

VARIATION. Variability in leaf color from pure green to almost completely flushed red is to be expected. Leaves can also vary greatly in size; in a very exposed situation, they can be tiny, but in a shady spot they are often more than 1 cm (0.4 in) long. 't Hart (1978) says that only the chromosome number 2*n* = 16 occurs.

HORTICULTURE. This species is a real challenge to a lowlander, for hot summer sun kills the plant. Often plants pull themselves down under gravel in baking conditions to emerge in autumn when temperatures moderate. A windy, semi-shaded spot is recommended, or a north-facing bank. *Sedum alpestre* is said to be a calcifuge, but experiments growing identical clones, one in a pot topped with quartz, the other with limestone chippings, showed no apparent differences in growth. It is an early flowerer for this group, usually flowering before the longest day of the year.

SEDUM ANNUUM L.

SYNONYM: *Etiosedum annuum* (L.) Löve & Löve

Rarely kept in cultivation for more than a few seasons, *Sedum annuum* becomes a spindly annual, branching from the base. It does not have a great deal to recommend it that cannot be offered by its close relatives, which are much more reliable. The light green, open plant produces two-branched cymes of yellow flowers, sometimes tinged with red.

HABITAT. *Sedum annuum* has an almost identical habitat to that of *S. alpestre*, but in addition is indigenous to Norway, Sweden, Finland, Iceland, and Greenland. It does not occupy such high areas as *S. alpestre* and is a plant associated with coasts in the far north.

MAIN POINTS OF DISTINCTION. Juvenile specimens are tight tufts of linear, pea-green leaves with papillose tips (Fig. 5.1e), but later the open nature of the plant on a short, stout stem, the obviously branched cymes, and the narrow, lanceolate, sharply pointed petals are good identifying characteristics. The uneven size of sepals and the relative length of petals, nearly twice as long as sepals, are also good indicators.

VARIATION. Some clones perpetuate themselves vegetatively if the conditions are right (Fig. 5.3). Situation plays a great part in producing variation. Plants grown in damp shade are up to 15 cm (6 in) high, with the whole plant appearing to be covered with flowers, while those in a dry, sunny spot, struggle to reach 3 cm (1 in) and are invariably tinged red. 't Hart (1978) reports that only the chromosome number $2n = 22$ occurs.

HORTICULTURE. The delicate nature of *Sedum annuum* is perhaps enough to encourage horticulturists to try to perpetuate it. A Swiss friend has no problems growing it and perpetuating small colonies, for it seeds itself readily, producing attractive carpets of yellow in midsummer.

Figure 5.3. *Sedum annuum*, a perenniating form from the Pyrenees.

Lowlanders, like myself, struggle to maintain a few plants. Plants seed themselves best in a scree of sharp gravel. They are a delightful accompaniment to a potted conifer where a top dressing of sharp quartz has been placed around the base of a dwarf tree. Perennial Pyreneean forms are worth acquiring.

SEDUM APOLEIPON 't Hart

Collected for the first time in 1856, plants were at first misidentified as *Sedum sexangulare,* but leaves of *S. apoleipon* are glaucous and much smaller than those of the former (Fig. 5.1f, k). Recent work by 't Hart (1983b) has shown this delightful little alpine to be a distinct species. Its glaucous blue-green creeping habit is most like that of *S. borrisovae,* but *S. apoleipon* is even rarer in collections.

HABITAT. Stony alpine meadows of Mount Timfristos, central Greece, and adjacent peaks above 1700 m (5600 ft) are the home of this species, mostly on north-facing and east-facing limestone.

MAIN POINTS OF DISTINCTION. *Sedum apoleipon* is so rare in cultivation, it is unlikely to be offered except from a specialist nursery. Dull, not shiny, glabrous leaves forming compact tufts, dead leaves adhering below, and green-yellow flowers are an almost unique combination of characteristics (Fig. 5.4). Subsessile flowers have very distinct blunt sepals that are noticeably unequal and fused into a receptacle tube. $2n = 44$.

VARIATION. More than likely, all plants in cultivation derive from 't Hart's collection on Mount Timfristos.

HORTICULTURE. Experiments in recent years seem to show that this species should be hardy in most temperate areas if given a well-drained site. It is not a particularly bright subject in flower, but plants soon form dense, attractive carpets. *Sedum apoleipon* is so low growing it needs to be observed in an elevated situation.

Figure 5.4. *Sedum apoleipon*—each tuft is 1 cm (0.4 in) across.

SEDUM BORISSOVAE Balkovsky

PLATE 4

Sedum borissovae is a relatively newly described, delicate species with very small, pruinose, grayish blue-green, minutely papillose leaves densely crowded on short, creeping, then erect stems (Fig. 5.1g). The relatively tall inflorescences carry only a few pale yellow flowers on lax cymes. It is a shy flowerer in cultivation, but the low, dense carpet produced by the sterile, procumbent shoots is most attractive.

HABITAT. Southern Ukraine in the former Soviet Union is the home of this species, which prefers granitic rock outcrops.

MAIN POINTS OF DISTINCTION. The very diminutive nature of plants with tight tufts of grayish blue-green leaves is similar to small forms of *Sedum laconicum*, but *S. borissovae* tends not to disintegrate in summer, and its leaves are very blunt, glaucous-pruinose blue, and tipped with tiny, very dark red spots. *Sedum laconicum*, in contrast, is very floriferous. Sepals of *S. borissovae* are uneven and less than half the length of the small, pale yellow petals, which are almost always tipped with red.

VARIATION. The species is only known from one location and presumably all plants in cultivation were derived from clones acquired by 't Hart. $2n = 26$.

HORTICULTURE. *Sedum borissovae* is a good plant for the alpine house though it can be grown outdoors in most temperate areas. It is slow, noninvasive, and a good subject for a raised bed or stone trough. It flowers in late summer.

SEDUM GRISEBACHII Boissier

PLATE 5

SYNONYMS: *S. flexuosum* Wettstein,
S. horakii Rohlena, *S. kostovii* Stefanov

Only a tetraploid form ("*Sedum kostovii*") is in general cultivation (Plate 5). The most distinctive feature of *S. grisebachii* is hyaline papillae on the leaf tips, clearly visible to those with reasonable close-vision (Fig. 5.1h). Tetraploid *S. grisebachii* is a tiny plant with narrow leaves in very congested tufts. It turns completely deep red in summer and is exceptionally floriferous. Golden-yellow flowers make a dense hemispherical mound, so it appears there are no sterile shoots left to perpetuate the plant. Fortunately the dying inflorescences reveal red densely tufted shoots at their bases.

HABITAT. Greece and Bulgaria are the home of this species, which is only found at high altitudes.

MAIN POINTS OF DISTINCTION. The density of hyaline papillae is only shared by two yellow-flowered species: this one and *Sedum laconicum*. The latter has leaves over 6 mm (0.2 in) long, while those of *S. grisebachii* are 4 mm (0.2 in) at most. The forms of *S. laconicum* in cultivation appear to remain a dull blue-green throughout the year, in contrast to the bright red assumed by *S. grisebachii*, even if both species are kept in the same sunny spot. As a further characteristic, *S. grisebachii* possesses long sepals.

VARIATION. Plants received from enthusiasts as far afield as Japan and Kansas show no noticeable variation. $2n = 32$.

HORTICULTURE. This is an excellent, colorful, diminutive specimen for a raised stone trough or bowl garden. It needs some protection in areas with very wet winters, but seeds quite generously—a relief when the main plant expires in a wet, cold spell. Gardeners are likely to retain the more familiar name "*Sedum kostovii.*"

SEDUM LACONICUM Boissier

PLATE 6

In autumn, all that exists of *Sedum laconicum* plants is tiny, pruinose, green, congested, rosettelike tufts at ground level. Like *S. flexuosum*, this species has hyaline papillae on the leaf tips, but is bluish gray-green. It is very floriferous and tends to disintegrate in late summer after the light yellow flowers, with petals showing a red mid-vein, die back.

HABITAT. *Sedum laconicum* is indigenous to Central and southern Greece and Crete at altitudes over 1000 m (3000 ft). It is also reported from the Middle East.

MAIN POINTS OF DISTINCTION. The best pointers are long, erect inflorescences of congested cymes with flowers of pale yellow, leaves tipped with hyaline papillae (Fig. 5.1i), and the formation of tiny tufts at ground level in autumn.

VARIATION. Several clones collected in Greece at different altitudes retain their variation of size in cultivation. In other respects they appear similar. $2n = 16$ and 32.

HORTICULTURE. *Sedum laconicum* is a delightful miniature. In the rock garden it tends to spread, but if grown in small containers, it seems to wish to occupy neighboring pots. Therefore, give it plenty of space. It is not invasive. On the contrary, it is slow to multiply, so does best in a large stone trough or raised bed. Unfortunately, it does not form a dense carpet.

SEDUM LITOREUM Gussone

Sedum litoreum is an annual species, which I have often failed to perpetuate. It is highly variable—at best growing to over 15 cm (6 in) and producing literally a hundred pale yellow flowers, each with only a single whorl of stamens. Runts of a colony may comprise only a simple stem with a few leaves and flowers. Leaves are ephemeral on all plants and become grooved above as they dry and fall.

HABITAT. Coastal zones of the east Mediterranean are the home of this species: from France to Israel, with a disjunct colony on the French shores of the Bay of Biscay. As its name suggests, *Sedum litoreum* favors sandy shorelines. It appears indigenous to Marseilles and Corsica but may have been introduced over a period of several hundreds of years. In medieval times and even before, traders spread their wares on beaches; fleeces or cloth from the east Mediterranean could easily have picked up seeds from *S. litoreum*. When cargoes were discharged at Mar-

seilles, a port with a long history of trade with the East, seeds could be cast and, in this way, plants today appear part of the native flora.

MAIN POINTS OF DISTINCTION. This species is a real oddity of the *Sedum acre* group: its stems thicken upwards (Fig. 5.5a) and its very short, stout, fleshy pedicels widen to huge sepals that unite to form a distinct tube (Fig. 5.5b). Bracts are often larger than flowers, and fleshy leaves (Fig. 5.1j) are often opposite on the stout stems which soon become woody.

VARIATION. Runemark and Greuter (1981) erected two new species: *Sedum praesidis* and *S. samium* for plants from Crete and Samos respectively, which were once considered to be *S. litoreum* or *S. annuum*. Therefore, it is possible that plants bearing the label *S. litoreum* and originating from the Aegean may not be of this species. I have been unable to study more than a dozen specimens of *S. litoreum* from France, Turkey, and Italy, but I would suggest that site and situation of plants in cultivation play a bigger part in variation than origin of the seed. All annual species of *Sedum* respond remarkably to site and

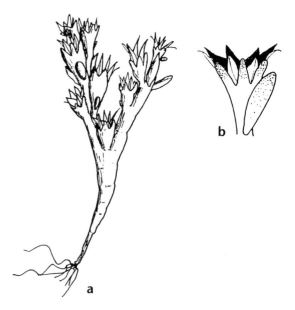

Figure 5.5. *Sedum litoreum*: (a) mature plants become woody and brittle; (b) old flower starting to fruit with bract; note stout pedicel widening into a distinct receptacle.

situation; this species is no exception. Hexa–ploids ($2n$ = 60) are the most common form in habitat, but $2n$ = 20 and 40 have been recorded.

HORTICULTURE. Emulating the habitat of a Greek shoreline to accommodate a winter-growing annual is no easy task in a cool, temperate area. Good luck to all who try.

SEDUM SEXANGULARE L.

PLATE 7

SYNONYMS: *S. boloniense* Loiseleur, *S. mite* Gilibert, *S. montenegrinum* Horak

COMMON NAME: Tasteless stonecrop

Sedum sexangulare is easily recognized by its six spirals of parallel-sided, oblong leaves, which are clearly visible when looking down on a sterile shoot (Plate 7). It has simple inflorescences with two or three branches carrying bright yellow flowers. Each flower has narrow, acutely pointed petals, and carpels with long narrow beaks. *Sedum sexangulare* does not have a bitter taste in the morning as does *S. acre*. It is a very common plant for ground cover, turning coppery in full sun.

HABITAT. This species is widespread across Central Europe: from the Baltic Sea margins to the Tyrrhenian Coast, from France to the Carpathian Mountains, and from sea level to montane areas of former Yugoslavia.

MAIN POINTS OF DISTINCTION. Linear-oblong, terete leaves (Fig. 5.1k) in six spirals are the best indicator. Other characteristics include persistent brown dead leaves that cover the lower stems and sepals that are not free.

VARIATION. Taller, less compact pentaploid forms of *Sedum sexangulare* from former Yugoslavia with finer, more deflexed leaves have been described as *S. montenegrinum* Horak.

Sedum tschernokolevii Stefanov is a recently described Bulgarian plant from the East Balkan Mountains in the locality of Scherba (Verna District). It is remarkably like the southern Yugoslavian forms of *S. sexangulare*, but the latter is said not to be indigenous to Bulgaria. Photographs of

herbarium specimens of *S. tschernokolevii* depict plants with long inflorescences. Whether these photographs reflect the true nature of plants or the result of etiolation or continuous growth in the herbarium presses is open to debate. Plants I have received under the name of *S. tscher-nokolevii* are virtually identical to pentaploid forms of *S. sexangulare*, though they are less rampant growers, and they have lighter yellow petals.

Sedum sexangulare subsp. *elatum* is a finer, greener eastern form now in the trade. It is very floriferous and has petals of green-yellow.

Grown in shade, *Sedum sexangulare* remains green, but it is much bronzer and more compact if grown in a stony, sunny spot. 't Hart (1978) reports that diploids ($2n$ = 74) are restricted to the East, tetraploids ($2n$ = 148) to the Mediterranean, and pentaploids ($2n$ = 185) like *S. montene-grinum* to the Dalmatian Coast, but triploids ($2n$ = 111) are the most widespread. *Sedum sexangulare* 'Weisse Tatra' is a regional variation from the Slovakian Tatra Mountains. It is very compact and is often labeled "compact form" or "new form."

Sedum sexangulare is often erroneously sold with the label "*S. acre*" in the United Kingdom. Several forms exist in cultivation with more than six spirals of leaves.

HORTICULTURE. This species is best contained, for it too rampant for a rock garden but, if desired, plants will soon smother a large area making an excellent ground-covering specimen. It is no more difficult to manage than *Sedum acre* and, like it, will grow well on a stone wall. *Sedum sexangulare* has the added interest of turning a beautiful copper shade in full sun.

SEDUM TUBERIFERUM
Stojanov & Stefanov

New to cultivation and still very rare, *Sedum tu-beriferum* is a very odd little plant producing subterranean, tuberlike propagules (Fig. 5.6a). These propagules have scalelike leaves, which, when they surface, become normal leaves. Early

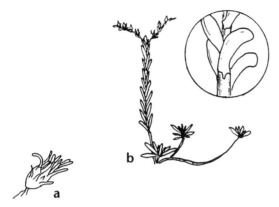

Figure 5.6. *Sedum tuberiferum*: (a) a subterranean propagule; (b) inflorescence, about 10 cm (4 in) high, with trilobed bracts.

growth is just a tiny, tufted rosette at ground level, but as the few bright green stems rise, laxly arranged leaves with very distinctive, three-lobed basal spurs are displayed (Fig. 5.1l). The inflorescences rise to about 15 cm (6 in) carrying few-branched cymes on which the bracts also have characteristic three-lobed spurs (Fig. 5.6b).

HABITAT. *Sedum tuberiferum* grows in Bulgaria and northern Greece in mountain areas.

MAIN POINTS OF DISTINCTION. Subterranean tuberlike propagules are unique. Three-lobed spurs at the bases of the leaves are also a good aid to identification. Flowers are pale yellow, and carpels have upturned beaks.

VARIATION. All plants in general cultivation originated from propagations of plants distributed by 't Hart. $2n = 32$. For a hybrid between this species and *Sedum multiceps*, see the description of *S. multiceps*.

HORTICULTURE. Plants have a complete summer rest. They survive outdoors in a wet temperate maritime climate, but would probably do far better in an alpine house. Growth is weak so I would only recommend this species for the true enthusiast.

SEDUM URSI 't Hart

Sedum ursi is a very recently described species from Turkey. At first it was considered a regional variation of *Sedum laconicum*, but there are no

hyaline papillae on the tips of the leaves (Fig. 5.1m). In other respects the two species somewhat resemble each other.

HABITAT. Mount Sandras was where the species was first discovered but it also grows in adjacent areas of southwestern Anatolia on limestone and serpentine scree at about 1650 m (5410 ft).

MAIN POINTS OF DISTINCTION. This glabrous species resembles *Sedum laconicum* except that the rounded leaf tips lack hyaline papillae. In addition, the sepals are fused into a receptacle, and the plant is distinct cytologically with $2n = 12$.

VARIATION. I have only grown a single clone and know of no others in cultivation.

HORTICULTURE. This species appears as hardy as *Sedum urvillei* and *S. laconicum*.

SEDUM URVILLEI De Candolle

PLATE 8

SYNONYMS: *S. hillebrandtii* Fenzl, *S. novakii* Domin, *S. sartorianum* Boissier, *S. stribrnyi* Velenovsky

Gardeners perpetuate the names "*Sedum stribrnyi*," "*S. sartorianum*," and "*S. hillebrandtii*" for they are so well known, and the plants in cultivation bearing these names appear distinct. These once apparently distinct species are all interlinked by intermediate forms in the wild. 't Hart's work (1978) has shown that *S. urvillei* incorporates them all and therefore is a variable, yet distinct species.

Sedum urvillei has fairly upright shoots, 5–12 cm (2–5 in) high, imbricately covered with gray-green or reddish, semi-terete leaves, each with a distinct, large, broad, truncate spur. Stems are shaggy with dead, silvery-gray leaves, and the inflorescence is a few-branched, short, compact cyme carrying yellow flowers, which could by the casual observer be taken for those of *S. acre*.

HABITAT. This polymorphic species is widespread in the far east of Europe and into the Middle East, from sea level to high mountain zones.

MAIN POINTS OF DISTINCTION. Large, broad, truncate spurs (Fig. 5.1n, o) differentiate this species from any other members of this group except for *Sedum borissovae*, which has much smaller leaves with very rounded tips and lax cymes of flowers.

VARIATION. Smaller forms of *Sedum urvillei* from Bulgaria and northern Greece, once referred to as *"S. strybrnyi,"* tend to be suffused red throughout the summer. Large forms from Greece, once referred to as *"S. sartorianum,"* tend to remain light green throughout the year, and the low, lax form from the Carpathians (i.e., *"S. hillebrandtii"*) has red stems and finer glaucous-green leaves. In Europe, tetraploids ($2n = 64$) appear to be most common; diploids ($2n = 32$) and triploids ($2n = 48$) are also common; hexaploids ($2n = 96$), heptaploids ($2n = 112$), and octoploids ($2n = 128$) have been found in southern Greece, and pentaploids ($2n = 80$) in former Yugoslavia, Greece, and Bulgaria. All levels of ploidy, although vegetatively very similar, retain slight differences in cultivation.

HORTICULTURE. *Sedum urvillei* is much slower than, and certainly not as dense as, *S. acre*. Plants become brittle in autumn when bits break off easily and root. This is a neat, easily controlled species that in all its forms is useful in raised stone troughs and beds, but is not easy to establish on a wall. Perhaps some protection will be needed in areas with extreme winters. Like *S. sexangulare*, this species tends to flower quite late in summer.

KYPHOCARPIC SPECIES WITHOUT YELLOW FLOWERS

This group consists of the following species in cultivation:

Sedum alberti Praeger (see *S. gracile*)
Sedum anglicum Hudson
Sedum arenarium Brotero (see *S. anglicum*)
Sedum atratum L.
Sedum bithynicum Boissier (see *S. pallidum*)
Sedum caespitosum De Candolle
Sedum glaucum Waldstein & Kitaibel
Sedum gracile C. A. Meyer
Sedum haematodes Scopoli (see *S. atratum*)
Sedum hispanicum L.
Sedum melanantherum De Candolle (see
    S. anglicum)
Sedum obtusifolium var. *listoniae* (C. A. Meyer)
    Fröderström
Sedum pallidum Bieberstein
Sedum rubens L.
Sedum rubrum Thellung (see *S. caespitosum*)
Sedum stefco Stefanov
Sedum stellatum L.
Sedum stoloniferum Gmelin
Sedum tymphaeum Quézel & Contandriopoulos

Plants of this group

- Have weak fibrous roots.
- Have kyphocarpic flowers.
- Have white, whitish pink, or purple petals.
- Are small-growing annual or perennial herbs from Europe or adjacent areas in the Middle East or North Africa.
- Flower in midsummer.

Figure 5.7 shows leaf shapes of European kyphocarpic species without yellow flowers.

The following is not intended to be a formal key, but merely an aid to identification of species within this group:

Leaves wide, flat, thin, plant perennial:
    S. stoloniferum
Leaves wide, flat, thin, plant perennial with
    subterranean propagules: *S. obtusifolium*
Leaves wide, flat, thin, plant annual:
    S. stellatum
Annual plants, single whorl of stamens only,
    mostly 4-partite flowers: *S. caespitosum*

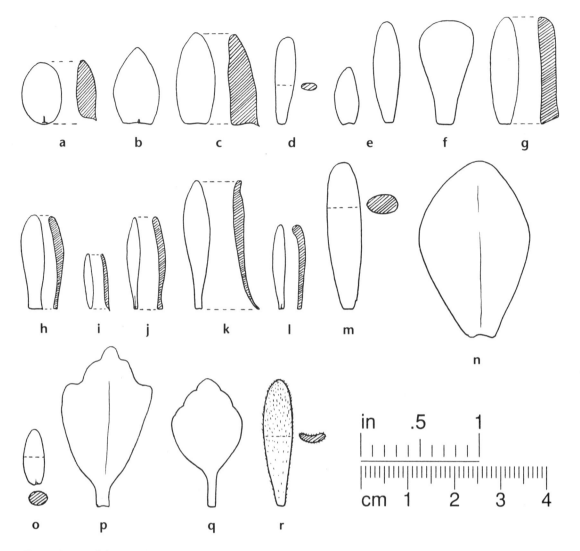

Figure 5.7. Leaf shapes of European kyphocarpic species without yellow flowers: (a) *Sedum anglicum* subsp. *anglicum* from St. David's Head, Wales; (b) *S. anglicum* var. *hibernicum* from Strangford Lough, Ulster; (c) *S. anglicum* var. *pyrenaicum*; (d) *S. anglicum* subsp. *anglicum* grown under glass; (e) contrasting leaves of *S. anglicum* subsp. *arenarium* plants—(left) an alpine form, (right) a lowland form; (f) *S. atratum*; (g) *S. caespitosum*; (h) *S. anglicum* subsp. *melanantherum*; (i) *S. gracile*; (j) *S. hispanicum* from Greece; (k) *S. pallidum*; (l) *S. hispanicum* var. *minus*; (m) *S. rubens*; (n) *S. obtusifolium* var. *listoniae*; (o) *S. stefco*; (p) *S. stellatum*; (q) *S. stoloniferum*; (r) *S. tymphaeum*.

Annual plants, single whorl of stamens only,
    5-partite flowers: *S. rubens*
Sepals free: *S. anglicum*
Leaves hirsute in dense rosettes: *S. tymphaeum*
Leaves hirsute, or at least upper inflorescence
    hirsute: *S. hispanicum* group
Leaves linear, shiny green: *S. gracile*
Annual with funnel-shaped calyx tube:
    S. atratum

Perennial with 4-partite flowers and 8 stamens:
    S. stefco

SEDUM ANGLICUM Hudson

PLATES 9, 10

COMMON NAME: English stonecrop

Sedum anglicum is a delightful and dainty, though not a particularly hardy, carpeting species. Some forms are nearly always perennial, but others are always annual. The type species is a lover of damp but not particularly saturated sites, and, as such, acts as an annual in abnormally dry conditions. Its green-tinged red foliage is usually not as bright as that of *S. acre*, but its charming pink-white flowers in June are most attractive.

HABITAT. Western Europe is the home of this species: from southern Scandinavia to Iberia, mostly on coastal sites with high rainfall.

MAIN POINTS OF DISTINCTION. Glaucous leaves have a broad spur (Fig. 5.7). Stems are bare and creeping below, but densely leafy and more erect above. The inflorescence is small and dense. Carpels are only somewhat spreading and each has an upturned beak. The best proof of identification is the free nature of the succulent, uneven sepals with spurs—a unique characteristic among white-flowered European *Sedum* species.

VARIATION. In many florae, *Sedum anglicum* and *S. arenarium* Brotero are considered distinct species because the former is strictly perennial and the later, annual. In *Flora Portuguesa*, Sampaio (1946) described *S. anglicum* subsp. *arenarium* Sampaio and *S. anglicum* var. *pyrenaicum* Lange. The latter is a bolder, more upright plant than the English stonecrop, and is associated with Iberia and southern France (Fig. 5.7c). In alpine areas of Iberia, tiny creeping forms of the type species, often referred to as *S. anglicum* var. *microphyllum* (Don) Fröderström, are often found near *S. anglicum* subsp. *arenarium*. A great deal of scientific investigation still needs to be carried out to justify the names presently used to classify this polymorphic species (Plate 9).

On the central plains of Portugal, *Sedum anglicum* subsp. *arenarium* appears to be perhaps the most common plant, growing as a marginal wherever rock breaks the surface—a feature occuring very frequently, for the granitic area was scoured by glaciers (Plate 10). Here plants are small, but in favorable locations it is possible to find individual specimens of 18 cm (7 in) stature with literally more than 100 flowers; generally

the species becomes more diminutive as one moves eastwards across Portugal or gains altitude (Fig. 5.7e).

Tiny forms of *Sedum anglicum* from the isles of Britain have been described as *S. anglicum* var. *minus* Praeger, but it is not always easy to assign a regional form to this name: a tiny form from Colonsay, Inner Hebrides, is compact and dark green; the form from the Lizard, Cornwall, England, is almost as small and brighter green, but can elongate more than Welsh or Scottish forms. The smallest form I have observed is from Mount Ventoux, France; it is similar to high alpine forms from the Pyrenees, the Sierra da Estrela, Sierra de la Pena de França and other mountain ranges of Iberia.

A large, somewhat downy form with patent fruit comes from Ireland and is known as *Sedum anglicum* var. *hibernicum* (Haworth) Don, but intermediate forms grow on the Isle of Man in the Irish Sea, geographically midway between the type species, which grows on rocky Welsh coasts, and the large, open, downy Irish form (Fig. 5.7b). The species generally is said to be calcifuge as it inhabits areas of very acid soils on the highlands and islands of Britain, but the prettiest form I have seen came from a limestone pavement gryke in Central Portugal (SF 198/1).

Sedum anglicum subsp. *melanantherum* (De Candolle) Jahandiez & Maire, a plant once associated with *S. album*, is from the mountains of Andalusia, southern Spain, and the Grand Atlas, Morocco. It is a very short, compact grower with silvery green, imbricate leaves (Fig. 5.7h). Inflorescences are much longer than those of the type species and carry only a few, small flowers. The plant I grow, verified by Liége Botanic Gardens, appears to have fully erect carpels in fruit, so I can understand why Fröderström assigned it to *S. album*. Few forms of *S. anglicum* have really patent carpels, but I would have expected them to be suberect in this instance to justify the alliance with *S. anglicum*. $2n = 48$ has been reported for the type species, and $2n = 24$ and 36 for *S. anglicum* subsp. *pyrenaicum*.

HORTICULTURE. High alpine forms are obviously the most hardy but they tend to be low, creeping, and less floriferous plants than lowland forms. During the very mild winters of the late 1980s, *Sedum anglicum* became a weed in peat-beds of several British botanic gardens, but a sharp winter will probably remedy this situation. Lowland, coastal forms of this species should be kept in an alpine house during periods of sharp frosts, but plants will become etiolated and uncharacteristic if kept there for more than a couple of months. Even etiolated specimens can be used for propagation, but introduce such plants back into the natural environment in stages. *Sedum anglicum* in any of its forms is unlikely to survive in areas with temperatures of over 25°C (77°F) for several consecutive weeks, unless moved to an airy, damp, shady spot. Although not very common in collections, it makes an excellent potted specimen plant (Fig. 5.8).

Figure 5.8. *Sedum anglicum* is a delightful, compact species for pot cultivation. The pot is 6 in (15 cm) across.

SEDUM ATRATUM L.

SYNONYM: *Sedella atrata* (L.) Fourreau

This tiny, annual species, rarely encountered in cultivation, comprises a simple stem, or several, branched at the base (Figs. 5.7f, 5.9). Each plant

Figure 5.9. *Sedum atratum* grows only a few centimeters (1.5 in) high.

is only a few centimeters (1.5 in) high, topped with a short, dense corymb of pink-white 5-partite or 6-partite flowers.

HABITAT. *Sedum atratum* grows on mountains of central and south Europe: from Greece to Spain, through the Carpathians and Alps, mostly on limestone.

MAIN POINTS OF DISTINCTION. Short pedicels widen into a funnel-shaped calyx tube from which deltoid sepals rise. Petals can be wavy, nectary glands are large, and stamens short. Carpels are not particularly wide spreading and have short, deflexed beaks.

VARIATION. In the wild, due to the many disjunct sites, many forms have been recorded and subspecies erected. Some regional variations have creamy petals. Dark red plants have been named *Sedum haematodes* Scopoli and can turn almost black. This dark form is generally accepted to be *S. atratum* subsp. *atratum*, while the greener, taller, more-likely-to-be-branched-from-the-base form from the southeast of its range has been named *S. atratum* subsp. *carinthiacum* (Hoppe ex Pacher) D. A. Webb. $2n = 18$ and 36.

HORTICULTURE. This diminutive species has little horticultural value, but it offers a challenge to the alpine enthusiast.

SEDUM CAESPITOSUM
De Candolle

SYNONYM: *S. rubrum* Thellung

A floriferous, fairly erect, 5-to 15-cm (2-to 6-in) high annual, *Sedum caespitosum* has 4-partite or sometimes 5-partite flowers but only a single whorl of stamens (Fig. 5.10a, b, c). This species is rarely seen in cultivation. Feeble, ephemeral petals are almost transparent. Very widespreading carpels are patent soon after the buds burst. The single whorl of stamens is often very difficult to locate, and seed seems to be formed during the bud stage. Flowers are feeble except for the colorful, rapidly forming, narrow, sharply pointed fruit. Green, oblong, terete leaves are quite attractive and turn red in full sun (Fig. 5.7g).

HABITAT. *Sedum caespitosum* can be found in almost every Mediterranean country, mostly at coastal sites. Small colonies grow at over 1000 m (3000 ft) in the Sierra Nevada, Spain, on level granitic scree, but the species is more usually spotted as a roadside marginal.

MAIN POINTS OF DISTINCTION. The rapidly spreading, very narrow, acute carpels of green then brown-red, a single whorl of stamens, and narrow, ephemeral petals are good indicators. The species is vegetatively very similar to *Sedum andegavense*, except the latter species has upright carpels.

VARIATION. A particularly bold, pretty form from Bouc-Bel-Air in southern France (Fig. 5.10d) has been distributed. It has mostly 5-partite flowers, is very colorful, and, in cultivation,

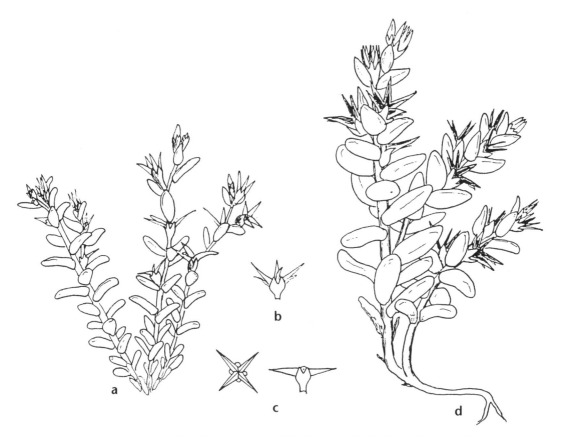

Figure 5.10. Contrasting forms of *Sedum caespitosum*: Turkish form (a) displaying lack of epipetalous stamens, (b) with mostly 4-partite fruit, (c) which soon become patent; (d) bold form from southern France with mostly 5-partite fruit.

makes a handsome specimen. Other examples from as far away as Turkey and the Balearic Isles seem remarkably similar. In one colony, the variation from very tiny, dark red plants, consisting of no more than a few leaves and a few flowers, to greener, sturdy, succulent plants of several centimeters, with dozens of flowers, is most contrasting. $2n = 12$ and 24.

HORTICULTURE. This species is rather dull as an annual (since the flowers have feeble petals), but it can produce a dense mat of colorful red foliage in a bright spot.

SEDUM GRACILE C. A. Meyer

PLATE 11

SYNONYM: *S. alberti* Praeger

Sedum gracile is vegetatively similar to smaller forms of yellow-flowered *S. sexangulare*, but it produces dull, whitish flowers. This bright green, carpet-forming species is fairly common in cultivation. It grows to about 5 cm (2 in) high and carries densely imbricate, linear leaves, each with a hint of a basal spur. The inflorescence comprises (usually) two patent branches about 3 cm (1 in) long, each carrying about half a dozen flowers. Carpels are erect at first, and, according to Praeger (1921) "later slightly spreading." Fröderström (1932), on the other hand, included the species in his section *Eurasiatica orthocarpia*, although the drawing in his monograph shows the typical bulge on the inner wall of the carpels that is generally associated with kyphocarpic flowers. Komorov (1939) said that the carpels are convex on the inside. This is true, and if one examines very old, dried fruit, there is no doubt that they do eventually become stellate-patent. Therefore I propose to include this species in the kyphocarpic group.

HABITAT. The Caucasus mountain range is the home of this species, which inhabits stony soils in subalpine and alpine zones.

MAIN POINTS OF DISTINCTION. Identifying characteristics are bright, narrow, linear, shiny, green foliage (Fig. 5.7i), two-branched (some-

times three or very rarely four), spreading inflorescences with sessile flowers, clearly visible nectary glands, and slowly spreading carpels firmly united at the base. In addition, lower stems are often shaggy with dead leaves. $2n = 12$.

VARIATION. Apiculate petals are often pale green and leaves can be tipped with red if plants are grown in full sun.

HORTICULTURE. This bright plant is especially useful against a dark background although its abundant flowers are rather dull. It is not particularly good in hot, drought conditions, but is relatively winter-hardy.

SEDUM HISPANICUM L.

PLATE 12

The *Sedum hispanicum* complex of plants comprises *S. hispanicum*, *S. rubens*, and *S. pallidum* but is in great need of expert attention to sort out the many anomalies and contradictions apparent in available literature. Even the name *S. hispanicum* is confusing, suggesting that such plants originate from Spain, when in fact they are only found much further east. Until recently some commonly grown plants of this group, which have been in cultivation for centuries, have had no documented details of their habitat. Little cytological work has been carried out on well-documented field specimens, and much confusion has been perpetuated by the scores of names published for regional variations.

Sedum hispanicum is a polymorphic species that generally can be persuaded to perenniate itself in cultivation, but is annual if summer conditions are hot and dry. Compact tufts of leaves can be glaucous green, gray, or pink-purple. In the past far too much emphasis has been placed on "annual versus perennial," for although it is true to say that some forms of *S. hispanicum* always act as perennial, others may change from season to season.

In collections today, especially in North American gardens, a plant often labeled "*Sedum hispanicum minus* purple form" is a European diploid form ($2n = 14$) that more correctly is called *S. hispanicum* var. *hispanicum*. Praeger (1921) described *S. hispanicum* var. *minus* (syn. *S. glaucum* Waldstein & Kitaibel) as the perennial form of *S. hispanicum*; as a result, any form that has perenniated itself in cultivation has been associated with Praeger's variety. The diploid form of *S. hispanicum* has white 6-partite to 10-partite flowers with wine-red veining. Boissier erected *S. hispanicum* var. *polypetalum* for 7-partite to 9-partite varieties, but often a single plant can produce mostly 6-partite flowers one season and fool the observer by producing a plethora of flowers with more numerous parts in following seasons.

Another form from Turkey is often introduced into cultivation. Like its Greek counterpart, it is a diploid, but because of its ability to produce 5-partite flowers and its less hardy nature causing it to act as an annual, it is more often incorrectly labeled *S. bithynicum*. It tends to be very floriferous, and as it is not particularly winter hardy, it is frequently lost after a single season.

Sedum bithynicum Boissier is a name upheld by several taxonomists, although occasionally one encounters the combination *S. hispanicum* var. *bithynicum* (Boissier) Chamberlain. According to Chamberlain (1972), this species should be assigned to *S. pallidum* as a variety because the carpels are "erecto-patent." Chamberlain also adds that this group is in need of further study. Perennial forms of *S. bithynicum* that I have observed from collections made in Turkey over a period of years have always had kyphocarpic, 5-partite flowers (patent rather than erect) but beaks are upturned. They have invariably been misidentified as *S. bithynicum*, but 't Hart (unpub.) claims that *S. bithynicum* is identical with *S. pallidum*.

Sedum hispanicum var. *minus* Praeger (Plate 12), also known as *S. glaucum* Waldstein & Kitaibel or glaucous stonecrop, is absent from all European and Turkish florae, for until very recently, it was only known as a garden plant. As such, it is exceptionally common and very high-

ly recommended for its glaucous blue-green tufts of leaves that form a very dense carpet, tinged pink below in drought conditions. It is not as floriferous as its near relatives, and therefore carries more sterile shoots. Flowers are produced on a short, flat-topped inflorescence of terminal scorpioid branches and are generally 6-partite, though several 5-partite flowers are often observed. Petals are abruptly pink in their upper two-thirds, but white at the base. Fruit are an attractive rust-red. This very distinct form of *S. hispanicum* is one of the best low forms of *Sedum* for scree, raised beds, stone troughs, and rock gardens. It is very easy to control, and, against a dark background, is most eye-catching. Recently it has been found in the wild in Turkey by Jean Metzger, but no cytological work has yet been carried out to justify its status. Vegetatively it is like *S. pallidum* var. *bithynicum*: the latter becomes a mass of long, tumbling inflorescences in summer that carry literally hundreds of white mostly 5-partite flowers with wine-red veining and leave only a few sterile shoots behind, while *S. hispanicum* var. *minus*, although not shy of flowering, has much shorter inflorescences and tends to remain glaucous blue-green at the tips of the sterile shoots throughout the summer. It is also fully hardy.

Praeger (1921, 301) mentioned a fourth variation on a theme: "There is a form of it with yellowish foliage known as *Sedum lydium aureum*. Though long in cultivation and most distinct, this plant appears to be undescribed. I have no information as to its native habitat." The situation has changed little since Praeger's time: the plant, which is commonly offered by garden centers, is usually named *Sedum hispanicum* var. *minus* f. *aureum*. It is not hardy, nor is it very floriferous; in fact, it is most shy of flowering. The sickly yellow hue of the leaf color is very pronounced, but on the few occasions it has flowered for me, flowers have been small, white, and mostly 6-partite. I have noticed recently the name "*S. bithynicum aureum*" used in association with this form, but, as far as I know, this combination is not official. Until its definite habitat is located, I am tentatively using the name *Sedum hispanicum* var. *minus* 'Aureum'. As this form appears not to have been formally described, it is probably better to refer to it as a cultivar. It (as well as other forms occasionally) produces cristate branches. The cristate parts are difficult to perpetuate alone, but with careful pruning, a most striking plant can be produced. In 1986, when radio-active fallout from the nuclear explosion at Chernobyl in the former Soviet Union rained over much of Europe, most plants of the form 'Aureum' showed some signs of fasciation.

HABITAT. *Sedum hispanicum* forms grow from Sicily to Turkey on both sides of the Mediterranean, in all countries except Egypt, and into the Middle East in a great multitude of sites and altitudes.

MAIN POINTS OF DISTINCTION. Upper parts of inflorescences are glandular-hairy in all vari-

eties and forms. With a magnifying glass, a line of hairs can be detected on the keel of petals and on the inner side of carpels. Plants are always very soft to the touch. Hyaline papillae at the leaf tips can often be detected, and the leaf bases are shortly spurred (Fig. 5.7j, l). Branching occurs from the bases of stems.

VARIATION. Three distinct forms are in cultivation but so are numerous regional variations:

Praeger's perennial *Sedum hispanicum* var. *minus* is the most common and most desirable form. It is least likely to lose its glaucous-blue color, and has mostly 6-partite, bicolored flowers.

Sedum hispanicum var. *minus* 'Aureum' is delicate and has tiny, 6-partite flowers.

Sedum hispanicum, a diploid form from Greece, sometimes acts as an annual, quickly tinges purple, and has many-partite flowers (it is often called "purple form" (Fig. 5.11).

HORTICULTURE. *Sedum hispanicum* var. *minus*

Figure 5.11. *Sedum hispanicum,* a Greek diploid form.

is the most useful and robust form, but the Greek diploid is recommended for raised stone troughs where it can mix with other plants. It is not dense enough to be showy by itself, but among other plants it will seed and produce new plants in both autumn and spring. It is never a menace. *Sedum hispanicum* var. *minus* 'Aureum' needs winter protection despite the fact it is usually sold as a hardy alpine.

SEDUM OBTUSIFOLIUM VAR. LISTONIAE (C. A. Meyer) Fröderström

PLATE 13

SYNONYM: *S. proponticum* Aznavour

Sedum obtusifolium var. *listoniae* is an exceptionally rare *Sedum* in cultivation and quite unlike any other species. Its growth pattern is most peculiar, for in autumn it is merely a group of very flat, few-leafed rosettes at ground level. It overwinters thus and in spring the stems elongate to display opposite-decussate, nearly orbicular to spathulate, dark green, well-spaced, flat leaves with blunt teeth (Fig. 5.7n). The upper stems are noticeably scabrid with deflexed glands. The terminal inflorescences of a few short branches, with a flower in the fork, carry sessile, 5-partite flowers. The petals, which are bright rose-purple in the upper two-thirds, become abruptly white at the base. Praeger (1921) stated that the carpels are upright, but the plants I have observed have relatively spreading carpels with the associated bulge on the inner wall, a feature of kyphocarpic species. After the flowering period of middle to late summer, the plants appear to die completely, but underground there are very peculiar white propagules, looking not unlike molars, from which the autumn rosettes spring.

HABITAT. Northwestern Anatolia is the home of this variety.

MAIN POINTS OF DISTINCTION. Flowers are large for *Sedum*, petals are deeply grooved on the upper surface, sepals are edged with beadlike cilia, glassy deflexed glands cover the stems, and the outer faces of carpels are papillose. Keels of petals have a line of hairs, but the most distinguishing features are the odd growth pattern and peculiar toothlike, subterranean buds. $2n = 30$.

VARIATION. The type species from northern Iran is not in cultivation as far as I know, but is reported to be smaller and have floral differences.

HORTICULTURE. This is a gem for the alpine specialist, with large, beautiful flowers. It grows well from seed. Unfortunately, it is exceptionally rare in cultivation. It must have winter protection. Praeger had difficulty keeping it outdoors in Dublin, Ireland, which has a reputation for mild winters; I bring my plant indoors for the worst two or three months.

SEDUM PALLIDUM Bieberstein

PLATE 14

Sedum pallidum is invariably annual in cultivation (Fig. 5.12). I have grown this pale plant on several occasions, and even managed to perpetuate a little colony, but it is rare in cultivation. Plants have linear leaves with long, spreading, flowering stems carrying strictly 5-partite flowers with 10 stamens.

HABITAT. The species is found in European Turkey and perhaps into the Middle East.

MAIN POINTS OF DISTINCTION. Inflorescences comprise two ascending branches. Flowers have white petals that are erect. Leaves are relatively long and narrow (Fig. 5.7k). *Sedum pallidum* var. *bithynicum* is colorful and floriferous and can be distinguished from *S. hispanicum* var. *minus* by its huge inflorescences and 5-partite flowers (Plate 14).

VARIATION. Plants of the type species are rarely seen in cultivation but *Sedum pallidum* var. *bithynicum* is becoming more easily available. Plants of either variety are highly contrasting if they are grown in diverse situations. Cytological variation is noted by 't Hart (1991): $2n = 20, 40,$ and 60.

HORTICULTURE. In cultivation, this is a frail

Figure 5.12. *Sedum pallidum* in a 3-in (8-cm) pot.

plant, but if it can be persuaded to seed in a mixed rock garden, it makes a delightful addition.

SEDUM RUBENS L.

PLATE 15

SYNONYMS: *Crassula rubens* L., *Procrassula pallidiflora* Jordan & Fourreau, *Aithales rubens* Webb & Berthelot

Sedum rubens, which is very closely related to *S. hispanicum*, is strictly a 5-partite, gray annual with usually only a single whorl of stamen(Fig. 5.13). Its leaves are larger and more succulent than those of *S. hispanicum*, but in most respects the two species are very similar (Fig. 5.7m).

HABITAT. The range of this species is even greater than that of *Sedum hispanicum*: from the Canary Islands right across Mediterranean margins to Turkey, extending into the Alps on a host of different aspects.

MAIN POINTS OF DISTINCTION. *Sedum rubens* is always annual, and its flowers have usually only five stamens. Plants are glandular pubescent throughout. Flower parts are much larger than those of *S. hispanicum*, with the in-

florescence made up of ascending branches. Carpels are spreading but turn up at the beaks. In the wild, where the species grows in association with *S. mucizonia*, young plants are almost impossible to distinguish; at the flowering stage the two are easily distinguished.

VARIATION. Fröderström (1932) erected *Sedum rubens* var. *praegeri* for a plant described as a "hexapetalous, dodecandrous *S. rubens*," which is said to be *S. hispanicum* × *S. rubens*. Such purported hybrids invariably have 6-partite flowers with two whorls of stamens. In the United Kingdom these "hybrids" are often offered as *S. hispanicum* 'Pewter' (Plate 14). 't Hart (unpub. 1994) says he has been unable to hybridize *S. hispanicum* and *S. rubens* successfully. Cytologically, this species is diverse: $2n$ = 10, 12, 14, 20, 40, 42, 60, 80, 94, and 100.

HORTICULTURE. Species and hybrids are pretty annuals, which proliferate without becoming pests. They are a delight in a scree garden or stone trough. They can be persuaded to grow on a dry stone wall and seem to be calciphiles. Seed germinates in autumn, and some in the following spring; the first wave is often wiped out by cold winters.

Figure 5.13. *Sedum rubens* from Sicily flowering in July in a 5-in (13-cm) pot.

SEDUM STEFCO Stefanov

Sedum stefco appears to be yet another variation on the *S. album* theme, but it is distinct and a very worthwhile carpet-forming plant (Fig. 5.7o). For much of the year its foliage is pink-red and its upright stems crimson-red. The few pink-white flowers are produced in late summer. It is still very rare in cultivation, but should become more common in the near future.

HABITAT. This species hails from southwestern Bulgaria.

MAIN POINTS OF DISTINCTION. The constantly 4-partite, pinkish flowers on short inflorescences are the best means of positive identification, and the kyphocarpic nature of the flower immediately separates *Sedum stefco* from any of the *S. album* complex, which vegetatively it most resembles. $2n = 14$.

VARIATION. Kept in shade, the leaves can revert to green.

HORTICULTURE. *Sedum stefco* is not as hardy

as one would expect in winter, so in extreme areas it is wise to take cuttings in autumn and pot them up in a cold frame or greenhouse. This is a splendid, bright subject for raised stone trough or rock garden. It is slow enough for the alpine house, but may become too lush and green if kept there permanently.

SEDUM STELLATUM L.

PLATE 16

SYNONYM: *Asterosedum stellatum* Grulich

Sedum stellatum is the only European annual with wide, flat leaves (Fig. 5.7p). The flowers are ephemeral, but the purple starlike fruit is very persistent and pretty. The dense, low, bushy plant has shiny green, short petiolate leaves, the lower ones being opposite. Papillose stems are 4–15 cm (2–6 in) long, and leaves have bluntly dentate margins. Mucronate petals are purple-pink and short lived.

HABITAT. This littoral species is found from

the Balearic Isles to Greece and south to Algeria. Recently it has been found further east.

MAIN POINTS OF DISTINCTION. *Sedum stellatum* is easily recognized by its wide, flat, opposite-decussate leaves in the early part of the year, and by the large starlike fruit, with short beaks, later in the season. These stars cover most of an ageing plant—hence the name. Long sepals, which have papillae, remain upright when the carpels become patent, so they appear like a crown on the star. $2n = 10$.

VARIATION. Tiny forms from the Balearic Isles appear to have a reduced inflorescence.

HORTICULTURE. This is one of the better annuals due to its more robust nature. It seems to produce enough seed to perpetuate itself. I save seed to grow in spring, but in the wild it is more likely to be a winter grower. Where plants seed themselves, they tend to attempt to grow in winter and therefore need some protection.

SEDUM STOLONIFERUM Gmelin

PLATE 17

Although this is a rare plant in cultivation, the name often appears in catalogs. Most growers who offer *Sedum stoloniferum* merely supply a form of *S. spurium*, which also has wide, flat, thin leaves and a similar sprawling habit. Together the two species cannot be confused. *Sedum stoloniferum* has tiny leaves by comparison and kyphocarpic flowers with outspreading petals. Often in botanic gardens, plants labeled *S. stoloniferum* are *S. spurium*, which does not necessarily indicate that the species have been initially muddled; it is just as likely that *S. stoloniferum* has expired and the more-common, fast-spreading *S. spurium* has jumped in its grave.

Unfortunately, in recent years more confusion has been created by equating *Sedum stoloniferum* with the yellow-flowered *S. hybridum* L. *Sedum hybridum* Urville ex Boissier is a synonym of *S. stoloniferum*, but *S. hybridum* L. is a member of *Aizoon* group.

Sedum stoloniferum is a fairly frail, creeping herb with small, opposite leaves (Fig. 5.7q) and scorpioid inflorescences of pink, stellate flowers.

HABITAT. This species is a forest plant in lower and middle mountain zones from Iran to the Caucasus Mountains.

MAIN POINTS OF DISTINCTION. Vegetatively, *Sedum stoloniferum* appears to be a miniature *S. spurium*, but spreading petals and fruit immediately distinguish it. No other species closely resemble *S. stoloniferum*. $2n = 14$, and 28.

VARIATION. I have noticed no variation, but I believe larger forms are in cultivation in mainland Europe.

HORTICULTURE. A shady spot is essential for successful cultivation of this species, which also needs room to spread as it languishes in pots. It is prudent to plant *Sedum stoloniferum* in several places as it is easily extinguished by adverse conditions. It needs some protection against heavy snowfalls, hot sunlight, and drought.

SEDUM TYMPHAEUM
Quézel & Contandriopoulos

Gardeners could be forgiven for thinking this species belonged to *Sempervivum* for it is made

Figure 5.14. *Sedum tymphaeum* in June in a 5-cm (2-in) pot.

up of dense, almost globose rosettes of glandular-pubescent leaves from which stolons radiate to perenniate the species via new rosettes (Fig. 5.14) When not in flower, it resembles *Sempervivum* more than *Sedum*. The 7-cm (3-in) inflorescence comprises only a few pink-white, 5-partite flowers, and is finely pubescent. This species is an exceptionally rare plant in cultivation.

HABITAT. *Sedum tymphaeum* is endemic to Greece in rocky, high limestone areas over 1700 m. (5600 ft), especially on Mount Timfi from which it gets its name.

MAIN POINTS OF DISTINCTION. This stonecrop is very like *Sedum tristriatum*, which has a very similar habit of growth and comes from Crete. The latter, however, has orthocarpic flowers, and much to my shame is not in cultivation, even though I received authenticated plants from Ron Evans. *Sedum pilosum* is vegetatively similar to *S. tymphaeum* but has lavender-pink flowers and rarely offsets. *Sedum hirsutum* in some of its forms could certainly be confused with *S. tymphaeum*, but it, too, has erect carpels. Leaves of *S. tymphaeum* are succulent and blunt (Fig. 5.7r), and cluster in tight rosettes. $2n = 14$.

VARIATION. No data available.

HORTICULTURE. This little gem is cold hardy but very difficult to acquire. It is ideal as a specimen alpine plant, but dreadfully slow to propagate.

YELLOW-FLOWERED ORTHOCARPIC SPECIES

The following species are in cultivation, most having been so for generations:

Sedum altissimum Poiret (see *S. sediforme*)
Sedum amplexicaule De Candolle
Sedum anopetalum De Candolle (see
    S. ochroleucum)
Sedum forsterianum Smith (syn. *S. rupestre* as used
    by Praeger and Evans)
Sedum montanum Songeon & Perrier
Sedum nicaeense Allioni (see *S. sediforme*)
Sedum ochroleucum Chaix
Sedum pruinatum Link ex Brotero
Sedum rupestre L. (syn. *S. reflexum* L. as used by
    Praeger and Evans)
Sedum sediforme (Jacquin) Pau
Sedum tenuifolium Sibthorp & Smith (see
    S. amplexicaule)
Sedum verloti Jordon (see *S. ochroleucum*)

This group of *Sedum* species has almost always been considered a natural group. It was referred to as section *Rupestria* of *Sedum* by Berger (1930). Grulich (1984) considered it so unique, he erected a new genus to accommodate species within: *Petrosedum*. There has been a great deal of misunderstanding and name changing within this section, but as an entity it has rarely been challenged.

The group comprises only six species and several subspecies in total, but literally hundreds of regional variations or levels of ploidy. In addition, there are several combinations of interspecific hybrids. Work in the field by Hébert (1983) and 't Hart (1972, 1974, 1978, 1987, 1991) in particular has resulted in a much better understanding of the group as a whole and the delimitation of the species within it.

Plants of this group

- Have carpels that remain upright until they shed their seed, as opposed to carpels that bulge on the inner wall spread out like a star, and then shed their seed.
- Have tall erect inflorescences topped with a dense cluster of flowers that are straw colored to deep yellow.
- Have apiculate leaves with basal spurs that are generally imbricate and many times longer than wide.
- Must be indigenous to Europe or neighboring areas of North Africa or the Middle East.

Leafshape is neither a sufficient nor reliable guide to identification of species in this group. Figure 5.15 combines leafshape with more consistent features.

To recognize species of this group with confidence, the following features need to be studied:

Inflorescence reflexed in bud: *S. amplexicaule,* *S. forsterianum, S. rupestre*
Inflorescence not reflexed (faces skywards throughout the full development): *S. montanum, S. ochroleucum, S. pruinatum, S. sediforme*
Flowers definitely yellow: *S. amplexicaule,* *S. forsterianum, S. montanum, S. pruinatum,* *S. rupestre*

Flowers light straw color: *S. ochroleucum,* *S. sediforme*
Plant dries up in summer: *S. amplexicaule,* *S. pruinatum, S. forsterianum* (sometimes)
Plant remains in growth in summer: *S. ochroleucum, S. montanum, S. pruinatum,* *S. sediforme, S. rupestre* (sometimes)
Glandular hairs on inflorescences (especially on sepals and bracts): *S. montanum,* *S. ochroleucum, S. rupestre* (sometimes)
Sepals long : *S. montanum, S. ochroleucum*
Sepals short: *S. forsterianum, S. sediforme*
Three lobed spurs at the bases of leaves: *S. amplexicaule*
Petals erect: *S. ochroleucum*

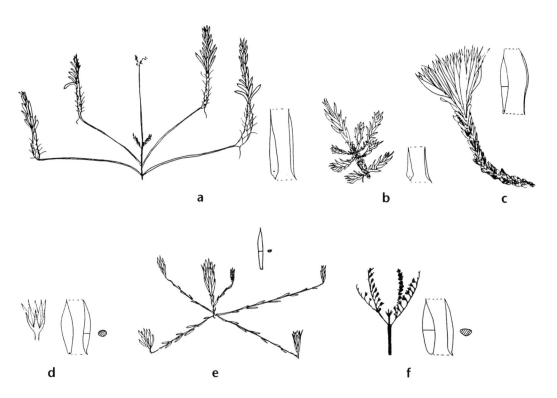

Figure 5.15. Leaf shape and other important diagnostic characteristics of European orthocarpic species with yellowish flowers: (a) *Sedum amplexicaule* subsp. a*mplexicaule* has large fleshy propagules, long stolons, and distinctly spurred leaves; (b) *S. amplexicaule* subsp. *ibericum* has tiny fleshy propagules, short stolons, and distinctly spurred leaves; (c) *S. forsterianum* 'Welsh Stonecrop' has stems shaggy with dead leaves and nonfleshy leaves that cluster into flat-topped tufts in winter; (d) leaves of *S. ochroleucum, S. montanum,* and *S. rupestre* are indistinguishable but flowers of *S. ochroleucum* have upright petals; (e) *S. pruinatum* has nonfleshy propagules and long stolons; (f) *S. sediforme* has fleshy flat-topped leaves and distinct inflorescences.

All the orthocarpic species of *Sedum* from Europe with yellowish flowers will hybridize with at least one other species of the same group. Offspring can be vigorous and fertile. Most species are geographically isolated from each other, so crossing in the wild is not widespread. Where species do intermingle, only certain levels of ploidy can interbreed, and, as a result, several hybrids have been reported in habitat. Often these hybrids have confused the understanding of the separate species and have frequently been misidentified. 't Hart (1978) has conducted a detailed series of experiments, attempting to artificially cross all combinations of species in this group; his findings show that the F_1 hybrids are generally mid-way between the parents. If fertile F_1 hybrids are produced in the wild, backcrossing surely must take place, so such hybrids will form a range of variation between the two parents. Hébert (1983) recorded a hybrid involving three species from Switzerland: *S. rupestre* × *S. montanum* × *S. ochroleucum*.

The most common hybrid in cultivation is *Sedum* ×*luteolum* Chaboisseau which is *S. rupestre* × *S. sediforme*. One distinct clone of this hybrid comes from from Spain, has very flat-topped, dark green leaves, and pale yellow flowers. Another distinct clone from southern France is glaucous with leaves more like *S. rupestre*, but also with very pale yellow flowers.

SEDUM AMPLEXICAULE
De Candolle

SYNONYM: *S. tenuifolium* Sibthorp & Smith

Sedum amplexicaule is a unique and very easily recognized species. It has a complete resting period in summer when all green is lost from the plant, leaving a tangle of brown-gray "propagules" (fleshy offsets) covered in dead leaves, and held together with very brittle, straight, threadlike stems (Fig. 5.15a). Because these stems break easily, the propagules may blow around in the wind. The propagules come to life in late September. During winter months the species produces soft, apiculate, imbricate leaves. In June, inflorescences rise, and by the time the flowers open, plants have dried out for their summer rest. The inflorescence is reflexed in bud, and yellow flowers can be as much as 11-partite, but 7-partite is more usual.

HABITAT. This stonecrop is a plant of the Mediterranean fringe from Iberia to Turkey, extending into northern Spain, Bulgaria, Tunisia, Algeria, and Morocco, in rocky, hilly, dry areas to relatively high zones in Spain and Greece. *Sedum amplexicaule* subsp. *amplexicaule* prefers shady sites and often grows on grassy banks where it is difficult to spot. *Sedum amplexicaule* subsp. *ibericum* is often a true alpine growing on level tundra just below the summer snowline in the Sierra Nevada and other high Iberian ranges.

MAIN POINTS OF DISTINCTION. Fleshy propagules can still be detected in the winter growing period as thickenings at the bases of stems (Fig. 5.15a). Bases of leaves have a distinct three-lobed spur, lax inflorescences are reflexed in bud, and golden-yellow many-partite flowers are often streaked with red. The best means of identification is the species growth pattern, which is unique.

VARIATION. Two subspecies exist: *Sedum amplexicaule* subsp. *ibericum* 't Hart has tiny stolons usually less than 2 cm (0.8 in) long. As the name suggests, this miniature form is restricted to Spain and Portugal, but is also found in southern France. Thin, brittle stolons attach the propagules to the main plant (Fig. 5.15b). Flowers are usually 6-partite, 7-partite, or 8-partite.

Sedum amplexicaule subsp. *amplexicaule*, has much longer propagules, produced on very long, straight, thin prostrate stolons.

't Hart (1978, 1991)) records chromosome counts of $2n = 24, 36, 48, 60$, and 72; Hébert (1983) adds $2n = 96$ for some Greek collections, but there appears to be no pattern to their distribution. A form reputed to be from Mount Ventoux, France, is particularly diminutive. I have discovered both flat-leaved and terete-leaved forms, green-leaved and glaucous blue-leaved forms, apiculate-leaved and blunt-leaved forms, all in southern Iberia.

HORTICULTURE. Both subspecies are worth acquiring just for the novelty of their growth. Horticulturally, as winter growers, they are of no interest for most of the active gardening period. Beware that a summer drought followed by high winds could leave you with no plants at all. It is prudent to push broken-off propagules into a sandy mixture during the summer. The larger subspecies is a very untidy plant, difficult to contain, but the smaller subspecies forms a dense carpet in summer, likened to dry oats, at which period flowers are formed (Fig. 5.16). The growth of leaves heralds winter's arrival. All forms are hardy in Mid Northumberland, England, but may need protection in more extreme areas.

SEDUM FORSTERIANUM Smith

PLATE 18

SYNONYMS: *S. rupestre* L. (as used by Praeger and later by Evans), *S. forsteranum*
COMMON NAMES: Rock stonecrop, Welsh stonecrop, Forsterian stonecrop

Most easily recognized in autumn when it dies back to rosettelike tufts, *Sedum forsterianum* has very thin leaves, which are soft and bend to the slightest touch (Fig. 5.15c). It is a very rapidly spreading, creeping ground cover. The 25-cm (10-in) tall inflorescences, which are reflexed in bud and upturn to display corymbs of distinct scorpioid branches, carry 6-partite or 7-partite yellow flowers. The long, soft stems are often clothed with dead leaves.

HABITAT. This western European species is indigenous to Herefordshire in England, France,

Figure 5.16. *Sedum amplexicaule* subsp. *ibericum* in late spring when all leaves have dried leaving only the 1.5-cm (0.6-in) long propagules and an 8-partite flower.

West Germany, Belgium, Spain, Portugal, and Morocco on lower damp, rocky areas and very often on the edges of glades with some shade. Hébert (1983) claimed that the Pyrenees Mountains act as a barrier between two isolated races.

MAIN POINTS OF DISTINCTION. Short, densely clustered, rosettelike tufts of soft, thin, linear leaves, reflexed inflorescences in bud, and pure yellow flowers with spreading petals are the best characteristics of identification. Tiny sepals are additionally helpful.

VARIATION. Several names have been published to distinguish extreme forms, but 't Hart (1978) reported that the morphological variation more or less forms a continuous series. A name still commonly used is *Sedum forsterianum* subsp. *elegans* Lejune, which refers to the common glaucous form with flat-topped inflorescences (Fig. 5.17). The name *S. rupestre* var. *forsterianum* was once reserved for the tiny green, glabrous, British form (i.e., 'Welsh Stonecrop', Plate 18), which is very short and does not creep but forms a dense, slowly spreading hummock. The tufts of leaves are flat-topped. Inflorescences are short (10 cm, 4 in) and hemispherical above with fewer flowers. In the trade it is often sold as *S. forsterianum* var. *minus*, which, according to Praeger (1921), originally referred to a very small, glaucous form—not this even smaller form from Herefordshire and the Brecon Beacons.

The North African form *Sedum forsterianum* f. *purpureum* Wilczek is sought after because of its glaucous, purple-violet hue retained for most of the year. There is such a wide range of leaf color and plant size within this species that gardeners will retain older names to acquire more-choice forms. 't Hart (1978) showed the British form as well as the common forms have $2n = 96$ (octoploid). Hébert stated that all octoploid forms are found north of the Pyrenees. 't Hart recorded plants with $2n = 48$, 60, and 72 from Portugal, and Hébert (1983) added that the North African form has $2n = 24$ (diploid), which has been described as *S. forsterianum* f. *purpureum*.

A cristate form of *S. forsterianum* has recently been distributed by Greenslacks Nursery, England. It is very much rarer than the cristate form

Figure 5.17. *Sedum forsterianum* subsp. *elegans* in habitat in the Montermuro Mountains, Portugal. Note the reflexed inflorescences forming (April) and the rounded tuft apices.

of *S. rupestre*, but, because of confusion of no-menclature, both cristates are likely to carry identical labels

HORTICULTURE. Except for the North African diploid or 'Welsh Stonecrop', this species is much too rampant for a rock garden. All forms are excellent as ground cover, especially accom-panying a potted conifer in a container from which they cannot escape. Plants seed them-selves regularly elsewhere, but are easily con-trolled. 'Welsh Stonecrop' (British form) is less colorful and less floriferous than most continen-tal forms, but has the advantage of being slow to spread—after 10 years it will only form a dense hummock less than a meter (3 ft) wide. In dry summer conditions accompanied by much sun, *S. forsterianum* in all its forms dries out and can disintegrate. If this happens, each densely clus-tered, rosettelike tuft reroots when the rains re-turn. This species should be fully hardy in all temperate zones, but it prefers half-shade and a much damper spot than its close relatives.

SEDUM MONTANUM
Songeon & Perrier

SYNONYMS: *S. ochroleucum* subsp. *montanum*
(Songeon & Perrier) D. A. Webb

Vegetatively this species is variable and indistin-guishable from small decumbent forms of *Sedum rupestre* or small forms of *S. ochroleucum* to which it is very closely related (Fig. 5.18) Normally creeping stems are clothed with imbricate, api-culate terete leaves (Fig. 5. 15d). Flowers are usu-ally 6-partite and always golden yellow. Several contrasting leaf-color forms are common in gar-dens, including the plant depicted by Evans (1983) as "*S.* 'Forsterianum' of Gardens," which is merely a green, more upright form of *S. mon-tanum.*

HABITAT. As the name suggests, this is an al-pine species from over 1000 m (3000 ft) in France, Switzerland, Italy, and former Yugoslavia.

MAIN POINTS OF DISTINCTION. When not in flower, *Sedum montanum* is likely to be more

creeping than *S. rupestre*, but identical to smaller forms of most species in this group. Leaves are much narrower than those of *S. sediforme* and much stiffer than those of *S. forsterianum*. The only true test is to observe inflorescences as they grow: they are upright-facing throughout their growth, not reflexed in bud, and flowers have glandular hairs on large sepals. Vegetatively, this species is almost identical to *S. ochroleucum*, but spreading petals are golden yellow on a flat-topped inflorescence.

VARIATION. Leaf color varies enormously: green, brown, and gray forms are in cultiva-tion—some glaucous, some glabrous, and others with individual leaves glaucous below and shiny glabrous above. Some forms with clusters of leaves at the ends of stems superficially resemble *Sedum forsterianum* plants. However, *S. monta-num*, has stiff leaves, and its stems are not usual-ly shaggy with dead leaves. 't Hart (1978) noted diploid ($2n = 34$), triploid ($2n = 51$), and tetra-ploid ($2n = 68$) plants.

HORTICULTURE. This species is suitable for rock gardens or raised beds. It is fully hardy in temperate zones, but may suffer in summers where day temperatures over 25°C (77°F) occur for several consecutive weeks.

SEDUM OCHROLEUCUM Chaix

SYNONYMS: *S. anopetalum* De Candolle,
S. verloti Jordon

Sedum ochroleucum is one of the less common species of this group in cultivation (Fig. 5.18). Its inflorescences are always upturned (never re-flexed in bud) and are topped with a flat corymb of straw-colored to almost white, mostly 6-par-tite flowers. Sterile shoots are most likely to be glaucous and decumbent.

HABITAT. This is a southern European species from Spain, southern France, Italy, former Yugo-slavia, Albania, Greece, Bulgaria, and Turkey, mostly below 1000 m (3000 ft).

MAIN POINTS OF DISTINCTION. Leaves are just about terete in cross section, as is true for *Se-*

dum rupestre, but petals are very distinct as they remain upright (Fig. 5.15d). Pedicels, bracts, and huge sepals have glandular hairs. Budding inflorescences are erect, fruiting inflorescences are concave, and plants usually have a fairly creeping habit. Out of flower this species is indistinguishable from *S. rupestre* or *S. montanum*.

VARIATION. Plants from Greece and former Yugoslavia are much larger than some forms from France which have been described as *Sedum verloti*. Glabrous forms from France are unusual in cultivation, but creeping glaucous forms from further east are often encountered. Some clones are quite green in spring and flush red in autumn, while others are almost pruinose thoughout the year. 't Hart (1978) shows that diploids ($2n = 34$) and tetraploids ($2n = 68$) can grow in association with one another, but in France and former Yugoslavia, plants of different levels of ploidy appear to occupy different altitudes or zones. Hébert (1983) adds that triploids ($2n = 51$) grow in former Yugoslavia and pentaploids ($2n = 85$) are found in the southwestern Alps.

HORTICULTURE. This species grows relatively more slowly than *Sedum forsterianum* and *S. rupestre*, so it is better for a rock garden. It is not useful as a rapid-growing ground cover. Geographically, it should be less hardy than its look-alike relatives, but it does not act differently, except perhaps in summer, when it seems to cope with higher temperatures without signs of distress.

SEDUM PRUINATUM
Link ex Brotero

PLATE 19

Sedum pruinatum, a very distinct member of the *Rupestria* group is unlikely to be confused with any other stonecrop. Like *Sedum amplexicaule*, this species grows in winter and is dormant in summer. It dries up but retains its leaves. The thin, threadlike stems become brittle, and often snap, casting propagation material into the wind. Terminal, conical tufts, often on long, straight, bare stems, grow as new plants in late September. Leaves are entirely covered with a thick, white, pruinose cuticle, and flowers are

Figure 5.18. Vegetatively, *Sedum montanum* (left, 3 clones), *S. ochroleucum* (middle), and *S. rupestre* (right, 2 clones) are indistinguishable.

usually 6-partite with pale yellow stellate petals.

HABITAT. According to 't Hart (1978), this species grows in two disjunct colonies in Portugal: in the north, along the River Homen (sic); and in the Algarve region (deep south) among heath. I have located sites on three sides of the Serra da Estrela in Central Portugal on vertical cliff faces at low altitudes and in Natural Parque do Alvão. After extensive exploration of the Algarve, I believe the similarity of *Sedum pruinatum* to *S. amplexicaule* has resulted in incorrect identification of plants in southern Portugal.

MAIN POINTS OF DISTINCTION. Summer-dormant conical leaf clusters on very thin, brittle stems are the best indicator. In winter, the species is a little more difficult to recognize, although the low, open, sprawling, pruinose growth helps (Fig. 5.15e). *Sedum amplexicaule* has thickened propagules, a feature not shared with this species. *Sedum pruinatum* has a spindly straight inflorescence topped with only a few light yellow flowers in contrast to *S. amplexicaule* with reflexed inflorescence and more golden-yellow flowers.

VARIATION. The basic chromosome number is $x = 13$, according to 't Hart (1978), who also has encountered plants with $2n = 26$ (the most common), $2n = 27, 28, 30$, and 36.

HORTICULTURE. The main plant usually dies each year, leaving offsets on long straight stolons to root and regenerate. It is a very untidy plant, almost impossible to contain in a pot, but in the wild it tends to grow in nearly two dimensions with stolons hugging the cliff faces. In this way it colonizes the cliff in all directions, and the network of stems and tufts is very pretty. I have not been able to simulate this situation in cultivation, but am working on it. The hardiness of this species in extreme areas is questionable, but I have always grown it outdoors without protection.

SEDUM RUPESTRE L.

PLATE 20

SYNONYMS: *S. reflexum* L. (as used by both Praeger and Evans), *S. albescens* Haworth

COMMON NAME: Crooked stonecrop

The foremost authority on European sedums, 't Hart (1978, 85), wrote,

> Ever since the beginning of the 19th century the description of *S. rupestre* has usually been misinterpreted and the species confused with *S. forsterianum* . . . however [this] view must be regarded as a misinterpretation of the differential characters in the Linnaean phrase names of *S. rupestre* and *S. reflexum*.

In other words, in the monographs most commonly available (those by Praeger and Evans), these names have been reversed. Thus, those who think they can identify members of this group with confidence will now have to reverse names well-known to them.

Sedum rupestre is a sturdy, fairly upright plant (Fig. 5.18) with 30-cm (12-in) tall inflorescences of bright yellow and 6- or 7-partite flowers, which are reflexed in bud. Leaves are stiff, succulent, apiculate, and terete (Fig. 5.15d). Plants do not die back to tight clusters of soft leaves at stem tips in summer, though some forms appear to be reduced to leaf clusters on the ends of fairly erect, stiff, sturdy, bare stems.

HABITAT. The crooked stonecrop is native to Central and Western Europe: Belgium, Holland, Denmark, Norway, Sweden, France, Germany, Luxemburg, Iberia, Italy, Switzerland, Czech Republic, Slovakia, and Poland; and has been introduced elsewhere in a multitude of settings from coastal sand dunes to about 2000 m (7000 ft) in the Pyrenees Mountains. It was probably introduced from Flanders in the Middle Ages to Ireland and England as a salad crop.

MAIN POINTS OF DISTINCTION. Vegetatively, *Sedum rupestre* is very similar to *S. sediforme*, but the latter usually has flatter-topped, wider leaves. It is also similar to *S. ochroleucum* and *S. monta-*

num, both of which are usually more creeping. *Sedum rupestre* has stiff leaves and reflexed inflorescences without bracts. Some glandular hair can be expected on inflorescences carrying, usually, 6- or 7-partite flowers with yellow, spreading petals.

VARIATION. This species is very variable and as a result has fooled experts over the centuries, causing much controversy. Nonetheless, it is distinct in all its forms, though plants need to be observed over a period of time for them to be identified with certainty. Propagations sold as *Sedum albescens* in England are in fact *S. forsterianum* f. *purpureum*. A particularly glabrous, green, upright, robust form known as *S. virescens* Willdenow is no more than a regional variation of *S. rupestre*. A particularly beautiful cristate form is often offered in the trade as *S. rupestre* f. *cristatum* or more usually *S. reflexum* f. *cristatum* (Plate 20).

't Hart (1978) reported that the basic chromosome number for *Sedum rupestre* is probably $x = 16$. Plants with $2n = 88, 112,$ and 120 have been discovered. Hébert (1983) records $2n = 56$ for a Spanish plant and several other anomalies from more northerly areas. He theorizes that this species has been produced through the introgressive hybridization between tetraploid races of *S. sediforme* ($2n = 64$) and tetraploid races of *S. forsterianum* or the diploid races of *S. montanum*.

Two variegated forms are commonly grown in the United States but are rarely seen elsewhere: 'Sandy's Silver Crest', a form that turns purple in strong sunlight and has particularly striking new growth of contrasting yellow-white and 'Sea Gold', a truly variegated slow-growing cultivar.

HORTICULTURE. Although *Sedum rupestre* is quite rampant, it is not unruly. It is a good species for the border, large rock garden, or indeed, any difficult spot in the garden. As ground cover, it is much more open and upright, and not as rapid as *S. forsterianum*. It grows well on a wall and often seeds itself around. The cristate form reverts very easily, so all normal shoots must be removed quickly. Only the cristate form requires some protection from rain in areas with particu-

larly wet winters. *Sedum rupestre* should be hardy in most cold-temperate zones.

SEDUM SEDIFORME (Jaquin) Pau

SYNONYMS: *S. altissimum* Poiret, *S. nicaeense* Allioni

Sedum sediforme is perhaps the most handsome member of the *Rupestria* group (Fig. 5.19). Its upright stems carry succulent leaves that are wider and flatter (on the upper surface) than the leaves of its cousins (Fig 5.15f). Leaves are usually glaucous green, but glaucous blue-green, glabrous olive-green, and brown-green forms are often encountered in cultivation. All forms can attain 25 cm (10 in) in height, and, with the addition of tall, straight inflorescences, plants can reach 50 cm (20 in) high. Inflorescences carry straw-colored flowers with spreading petals on scorpioid branches. In fruit, the scorpioid branches of the corymb stand up like the fingers of a cupped hand (Fig. 5.15f).

Figure 5.19. *Sedum sediforme* in a 6-in (15-cm) pot.

HABITAT. This stonecrop is widespread in southern Europe and North Africa: Portugal, Spain, southern France, Italy, Adriatic coastlines, Greek coastlines, Mediterranean islands, Turkey, Israel, Libya, Syria, Tunisia, Algeria, and Morocco, as a lowland dweller, usually not far from the sea on dunes or coastal cliffs, but up to about 1000 m (3000 ft) in the French Alps and 1750 m (5740 ft) in the Sierra Nevada.

MAIN POINTS OF DISTINCTION. 't Hart says that it is impossible to distinguish *Sedum sediforme* vegetatively from *S. rupestre*, *S. ochroleucum*, or *S. montanum*. On the basis of the 30 diverse regional forms I have examined in cultivation, *Sedum sediforme* is usually very upright on sturdy stems and has distinctly flat-topped, succulent leaves. The inflorescence, without any glandular hair, is not reflexed in bud, and flowers are straw colored, followed by a drying inflorescence of distinct shape. Other identifying characteristics are stamens, which are particularly papillate at their bases, and tiny sepals.

VARIATION. The wide-leafed Portuguese and Spanish forms are exceptionally beautiful due to their compact nature. The greener French forms from higher altitudes are less spectacular, although they are far more hardy. Maire (1977) described *Sedum nicaeense* var. *brevirostratum* Faure & Maire with smaller flowers from the Grand Atlas Range, but of the dozen or so collections I have observed from this region, it seems impossible to group plants into two distinct forms with regard to flower size. Smaller olive-green or browner Spanish forms are dull plants, but strangely, plants from Israel—at the opposite end of the range—appear identical to some forms from Iberia. In the Sierra Nevada, I noted visually contrasting forms growing side by side. 't Hart (1978, 1991) recorded plants with $2n = 32, 48, 64, 80, 96$, and 128, saying that the diploid forms prefer lowland habitats, tetraploids have no preference, and hexaploids occur predominantly in mountain habitats. Hébert (1983) added $2n = 60$ for Spanish, Greek, and Turkish plants, plus numerous anomalies. A particularly beautiful cristate form, which grows true from seed, has been distributed by a French enthusiast.

HORTICULTURE. The wide-leafed, glaucous forms make excellent specimen plants. All forms are hardy in maritime Northumberland, England, although precautions need to be taken in areas experiencing cold winters, except perhaps with French or Spanish hexaploids. Generally this species has more elegance than other species of this group, but it tends to become quite tall.

ORTHOCARPIC SPECIES WITHOUT YELLOW FLOWERS

This group consists of the following species in cultivation:

Sedum acutifolium Ledebour (see *S. subulatum*)
Sedum album L.
Sedum andegavense De Candolle
Sedum athoum De Candolle (see *S. album*)
Sedum brevifolium De Candolle
Sedum caeruleum L.
Sedum cepaea L.
Sedum coeruleum (L.) Vahl (see *S. caeruleum*)
Sedum corsicum De Candolle & Duby (see

S. dasyphyllum)
Sedum cruciatum Desfontaines (see *S. monregalense*)
Sedum dasyphyllum L.
Sedum fragrans 't Hart
Sedum gypsicola Boissier & Reuter
Sedum hirsutum Allioni
Sedum involucratum Marschall von Bieberstein (see *S. spurium*)
Sedum lydium Boissier
Sedum magellense Tenore
Sedum monregalense Balbis

Sedum oppositifolium Sims (see *S. spurium*)
Sedum serpentini Janchen
Sedum spurium Marschall von Bieberstein
Sedum subulatum (C. A. Meyer) Boissier
Sedum tenellum Marschall von Bieberstein
Sedum villosum L.
Sedum winkleri Wolley-Dod (see *S. hirsutum*)

Plants of this group

- Have carpels that remain upright until they shed their seed, as opposed to carpels that bulge on the inner wall, spread out like a star, and then shed their seed.
- Have white, pink, red, purple, or, in one instance, blue petals.
- Have small terete or flattened leaves that cluster in tufts for at least part of the year.
- Have their main habitat in Europe with colonies beyond into North Africa or western Asia (especially Anatolia).
- Are low-growing evergreen annual or biennial species that flower around midsummer.
- Have 5-partite flowers generally, with several exceptions.

Figure 5.20 shows leaf shapes of European orthocarpic species without yellow flowers.

Grulich, in 1984, removed most of this group from *Sedum* and erected a new genus: *Oreosedum*. *Oreosedum* is characterized by inflorescences with thin pedicels that are never scorpioid but remain simple, and by orthocarpic flowers without yellow enzymes. He did not include *Sedum cepaea* because of its huge pyramid of flowers, nor *S. lydium* for it has a very compact inflorescence. He also excluded the annual *S. andegavense*, which has a single whorl of stamens. For reasons unknown, he included two species with kyphocarpic flowers, namely, *S. farinosum* and *S. stefco*. He also erected a new genus *Asterosedum* to accommodate the group of *Sedum* with flat leaves and scorpioid inflorescences centered on the Caucasus Mountains in which he included *S. spurium* alongside the kyphocarpic *S. stoloniferum* and *S. stellatum*.

The following is not a formal key, but a general guide to the reader:

Leaves wide and flat on both surfaces, plants perennial: *S. spurium*

Leaves spathulate and flat on both surfaces, plants annual with a huge pyramid of white flowers: *S. cepaea*

Leaves narrow and flat on both surfaces, leaves in whorls of four on the inflorescence: *S. monregalense*

Leaves narrow and flat on both surfaces, inflorescence has the outline of a narrow cone or cylinder (spike): *S. magellense*

Plants of a rosulate nature, leaves pubescent, flowers tiny and campanulate: *S. fragrans*

Plants of a rosulate nature, leaves pubescent, flowers stellate with patent petals, united somewhat at the base: *S. hirsutum*

Leaves terete, sharply pointed, petals erect: *S. subulatum*

Leaves globose, tightly packed in four columns: *S. brevifolium*

Leaves globose, tightly packed in five spirals: *S. brevifolium*

Leaves terete, glabrous, usually shiny, inflorescence reflexed in bud: *S. album*

Leaves terete, imbricate, downy: *S. gypsicola*

Leaves terete, very narrow with compact inflorescence: *S. lydium*

Narrow leaves triangular in section, flowers red: *S. tenellum*

Leaves semi-terete and shiny, tall monochasial inflorescence reflexed in bud: *S. album*

Leaves semi-terete and shiny, tall inflorescence dichotomous: *S. serpentini*

Leaves semi-terete, upper surface flat, not shiny, but glaucous or hairy or both, inflorescences short: *S. dasyphyllum*

Leaves semi-terete, shiny, somewhat hairy: *S. villosum*

Flowers blue: *S. caeruleum*

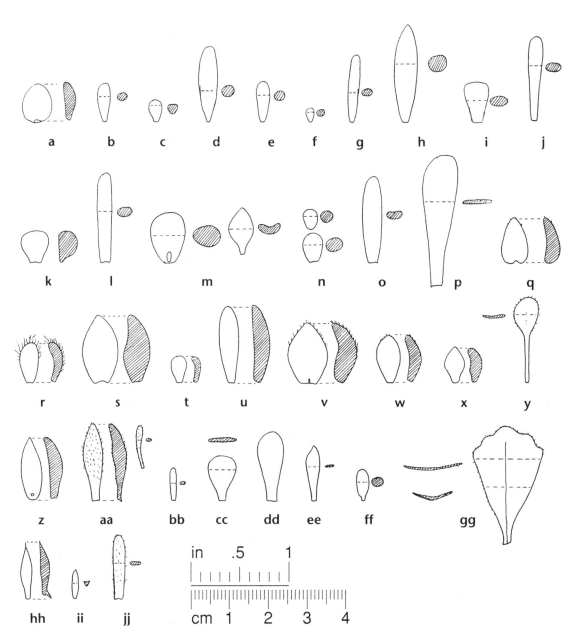

Figure 5.20. Leaf shapes of European orthocarpic species without yellow flowers: (a) *Sedum album* 'Athoum'; (b) *S. album* var. *balticum*; (c) *S. album* var. *micranthum* subvar. *chloroticum*; (d) *S. album* subsp. *clusianum*; (e) *S. album* 'Coral Carpet'; (f) *S. album* 'Fårö Form'; (g) *S. album* 'Hillebrandtii'; (h) *S. album* 'Ibiza'; (i) *S. album* 'Laconicum'; (j) *S. album* f. *murale*; (k) *S. album* var. *turgidum*; (l) *S. album* subsp. *teretifolium*; (m) *S. andegavense* (left) lower leaf, and (right) upper leaf; (n) *S. brevifolium* contrasting clones; (o) *S. caeruleum*; (p) *S. cepaea*; (q) *S. dasyphyllum* typical cultivated form; (r) *S. dasyphyllum* 'Lloyd Praeger'; (s) *S. dasyphyllum* var. *macrophyllum*; (t) *S. dasyphyllum* var. *mesatlanticum*; (u) *S. dasyphyllum* subsp. *oblongifolium*; (v) *S. dasyphyllum* var. *suendermannii*; (w) *S. dasyphyllum* 'Lilac Mound'; (x) *S. dasyphyllum* 'Opaline'; (y) *S. fragrans*; (z) S. *gypsicola*; (aa) two contrasting forms of *S. hirsutum*; (bb) *S. lydium*; (cc) S. *magallense* subsp. *olympicum*; (dd) *S. magallense* subsp. *magallense*; (ee) *S. monregalense*; (ff) *S. serpentini*; (gg) S. *spurium*; (hh) *S. subulatum*; (ii) *S. tenellum*; (jj) *S. villosum*.

SEDUM ALBUM L.

PLATES 1, 21

SYNONYMS: *S. athoum* De Candolle,
S. clusianum Gussone, *S. micranthum* Bastard,
S. teretifolium Lamarck, *S. turgidum* d'Urville,
Oreosedum album (L.) Grulich
COMMON NAME: White stonecrop

Surely this must be the most common garden plant in Europe. It is also frequently encountered in gardens in other temperate areas. In the right spot it can be a choice plant, but generally it is a pest and a weed. As a ground cover, the common forms spread rapidly, smother less rampant plants, and regenerate from a single fallen leaf. This is the species that has given the genus a bad name, but it should not be written-off or banned from the garden. On the contrary, in a dry summer, *Sedum album* on a stone wall looks a delight when all else has burned or shriveled.

White stonecrop changes dramatically with the seasons: in a wet period it can be green and lush, but in a dry spell it can turn red, bronze, or brown. The size of the leaves changes with the seasons and, if identical plants grow in contrasting sites, it could appear as though several varieties or species exist. The plant is stunted, tortuous, and deeply colored on dry walls, but turgid and insipid in damp spots or on rich loam. Despite the impact of site on the common clone, countless sharply contrasting forms remain distinct in cultivation, in addition to more choice regional variations. Among the number of choice forms available, several can be described as relatively slow growing.

HABITAT. Indigenous to every country in Europe except Ireland and Iceland, *Sedum album* also grows in North Africa and has apparently been reported as far east as Mongolia, though this sounds rather dubious. Throughout its range it grows at very contrasting altitudes and in a great variety of soils. It has been widely introduced elsewhere. As it is commonly associated with people, it is probably not indigenous to many locations where it appears abundant.

MAIN POINTS OF DISTINCTION. *Sedum album* is easily recognized by its blunt, scattered leaves (Fig. 5.20a–l) and reflexed inflorescences (when the flowers are in the bud stage), which turn upright to form flattish cymes, each carrying many small white or pink-white flowers.

VARIATION. This species is probably more varied than any other species of *Sedum*. In its common forms, it is generally about 12 cm (5 in) high, adding the same again for the inflorescences, but there are many shorter, more compact, very worthwhile variations.

Sedum album 'Athoum' (syn. *S. athoum* De Candolle) is a form with particularly globose leaves, which are flat on the upper surface and turn somewhat orange then rich, deep red in summer. Flowers are small and pink. It is relatively slow growing and, if grown in a sunny spot, can be most rewarding. This form is from Greece and former Yugoslavia.

Sedum album var. *balticum* Hartman is an upright green form with relatively flatter, more imbricate leaves, and pure white flowers (Fig. 5.20b). Its status is very questionable as it resembles many other distant regional forms.

Sedum album var. *micranthum* subvar. *chloroticum* Rouy & Camus is a fairly common, very low-growing plant with tiny, almost spherical leaves without any hint of red coloring (Plate 1; Fig. 5.20c). The bright yellow-green leaves and stem form a loose mat no more than 2 cm (0.8 in) high with the inflorescences only doubling this height.

Sedum album subsp. *clusianum* Gussone is a large but dainty, bright, colorful, upright form with long club-shaped leaves that tinge pink (Fig. 5.20d). It hails from Iberia (Plate 21).

Sedum album 'Coral Carpet' is a common, red, low-growing cultivar, but buyers often acquire a common, fast-growing form instead of the true cultivar (Fig. 5.20e). The true 'Coral Carpet' should only rise several centimeters (1.5 in) and be red all over in full sun. Several recently distributed forms from central Portugal and North Africa are lower, redder, slower, and therefore more choice.

Sedum album 'Fårö Form' is the smallest form (Fig. 5.20f). Originating from a Swedish isle in the Baltic, it has leaves that are only 3 mm (0.1 in) long and forms a compact carpet that is only about 1 cm (0.4 in) high. The plant turns purple-red then brown in summer. Inflorescences are very short.

Sedum album 'Hillebrandtii' is a large green form that turns orange-red in summer (Fig. 5.20g). It is very similar to *S. album* subsp. *clusianum* except it is less upright. It grows in the Rhine Valley.

Sedum album 'Ibiza' from the island of the Balearics with this name has almost apiculate (pointed) leaves and is dull, papillose brown-green. It is not particularly hardy. It resembles some of the giant forms from Spain, which also have almost-apiculate leaves.

Sedum album 'Laconicum' (Fig. 5.20i) like *S. album* 'Hillebrandtii' has been christened with a most inappropriate, undesirable name that can only cause confusion. Plants are large with partly green, partly red-brown leaves, vegetatively midway between the type species and 'Athoum' with pink carpels.

Sedum album f. *murale* Praeger is a brown, bronze, or purple form with pink flowers (Fig. 5.20j). It is a fairly tall and open form that can flower itself to death. It probably originates from North Africa.

Sedum album 'Rubrifolium' is a European garden sport of *S. album* f. *murale* with leaves more red than brown in summer and dark green with a purple tinge in winter. Flowers are light pink.

Sedum album var. *turgidum* De Candolle is similar to 'Athoum', but its leaves are almost spherical and gray-purple (Fig. 5.20k). It is a stately, very slow-growing form, with small pink flowers, from the Atlas Mountains.

My reference collection contains in excess of 40 distinct clones of *Sedum album*. Many names have been used to classify them, but there are so many intermediate variations that this task is pointless. For example: small-leaf forms with small, pink flowers seem to exist throughout the full range of the species, while highly contrasting forms can exist in the wild within a few kilometers of each other. Several beautiful forms with imbricate leaves have recently been introduced from North Africa. These should perhaps be assigned to *S. gypsicola*, a very closely related Iberian species. As botanic expeditions explore Spain and the mountains of North Africa, new clones that tend to be more choice are entering cultivation.

The most common and widespread forms belong to *Sedum album* subsp. *teretifolium* (Lamarck) Syme. These terete-leaved forms are tetraploids (Fig. 5.20l). Pentaploids, hexaploids, and octoploids occur only in southern Europe, and diploids ($2n = 34$) are generally lowland plants in northern Europe. Unfortunately, the patterns are never as simple as this, with pockets of polyploids being discovered in diverse areas: $2n = 32, 34, 36, 48, 51, 56, 64, 68, 80, 85, 96, 102, 112, 128,$ and 136.

HORTICULTURE. This is the Jekyll-and-Hyde *Sedum* species which generally needs to be carefully contained. The common forms are best grown on a tiled roof or a dry stone wall, though the low mat-producing forms are excellent for scree or rock gardens and are an important element in pictorial bedding displays in parks and gardens. Rapid-growing forms make an excellent substitute for lawn in areas with dry summers and require no mowing or watering! In drought, the stonecrop lawn could be bright red. Furthermore, many weeds are smothered by the dense growth of *S. album*, and once taller weeds that manage to get a foothold are removed, the stonecrop soon fills the gap.

SEDUM ANDEGAVENSE
De Candolle

SYNONYM: *Crassula globilifolia* Moris

This simple, upright annual (Fig. 5.21). was once considered to be a *Crassula* species because of its single whorl of stamens. Only a few centimeters (1.5 in) high, this single-stemmed plant is furnished initially with turgid, opposite-decussate leaves (Fig. 5.20m). At this stage, the little upright stonecrop very much reminds one of South African *Crassula* species. Simple plants turn a deep purple throughout before the terminal inflorescence of a few short branches displays 4-partite, white flowers with upright petals and fat, upright carpels. The four stamens are often difficult to locate between the four petals.

HABITAT. This is a very localized species from the Grand Atlas Mountains of North Africa, Portugal, Spain, France, Mediterranean islands, and Italy, on damp or shaded horizontal sites of quartzite or igneous rock outcrops.

MAIN POINTS OF DISTINCTION. There are no other annual European *Sedum* species with opposite-decussate leaves and orthocarpic, 4-partite flowers with a single whorl of stamens. The species has often been confused with *S. caespitosum*, a species with distinctly kyphocarpic flowers. $2n = 50$.

VARIATION. Five-partite flowers exist but are rare. The runts of a colony, or those plants seeded in less favorable spots, comprise little more than a few leaves topped by several flowers. Those more fortunate plants, seeded in a favorable spot, can be 10 cm (4 in) tall and carry 50 flowers. The upper leaves tend to spiral and can be green in a shady place.

HORTICULTURE. Seeds germinate in late au-

Figure 5.21. *Sedum andegavense* in habitat near Cabo da Roca, Portugal. A single seedling of *S. brevifolium* is visible bottom, right of center.

tumn, so it is prudent to keep seedlings in an alpine house in the worst of the winter. Plants are very neat, compact annuals, and small colonies can invoke much attention especially if grown in a terra-cotta bowl.

SEDUM BREVIFOLIUM De Candolle

PLATE 22

SYNONYMS: *S. quinquefarium* (Praeger) Evans (?), *Oreosedum brevifolium* (De Candolle) Grulich

The four straight columns of tightly packed spherical pruinose leaves on wiry stems make this a most desirable species. Neat, compact mounds created by crowded stems flush with cherry pink in summer. Inflorescences usually have leaves arranged in five spirals, and often sterile shoots show this leaf arrangement. Praeger erected *Sedum brevifolium* var. *quinquefarium* for this spiraled form, not realizing that in the wild both forms grow alongside each other. In addition, occasionally both leaf arrangements exist on the same plant. The white, chalky coating of the leaves gives plants a very eye-catching appearance, but it is not the easiest of species in this group to cultivate successfully, though it is most rewarding to those who manage.

HABITAT. This stonecrop is most widespread in Iberia but also grows in France, Corsica, Sardinia, and adjacent North Africa, from a great variety of altitudes and habitats: in rock niches in lowland granitic areas, on precipitous slopes, and even on flatter areas above the winter snow line—a true alpine in its southern extremities.

MAIN POINTS OF DISTINCTION. Once you have seen a true specimen of this species, you cannot confuse it with any other. Unfortunately, it has been confused in the trade, especially with certain forms of *Sedum dasyphyllum,* which are never pruinose and always have leaves that are flat on the upper surface (Fig. 5.20n). Inflorescences of *S. brevifolium* are short and leafy, carrying only a few flowers. China-white petals, with obvious red nerves on the back, are particularly wide for their length, and although Prae-

ger (1921), Fröderström (1932), and Evans (1983) stated that the petals are apiculate, they are often very obtuse. Plants are stiff, usually upright, and hard to the touch. $2n = 36$ and 72.

VARIATION. *Sedum brevifolium* is tremendously variable (Plate 22). *Sedum brevifolium* var. *induratum* Cosson, often referred to as *S. brevifolium* "minor form," is a very small form that is so stiff and hard it can hardly be squeezed between two fingers. It comes from North Africa and is tiny with particularly wiry stems (Fig. 5.22). Stems are merely a few centimeters (1 in) long, and individual leaves are little more than 2 mm (0.08 in) across. This tiny form is the one depicted by Praeger as being the true *S. brevifolium*. Therefore, it is not surprising that when he encountered the very much bolder form with leaves in five spirals, he thought it different enough to erect a new variety. The true *S. brevifolium* is almost as stiff and hard (to the touch) as the smaller variety, but the bare, lower stems can be 10 cm (4 in) long below the tightly packed leaf arrangement. It is understandable that gardeners prefer to retain Praeger's name *S. brevifolium* var. *quinquefarium* for forms with leaves mostly in five spirals, but I think *S. brevifolium* f. *quinquefarium* is sufficient rank as, in a single wild colony, both forms are likely to be encountered if the explorer has patience.

In recent years, exploration of Iberia has brought about the introduction of several very extreme clones, which have been tentatively assigned to *Sedum brevifolium*. The Royal Botanic Garden Edinburgh (R.B.G.E.) found a glabrous, green clone of *S. brevifolium* in the roots of a plant of a different genus, which had been collected in the Sierra Nevada (of Spain). Petals of this extreme form of *S. brevifolium* are particularly obtuse, and several other similar forms from other parts of Spain and Portugal have much in common with it. The R.B.G.E. plant turns yellow, then red in full sun, but a similar upright form from Laguna Negre, Picos de Urbion, central Spain, remains yellow-green in full sun. A cherry-red form from the Serra da Estrela (Portugal) has four columns of shiny leaves, decreasing in size up the decumbent stems. On the neighboring range, the Serra da Lapa, lives a similar form with a more-upright growth and with leaves mostly arranged in five spirals. Such new introductions tend to be available as "forma nova" or "subsp. novum." According to 't Hart (1991) the phyllotaxis (decussate or alternate) and color of the leaves (glaucous, shiny, green, or red) are not correlated with the four known chromosome numbers: $2n = 36, 54, 72,$ and 90. Moreover, the different forms are fully interfertile, often intermingling in the wild. In the schist outcrops of the Serra de Alvão and Serra do Marão, likelihood of encountering glabrous forms increases with altitude.

HORTICULTURE. This species must have a very well-drained spot. Although I have rescued plants from melt-pools below a spring snow line in habitat, in cultivation anything less than perfect drainage is not recommended. All forms of this species make excellent potted plants for the alpine house, and as specimen plants they are choice for alpine displays. All forms of this species are very slow to grow and propagate, while forms of *Sedum dasyphyllum* masquerading as *S. brevifolium* are rapid and less colorful. (See *S. dasyphyllum* var. *macrophyllum* for further information on differences between these two species.)

By drilling a hole on the vertical face of a stone, or utilizing a natural niche, superb compact hemispherical clusters can be grown. In such a situation, they are much less likely to succumb to winter wet.

SEDUM CAERULEUM L.

PLATE 23

SYNONYMS: *S. coeruleum* L., *S. azureum* Desfontaines, *Oreosedum caeruleum* (L.) Grulich

Sedum caeruleum is the only blue-flowered Crassulaceae. Once it was a common annual in gar-

Figure 5.22. *Sedum brevifolium* var. *induratum.* Each stem is only 2 cm (0.8 in) long.

dens—spring-sown seeds were germinated with heat and sold with other annual bedding plants —but seeds are now difficult to acquire. This very open and delicate bushy annual can range from a tiny, almost leafless plant with a few sky-blue 7-partite to 9-partite flowers to a plant topped with a tangle of long pedicels. Large plants can reach 25 cm (10 in) high, carrying literally 100 or more such flowers in various stages, and giving the appearance of a huge hemisphere of tiny azure stars.

Bright red foliage, the result of a sunny aspect, is an added bonus (Fig. 5.20o). Each carpel contains only one seed, or rarely two. This fact, in addition to the high number of flower parts, plus the unique petal color (which is elusive to photographers), has led many to attempt to remove this species from *Sedum*.

HABITAT. *Sedum caeruleum* is a littoral species indigenous to Italy, Corsica, Sardinia, Sicily, Malta, and North Africa into the Atlas Mountains, especially in sandy areas including shorelines.

MAIN POINTS OF DISTINCTION. Once it has flowered, *Sedum caeruleum* can be confused with nothing else. $2n = 26$.

VARIATION. Plants can vary tremendously in size. In shade, the leaves and stems are green, but in full sun they turn bright red.

HORTICULTURE. Plants thrive if grown indoors in pots or flats; outdoors, seeds tend to germinate in late autumn and seedlings perish in cold winters. Perhaps in milder areas, it is easier to establish a perpetuating colony on a scree or well-drained part of the border. As long as the soil is not disturbed, the seeds germinate easily.

SEDUM CEPAEA L.

This winter-growing annual or biennial starts its life as a flat rosette which usually elongates the following spring to produce a huge, 30-cm (12-in) high, open, terminal, hirsute pyramid of white flowers (Fig. 5.23). The leaves at this stage are in definite whorls (usually in fours) and are flat, thin, and limp (Fig. 5.20p).

HABITAT. *Sedum cepaea* is indigenous to Spain, France and adjacent isles, Italy and adjacent isles, former Yugoslavia, Albania, Bulgaria, Greece and adjacent isles, Turkey, Libya, Syria, Tunisia, and Algeria, in fact, almost right around the Mediterranean—plus Switzerland and Romania (and introduced elsewhere), in shady, rocky subalpine zones.

MAIN POINTS OF DISTINCTION. Tall, open, pubescent pyramids of white stellate flowers and whorled leaves make the species unique.

VARIATION. A rather fine cristate (crested form) has been distributed, which tends to come true from seed. Flowers of the crested form become fasciated and can be 6-partite to 10-partite. In full sun leaves can turn violet-brown. Often plants are biennial and pyramidal sprays of flowers can be large; in contrast, runts can flower from seed in a few months, and the inflorescences, although still pyramidal, are meager.

Sedum cepaea var. *gracilescens* Maire & Weiller

Figure 5.23. *Sedum cepaea* inflorescence.

is a form with much neater, flatter rosettes. As the species is from a very large range of habitats, many variations exist and several other names have been erected to account for some of them. $2n = 20$, 22, and 44.

HORTICULTURE. As with all annuals, perpetuating the species involves an element of risk: plants seed themselves without ever becoming a pest. This species is used as an attractive bedding plant at Cambridge Botanic Gardens, Cambridge, England.

SEDUM DASYPHYLLUM L.

PLATES 24, 25

SYNONYMS: *S. corsicum* De Candolle & Duby, *Oreosedum dasyphyllum* (L.) Grulich

COMMON NAME: Thick-leaved stonecrop

Sedum dasyphyllum is a polymorphic species. Generally it is a very low, compact plant only a few centimeters (1.5 in) high, producing a dense mat of glaucous-gray foliage. Some forms are particularly hairy, others completely glabrous, but the majority of common forms have some short hair on the plants, especially on the inflorescences. Imbricate, ovoid, flat-topped leaves are very succulent and tightly packed (Fig. 5.20q). White flowers are produced on short, simple, few-flowered monochasiums.

HABITAT. Central Europe to the Mediterranean coastlines is the main habitat of *Sedum dasyphyllum* with several distinct forms being endemic to the Atlas Mountain region of North Africa, Spain, and adjacent isles. It is indigenous also to France, Italy and adjacent isles, Switzerland, Austria, Germany, former Yugoslavia, Albania, Bulgaria, Romania, Greece, Anatolia, Algeria, Morocco, and Tunisia, on a great diversity of sites, at a great range of altitudes. Small hirsute forms grow above the winter snow line in the Sierra Nevada on calcareous cliffs. The species has also been introduced into many other areas. Normally found in dry, rocky areas, it also grows on stone walls, often closely associated with people.

MAIN POINTS OF DISTINCTION. Leaves of *Sedum dasyphyllum* are never shiny, but are glaucous, papillose, pubescent, or a combination of all three. One subspecies, *S. dasyphyllum* subsp. *oblongifolium*, has elongated leaves. The only species that could be confused with *S. dasyphyllum* is *S. brevifolium*, which for many years was considered a form of *S. dasyphyllum*. *Sedum dasyphyllum* is soft to the touch, being easily squashed between the fingers. Moreover, the leaves tend to fall off in profusion if the plant is disturbed, in contrast to leaves of *S. brevifolium*, which do not fall off easily. Carpel beaks of *S. dasyphyllum* are very short and sharply turned out.

VARIATION. Due to the wide range of this species, many varieties and subspecies have been described. Unfortunately, most of these are not distinct but are linked by intermediate forms. Often plants are difficult to confidently assign to one variety. Several particularly distinct forms in cultivation appear to be without specific names, but perhaps these, too, are linked with intermediate forms in the wild (Fig. 5.24).

Sedum dasyphyllym var. *adenocladum* f. *oppositifolium* (Burnat) Maire is very similar to the type species, except its gray leaves are normally arranged in four columns. Stems are short and upright—a feature somewhat reminiscent of *S. brevifolium*, but *S. brevifolium* has tiny, pruinose (not gray), almost globular leaves that are not easily detached. It is a prolific flowerer.

Sedum dasyphyllum var. *glanduliferum* (Gussone) Moris (syn. *S. corsicum* Duby) is the form from Corsica and Sicily, which is given status because of its hairy nature. The plant is the same size as the type species, but is glandular-pubescent. This pubescence is variable and certainly not as marked as on one particular form commonly cultivated and mentioned by Praeger (1921, 179):

> I have grown a large series of *dasyphyllum* forms, collected mainly from garden sources and find them puzzling . . . one very hairy form has leaves which readily drop off, so that

after heavy rain, the stems are almost bare and the fallen leaves soon form a dense mat of young plants.

As far as I can ascertain, this extreme form has never been formally named. It is light green if grown in shade or half shade, but becomes gray later in the season. Unlike many other forms it has no propensity to turn lilac-mauve in full sun. As this plant is so distinct and without a handle I propose to refer to it as *S. dasyphyllum* 'Lloyd Praeger' (Figs. 5.20r; 5.25). In the United Kingdom it is often sold as *S. dasyphyllum* var. *rifanum* Maire, a valid name, but one which refers to a glabrous form, probably no more than a slight variation of the type species. Climbing over 2500 m (8200 ft) in the Sierra Nevada, I noted that almost-glabrous forms were found at low altitudes, very hairy forms in high alpine zones, and every intermediate form between.

Sedum dasyphyllum var. *macrophyllum* Rouy & Camus is a very common form in gardens. As the name suggests, it is much larger than the type species (Fig. 5.24). The turgid leaves are white-green and without hair, turning pink in

Figure 5.24. Variation within *S. dasyphyllum*: (top row, left to right) *S. dasyphyllum* var. *mesatlanticum*, *S. dasyphyllum* var. *glanduliferum*, a form from the Pyrenees, *S. dasyphyllum* var. *macrophyllum*; (second row) a particularly hairy form from the Atlas Mountains that is difficult to separate from *S. hirsutum*, *S. dasyphyllum* var. *adenocladum* f. *oppositifolium*, and (right) *S. dasyphyllum* 'Lilac Mound'; (bottom row) *S. dasyphyllum* subsp. *oblongifolium*, *S. dasyphyllum* 'Opaline', *S. dasyphyllum* var. *suendermannii*.

full sun. Plants are decumbent with succulent leaves packed tightly into five spirals. Because of this feature, the variety has been wrongly identified in numerous works, including Evans's *Handbook of Cultivated Sedums* (1983), which depicts this plant as *S. quinquefarium*. The latter is a form of *S. brevifolium* with wiry, upright stems and very hard leaves (to the touch) with a pruinose coating. *Sedum dasyphyllum* var. *macrophyllum* is a fast grower with turgid, subglobose, tightly packed leaves and relatively large flowers with sepals that stick out nearly at right angles to the closed petals (Fig. 5.20s). The stems of this variety collapse with the weight of the succulent leaves and tend to creep; they are thin but not wiry like those of *S. brevifolium*.

Sedum *dasyphyllum* var. *mesatlanticum* is a North African form usually grown under the label "*S. atlanticum*." The true *S. atlanticum* (Ball) Maire, a yellow-flowered species from the Atlas Mountains, has a very open nature and is closely related to *Monanthes*. It is not in cultivation. *Sedum dasyphyllum* var. *mesatlanticum* is a choice low grower with flat-topped, crowded, almost-white leaves lying very imbricate to the very short stems, which for much of the year are rosetted (Fig. 5.20t). A monstrous form of this variety has very dense, tiny rosettes that hardly elongate at all but turn a beautiful pink-gray. In cultivation it is generally labeled "*S. hispidum* Desfontaines." This is a valid name but for a very hairy annual from the same region in North Africa, which is only a very distant relative of *S. dasyphyllum* var. *mesatlanticum* f. *monstrosum*. (*Sedum dasyphyllum* var. *mesatlanticum* f. *monstrosum* is sometimes offered as "*Sedum hispidulum*," an invalid name.) Had the monstrous form not reverted to *S. dasyphyllum* var. *mesatlanticum* for me on several occasions, I would still be puzzled about its relation to other plants in this group. *Sedum dasyphyllum* var. *mesatlanticum* f. *monstrosum* is a choice diminutive form

Figure 5.25. *Sedum dasyphyllum* 'Lloyd Praeger'.

that is particularly susceptible to overwatering and winter rains. In fact, all forms of *S. dasyphyllum* var. *mesatlanticum* are safer in the unheated alpine house.

Sedum dasyphyllum subsp. *oblongifolium* (Ball) Maire (Plate 24) is so different from the type species, it was actually distributed by the International Succulent Institute as *S. album*. Generally it is known as *S. dasyphyllum* 'Atlas Mountain Form'. The elongated leaves are like those of *S. album* in shape but are glaucous-gray at first and then turn a beautiful pink-lilac in full sun. The dichotomous inflorescence can be tall for this species, to about 12 cm (5 in). This is perhaps the choicest plant in the group, and one which I recommend for the alpine house. It resembles *S. dasyphyllum* var. *mesatlanticum*, but has much larger leaves that are well attached (Fig. 5.20u). Unfortunately, other forms of this species, if grown in the alpine or greenhouse, can become leaf-shedding weeds and therefore troublesome.

Sedum dasyphyllum var. *suendermannii* (L.) Praeger is a fairly hirsute form, similar to *S. dasyphyllum* var. *glanduliferum*, except much larger, with leaves being particularly flat-topped and imbricate (Fig. 5.20v). In addition, it has a preponderance of 6-partite, rather than 5-partite, flowers. This variety is found in Spain, but Praeger described it from a garden plant and was not aware that smaller forms exist in the Pyrenees Mountains, which link it with several other described varieties.

There are countless forms of *Sedum dasyphyllum* in cultivation, and it is most interesting and visually pleasing to see contrasting forms intermingled. A particularly dense form (so dense you could not squeeze a blade of grass through the tight hummock) with small leaves, sold in the United Kingdom under the invalid name of "Mucronatis," turns a beautiful shade of purple-gray in full sun. It probably originates from North Africa, and I propose to give it the cultivar name *S. dasyphyllum* 'Lilac Mound' (Plate 25; Fig. 5.20x). A light glaucous-green form or cultivar with leaves in four columns without any hint of red is sold as 'Opaline' and may have a few short bristles (Plate 25). It probably originates from the Pyrenees, but has not been formally described as a regional variety.

Most forms of *Sedum dasyphyllum* have 5-partite flowers but some clones have predominantly 6-partite flowers. Maire (1977) lists dozens of subspecies, varieties, and forms, but I think we must accept that the species is exceptionally polymorphic, that *S. dasyphyllum* in Spain is quite different from *S. dasyphyllum* in Turkey, and that *S. dasyphyllum* at 500 m (1600 ft) in the Sierra Nevada is quite different from *S. dasyphyllum* at 2500 m (8200 ft) in the same range. $2n = 28, 42, 56, 70,$ and 84.

HORTICULTURE. *Sedum dasyphyllum* is indispensable as a ground cover. It is being used by professional horticulturists and serious gardeners to cover soil in potted plants such as bonsai. In tubs containing a shrub or conifer, this stonecrop is a perfect ground cover and, as it tumbles over the container lip, it breaks up the straight lines of the subject. It is a very suitable companion plant for cacti in a container. In the United Kingdom, *S. dasyphyllum* is grown on sheets of rock wool that are glued to rigid boards and used in the construction of lasting floral displays. Cathedrals, cottages, or windmills that appear to be encrusted with living plants often emphasize detail with *Sedum* species of contrasing colors.

Beware that falling leaves of the common forms can become troublesome in the greenhouse if, for example, they fall into a pot containing a spiny cactus and you do not wish the plants to grow together. It is almost impossible to remove new plants cleanly, and attempts to do so will merely result in leaving behind even more leaves.

Choice forms of *Sedum dasyphyllum* are eye-catching alpines with overall pink-purple coloring. They make an excellent contrast to plants with dark foliage. In many forms *S. dasyphyllum* is suitable for scree, rock gardens, raised pots, and stone troughs. It is fully hardy in its common forms.

SEDUM FRAGRANS 't Hart

Sedum fragrans is the perennial form of *S. alsinefolium*, a species not in general cultivation. For many years descriptions of the latter were conflicting, as two apparently disjunct colonies had contrasting features: *S. alsinefolium* from the Italian/French border is an annual calcifuge, while work by 't Hart (1983a) showed that perennial plants of the limestone districts further south, once considered synonymous, have a different chromosome count. In addition, the annual form has simpler inflorescences and smaller flowers with shorter tubes.

Sedum fragrans is a most unusual species (Fig. 5.26). In winter it is a mat of very low, almost flat rosettes of spathulate leaves, which are very soft, velvety, and slightly sticky to touch (Fig. 5.20y). The root system is meager, so plants can be easily lifted from the soil without effort, suggesting plants grow on solid rock in the wild. Rosettes elongate in spring and 25-cm (10-in) long, weak, open, pubescent inflorescences carry small, white, campanulate flowers with petals erect at the base.

HABITAT. This is a localized species from the Italian-French Alps in shady spots on limestone just to the north of Monte Carlo.

MAIN POINTS OF DISTINCTION. Tiny, campanulate flowers on long pedicels are very dis-

Figure 5.26. *Sedum fragrans* in a 3-in (8-cm) pot.

tinct. The plant is more likely to be taken for a *Monanthes* species or a lax *Rosularia* species than for a *Sedum* species. Glandular hairs emit a distinct musty odor, and, when in flower, the whole plant has a faintly sweet smell. $2n = 26$. *Sedum alsinefolium* has $2n = 20$.

VARIATION. Probably most plants in habitat are those distributed by Ron Evans (as *Sedum alsinefolium*) and therefore constant. In an open site, the rosettes are less lax and leaves less limp.

HORTICULTURE. This is a pleasant indoor plant for a north-facing windowsill. I put my specimen outdoors for summer in a semi-shady spot, and even here it turns bronze. I keep spare plants under a greenhouse bench for safety. The species is not hardy nor does it travel well. While most other *Sedum* species are renowned for the amount of time they can spend out of soil without wilting, *S. fragrans* is limp hours after picking and almost completely shriveled in a day or two. Fortunately, seed is viable and the species is self-fertile. Excellent results can be obtained by growing it in shade in a clay pot standing in a shallow bowl of water.

SEDUM GYPSICOLA
Boissier & Reuter

SYNONYMS: *S. album* var. *gypsicola* Hamet, *Oroesedum gypsicola* (Boissier & Reuter) Grulich

Often referred to as a subspecies of *Sedum album*, *S. gypsicola* obviously is very closely related to it. It is low growing, carpet-forming, and much slower growing than most forms of *S. album*, but both species have a basic chromosome count of $x = 17$. 't Hart and Van den Berg (1982) believed that both species have evolved from a common diploid ancestor. The wine-red, overlapping leaves in clusters have been likened to pine cones. Evans (1983) said it was quite common in cultivation, but this is not my experience.

HABITAT. This species is endemic to Iberia and adjacent North Africa, commonly on calcareous sites—hence its name. It grows from relatively low levels to the spring snow line in the

Sierra Nevada (2500 m/8200 ft), almost always on rock (Fig. 5.27).

MAIN POINTS OF DISTINCTION. *Sedum gypsicola* is a creeping species with imbricate, downy leaves that cluster at the stem tips. In every other respect, it matches the small-flowered forms of *S. album* with leaves somewhat flattened on the upper surface (Fig. 5.20z).

VARIATION. 't Hart and Van den Berg (1982) say that no hybrids have been reported between *Sedum gypsicola* and *S. album* in the wild though the two can hybridize in cultivation. Many new forms collected in the Atlas Mountains in northwestern Africa appear difficult to confidently assign to either species, for they have fairly imbricate leaves that are not downy but faintly papillose. I have observed considerable variation in such plants new to cultivation but several distinct clones have been in collections for a long time. One of these has particularly flat-topped leaves. In shade, leaves can be very dark green. $2n = 34$, 68, and 102.

HORTICULTURE. *Sedum gypsicola* is not at all invasive, so it is much more highly recommended than most forms of *S. album*. Because of its dull hue, however, it can be lost against a dark

Figure 5.27. *Sedum gypsicola* on the vertical face of a limestone erratic on the north side of the Sierra Nevada, southern Spain.

background. It is seen at its best on raised stone troughs. It requires a well-drained site, but limestone does not seem to improve its growth.

SEDUM HIRSUTUM Allioni

PLATE 26
SYNONYMS: *S. winkleri* Wolley-Dod,
Oreosedum hirsutum (Allioni) Grulich,
Rosularia hirsuta (Allioni) Eggli

Densely hairy rosettes of this species can range from a mere centimeter (0.4 in) across in tightly packed hummocks to larger (4 cm/1.5 in), stalked rosettes in a fairly open mound. Each inflorescence carries a few large white flowers on a simple monochasium. Petals with wavy margins are united somewhat at the base. Carpels are pubescent on the inner side.

Sedum winkleri Wolley-Dod (syn. *S. hirsutum* subsp. *baeticum* Rouy) has been erected to describe the large extreme form (Fig. 5.28). It has long runners between the sterile rosettes, petals united to one-quarter of their length, and free sepals with slight spurs. Throughout Iberia every combination of intermediates can be seen.

HABITAT. This species is found in Iberia and adjacent North Africa, France, and Italy, mostly on sheer cliffs, generally as a lithophyte, and sometimes above the winter snow line (Plate 26).

MAIN POINTS OF DISTINCTION. The densely pubescent rosettes never elongate in full light. Some North African forms are very difficult to separate from compact, hairy forms of *Sedum dasyphyllum*, but the latter has free petals, glabrous carpels, and sepals that are never spurred.

VARIATION. A complete range of forms exist from the large "*Sedum winkleri*" with stout stolons, to the tiny, compact forms growing like mosses (Fig. 5.20aa). Fröderström (1932) claimed these stolons are subterranean. This may sometimes be so in cultivation, but in habitat, where the plants grow on sheer solid rock faces, this is impossible. It is suggested that the large forms are more southerly in nature, but I have observed them in central Portugal. Tiny

Figure 5.28. *Sedum hirsutum* f. *baeticum*, a large form from Central Portugal.

forms appear to be indigenous to the Cantabrian Mountains, Serra da Lapa, and Grand Atlas Mountains. $2n = 18$, 20 and 60.

HORTICULTURE. The hirsute nature of the plants means that winter rain can accumulate in the hairs and cause rot. Plants are hardy in maritime Northumberland with 30 cm (12 in) of winter rain, but a few miles further inland, they are not. All forms make excellent alpine potted plants. It is prudent to place pots on their sides in winter to provide a more natural situation (i.e., better drainage).

SEDUM LYDIUM Boissier

Sedum lydium is a fairly common, tiny, 4-cm (1.6-in) high, carpet-forming, tufted species with narrow, linear, bright green leaves that turn copper-red in full sun (Figs. 5.20bb; 5.29). A shy flowerer, it sometimes produces pink-white flowers on a dense, comparatively long inflorescence. The plant's diminutive nature makes it a most useful and popular species.

HABITAT. This stonecrop inhabits moist soils in subalpine zones from Turkey to Armenia, especially in the province of Lydia in Anatolia.

MAIN POINTS OF DISTINCTION. *Sedum lydium* is a low-growing, tufted species that branches from the base and has a distinct, compact, almost spherical inflorescence made up of tiny flowers. Flowers have white carpels, which soon turn red, giving the flowers an impression of pink. *Sedum lydium* has many sterile shoots and thin, creeping rhizomes from which new shoots rise.

VARIATION. Although several names, such as 'Bronze Queen', are used, plants appear relatively constant. $2n = 12$.

HORTICULTURE. Unfortunately, this species soon dies in a pot as it needs to put its roots in a cool damp spot. It is seen at its best growing in the cracks between paving stones. Dick Caven-

Figure 5.29. *Sedum lydium*—each tuft is 0.8 cm (0.3 in) across.

Figure 5.30. *Sedum magellense* subsp. *magellense* in a 4-in (10-cm) pot.

der (1991) reported that the cracks between the stone slabs which pave the site of J. F. Kennedy's grave, just across the river from Washington, D.C., are tightly packed with *Sedum lydium* and another species.

SEDUM MAGELLENSE Tenore

SYNONYM: *Oreosedum magellense* (Tenore) Grulich

Sedum magellense subsp. *magallense* is an unusual and rare species in collections (Fig. 5.30). It is a very distinct little plant having leafy, racemous inflorescences, each with the outline of a cone or cylinder, rising to about 12 cm (5 in). Bright green, flat leaves can turn bright red in full sun, and white flowers are often tinged with purple or green.

HABITAT. This south European stonecrop comes from the Apennines Mountains of Italy (especially Monte Majella), former Yugoslavia, Albania, Bulgaria, Greece, Crete, Asiatic Turkey, and Algeria, often in shade, but as a true alpine.

MAIN POINTS OF DISTINCTION. As this species is unlike any others in the group, it is unlikely to be misidentified. Flat, bright green, glabrous leaves without spurs and tall, narrow flower spikes are the best guides. Also carpels, abruptly tipped with a short and broad style, and clearly visible yellow nectary glands help confirm identity.

Figure 5.31. *Sedum magellense* subsp. *olympicum* in a 2-in (5-cm) pot.

VARIATION. Two distinct forms exist: *Sedum magellense* subsp. *magellense* from Italy with alternate leaves, and *S. magellense* subsp. *olympicum* (Tenore) Fröderström from Greece and probably elsewhere, which tends to have opposite leaves (Figs. 5.20cc; 5.20dd; 5.31). The type species is an extreme form that has probably evolved from *S. magellense* subsp. *olympicum*. It is taller and more open. $2n = 28$ and 30. Greek and Yugoslavian plants, often encountered in cultivation, are compact and very low growing. Some leaves turn bright red, a superb contrast to others on the same plant that remain bright green.

HORTICULTURE. This is a very bright green carpeter. If cultivated in pots, it needs to have its roots under a stone to stop baking in hot summers. I highly recommend it for raised beds and deep troughs. It likes a lot of water in summer.

SEDUM MONREGALENSE Balbis

SYNONYMS: *S. cruciatum* Desfontaines, *Oreosedum monregalense* (Balbis) Grulich

Sedum monregalense is a very short, slender, bright green, carpet-forming species with whorls of flat, thin leaves which group in fours on the inflorescences and less noticeably on sterile shoots (Fig. 5.32). All parts of the plant, save the leaves, are sparsely pubescent; a little magnification will show lines of hair on the sepals, petals, and inside the carpels. Pubescent inflorescences are lax, and white flowers are carried on long pedicels.

HABITAT. This southeast European subalpine grows in shady spots in Italy (Monregal, for which the species is named, is on the Italian Piedmont), southern France, and Corsica.

MAIN POINTS OF DISTINCTION. The well-spaced leaves in whorls of four on inflorescences are a very distinct feature only shared with the biennial or annual *Sedum cepaea*, which starts its life as a flat rosette. *Sedum monregalense* is tufted in winter and spring, and the imbricate leaves are flat on both the upper and lower surfaces (Fig. 5.20ee). $2n = 30$.

VARIATION. Contrasting position and varying amounts of water result in dissimilar plants. In dry, sunny spots, tufts of leaves remain tightly packed throughout summer and turn tan. In this state, plants are shy to flower and can extinguish. Grown in a damp, shady spot, the species is soft, green, and open.

HORTICULTURE. This stonecrop probably requires some protection in areas with extreme winters, and it prefers a shady, damp niche.

Figure 5.32. *Sedum monregalense*—note the verticillate leaves on the inflorescence on the right.

SEDUM SERPENTINI Janchen

SYNONYM: *Oreosedum serpentini* (Janchen) Grulich

Appearing to be a pleasant variation on the *Sedum album* theme, *S. serpentini* is usually brown-red throughout, tortuous, and creeping (Fig. 5.20ff). Small, pink flowers are carried on a dichotomous inflorescence. The differences between it and short forms of *S. album* are few, but *S. serpentini* dies back considerably in winter, leaving only a mat of tangled, tortuous stems.

HABITAT. Serbia, Croatia, Albania, and Greece are the home of this diminutive stonecrop which, as its name infers, prefers serpentine rocks.

MAIN POINTS OF DISTINCTION. The tenuous differences between this species and forms of *Sedum album* from Adriatic Italy make for very difficult positive identification. To label plants with any certainty, field documentation is essential. Plants of the true species become almost leafless in winter, but the described inflorescence is a less reliable feature on which to base a decision.

VARIATION. The inflorescence branching in the lower quarter is not always a constant feature.

HORTICULTURE. This species is not distinct enough to warrant special interest, but is a very easily cultivated, low-growing plant that never becomes a pest.

SEDUM SPURIUM
Marschall von Bieberstein

PLATE 27

SYNONYMS: *S. oppositifolium* Sims, *S. involucratum* Marschall von Bieberstein, *Asterosedum spurium* (Marschall von Bieberstein) Grulich, *Spathulata spuria* (Marschall von Bieberstein) Löve & Löve

In its numerous forms, perhaps *Sedum spurium* is the most common stonecrop in cultivation. It is usually used for rapid ground cover, which ranges from white-flowered, green carpets (i.e., *S. oppositifolium*), right through to rich, purple-flowered, deep bronze carpets, with almost every combination in between. The forms with the greenest leaves usually have the lightest flowers, and through the range of wine-red, copper, and deep purple foliage, flower color darkens. Numerous cultivars exist, many unworthy of note as they lack unique qualities.

Large, flat, crenate-serrate leaves, which are opposite-decussate, are reduced to terminal buds in winter, when the long, creeping, very branched stems scarred with former leaves are exposed. The flowers have upright petals produced on a flat, dense cyme.

HABITAT. This stonecrop originates from subalpine meadows in the Caucasus Range to Armenia and northern Iran, but the white-flowered form described as *Sedum oppositifolium* is said to be from drier sites. This species is an escape in many countries.

MAIN POINTS OF DISTINCTION. Large, flat leaves, creeping habit, and evergreen nature differentiate this species from any other species (Fig. 5.20gg). In spring it is often very difficult to differentiate young plants of *Sedum hybridum* or *S. ellacombianum* from *S. spurium*, but once the plant in question flowers, there can be no doubt: *S. hybridum* and *S. ellacombianum* have yellow flowers. The white-flowered forms of *S. spurium* are less floriferous than the type species, but they creep in all their forms, and after a few years, tangled stems can be 30+ cm (12+ in) long. No other species in this group acts in this fashion.

VARIATION. The type species has pink-purple flowers and green leaves that tinge red in full sun. The following cultivars are listed from lightest to darkest:

'Album' (syn. *Sedum oppositifolium*) has constantly green foliage and white flowers, and is reluctant to flower.

'Green Mantle' (syn. 'Album Superbum') has large, constantly green leaves. It is less reluctant to flower and the flowers are white fading to very light pink.

'Salmoneum' is a North American garden form, little different from the type species, except the flowers are perhaps more salmon-pink.

'Roseum' is an old cultivar little different from the type species.

'Coccineum' (syn. 'Splendens') has redder flowers and leaves that tinge red. It has been in cultivation more than 100 years.

'Erd Blut' has purple flowers and leaves that are more suffused.

'Bronze Carpet' is a North American garden form with leaves that turn bronze and flowers that are perhaps a little deeper than the type species.

'Fulda Glut' is slightly darker throughout.

'Ruby Mantle' has deep red foliage and purple flowers.

'Purpurteppich' ('Purple Carpet'), as the name suggests, has purple flowers. This form has noticeably large leaves, which in spring can be brown-violet.

'Schorbuser Blut' is often sold under the translation of 'Dragon's Blood'. It starts the season with bright green leaves margined with red but by autumn is the darkest and one of the slowest forms, so therefore more choice.

In addition to the cultivars mentioned, the following are also of interest:

'Tricolor' is the North American name for the variegated form sold in Europe as *Sedum spurium* var. *variegatum*. The North American name is more appropriate because the plant is not found in the wild and the green leaves are edged in creamy-white, which in turn is flushed wine-red in the sun, giving a three-colored effect. Leaves are a different shape from the type species and 'Tricolor' is sometimes taken for a different species: it is often seen masquerading as *S. kamtschaticum* var. *variegatum*, which is vegetatively similar but more upright with yellow flowers. Flowers of 'Tricolor' are a very pleasant light pink-purple. Plants often revert.

Sedum spurium var. *involucratum* is very rare in cultivation. It can be recognized by its huge sepals, as long or nearly as long as the petals. It is a small form of *S. spurium* with eroded, light-colored petals. $2n = 28$ and 42.

HORTICULTURE. *Sedum spurium* is a very vulgar spreader, far too prolific to plant on a small rock garden, but excellent for rapid groundcover. It is ideal for smothering a metal drainage hatch or for planting in a rocky part of the garden where nothing else will grow. Unfortunately, it smothers choicer plants and needs to be contained. Having said that, this stonecrop languishes in pots, needing plenty of room to spread. Dark forms are slower, as is the variegated form, and together they make good foliage-contrasting plants for the border. Filling whole beds in parks, this stonecrop is a picture. It is said to be spontaneous in most countries to 60° north of the equator.

SEDUM SUBULATUM
(C. A. Meyer) Boissier

SYNONYMS: *S. acutifolium* Ledebour,
Oreosedum subulatum (C. A. Meyer) Grulich

Sedum subulatum is exceptionally rare in cultivation. Having been lost to cultivation several times, it has recently been reintroduced. The species is very new to me, but Ron Evans grew it for a few years and depicted it well. Roots are thickened, and stems are mainly simple to about 10 cm (4 in) high, carrying fleshy, gray linear leaves with a pronounced spur on the base and apiculate tips (Fig. 5.20hh). The dense inflorescences of scorpioid branches carry white flowers with erect petals, and carpels have a long subulate (wide-based but sharply pointed) beak (Fig. 5.33).

HABITAT. Found in calcareous stony soils in mountains to over 2000 m (7000 ft) in the Caucasus Range, this stonecrop is widespread from Armenia to Iran and Turkey, but apparently not in the Balkans as has been suggested.

MAIN POINTS OF DISTINCTION. Vegetatively, plants of this species resemble those of the

Figure 5.33. *Sedum subulatum* petals are erect and united at the base.

common *Rupestria* group, which have yellow spreading petals. Because of their upright, white petals connate for 2 mm (0.08 in), flowers of *Sedum subulatum* are so unusual that the plant has been referred to the genera *Umbilicus* and *Cotyledon*. Stems have a very thick base, unlike those plants of the *S. rupestre* group, except for *S. tenuifolium*. Recently in the United Kingdom, a small Turkish form of *S. sediforme* has been distributed as *S. subulatum*. *Sedum sediforme* does not have terete, apiculate leaves, and the flowers are most contrasting. $2n = 18$.

VARIATION. Plants distributed as *Sedum acutifolium* by the International Succulent Institute are yellow-flowered *S. sarmentosum*.

HORTICULTURE. This plant appears difficult to grow in temperate, maritime lowlands, preferring to grow in winter when perhaps it needs some warmth and water.

SEDUM TENELLUM
Marschall von Bieberstein

PLATE 28

SYNONYM: *Oreosedum tenellum* (Marschall von Bieberstein) Grulich

Sedum tenellum is new to cultivation and still exceptionally rare. Short stems are clothed with narrow, densely tufted, imbricate leaves (Fig. 5.20ii). The few white flowers, on a short, simple inflorescence are tinged red but give the appearance of being red overall. Vegetatively, the plant is like a small *S. gracile* or *S. lydium*.

HABITAT. This stonecrop grows from the Elburz Mountains in Iran to the Caucasus Mountains in Turkey between 2000 and 3000 m (7000 and 10,000 ft) on pebble soils and rocky areas in high mountain zones.

MAIN POINTS OF DISTINCTION. *Sedum tenellum* is exceptionally rare in cultivation. Unfortunately a bold form of *S. kamtschaticum* has been widely distributed with this name, particularly in Scotland. No other *Sedum* species has similar vegetative characteristics, namely, red petals which, incidentally, have unusually wavy margins. The large nectaries and the dwarf 3-cm (1-in) high stems, carrying terete leaves, each with a distinct obtuse spur, are also good pointers. $2n = 40$

VARIATION. No data available.

HORTICULTURE. The plant has survived a mild Northumbrian winter outdoors, but obviously is a candidate for the cold frame or alpine house.

SEDUM VILLOSUM L.

PLATE 29

SYNONYMS: *S. glandulosum* Moris, *S. insulare* Moris, *Oreosedum villosum* (L.) Grulich, *Hjaltalinia villosa* (L.) Löve & Löve.
COMMON NAME: Hairy stonecrop

Sedum villosum is one of the most difficult *Sedum* species to perpetuate in cultivation due to its

Figure 5.34. *Sedum villosum* from the beaches of Iceland, here in a 4-in (10-cm) pot.

observed through a lens to locate the short hairs.

VARIATION. Due to the extreme range and highly disjunct habitats of this species, a number of varieties have been named. Glabrous subarctic forms such as *Sedum villosum* var. *glabratum* Rostrup (Fig. 5.34) are often in cultivation in the short term. I managed for several seasons to perpetuate such a variety which grows on sandy shorelines of Iceland. Unfortunately, a hot, dry summer extinguished it. $2n = 30$

HORTICULTURE. As part of a garden feature with running water, this species would probably thrive and give much pleasure. Otherwise, grow it in a clay pot of peaty soil, standing in a large dish of water, in half shade, in an airy spot.

odd habitats of peat bog, saturated, shady rock faces, and the edges of rivulets. It seems very contrary for a succulent to adapt to areas that are soaking wet for much of the time. Despite acting as an annual or biennial, or often perpetuating itself by vegetative means, it would appear as though this species is declining rapidly in the wild—certainly it is not apparent in many of the sites in the United Kingdom where it was reported a hundred years ago.

HABITAT. Wetter, west margins of Europe are the home of the hairy stonecrop, with disjunct, very localized sites extending into Baltic margins, and even into northern Italy, former Yugoslavia, and North Africa.

MAIN POINTS OF DISTINCTION. The solid, rose-lilac petals are unusual, and the glandular-pubescent nature of the plant as a whole is an immediate indication of its identity (Fig. 5.20jj). This pubescent covering changes with the seasons. At times, the pea-green plants need to be

CHAPTER 6

Far Eastern Species of Subgenus Sedum

Few species in subgenus *Sedum* are found between the two major Old World areas of concentration: one centered on the Mediterranean, the other in the Far East. However, it has been suggested by several taxonomists that there is a close relation and affinity between Oriental species and some stonecrops of Eurasia.

The volcanic string of islands comprising part of the Pacific Ring of Fire—from the Kamchatka Peninsula through the Kurile Islands, Japan, Ryukyu Islands, and Taiwan to the Philippines—has a rich variety of endemic *Sedum* species and others it shares with the adjacent mainland. East Siberia, Korea, and China have a rich *Sedum* flora. Unfortunately, scores of stonecrops collected in the Chinese interior and described in the early 1900s or before have never been introduced to cultivation and therefore are only names in ageing florae. Some species that were successfully introduced were not perpetuated in cultivation. For this reason, and because China

has been closed to botanists for most of the twentieth century, there are few Chinese species of *Sedum* in cultivation. As a result of agricultural and social revolutions in China and consequential utilization of virgin land, many species could now be extinct.

Fröderström (1931) did not accept many of the species described from the Far East. He suggested that only a few very polymorphic species existed as a plethora of species were linked by intermediate forms. The work of Uhl and Moran (1972, 75), "besides [deciphering] chromosome number[s], several other parameters of nuclear cytology . . . notably nuclear volume and mass, and the quantity of DNA associated with a chromosome set," has helped validate certain species and shown relation between others. Oriental species in cultivation can be divided into two groups: *Aizoon* group and the group of species with fibrous roots.

AIZOON GROUP

Aizoon group comprises the least succulent group within the genus *Sedum* and consists of the following species in cultivation:

Sedum aizoon L.
Sedum ellacombianum Praeger
Sedum hybridum L.

Sedum hyperaizoon Komarov (see
  S. maximowiczii)
Sedum kamtschaticum Fischer & Meyer
Sedum kurilense Woroschilov (see
  S. kamtschaticum)
Sedum litorale Komarov
Sedum maximowiczii Regel

Sedum middendorffianum (Maximowicz)
   Borissova
Sedum selskianum Regel & Maack
Sedum sichotense Woroschilov
Sedum sikokianum Maximowicz (see
   S. kamtschaticum)
Sedum takesimense Nakai

With two exceptions, *Aizoon* group comprises plants of the temperate and sub-Arctic Far East. *Sedum hybridum* has a range extending into the Ukraine, and *S. sichotense* is also found as far west. All members of *Aizoon* group are intolerant of summer drought, but can cope with poor, stony soils, where they tend to be more stunted. Inflorescences are usually produced on all stem tips, though sterile rosettes or branches are sometimes encountered. Flower color ranges from pale yellow to rich orange, though petals themselves are rarely deeper than gold. Carpels often turn deep orange or red and are retained for a month or more after petals have faded. Plants of this group set viable seed and are reputed to cross in cultivation. Although I grow plants that are said to be of hybrid origin, in my many years of growing a large range of plants of *Aizoon* group side by side, I have never noticed such a phenomenon, despite hundreds of self-sown seedlings which have sprouted up.

Species of *Aizoon* group come to life in early spring and flower around midsummer. Like many early flowerers, they need to be tidied up after flowers are spent. The two best methods of propagation are by taking cuttings in spring (see chapter 2 for details of propagation by vegetative means) or by dividing the woody rootstock with a sharp knife in late autumn after stems have turned brittle and preferably when next year's growth in the form of overwintering buds of tightly packed leaves has formed near soil level. By making sure each division has such a bud, there is a good chance of success. If this second method of propagation is chosen, it would be prudent to let divided rootstocks dry before replanting them in the garden. Alternatively, each divided rootstock can be safely potted in a gritty compost under cover if water is withheld for a week or so. Generally, *Aizoon* group species are exceptionally easy to grow, and no special treatment is required.

The most commonly available plants in the trade appear to be *Sedum ellacombianum* and a few forms of *S. kamtschaticum*. Names, such as *S. wallaceum*, *S. hallaceum*, *S. stevanianum*, and *S. tenellum*, are commonly seen on *S. kamtschaticum* clones, but these are worthless names or names valid only for unrelated species. Sometimes in the United States, *S. kamtschaticum* 'Golden Carpet' is incorrectly offered as *S. spurium* 'Golden Carpet'. In spring it is very difficult separating the many *S. spurium* forms from the *S. kamtschaticum* forms, but the former usually have terminal clusters of leaves in rosettes on very long, bare, creeping stems, while the latter grow immediately from a rootstock. No doubt about the identity of *S. spurium* and *S. kamtschaticum* clones is possible when plants flower, as the former have deep purple to white flowers. Plants stubborn to flower are much more likely to be white-flowering *S. spurium* forms rather than *S. kamtschaticum* clones.

Plants of *Aizoon* group

- Are herbaceous (although *Sedum hybridum* and *S. takesimense* keep leaves overwinter, and most species produce overwintering buds or rosettes at ground level which become next year's stems).
- Have flat leaves, dentate near the apex.
- Have thick, woody rootstocks (Fig. 3.10e).
- Have yellow flowers produced on terminal, clustered inflorescences.
- Have flowers with mucronate petals.
- Have kyphocarpic fruit.

Aizoon species are a closely related group of mostly east Asian herbs, which range from very tall, erect plants with unbranched stems 80 cm (31 in) long topped with bright yellow clusters of flowers, to much smaller, ground-hugging plants with stems branching from the base and carrying smaller clusters of flowers. As an entity, *Aizoon* group is easy to define (so much so that Grulich [1984] erected a new genus to accommodate it—*Aizopsis*), but the group is exceptionally difficult to break up into easily defined distinct species.

Very tall, upright *Sedum aizoon* has been described in a number of forms and under a number of names. So, too, has *S. kamtschaticum*, a low, more creeping species. Dozens of forms—apparently uniting all the accepted species in this group—exist in cultivation, making one question the point of trying to describe all species within *Aizoon* group. As far as the gardener is concerned, a tall, erect specimen has quite different uses from a creeping, carpet-forming specimen, and, if the two contrasting forms displayed the same name, it would lead to much confusion. To be honest, upon growing plants that have been propagated from wild collections, I have often been in a dilemma as to which species to assign each clone: short clones of *S. aizoon* are almost indistinguishable from tall clones of *S. kamtschaticum*.

Fröderström (1931) recognized only two species, lumping all plants in this group under *Sedum aizoon* except *S. hybridum*, which geographically is an oddity and has evergreen tendencies. In more recent times, several forms and varieties of *S. kamtschaticum* have been given specific rank, but overall, hundreds of regional variations comprise a polyploid complex with a basic chromosome number of $x = 16$. Figure 6.1 shows leaf shapes of *Aizoon* group species.

The following is not a formal key, but an aid to identification of plants in *Aizoon* group:

Stems long (40 cm+, 15 in), thick (5 mm+, 0.2 in), erect : *S. aizoon*
Stems long, thick, outer ones prostrate:
    S. maximowiczii
Stems long, thick, all prostrate: *S. takesimense*
Stems shorter (30 cm, 12 in), semi-erect,
    thinner: *S. litorale*
Stems shorter (15 cm, 6 in), thin:
    S. kamtschaticum

Unless

Plant hairy all over: *S. selskianum*

Leaves long, very narrow, and deeply V-shaped
    in cross section: *S. middendorffianum*
Leaves bright, fresh green, and fruit orange:
    S. ellacombianum
From western Asia and leaves small, narrow
    and deciduous: *S. sichotense*
From western Asia and leaves evergreen, small
    but wide: *S. hybridum*
From Ullong-Do and leaves evergreen, large
    and wide: *S. takesimense*

SEDUM AIZOON L.

PLATE 30
COMMON NAME: Hoso-ba-no-kirin-sō

Plants of *Sedum aizoon* can be 40 cm (16 in) or more tall. All forms of the species are herbaceous plants comprising straight, simple, upright stems with large, usually light green leaves, topped with a clustered cyme of pale yellow flowers. *Sedum aizoon* is an old-fashioned cottage garden herb with not a great deal to recommend it—except perhaps as a useful addition to the back of a border. A much more colorful form, *S. aizoon* 'Euphorbioides' is more desirable.

Plants of all forms are at their best in the first half of the year. After flowering by July plants slowly dry, lose their leaves, and, except for a few woody stems, just about disappear by September. *Sedum aizoon* is best planted among later flowering species of *Hylotelephium* group, which will grow over spent plants of *S. aizoon*. This stonecrop seeds itself quite readily but could not become a pest.

HABITAT. *Sedum aizoon* is widespread across the eastern third of the former Soviet Union, from the Yenisei River in Siberia to the east coast, and from Mongolia to Japan. It is not indigenous to particularly dry areas.

MAIN POINTS OF DISTINCTION. This is an exceptionally polymorphic species, so if a plant in question is a tall, herbaceous member of *Aizoon* group, then it is likely to be *Sedum aizoon*. Only *S. maximowiczii* could cause confusion, and many taxonomists believe it is merely another form of *S. aizoon*. *Sedum maximowiczii* has more

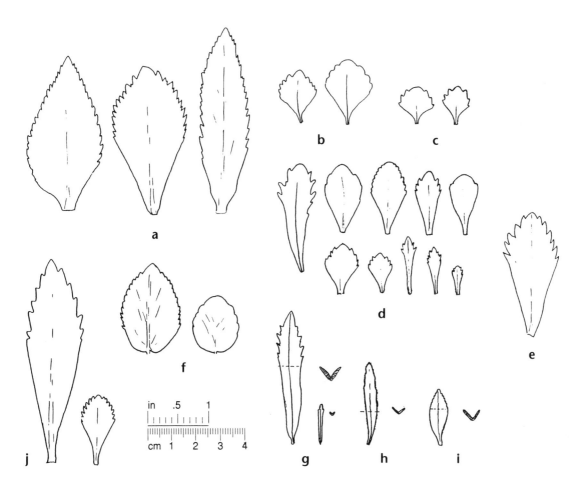

Figure 6.1. Leaf shapes of species of *Aizoon* group: (a) *Sedum aizoon*; (b) *S. ellacombianum*; (c) *S. hybridum*; (d) *S. kamschaticum*; (e) *S. litorale*; (f) *S. maximowiczii*; (g) *S. middendorffianum*; (h) *S. selskianum*; (i) *S. sichotense*; (j) *S. takesimense*.

stem-clasping leaves with broader bases, but its color resembles darker forms of *S. aizoon*, which currently are more popular in the United Kingdom than their lighter counterparts.

VARIATION. Plants of *Sedum aizoon* are quite varied in height, leaf color, and leaf shape. *Sedum aizoon* f. *latifolium* is a broad-leaved form from the Far East, and *S. aizoon* f. *angustifolium* is a narrow-leaved form from the interior of Siberia, but many transitional forms exist (Fig. 6.1). A dark form *S. aizoon* 'Euphorbioides' (syn. *S. aizoon* var. *aurantiacum* hort.) is a much more eye-catching plant with dark red stems, leaves that turn bronze, and bright orange-yellow flowers. $n = 48$ and $n = 64$.

HORTICULTURE. *Sedum aizoon* is a very easy plant for a border only, preferably in a semishaded spot. It dislikes spring drought.

SEDUM ELLACOMBIANUM Praeger

PLATE 31

SYNONYMS: *S. kamtschaticum* var. *ellacombianum* (Praeger) Clausen

COMMON NAME: Hirohano-Kirinsho

Sedum ellacombianum is a vibrant green, dense, carpet-forming species with bright orange fruit. It tends to spread quite quickly and is happy to trail over trough edges, stones in a rock garden, and even concrete steps and adjacent paving.

Dense mounds, 10 cm (4 in) high, of bright green foliage are very eye-catching as they take on the shape of whatever they engulf. Although this species seeds itself from time to time, it is very easily controlled and can never become a pest. Considered by many to be merely a form of *S. kamtschaticum*, this stonecrop is a very desirable plant with pleasing habits.

HABITAT. Early literature is vague about the actual habitat of this stonecrop, but it certainly grows on Hokkaido, Japan, not at particularly high altitudes.

MAIN POINTS OF DISTINCTION. Leaf shape (Fig. 6.1b) and color, although quite variable, are reasonably distinct. In spring, leaves in shaded areas are yellow-green, and in full sun or drought conditions, they never blush red. In other respects this species resembles creeping, wider-leaved forms of *Sedum kamtschaticum*, except fruit of *S. ellacombianum* are bright orange to rust-red. *n* = 16.

VARIATION. Plants in gardens are constant since they all have been propagated from material that has been in cultivation since the early 1900s. Wild clones collected in recent years are not quite as bright as plants in cultivation and very similar to the U.S. cultivar 'Golden Carpet', which is perhaps better assigned here than with *S. kamtschaticum*.

HORTICULTURE. *Sedum ellacombianum* deserves its popularity because of its many uses. It is perfect for brightening up a dull spot in the corner of a border, or in a rock garden, stone trough, raised bed, or dark scree. It is a point of interest into late summer because of the fruit that remains colorful till autumn. For inexplicable reasons, a plant can disappear rapidly from a given location, so it is prudent to have more than a single specimen. Perhaps plants are too fast for a small rock garden, but they make excellent solid summer ground cover.

SEDUM HYBRIDUM L.

Sedum hybridum is similar in many ways to other low-growing members of *Aizoon* group (Fig. 6.2).

It is noted for the fact that some leaves are retained throughout winter and for the fact that in favorable conditions it appears to have two distinct flowering seasons: one in late spring, and another more floriferous season about eight weeks later.

HABITAT. Indigenous to stony and gravelly soils on open, upland steppe to the south of the Taïga (the great coniferous forest that stretches across Eurasia as the Boreal Forest stretches across North America), this stonecrop is widespread from the Ural Mountains to Mongolia.

MAIN POINTS OF DISTINCTION. Relatively wide leaves with only several shallow notches are confined to terminal clusters on short, bare decumbent stems (Fig. 6.1c). The species is similar to *Sedum ellacombianum*, but its evergreen nature separates the two. In spring *S. hybridum* is very similar vegetatively to forms of *S. spurium* with bright green leaves.

VARIATION. A light green form of *S. hybridum* with paler flowers is sold in Europe under the

Figure 6.2. *Sedum hybridum* covering a damp bank.

name 'Immergrünchen', a reference to its ever-green nature. A form distributed as *S. hybridum* var. *dentatum* has leaves that appear to be slight-ly more dentate, but I am unaware that the name is valid.

HORTICULTURE. This stonecrop is slow-grow-ing but very tolerant of extreme conditions. I recommend it for stone troughs, raised beds, rock gardens, scree gardens, and the front of a border. It is a better ground cover than any other species of *Aizoon* group in that it has some win-ter color, but because it is slow to spread, I rec-ommend spacing plants 30 cm (12 in) apart.

SEDUM KAMTSCHATICUM
Fischer & Meyer

PLATE 32

SYNONYM: *S. kurilense* Woroschilov
COMMON NAME: Kirin-sō

Sedum kamtschaticum is a very variable, creeping member of *Aizoon* group and some forms are ex-ceptionally common in cultivation. Unfortu-nately, common forms are not particularly col-orful, but spread quite quickly to form a dense, herbaceous carpet. Other forms turn a beautiful, bright cherry-red in autumn after yellow flowers have faded (Plate 32). Most forms grow no high-er than 20 cm (8 in), but 10 cm (4 in) is more common.

HABITAT. This species grows in areas all the way down the eastern margin of Siberia to Cen-tral China, including most neighboring island groups.

MAIN POINTS OF DISTINCTION. Some tax-onomists include *Sedum middendorffianum*, *S. selskianum*, and *S. ellacombiamum* as varieties or forms of *S. kamtschaticum*. Although these spe-cies have distinct descriptions, intermediate forms of most combinations are known. I grow several of these intermediates in my reference collection; the majority are wild propagations rather than hybrids. *Sedum selskianum* is hairy in all its visible parts, *S. middendorffianum* has very narrow leaves V-shaped in section, and *S. ella-*

combianum has wide, fresh-green leaves with a tendency to be opposite-decussate. *Sedum hybri-dum* is very similar to *S. ellacombianum* but has evergreen leaves. Thus, *S. kamtschaticum* can be distinguished by its medium-to-dark green her-baceous leaves that are not V-shaped in section, not hairy, and not opposite-decussate (Fig. 6.1d)

VARIATION. *Sedum kamtschaticum* is a very polymorphic species. The most common forms in cultivation are *S. kamtschaticum* var. *floriferum* (Fischer & Meyer) Praeger (Fig. 6.3) and its culti-vated form 'Weihenstephaner Gold'. The former is very floriferous as suggested by its name and can be recognized by its very branched nature. Flowers are smaller and more abundant than those of the type species, and are greenish or paler yellow as they open. Petals turn medium yellow, and carpels fade red-brown. 'Weihen-stephaner Gold' is an exceptionally common plant, ideal for rapid ground cover, but its popu-larity puzzles me. Its leaves are rather dull, dark green, with a greater propensity to turn bronze than those of *S. kamtschaticum* var. *floriferum*, and its flowers are not golden; in fact, it is per-

Figure 6.3. *Sedum kamtschaticum* var. *floriferum* branches copiously, and each branch becomes an inflorescence.

haps the least interesting form of *S. kamtschaticum* in cultivation.

Sedum kamtschaticum f. *variegatum* is a delightful, slow-growing form with almost entire leaves edged in cream. Leaf margins are blushed orange or pink in full sun giving the leaves a tricolored effect. Flowers of this variety are large (2 cm/0.8 in across) and deep yellow fading to orange. I highly recommend this form.

Sedum kamtschaticum 'Golden Carpet', a favorite in the United States, is a bright, low-growing floriferous plant with leaves not unlike those of *S. ellacombianum* in color and shape. It is not as fresh green as *S. ellacombianum* and not so rapid spreading.

"*Sedum kurilense*" is a validly published name for tiny forms of *S. kamtschaticum* from the Kurile Islands (which stretch from the Kamchatka Peninsula of Siberia to Hokkaido, the northernmost of the larger Japanese islands). A particularly compact clone was distributed as *S. kamtschaticum* 'Takahira Dake'—the name of the mountain on which this plant is endemic. I question the desirability of erecting *S. kurilense* as a distinct species, as other regional forms from Japan are just as compact, yet unique in their own ways (e.g., *S. kamtschaticum* from Hikari-Dake, *S. kamtschaticum* from Kita-Dake, *S. kamtschaticum* from Tekari-Dake). Kurile Island forms do not creep but form compact hummocks, and some of them have 4-partite rather than 5-partite flowers. Other forms (e.g., from Ishimaka or Kogane Coast) root as they spread and form a dense mat of greenery.

Several worthless names, such as 'Gold Star', are associated with this group, but generally, plants in cultivation are correctly named—though names are often shortened to *S.* 'Weihenstephaner Gold', *S. floriferum*, *S.* 'Golden Carpet', and so forth. *n* = 16, 32, 48, 64, and some oddities have been reported.

HORTICULTURE. *Sedum kamtschaticum* in its numerous forms offers useful plants for the garden. The faster growing forms, such as *S. kam-*

tschaticum var. *floriferum* and its cultivar, can quickly hide a troublesome stony area. The miniature regional gems or the more upright, variegated form make superb plants for a rock garden or raised trough. All forms originate from areas that have heavy summer rainfall and higher-than-average winter rain. Plants are not particularly succulent, so they suffer in long, dry spells for want of irrigation.

Most forms in cultivation are plants originating from maritime climates where prolonged spells of frost or snow are unknown, while some grow near the coast of northeastern Siberia (which experiences the same bitter winters as Labrador), or at high altitudes just below the snow line. Oddly, as plants are quite dormant in winter, their origin does not seem to influence their growth in cultivation the following spring. The only *Sedum kamtschaticum* form I have lost as a result of frost was one collected from Kyushu—the most southern of the Japanese islands (probably the plant often called *S. sikokianum* Maximowicz). This particular regional form showed no signs of distress after a bitter, wet winter with periods of freeze, but warm sun in April brought the plant to life and frosts that followed killed it. In areas that do not have distinct seasons it is advisable to take frost precautions by covering specimens that have started to grow with leaves, straw, or plastic sheets.

SEDUM LITORALE Komarov

Sedum litorale is a medium-size member of *Aizoon* group, midway between *S. aizoon* and *S. kamtschaticum*. It grows to about 30 cm (12 in) and has leaves that tend to be opposite in the upper half of the stems, but can be ternate in the lower half (Fig. 6.1e). Generally, medium green leaves are less scattered than are leaves in *S. aizoon*. Flowers are deep yellow.

HABITAT. This is a very localized species only found on Popov Island near Vladivostok on sandy sea shores.

MAIN POINTS OF DISTINCTION. An undocumented plant is almost impossible to identify with confidence as intermediate forms or questionable hybrids of *Sedum aizoon* and *S. kamtschaticum* are very similar. Sepals of *S. aizoon* are exceptionally long and narrow, but those of *S. litorale* are more deltoid. This factor differentiates *S. litorale* from *S. aizoon* and also from taller forms of *S. kamtschaticum*; in addition, inflorescences of *S. litorale* are often very branched (Fig. 6.4).

VARIATION. As *Sedum litorale* is endemic to a tiny island, it is unlikely to show much variation, but as a species it is not particularly distinct.

HORTICULTURE. Perhaps this is a more useful herb to an alpine enthusiast than *Sedum aizoon* due to its lower stature. It is certainly not out of place in a large rock garden and is ideal for areas experiencing very high rainfall and cold winters—as long as drainage is good. Areas of very sandy soils should also benefit by its presence.

Figure 6.4. *Sedum litorale* inflorescences in fruit are far more branched and open than those of *S. aizoon*.

SEDUM MAXIMOWICZII Regel

SYNONYM: *S. hyperaizoon* Komarov

This tall, robust herb is very closely related to *Sedum aizoon*, if not actually a form of it. If grown as a border plant, *S. maximowiczii* can reach a stature of 80 cm (32 in), but if contained in a pot, it is stunted and tends to be decumbent throughout. Outer stems of a mature plant in a border tend to be more sprawling than those of typical *S. aizoon* forms. *Sedum maximowiczii* plants are colorful, having bronzed leaves and deep yellow flowers.

HABITAT. This giant stonecrop is frequently found in cultivation in Japan, but its native habitat is unknown, although it is almost certainly a cultivated form of *S. hyperaizoon* from Russkii Island.

MAIN POINTS OF DISTINCTION. Broader in leaf than *Sedum aizoon* (Fig. 6.1f), *S. maximowiczii* has foliage and flowers very similar to those of *S. aizoon* 'Euphorbioides'. *Sedum maximowiczii*, however, has leaves with relatively wide bases, which are amplexicaul, and in one form, opposite-decussate (Fig. 6.5). Inflorescences are large, more branched than those of *S. aizoon*, and therefore less compact, so carry more flowers than specimens of *S. aizoon*. "*Sedum hyperaizoon*" (the wild form of *S. maximowiczii*) is green, has scattered leaves, as does *S. aizoon* proper, but in other respects it is identical to *S. maximowiczii*.

VARIATION. In reality, this is just a major form of *Sedum aizoon* which is reported to cross with it and produce viable seed. Thus, hybrids must exist in cultivation.

HORTICULTURE. *Sedum maximowiczii* is preferable to other tall-growing *Aizoon* species and is an excellent foliage-contrast plant if grown among lighter-colored members of this group. If a whole bed is planted with a range of *Aizoon* group plants, the spectacle in early summer is a very special harmony of foliage colors ranging from a very bright green to bronze, and with flowers from light yellow to orange. *Sedum maximowiczii* is most useful in this situation. It could also be a feature plant on a very large rock garden. As with other stonecrops of this group, high rainfall and partial shade seem to produce more robust specimens.

Figure 6.5. Opposite leaves half-clasp the inflorescence on one form of *Sedum maximowiczii.*

SEDUM MIDDENDORFFIANUM
(Maximowicz) Borissova

PLATE 33

COMMON NAME: Hina-kirinsho

Sedum middendorffianum comprises a polymorphic range of herbs very closely related to *S. kamtschaticum*. Variation is great: from robust plants at one end of the range with 30 cm (12 in), semierect stems carrying 8 cm (3.2 in) long, linear-spathulate, green leaves, obtusely crenate in the upper half, to tiny creeping purple-brown plants with linear leaves displaying only a couple of notches near apices at the other (Fig. 6.1g). In cultivation both extremes exist along with several intermediate and variable forms. Flowers are produced on many-flowered inflorescences, and bright orange anthers add to the overall picture.

HABITAT. Indigenous to stony soils, rock crevices, and forest glades from the valley of the River Lena in northeast Siberia to the Okhotsk district, through northern China and Japan, this stonecrop is widespread from fairly coastal sites to alpine slopes.

MAIN POINTS OF DISTINCTION. Shapes of the leaves, although quite varied, have very similar cross sections. This attribute plus carpels with extremely short beaks are the best means of identification.

VARIATION. Although names have been given to some extreme forms of *Sedum middendorffianum*, other forms remain anonymous. Almost every intermediate form exists in cultivation. *Sedum middendorffianum* var. *diffusum* (Maximowicz) Praeger is a tall form so close to forms of *S. kamtschaticum* that only carpels give a clue to its identity. *Sedum middendorffianum* 'Striatum' is a name bestowed upon a tiny, extreme form with very narrow, brown-purple leaves, but if given richer soil, this form changes somewhat. I am not suggesting that conditions are totally responsible for the form a plant takes in cultivation, as there are considerably contrasting clones, but the same clone, grown in contrasting sites, can take on remarkably different forms.

HORTICULTURE. Tall forms make excellent plants for the front of a border, and all are very suitable for rock gardens, though very dark, tiny forms can be visually lost without a contrasting background. Few nurseries offer this species for sale, but it is not too difficult to acquire a specimen. As with *Sedum kamtschaticum*, one must experiment with the plant to decide whether the clone acquired is one of the quick-spreading kinds or one of the diminutive slow-growers.

SEDUM SELSKIANUM
Regel & Maack

Sedum selskianum is an exceptionally rare plant in cultivation. Unfortunately it has been confused with *S. ellacombianum*, and plants of *S. ellacombianum* have been widely distribed under an incorrect name, often by those who should have known better. There is absolutely no way in which one could mistake the true *S. selskianum* for any other species, as it is hairy in all its parts (Fig. 6.6). With an eyeglass, or if one's near vision is good, it is fascinating to see hirsute sepals, petals, and carpels. This slender, painfully slow-growing species of *Aizoon* group must be observed at close hand for its beauty to be enjoyed. It attains a stature of only 15 cm (6 in), but in the wild, plants of twice this size are more usual.

HABITAT. From the border region of China and the former Soviet Union, this stonecrop is native to rocky slopes of the River Amur and adjacent forest glades.

MAIN POINTS OF DISTINCTION. Narrow, hirsute leaves (Fig. 6.1h), densely ciliate flowers, and pubescent stems are the major points for identification. Flowers are very like those of *Sedum kamtschaticum*. Woody rootstocks are huge for the size of plant.

VARIATION. This species hybridizes with *Sedum kamtschaticum* in cultivation, and recently a hybrid was distributed in the United Kingdom under the name of an unrelated west Russian species. Like true plants of *S. selskianum*, hybrids display more hair on the undersides of leaves, but generally the hirsute nature is less pronounced, and leaves are wider and darker green.

HORTICULTURE. Plants are interesting for their unusual pubescence, but need to be grown on an elevated site to be observed.

SEDUM SICHOTENSE Woroschilov

SYNONYM: *S. middendorffianum* var. *sichotense* Woroschilov

Sedum sichotense is a very small, slow-growing, tufted, upright, and particularly neat variation on a theme. Rising to only 10 cm (4 in), it is

Figure 6.6. *Sedum selskianum* is hairy in all its parts.

rather floriferous for such a diminutive plant, but rare in cultivation (Fig. 6.7).

HABITAT. Indigenous to Eastern Ukraine, this stonecrop is geographically extreme for *Aizoon* group.

MAIN POINTS OF DISTINCTION. Unless the origin of a plant is known, it is just about impossible to separate this species from tiny forms of *Sedum kamtschaticum* from east Hokkaido or Kurile Isles, Japan. Geographically, *S. sichotense* is distinct, for nothing like it grows for 4800 km (3000 miles) to the east, but to a keen gardener there is no real key to its identity, save tiny leaves (Fig. 6.1i), which tend to be quite upright, and purple stems. Several clones of *S. kamtschaticum* could fit this description, but they have more patent leaves and very narrow, linear sepals (the sepals of *S. sichotense* are marginally more deltoid). Plants received from a botanic

Figure 6.7. *Sedum sichotense* growing at the Royal Botanic Garden Edinburgh in a very rich border. My plants are lower and more compact than these 14-cm (5-in) high specimens.

garden in the former Soviet Union with a *S. sichotense* label turned out to be *S. spurium*.

VARIATION. This stonecrop is so rare in cultivation, all plants may have been propagated from the same source.

HORTICULTURE. *Sedum sichotense* will give pleasure for decades without requiring any cutting back or tending. It is so diminutive, it needs to be in a raised position to be noticed. It is the best species of *Aizoon* group to cultivate as a specimen plant in an alpine house, where it will form a neat mound. Either clay or plastic pots would be suitable containers as this species is not fussy; on the contrary, it is most resilient.

SEDUM TAKESIMENSE Nakai

COMMON NAME: Takeshima-kirinsho

Sedum takesimense is a recent introduction grown from seed collected in habitat. When I first grew it in my collection, I thought it to be merely another form of *S. aizoon*, but stems are very thick and decumbent (Fig. 6.8). Large, light green leaves are also reminiscent of *S. aizoon*, but plants have the creeping habit of *S. kamtschaticum*. *Sedum takesimense* is a very floriferous species with additional branches that carry flowers rising from below the main cyme. The real surprise is that the large leaves are retained throughout winter (Fig. 6.1j). This oddity flowers in August like *S. kamtschaticum* rather than earlier in summer like *S. aizoon*. Plants became available in the trade in the 1990s.

HABITAT. *Sedum takesimense* is endemic to mountains of Kyŏngsang, North Province of Ul-long-Do, a remote island between Korea and Japan.

MAIN POINTS OF DISTINCTION. Very thick, decumbent stems with large, light green, evergreen leaves are unique in this group. Bracts are leaflike and large. The species is diploid with $n = 16$.

VARIATION. None.

HORTICULTURE. Having only overwintered this species for two years, through winters that

Figure 6.8. *Sedum takesimense*; the tied label measures 10 cm (4 in).

have not been harsh, I doubt the full hardiness of a plant from such a maritime area at fairly low latitudes, but it has also survived without protection in colder, wetter parts of England. My propagations were heavily damaged by a frost in late June when plants were in full growth, but more severe frosts were not damaging at all when plants were dormant (but leafy). This is too large a plant for a small rock garden, but excellent for a large scree or near the front of a border. Oddly, plants appear self-sterile.

SPECIES WITH FIBROUS ROOTS

Plants of this group

- Are perennial or very rarely annual or biennial.
- Have mostly 5-partite flowers with yellow mucronate petals. Thus, anomalous 4-partite flowers are a good aid to identification.
- Have kyphocarpic flowers, with yellowish anthers, carpels, and nectaries.
- Are small, creeping or upright, glabrous species with fine, fibrous roots.

The following species are in cultivation:

Sedum alfredi var. *nagasakianum* (Hance) Hara (see *S. nagasakianum*)
Sedum bulbiferum Makino (see *S. rosulatobulbosum*)
Sedum drymarioides Hance
Sedum formosanum Britton
Sedum hakonense Makino
Sedum japonicum Siebold
Sedum kiusianum Makino (see *S. polytrichoides*)
Sedum lineare Thunberg

Sedum makino Maximowicz
Sedum nagasakianum (Hara) Ohba
Sedum onychopetalum Fröderström
Sedum oryzifolium Makino
Sedum polytrichoides Hemsley
Sedum rosulatobulbosum Koidz
Sedum rupifragum Koidz
Sedum sarmentosum Bunge
Sedum senanense Makino (see *S. japonicum*)
Sedum sp. RBGE 763791
Sedum subtile Maximowicz
Sedum tetractinum Fröderström
Sedum tosaense Makino
Sedum yabeanum Makino (see *S. polytrichoides*)
Sedum zentaro-tashiroi Makino (see *S. subtile*)

Sedum drymarioides is an anomalous annual with white flowers. Plate 34 shows leaf shapes and leaf arrangements of Far Eastern species with fibrous roots. The following is not a formal key but an aid to identification of yellow-flowered Far Eastern species with fibrous roots:

Annual with massive stems: *S. formosanum*
Propagated by bulbils: *S. bulbiferum*, *S. rosulato-bulbosum*
Leaves about the size and shape of grains of rice: *S. japonicum*, *S. oryzifolium*, *S. senanense*
Leaves long, narrow, thin, lanceolate, ternate: *S. lineare*
Leaves long, succulent, ternate: *S. sarmentosum*
Leaves long succulent, scattered: *S. nagasakianum*, *S. rupifragum*
Leaves flat, spathulate: *S. makinoi*, *S. tetractinum*, *S. tosaense*
Leaves long, narrow, scattered: *S. polytrichoides*
Leaves on inflorescence spathulate and opposite: *S. subtile*
Leaves on inflorescence spathulate and verticillate: *S. zentaro-tashiroi*
Flowers 4-partite: *S. hakonense*, *S. tetractinum*
Tiny plant with huge inflorescence: *S. onychopetalum*

SEDUM DRYMARIOIDES Hance

Sedum drymarioides is unlike any other Oriental species in cultivation (Fig. 6.9). Flat, entire, glandular-pubescent, opposite, spathulate leaves are noticeably stalked. The plant is very spindly and feeble, rising to 15 cm (6 in) high. In a warm greenhouse it can sometimes be persuaded to perpetuate for several seasons. Loose inflorescences carry white, pubescent flowers.

HABITAT. Lowland southeast China and Taiwan are the home of the type species, but *Sedum drymarioides* var. *toyamae* (?) is reported from southern Japan.

MAIN POINTS OF DISTINCTION. Plants could not be confused with any other species in cultivation. The soft, hairy, petiolate-spathulate leaves are not particularly succulent, but they are unique in the genus. All flower parts, except carpels, are pubescent. Carpels remain quite upright, and petals only partly open to about 60°. Blackish seeds are large for *Sedum*, being about 0.5 mm (0.02 in) long.

VARIATION. Unable to comment.

HORTICULTURE. This species is best grown on a heated tray full of sandy material near an open door. It is of little horticultural impor-

Figure 6.9. *Sedum drymarioides.*

tance, but if a small colony can be perpetuated, the resulting display is certainly different and can give much pleasure to the grower.

SEDUM FORMOSANUM N. E. Brown

SYNONYM: *S. alfredi* Hance
COMMON NAME: Hama-mannengusa

Upon first growing this species, I was amazed at the stature plants attained. Bases of stems developed a girth of nearly 2 cm (0.8 in), and annual plants, resembling little bonsai trees, exceded 25 cm (10 in) in height (Fig. 6.10). Well-spaced, very blunt, thin, bright green, obovate-spathulate leaves are alternate or sometimes opposite. The large cymes of flowers are not particularly bright, but carry a lot of sessile flowers.

HABITAT. Ryukyu Islands, China, Philippines, and Taiwan are the homes of this species, mostly along seashores.

MAIN POINTS OF DISTINCTION. The form in

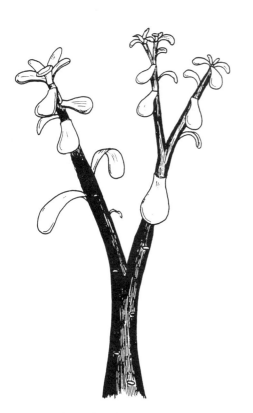

Figure 6.10. *Sedum formosanum.*

cultivation bears little resemblance to other yellow-flowered Far Eastern sedums. It is a stout, upright annual or biennial. Stems are forked, and eventually spread. Flowers have slightly spurred, spreading, leaflike sepals. Carpels are only slightly divergent in fruit. $n = 32$.

VARIATION. Drawings of plants collected from habitat indicate some plants can be quite feeble. Plants have been reported that geographically and vegetatively are midway between *Sedum nagasakianum* and the species.

HORTICULTURE. It is said that this species can be persuaded to act as a perennial, as it often does in the wild, but so far I have not succeeded. I was disappointed when rooted cuttings flowered at exactly the same time as the parent plants, neither producing sterile shoots.

SEDUM HAKONENSE Makino

PLATE 34
COMMON NAME: Matsu-no-ha-mannengusa

Sedum hakonense is a fairly typical Japanese sedum resembling *S. rupifragum* and others. It is a creeping, then ascending plant, much branched from the base, with linear, loosely tufted, scattered leaves that are more succulent than those of *S. lineare*. Plants are usually no more than 5 cm (2 in) tall, but stems are often twice this length. Many 4-partite, pale yellow, sessile flowers of late summer are carried on a 3-branched cyme (Fig. 6.11). The species is exceptionally rare in cultivation, even in Japan.

HABITAT. This stonecrop is indigenous to mountains of southern Honshu, Japan.

MAIN POINTS OF DISTINCTION. Leaves are not particularly distinct, but 4-partite flowers are rare in this group. Tiny sepals are unequal and fairly deltoid. Turgid fruit are pronounced kyphocarpic.

VARIATION. Unable to comment.

HORTICULTURE. *Sedum hakonense* is almost hardy. If you manage to acquire a piece to propogate, give plenty of cuttings away so you can beg one back if you lose your plant.

Figure 6.11. *Sedum hakonense.*

SEDUM JAPONICUM Siebold ex Miquel
S. SENANENSE Makino

PLATES 34, 35

COMMON NAMES: Me-no-mannengusa;
Miyama-mannengusa

Sedum japonicum (Fig. 6.12) is a tufted species growing to 15 cm (6 in) high; it resembles European *S. album* but has flatter, brighter leaves, and yellow flowers. Smaller, redder, and more common forms in cultivation tend to be labelled "*S. japonicum* var. *senanense*," but they are best referred to as *S. senanense*. While *S. japonicum* plants are bright green and more sturdy than plants of *S. senanense*, the latter have slender, much branched, decumbent, then rising stems that carry alternate, imbricate at first, linear-ovate leaves with spurs in loose tufts. Inflorescences of summer carry many subsessile flowers on three or four branches. Cytological evidence points to keeping the two species separate.

HABITAT. *Sedum japonicum* grows on rocky, open-wooded, lower hillsides on Honshu island, Japan, while *S. senanense* is from higher altitudes in Honshu—to 2500 m (8200 ft)—often partly shaded.

MAIN POINTS OF DISTINCTION. These species are difficult to differentiate from *Sedum oryzifolium* in this group and are also similar to larger species in the European *S. acre* complex. Leaves of *S. japonicum* and *S. senanense* are longer than all the leaves of plants of the *S. acre* group, except for *S. sexangulare*, which has neat spirals of leaves, and *S. urvillei*, which has acute leaf apices. *Sedum japonicum* and *S. senanense* have blunt, more loosely scattered, reflexed leaves, which are flat on both surfaces. (For ways of differentiating these species from *S. oryzifolium*, see under that species.) Sepals of both species are unequal in length, free, and spurred. Epipetalous stamens are inserted noticeably above the bases of petals and are very short. Carpels are erect at first, but then spread widely.

Work by Uhl and Moran (1972) has shown these two species to be cytologically distinct, so they uphold the name *Sedum senanense* with $n = 9$. *Sedum japonicum* has a chromosome count of $n = 19$ and is a more robust plant than *S. senanense* (Plate 35). I have not yet acquired a clone that remains pure green when in full sun, but *S. japonicum* plants are about 6 cm (2 in) tall and only slightly flush with red, even if grown in a very exposed spot. *Sedum senanense* is bright red for much of the year, and plants do not usually

Figure 6.12. *Sedum japonicum* in a 5-in (13-cm) pot.

grow more than 4 or 5 centimeters (1 in) high.

VARIATION. Neither species is particularly common in cultivation, but both respond to situation considerably. Grown indoors, etiolated specimens become uncharacteristic. A species with affinity to *Sedum japonicum* was collected in Taiwan by the Royal Botanic Gardens Edinburgh and can be found under *Sedum* sp. RBGE 763791.

HORTICULTURE. These plants make very bright subjects. They tolerate wet conditions if well-drained sites are chosen, but are questionably hardy in areas of long, bitter winters. They are just hardy for me in Mid Northumberland. *Sedum senanense* is most suitable for alpine cultivation. Neither species grows fast enough for ground cover, as the carpet produced is too open, but both are most attractive in containers and on raised beds.

SEDUM LINEARE Thunberg

PLATE 34

COMMON NAME: O-no-mannengusa

Sedum lineare is exceptionally common in its variegated form, which is invariably grown in a hanging basket. Very long, rising, creeping, then falling stems, carry flat, linear, acute leaves in whorls of three (Fig. 6.13). Yellow flowers of summer, on flat-topped, lax, few-flowered inflorescence, are hardly ever produced on variegated plants. It can be most confusing to read that synonyms of this species comprise a long list of most other Oriental species, a consequence of Fröderström, in particular, generally ignoring vegetative form and lumping together all Far Eastern species with similar flowers. Here, following more recent opinion, *S. subtile*, *S. zentaro-tashiroi*, and *S. makinoi* are treated as distinct species.

HABITAT. The true habitat is confused by garden escapes in the Japanese islands of Honshu, Shikoku, and Kyushu, but the species is indigenous to the Ryukyu Islands and possibly mainland China.

MAIN POINTS OF DISTINCTION. This stonecrop is only likely to be confused with *Sedum sarmentosum*, which also can produce 30-cm (12-in) creeping stems with long, spurred ternate leaves. Cytologically, *S. sarmentosum* is distinct from *S. lineare*, which has *n* = 36. Uhl and Moran (1972) noted that the related *S. sarmentosum* may have approximately the same *n* number, but the latter usually displays considerable irregularity at meiosis, suggesting it is a hybrid. Width and thickness of leaf are the only real guides upon which the amateur can rely to distinguish the two species: *S. lineare* has thin, narrow leaves that are not very fleshy, those of *S. sarmentosum* are leathery and more lanceolate. Both stonecrops have free sepals without spurs, but those of *S. lineare* tend to be upright and stand up between petals. Highly fused carpels only spread a little. *Sedum lineare* resembles, and is obviously closely related to, *S. mexicanum*, which has nearly terete leaves in whorls of four.

VARIATION. Praeger described *Sedum lineare* var. *robustum*, but all the plants I have received with this label have turned out to be *S. sarmentosum*. If grown outside, *S. lineare* becomes more

Figure 6.13. *Sedum lineare*; the commonly cultivated variegated form in a hanging basket 6 in (15 cm) in diameter.

robust, more upright, and has shorter, denser shoots. *Sedum lineare* f. *variegatum* has leaves with cream edges and is a very popular potted plant for the home, although it tends to be leggy indoors.

HORTICULTURE. Frosts tend to sear plants at ground level, but they often regenerate. Even after a bitter winter, end pieces left blowing around, if pushed into soil, soon start growing. It is prudent to keep some stock under cover in the worst months. In milder areas, this species and its variegated form produce very dense ground cover, pouring over the edges of stone troughs or raised beds.

SEDUM MAKINOI Maximowicz

PLATES 34, 36
COMMON NAME: Maruba-mannengusa

Plants of *Sedum makinoi* form a dense ground cover only a few centimeters high. In winter, stems are short and crowded with almost orbicular leaves, but they lengthen considerably in the growing season so that long, creeping stems carry opposite-decussate, flat, fleshy, shiny, spathulate leaves. Flat-topped inflorescences of scorpioid branches with large leaflike bracts and green-yellow flowers of summer are not very colorful. This stonecrop is still uncommon in cultivation, but is becoming more widely available

HABITAT. Honshu, Shikoku, and Kyushu islands, Japan, are the homes of *Sedum makinoi*, which inhabits fairly wet, rocky, shaded areas in valleys.

MAIN POINTS OF DISTINCTION. Almost round, spathulate leaves, and creeping habit are a good general guide. Sepals are rather hourglass-shaped, free, and spurred. Petals are pale green-yellow and somewhat ephemeral.

VARIATION. A number of clones exist in cultivation. Leaves of each vary considerably in size and shape. A delightful, half-hardy variegated clone is perhaps as common as the type species in cultivation. Leaves are margined, splashed or completely cream-yellow, and the variegation

flushes pink in full sun. In all forms, leaves are often more scattered above. Two levels of dysploidy have been discovered: $n = 35$, and $n = 36$, but they are not geographically unique. Forms with narrower leaves are difficult to differentiate from other Japanese species.

HORTICULTURE. This stonecrop is only questionably hardy. It is best kept inside for the worst months. The variegated form is even more delicate, but I have successfully kept it outdoors, adjacent to the house for many winters. This species would make an ideal ground cover in warmer areas, reducing only somewhat in winter. Unfortunately, like all Oriental, creeping species, it tends to break up in autumn.

SEDUM NAGASAKIANUM
(Hara) Ohba

PLATE 34
SYNONYM: *S. alfredi* var. *nagasakianum* (Hance) Hara

Sedum nagasakianum has the appearance of a fairly typical Japanese sedum, but is more upright and has wider leaves than those of *S. lineare* and *S. sarmentosum*. It forms a low, fairly open, bushy plant to about 15 cm (6 in) high. Opposite at first, flat, lanceolate leaves are midway betwen those of *S. makinoi* and those of *S. sarmentosum* (Fig. 6.14). Flowers of midsummer are produced on simple or branched inflorescences. Plants are rare in cultivation, even in Japan, though they are easy to grow.

HABITAT. Kyushu, the most southerly of the large Japanese islands, is the home of this stonecrop.

MAIN POINTS OF DISTINCTION. Shape, size, and disposition of leaves are the best means of identification. Relatively acute apices of leaves immediately separate this species from *Sedum makinoi*, and width of leaves differentiates it from *S. sarmentosum*. Sessile flowers have unequal, free sepals without spurs, mucronate petals, and short stamens. Carpels are not particularly wide spreading.

VARIATION. Leaves are sometimes ternate be-

Figure 6.14. *Sedum nagasakianum* is best identified by the shape, size, and disposition of its leaves.

low and scattered above. $n = 62$, and possibly $n = 65$.

HORTICULTURE. This is only a half-hardy species; plants prefer shade and damper spots. They easily damp-off in warm, still winters in a greenhouse. *Sedum nagasakianum* would make a superb ground cover in warmer temperate zones. Its sprawling nature necessitates growing the species in hanging baskets in cooler areas.

SEDUM ONYCHOPETALUM
Fröderström

PLATE 34

Sedum onychopetalum is one of the few mainland Chinese species to survive in cultivation. It is vegetatively very similar to *S. rupifragum* but

smaller and even rarer (Fig. 6.15). In winter, much of the vegetation of the 8-cm (3-in) stems is reduced, and buds are formed at soil level. Spurred leaves are whorled on huge inflorescences of late summer. Floriferous stems are over 10 cm (4 in) long and carry numerous flowers on scorpioid branches.

HABITAT. This species is localized to the Nanking area, China, where it grows on cliffs.

MAIN POINTS OF DISTINCTION. Inflorescences are very large for such small plants. Petals are constricted in width at the base and ephemeral. Epipetalous stamens are inserted almost one-third up the petals. Long carpels have short, stout beaks.

VARIATION. Unknown.

HORTICULTURE. This stonecrop appears reasonably hardy. I have been reluctant to experiment due to its great rarity in cultivation.

SEDUM ORYZIFOLIUM Makino

PLATE 34

COMMON NAME: Taitōgome

Clones of *Sedum oryzifolium* can be difficult to separate from the range of *S. japonicum* clones in cultivation. At times differences seem too meager to be considered, and the plants seem to be one and the same species. Work by Uhl and Moran (1972), however, showed them to be cytologically distinct. *Sedum oryzifolium* has $n = 10$; *S. japonicum* has $n = 19$. Tomitara Makino (1891, 2) said of *S. oryzifolium*, "This plant grows near the sea; it resembles very much *S. japonicum*, but differs from it by its erect-patent follicles, shorter leaves, long creeping stems, sterile end of the main stem and flowering time." Not all these points are particularly helpful:

- "This plant grows near the sea" is most helpful to field botanists or enthusiasts who encounter plants in the wild, for *Sedum japonicum* is associated with hilly terrain, but it does not help a gardener to identify plants in the garden with any certainty.

Figure 6.15. *Sedum onychopetalum* in a 3-in (8-cm) pot.

- "Erect-patent follicles" is a contradiction in terms that refers to carpels as being only somewhat spreading. *Sedum japonicum* has widely spreading carpels, but differences between its carpels and those of *S. oryzifolium* are not particularly marked.
- "Shorter leaves" is a description with which I disagree completely. A giant form of *Sedum oryzifolium* from Jogashima Island has longer leaves than *S. japonicum*. In general, leaves of *S. oryzifolium* are more succulent, thicker, and wider than those of *S. japonicum*, and therefore they appear shorter with respect to girth.
- "Long, creeping stems" is probably the most useful aid to identification, but stems are only long and creeping after several seasons. *Sedum japonicum* tends to die back to its origin, though broken-off pieces root in the vicinity of the parent. *Sedum oryzifolium*, on the other hand, creeps, and roots as it creeps. After many seasons, its stems can be exceptionally long, with tufts rising at intervals as plants spread and form carpets.
- "Sterile end of the main stem" is fairly helpful with mature plants, but not with young cuttings. *Sedum japonicum* tends to flower at all stem tips (Fig. 6.12), and as inflorescences die back, new tufts are revealed below.

Sedum oryzifolium, if a large plant, has lots of sterile stems.
- "Flowering time" for *Sedum oryzifolium* is earlier in the wild, but this is most probably due to the species low-altitude, maritime habitat. In cultivation there is no marked difference between flowering time of the two species.

Upright, tufted stems carrying loose, spirally arranged, spurred leaves make *Sedum oryzifolium* very similar in appearance to some of the yellower forms of *S. album* from Europe. Both species change remarkably with site, although, at least three very distinct clones of *S. oryzifolium* are in cultivation.

HABITAT. This stonecrop is indigenous to coastal rocks of southern Honshu, Shikoku, and Kyushu islands of Japan and neighboring offshore Pacific islands.

MAIN POINTS OF DISTINCTION. *Sedum oryzifolium* sometimes produces eroded petals, an odd feature for the genus. Two-or three-branched inflorescences carry flowers with fairly upright, linear, terete sepals of equal length. The name suggests that leaves are like grains of rice. Compared to other Far Eastern species this is a reasonable guide, but leaves of some occidental species resemble rice grains more accurately.

VARIATION. A particularly eye-catching form from Jogashima Island off the Miura Peninsula is a large, sturdy, upright plant that tinges red in summer, especially on leaf margins. Looking at the blush closely, it is made up of a myriad of tiny wine red dots (Fig. 6.16). A form from Niijimar Island (160 km [100 miles] south-southwest of Tokyo Bay) is very similar.

An exceptionally minute form, which may in fact be a tiny form of *Sedum uniflorum* Hooker & Arnott (common name: Kogome-mannengusa), a closely related species, forms a dense mound of long stems and tiny leaves, which together turn bronze then wine red in a sunny spot. Flowers are often produced singly or in small numbers and again are often eroded. This form is far more common in Japan than elsewhere and is usually referred to in cultivation as *S. oryzifolium* 'Tiny Form' (Fig. 6.17).

If grown indoors, all forms become pale, creeping plants without upright tufts, and they lose their individual identity.

HORTICULTURE. Bright, pea-green leaves are very striking and similar, in many respects, to *Sedum acre*, except for shape. No forms of *S. oryzifolium*, unfortunately, are particularly hardy, but all are recommended for alpine collections despite their low-altitude origins. In drought conditions, plants sometimes act as annuals. In warm temperate lands, this species would be perfect for ground cover as it is dense and highly colorful. It is also ideal for growing between paving stones.

SEDUM POLYTRICHOIDES Hemsley

PLATE 34

SYNONYMS: *S. kiusianum* Makino, and apparently includes *S. yabeanum* Makino
COMMON NAMES: Unzen-mannengusa; Tsushima-mannengusa (for *S. yabeanum*)

Densely tufted stems of *Sedum polytrichoides* are very reminiscent of the European *S. rupestre* group. They are said to be somewhat upright in the wild, but become procumbent for me in cultivation (Fig. 6.18). Linear leaves turn deep purple, and dead leaves make lower stems shaggy. Summer inflorescences have few flowers. A very polymorphic species, Fröderström included the vegetatively contrasting *S. oryzifolium* in it. Uhl and Moran's findings (1972, 64), as a result of studying species of Korea and Japan, are very surprising:

> The species or complex most notable cytologically is *S. polytrichoides*. . . . The plants we include in this complex are fairly diverse; but chromosome number is very imperfectly correlated with morphology and distribution. . . . The best taxonomic treatment of this complex remains a problem . . . in view of the diversity of chromosome numbers . . . $n = 11$, $n = 12$, $n = 14$, $n = 16$, $n = 20$, $n = 21$, $n = 23$, $n = 24$, $n =$

Figure 6.16. *Sedum oryzifolium*; a bold form from Jogashima Island off the Miura Peninsula. Leaves are up to 1 cm (0.4 in) long.

Figure 6.17. *Sedum oryzifolium* 'Tiny Form' makes dense hummocks of copper foliage. Each leaf is about 4 mm (0.2 in) long.

25, $n = 26$, $n = 27$, $n = 35$, [and a number of oddities].

The plant described as "*S. kiusianum*," long thought to be synonymous with *S. polytrichoides*, is particularly narrow leaved; it is in cultivation in specialists' collections in Japan and the United States, but is still exceptionally rare in Europe. Wider- and flatter-leaved, more upright forms originally described as "*S. yabeanum*" are delightful, more floriferous, and vegetatively unlike the narrow-leaved forms (Fig. 6.19).

HABITAT. Kyushu Island, Japan, and Korea are the homes of this polymorphic species. In Korea, in particular, plants are mostly found at low altitudes, but up to 1200 m (3900 ft).

MAIN POINTS OF DISTINCTION. Two clones in cultivation have very contrasting leaf shapes. Sepals are equal, short, deltoid, not free, and not spurred. Epipetalous stamens are inserted some way from bases of petals, and are noticeably short. Carpels are only somewhat spreading.

VARIATION. Two highly contrasting clones are grown in the United States. Other intermediate forms could enter cultivation.

HORTICULTURE. I overestimated the hardiness of *Sedum kiusianum* 'Yabeanum' and lost a large stand one winter. The narrow-leaved forms are very difficult to perpetuate, even in a cold greenhouse, as plants like a lot of water.

SEDUM ROSULATOBULBOSUM Koidz.
S. BULBIFERUM Makino

PLATE 34

COMMON NAMES: Korai-ko-mochi-mannengusa; Ko-mochi-mannengusa

Sedum bulbiferum has been included with *S. alfredi* and *S. lineare* in the past, but together with *S. rosulatobulbosum* it is unique in disintegrating and casting a multitude of adventitious buds or bulbils to the wind. Uhl and Moran do not differentiate between these two species for cytolog-

Figure 6.18. *Sedum polytrichoides* in a 3-in (8-cm) pot.

Figure 6.19. *Sedum polytrichoides* 'Yabeanum'. Leaves are about 2 cm (0.8 in) long.

ically as well as vegetatively they have much in common. Dwellers of heavily shaded valleys in damp places, even on rocks in the middle of mountain rivulets, these oddities need special cultivation.

Stems rise to as much as 20 cm (8 in) high before flowering, producing copious quantities of bulbils, and then collapsing. In my experience, *Sedum rosulatobulbosum* is the most robust species with large adventitious bulbils, consisting of rosettes of almost-round leaves more than 1 cm (0. 4 in) across (Fig. 6.20). In addition, the species tends to be perennial with the main plant regenerating in spring.

Sedum bulbiferum is much smaller, with narrower leaves and tiny bulbils consisting of only a couple of pairs of opposite-decussate leaves. It tends to be annual or biennial. Makino says that in the wild all parent plants perish and that together these stonecrops are the most common in Japan. He says that only sterile seed is produced.

HABITAT. *Sedum rosulatobulbosum* is said to be Korean and from Hachijo Island in Izu Province of Japan, while *S. bulbiferum* is indigenous to Honshu, Shikoku, and Kyushu islands, Japan.

MAIN POINTS OF DISTINCTION. Plants are very similar to *Sedum* subtile, but the development of bulbils is unique to *S. rosulatobulbosum* and *S. bulbiferum*. In addition, stems of these species are very unusual for the genus as they are grooved in the upper part until they are almost square or hexagonal in section. Leaves are spurred. Lax, branched inflorescences carry flowers with unequal, free, spurred sepals, ephemeral petals, and somewhat divergent carpels.

VARIATION. Perhaps intermediate forms exist. Uhl and Moran show that both Korean and Japanese plants have $n = 19$ and that triploids exist in the wild.

HORTICULTURE. Fascinating perhaps, but these oddities are somewhat of an anathema to growers of xerophites or alpines. Perhaps the plants would benefit from being grown in a water garden or beside an artificial waterfall. I have never managed to perpetuate the minor of the two forms for more than consecutive seasons. Shade and damp conditions are essential, but plants soon rot if overwintered in an unventilated, damp environment.

Figure 6.20. *Sedum rosulatobulbosum* in a 5-in (13-cm) terra-cotta pot.

SEDUM RUPIFRAGUM Koidz

PLATES 34, 37

SYNONYM: *S. hakonense* var. *rupifragum* (Koidz) Ohwi

COMMON NAME: Ō-me-no-mannegusa

Usually an erect, tufted stonecrop, *Sedum rupifragum* grows to about 8 cm (3 in) high. Stems, particularly in winter, are topped with loose rosettes of bright, flat, quite narrow, elliptic, patent leaves (Plate 37). Leaves have a median groove on upper surfaces and are deflexed towards their tips. In summer, rosettes are less well-defined as stems elongate, and leaves are present on the upper two-thirds. Flowers in early summer are on 3-branched inflorescences.

HABITAT. This species is native to mountains of southern Honshu.

MAIN POINTS OF DISTINCTION. Three features are the best means of identification: rosettes in winter are very distinct, the neat upright nature of short stems, and the shape of leaves. Small, unequal, deltoid sepals are neither free nor spurred. $n = 68$.

VARIATION. Due to the limited range of this species in the wild, little variation is expected.

HORTICULTURE. The species is a very neat, slow to propagate, and almost always hardy in Mid Northumberland. It makes an excellent alpine plant for a shallow pan, but is equally beautiful in a rock garden, a raised bed, or a stone trough. It is one of the most refined species in the Far East group, but its diminutive nature necessitates that it be grown on an elevated site.

SEDUM SARMENTOSUM Bunge

PLATES 34, 38

COMMON NAME: Tsuru-mannengusa

Often found in parks or used as a ground cover, *Sedum sarmentosum* is probably the most common of the Oriental species in cultivation, if indeed it is a true species. Its type locality is reported to be near Peking, but it is so widespread, its origins are fogged. Known in cultivation long before it was formally described, it has escaped in North and Central America, Europe, and Asia. It is no pest for me, but in areas with milder winters it can become a weed. Uhl and Moran (1972, 65) stated "it can become a nuisance in a rock garden where it propagates itself by means of runners and broken bits of stem . . . [also] it usually displays considerable irregularity at meiosis." This explains why flowers are sterile and suggests that perhaps the plant is of hybrid origin.

Sedum sarmentosum is almost identical to *S. lineare*, but has wider, more succulent leaves. Rising, then creeping stems, with pale green, ternate leaves, can be exceptionally long if they are not checked by winter frosts. The plant is a rapid spreader, producing dense carpets of sterile stems that billow over trough edges, window boxes, and rock gardens. It is known to have medicinal properties.

HABITAT. The species is probably a very old garden hybrid.

MAIN POINTS OF DISTINCTION. Lanceolate leaves in threes on long decumbent stems are the best indicator for identification. Free sepals without spurs are nearly as long as petals. Epipetalous stamens are inserted some way from bases of petals. Unfortunately, this species was recently erroneously distributed by the International Succulent Institute as "*Sedum acutifolium.*"

VARIATION. Leaf color can vary from bright pea-green to bronze-green.

HORTICULTURE. Use *Sedum sarmentosum* cautiously in areas of mild winters for this bright, rapid ground cover can overrun choicer plants. As an accompaniment to a potted conifer, it tumbles out of the container, producing cascades of light green. It is excellent in a window box.

SEDUM SPECIES AFFIN. S. JAPONICUM RBGE 763791 Collected Taiwan

PLATE 34

Ron Evans believed this specimen to be a hitherto undescribed species when he received it from an expedition of the Royal Botanic Garden Edinburgh to Taiwan. He distributed it under the unpublished and therefore invalid name of *Sedum rubromucronatum*. Unfortunately, his untimely death prevented him from validating this suitable name. In many respects this stonecrop is similar to *S. japonicum*, but it tends to spread considerably more with the habit of *S. oryzifolium* (Fig. 6.21). It is more vigorous, resilient, and firm to touch than either of these species. Flower buds show bright red markings on petal tips—hence Evans's suggested name.

HABITAT. Original collections were made in Taiwan on rocks above the tree line, and notes emphasize that the plants are not epiphytes.

MAIN POINTS OF DISTINCTION. Until cytological work proves or disproves the relationship with *Sedum japonicum*, this specimen may be nothing more than an endemic form of an already described species. Red mucrons are very pronounced, though some tinges of red are occasionally observed on flowers of *S. japonicum*. Plants are very twiggy to touch and certainly do

not feel soft and succulent like *S. japonicum*. Wiry, almost woody stems are very reluctant to root from cuttings. Leaves are thin and flat on both faces. Small, free, fairly equal sepals are deltoid. Stamens are long and carpels become patent.

VARIATION. All plants in cultivation have been propagated from one clone.

HORTICULTURE. Plants are fully hardy at Edinburgh where, in a few years, a delightful patch of medium green, upright, tufted heads was produced, covered with bright orange-yellow flowers in midsummer.

SEDUM SUBTILE Maximowicz
S. ZENTARO-TASHIROI Makino

PLATE 34

COMMON NAMES: Hime-renge; Ko-mannengusa

Closely related, *Sedum subtile* and *S. zentaro-tashiroi* have at times been considered synonymous, but Uhl and Moran (1972) showed the former to

Figure 6.21. *Sedum* species RBGE 763791 from Taiwan.

have $n = 28$ and the latter to have $n = 17$. Both are light green, slender, fairly feeble species. Spathulate leaves of *S. subtile* are opposite and more obovate, while longer leaves, in whorls of 4 (verticillate), are carried on inflorescences of *S. zentaro-tashiroi*. Otherwise, the two species are similar vegetatively.

Although both species are made synonymous with *S. lineare* by Fröderström, vegetatively they are not even vaguely similar (Fig. 6.22). Both are rare in cultivation.

HABITAT. Honshu, Shikoku, and Kyushu islands, Japan, are the homes of *Sedum subtile*, usually on mossy rocks in shaded spots in mountain forests. *Sedum zentaro-tashiroi* is endemic to Tsushima Island.

MAIN POINTS OF DISTINCTION. Leaf shape and arrangement, particularly on inflorescences, are helpful guides to separate the two species that are invariably feeble plants. Narrow sepals are long, free, and unequal, but not spurred. Petals are ephemeral, stamens are short, and carpels are only vaguely spreading.

VARIATION. Leaves of *Sedum subtile* are often alternate on inflorescences, and can be whorled in 3s or 5s in *S. zentaro-tashiroi*.

HORTICULTURE. Both species demand shady spots, regular water, and good drainage without extreme temperatures. Neither is of horticultural importance, but both are bright green subjects for a shady spot.

SEDUM TECTRACTINUM Fröderström

PLATE 34

For several years, a rising then creeping plant has been distributed as "affin. *Sedum makinoi* from China." Opposite, ternate or alternate shiny leaves are orbicular-spathulate and somewhat petiolate. For several seasons I was unsure whether this stonecrop was *S. bracteatum* Diels or *S. tetractinum*. The two species are closely related, but the latter has 4-partite flowers. My specimen produced only 4-partite flowers in its first season, but the following season, only central flowers of the forks of scorpioid branches were consistently

Figure 6.22. *Sedum subtile*; winter rosettes in a 3.5-in (9-cm) square pot.

4-partite; others were often 5-partite. The clone in cultivation deviates from the original description of *S. tetractinum* in that leaves are said to be mammillate in the upper part. I have failed to observe such a feature in my plant, but plants in cultivation appear nearer *S. tetractinum* than any other described species.

HABITAT. This Chinese stonecrop is from the Hunan-Kwangtung border from 700 to 900 m (2300 to 3000 ft).

MAIN POINTS OF DISTINCTION. Orbicular, petiolate leaves, and 4-partite flowers are a unique combination (Fig. 6.23).

VARIATION. Only a single clone appears to have been very widely distributed among enthusiasts.

HORTICULTURE. I have not tried growing this species outdoors but imagine it to be of similar hardiness to *Sedum makinoi*. It makes quite a dense, interesting ground cover, and is an excellent subject for hanging baskets, window boxes, or edges of stone troughs.

SEDUM TOSAENSE Makino

PLATE 34

COMMON NAME: Yahazu-mannengusa

Sedum tosaense is exceptionally rare in cultivation even in Japan (Fig. 6.24). Upright stems to 18 cm (7 in) high carry alternate, spathulate, fleshy, rounded, and somewhat retuse leaves. Uhl and Moran did not accept *S. tosaense* as a distinct species, but they accepted *S. tricarpum* Makino (common name: takane-mannengusa), which vegetatively is very similar. On two occasions I have been given cuttings purporting to be *S. tricarpum*, but as the name suggests, the very distinct feature of *S. tricarpum* Makino is that it has only 3 carpels per flower, even though 5 petals are present. Thus, the normal 5-partite flowers that grew on my cuttings showed them to be *S. tosaense*.

HABITAT. Tosa is a province of Shikoku.

MAIN POINTS OF DISTINCTION. Leaf shape and arrangement will help identification, but the species is not very distinct. Sepals are fairly equal, upright, and spathulate, and anthers tinge red. Carpels are wide spreading.

VARIATION. Variation seems unlikely.

HORTICULTURE. *Sedum tosaense* is not particularly succulent nor is it hardy. It is somewhat gangling and of little horticultural merit, but it is bright and cheerful.

Figure 6.23. *Sedum tetractinum* creeping over the edge of a 12-in (31-cm) container.

Figure 6.24. *Sedum tosaense* in a 6-in (15-cm) pan.

CHAPTER 7

Eurasian Oddities of Subgenus Sedum and Related Rosularia

This chapter presents seven genera whose member species are often included with *Sedum*. These Eurasian oddities have a single feature anomalous in *Sedum*, but in most respects have much in common and are best considered part of the cosmopolitan genus (see "Natural Groups of Stonecrops" in Chapter 4). In this volume, six genera are treated as groups within *Sedum*:

GROUP	SPECIES
Meterostachys	*Sedum leveilleanum* Hamet
Mucizonia	*Sedum mucizonia* (Ortega) Hamet
Orostachys	*Sedum aggregeatum* (Makino) Makino
	Sedum boehmeri (Makino) Makino
	Sedum chanetii (Léveillé) Berger
	Sedum erubescens (Maximowicz) Ohwi
	Sedum furusei (Ohwi) Ohwi

GROUP	SPECIES
	Sedum iwarenge (Makino) Makino
	Sedum limuloides Praeger
	Sedum spinosum (L.) Willldenow
Prometheum	*Sedum pilosum* Marschall von Bieberstein
	Sedum sempervivoides Fischer ex Marschall von Bieberstein
Pseudosedum	*Sedum multicaule* Lindley
Sinocrassula	*Sedum indicum* (Decaisne) Hamet

In addition to these six genera within subgenus *Sedum*, one borderline species of *Rosularia*, which is more generally labelled "sedum," is included with the Eurasian oddities, as is *S. adenotrichum* Wallich ex Edgeworth, although the latter is often included within the genus *Rosularia*.

METEROSTACHYS GROUP

Meterostachys group comprises a single species with open cymes of flowers, each with connate petals.

SEDUM LEVEILLEANUM Hamet

SYNONYMS: *Sedum sikokianum* (Makino) Hamet, *Cotyledon sikokiana* Makino, *Meterostachys sikokianus* (Makino) Nakai

From a short, fleshy rootstock, dense tufts of linear, almost terete, apiculate leaves form overwintering rosettes (Fig. 7.1). In summer, stems rise with leaves less clustered and often ternate below but opposite above. Lax cymes of pink-white flowers are produced in autumn. The species is exceptionally rare in cultivation except in Japan.

HABITAT. *Sedum leveilleanum* is indigenous to Cheju-do, western Honshu, Shikoku, Kyushu, and mountains of Korea at 650 to 1500 m (2130 to 4900 ft).

MAIN POINTS OF DISTINCTION. Fusion of petals to almost half their length immediately differentiates this species from any *Orostachys* species, although vegetatively there is a resemblance, especially in winter when rosettes are dormant. Carpels are like those of subgenus *Sedum* rather than those of *Orostachys* group. Stamens are inserted near the top of the floral tube at about the level petals become free. $n = 16$.

VARIATION. I have never been able to grow lush plants matching those shown in habitat photographs.

HORTICULTURE. As the habitat has a monsoon maritime climate, low winter temperatures should not be too prolonged, moisture should be frequently applied, and drainage should be good. Unfortunately, plants have always acted

Figure 7.1. *Sedum leveilleanum* in a 2.5-in (6-cm) pot.

as annuals for me; perhaps I have been overly cautious and kept them too dry.

MUCIZONIA GROUP

Mucizonia group was associated with the genus *Cotyledon* for a long time and then with the genus *Umbilicus*; all three have well-developed floral tubes. Only the fusion of petals in *Mucizonia* group sets it apart from subgenus *Sedum*. I found young members of *Mucizonia* group growing alongside *Sedum* species in the Sierra da Arrábida, Portugal, and until they flowered, took them to be *S. rubens*. Apart from a few short, bristlelike hairs, young plants are indistinguishable vegetatively from *Sedum* proper. Recent cytological studies seem to point toward a very close affinity between the two genera so I include *Mucizonia* as a group within *Sedum*. Only one species is in cultivation.

SEDUM MUCIZONIA
(Ortega) Hamet

PLATE 39

SYNONYMS: *Cotyledon mucizonia* Ortega,
Umbilicus hispidus De Candolle [nom. illeg.],
Mucizonia hispida (Lamarck) Berger

In spring, tight clusters of turgid, gray-green leaves hide stems. Sometimes by this stage, short bristles can be seen on leaves, but these become more apparent as stems elongate. Flower buds

are exceptionally bristly, and distinctly tubed flowers are produced in summer. At first they appear white-pink, but throats soon flush yellow. Some forms of this species can act as perennials if treatment is perfect. By late summer, stems elongate and leaves shrivel, so plants are lax and soon desiccate.

HABITAT. Southern Iberia, Algeria, and Morocco are the homes of this delightful stonecrop, from sea level to fairly high altitudes in the south, especially on rocky scree or solid limestone, in half-shaded nooks.

MAIN POINTS OF DISTINCTION. Branching only takes place at the very base of the plant. Bristles on buds, the hirsute nature of the stems, and tubed flowers are good indicators. Fusion of petals is the most easily observed feature. Fused for much more than half their length, they form a floral tube which is very pronounced.

VARIATION. Sometimes North African variations enter cultivation, but they tend not to be perpetuated.

HORTICULTURE. Treat the species as an annual, but, as seed tends to germinate in autumn, either (1) allow self-seeding and remove the container from frosty conditions to overwinter in an alpine house, or (2) save the seed to sow in spring.

OROSTACHYS GROUP

Carpels of *Orostachys* group are identical to those of subgenus *Hylotelephium*, so, if the former is beyond the boundaries of *Sedum*, then *Hylotelephium* should also be beyond its boundaries. As inflorescences of *Orostachys* group are in most instances extreme for the genus *Sedum*, *Orostachys* forms a natural group. Despite the stipitate carpels of both subgenus *Hylotelephium* and *Orostachys* group and the elongated inflorescence of the latter, some botanists prefer to keep both within *Sedum* rather than as separate genera.

Orostachys is a natural group of rosetted species rising from feeble root systems, having typically very congested, elongated spikes of sedumlike flowers. Spurless leaves are flat to terete, with all stages between. They are sometimes sharply apiculate but can be blunt. Overwintering rosettes are often surrounded by a protective mass of dead leaves resembling onionskins. Inflorescences are terminal, and, where species do not propagate vegetatively via stolons, plants act as annuals. In recent years, there has been a terrific surge of interest in these fascinating alpines especially by lovers of *Sempervivum*, though species of *Orostachys* group tend not to be so easy to overwinter.

Much hybridization has been done in cultivation, a lot of it haphazard in nature, with the result that stronger, more eye-catching strains have been produced, but most are of debatable parentage. More desirable named hybrids that unite the large features of the annual species with the ability to be vegetatively propagated will soon be available in the trade. *Sedum* 'Bountiful' by Ed Skrocki of Ohio is a strong plant that lives up to its name (Fig. 7.2). Ed has produced many eye-catching hybrids, and the demand for such attractive plants has grown immensely in recent years. 'Yatsugashira' is a much slower, miniature Japanese introduction (Fig. 7.3).

Eastern Asia is the main habitat for group *Orostachys*—though some species extend through central Asia, north of the Himalayas, but not beyond the Aral Sea. Species inhabit sites from sea level in Japan to 4400 m (14,400 ft) in Mongolia.

All species in cultivation are rosetted except for rapidly grown annuals, which go from seed-

Figure 7.2. *Sedum* 'Bountiful'.

Figure 7.3. *Sedum* 'Yatsugashira'.

ling to flowering stage rather quickly. Ortho-carpic flowers have stipitate or attenuate carpels as do plants of subgenus *Hylotelephium*. In general, individual flowers are produced horizontally on lupinlike spikes that are produced very late in the year.

SEDUM AGGREGEATUM Makino

SYNONYMS: *Cotyledon aggregeata* Makino, *Cotyledon malacophylla* (Pallas) Fischer, *Orostachys aggregeatus* (Makino) Hara
COMMON NAMES: Ao-no-iwarenge, ko-iwa-renge

SEDUM BOEHMERI

PLATE 40
SYNONYMS: *Cotyledon boehmeri* Makino, *Orostachys boehmeri* (Makino) Hara
COMMON NAME: Ko-mochi-renge

Often *Sedum boehmeri* is considered a variety of *S. aggregeatum*, and unless viewed side-by-side, the two species are very difficult to distinguish. Both are shiny, glabrous species with rosettes about 4 cm (2 in) in diameter. Both produce copious stolons, which, from above, resemble spokes of a wheel. In this way, if conditions are right, the two species can produce open carpets of light green rosettes. All leaves are flat: inner ones cupped, more upright, and more apiculate; outer leaves are spreading and more rounded. Both species have short, wide-based pyramids of densely clustered white flowers. Flowers have barely connate, long, thin petals that spread fully. Plants in flower in October or November are startlingly beautiful. Contrasting anthers are dark red. In winter, conical buds of rosettes close, and outer leaves dry to form a protective coat of dead leaves resembling onionskins.

Sedum boehmeri has long, stout stolons that appear from below rosettes (Fig. 7.4). *Sedum aggregeatum* has shorter stolons, which are produced from between leaves of rosettes (Fig. 7.5).

Figure 7.4. The true *Sedum boehmeri*. Glabrous, succulent rosettes are about 2 cm (0.8 in) across.

The latter species is the one that gardeners are most likely to encounter, and it is the most hardy in the group *Orostachys*.

HABITAT. *Sedum aggregeatum* is a littoral species from the Pacific side of Honshu island, Japan. *Sedum boehmeri* is also a littoral species but from western Hokkaido and Honshu islands.

MAIN POINTS OF DISTINCTION. Small, green, flat, blunt, shiny leaves, prolific production of stolons, and young rosettes never appearing as though leaves are opposite-decussate are the best distinguishing points.

VARIATION. Variation exists in the wild, and several forms of each species are in cultivation. Unfortunately, a widely distributed glaucous clone of *Orostachys* group, bearing the name *Sedum boehmeri*, is more common in cultivation than the true species. The impostor could be a form or a hybrid of *S. furusei*. Ohba (1981a) referred to the presence of such glaucous forms with blunt leaves, but the type species is said to

be shiny green. I propose 'Keiko' as the name for the very beautiful glaucous form now quite well-known in cultivation; to date it has merely been labelled "powdery form" (Plate 40).

HORTICULTURE. Even these maritime species appear to be fully hardy if dry. They are best left in an airy, dry, light position. I find that they often decide not to flower till late November or after, by which time I am no longer watering them, and therefore growth is curtailed. Excellent drainage is essential.

SEDUM CHANETII
(Léveillé) Berger

SYNONYMS: *S. pyramidalis* Praeger,
Orostachys chanetii (Léveillé) Berger
COMMON NAME: Pe-tche-li

Small rosettes only 2 cm (0.8 in) across have leaves of two lengths, as do plants of *Sedum spinosum*. Outer leaves are almost terete and lin-

Figure 7.5. *Sedum aggregeatum* in a 3-in (8-cm) pot.

ear, half spreading, and tipped with long, soft spines. Leaves in the center of rosettes are short and so densely packed that they feel a solid mass. The overall effect is that rosettes resemble half-open daisy flowers. A flower spike is tall and narrow throughout its length, cylindrical in shape rather than conical (Fig. 7.6).

Individual flowers are white with only a hint of fusion at the bases of petals. In cultivation, plants can often be frustratingly monocarpic, but once established, offsetting, on very short stolons, can be expected.

Figure 7.6. *Sedum chaneti* in flower in late October in a 2.5-in (6-cm) pot.

HABITAT. *Sedum chanetii* comes from Kansu Province, China, near the Mongolian border at 1800 to 2500 m (5900 to 8200 ft), but is commonly found growing on pagoda roofs and even on the thatch of dwellings on coastal plains of China. Plants may have been introduced by humans or they may have spontaneously generated as a result of bird migration.

MAIN POINTS OF DISTINCTION. Terete leaves of two distinct lengths and tall, narrow inflorescences are the best distinguishing features.

VARIATION. Grown lushy, plants turn glaucous green, but in full sun they are lilac-gray.

HORTICULTURE. Do not be too generous at first by giving away offsets, as the over-floriferous nature of this species could leave you with only a hope of setting seed.

SEDUM ERUBESCENS
(Maximowicz) Ohwi

PLATE 41

SYNONYMS: *Umbilicus erubescens* Maximowicz,
Cotyledon erubescens Franchet & Savatier,
Orostachys erubescens Maximowicz
COMMON NAME: Tsume-renge

Often *Sedum erubescens* is included with *S. spinosum*, but geographically it is more easterly. Dense rosettes (6 cm/2 in across) of linear-lanceolate, succulent leaves appear midway between those species with terete leaves and those with flat leaves. Leaf apices have a short, soft spine tip and often several teeth. Solitary, terminal spikes of white flowers are short and often half as wide as high. Anthers are dark purple. A few offsets are produced, but often inflorescences outnumber new growth.

HABITAT. This species is from rocky, dry slopes of the three southern Japanese islands, northern China, adjacent parts of the former Soviet Union, and Korea.

MAIN POINTS OF DISTINCTION. Leaves have a broad base, are very succulent and only slightly flattened. Flower spikes are short.

VARIATION. *Sedum erubescens* var. *japonicum* (Maximowicz) Ohwi is a more narrow-leafed, softer-to-the-touch form from rocky coastlines of Honshu. It tends to be very floriferous, often with secondary flowering branches that have tall spikes of flowers. Invariably it flowers itself to death. Many other regional variations show beautiful glaucous colors. A striking form from Tschuchima district, Japan, starts the season glaucous-purple but ends up glaucous-orange (Plate 41).

HORTICULTURE. Despite its lowland origins, this is a dynamic plant for the alpine enthusiast though it is still rare in cultivation.

SEDUM FURUSEI (Ohwi) Ohwi

PLATE 42

SYNONYM: *Orostachys furusei* Ohwi
COMMON NAME: Rebun-iwa-renge

Glaucous rosettes can be gray, blue, or violet, and appear, when young, to be made up of opposite-decussate pairs of leaves (Plate 42). Rosettes often remain sterile for several seasons and offsets are produced regularly. Leaves are not dimorphic, but gradually grade from outer ones to inner ones. They are flat, entire, and almost rounded. Spikes have many bracts. Green-white flowers have upright petals and very long, upright sepals.

HABITAT. This is a littoral species from Rebun and Hokkaido islands, Japan.

MAIN POINTS OF DISTINCTION. Young, almost pruinose rosettes with opposite-decussate flat, rounded leaves are a good indicator.

VARIATION. A beautiful hybrid, *O. furusei* × *O. aggregeatus* 'Noordwijk', was created by Ben Zonnevelt of the Netherlands. *Sedum furusei* 'Showa', a Japanese cultivar, appears to be of similar parentage.

HORTICULTURE. This tiny, delightful species is a choice plant for alpine collections. It requires frequent watering and perfect drainage.

SEDUM IWARENGE
(Makino) Makino

SYNONYMS: *Cotyledon iwarenge* Makino, *Orostachys iwarenge* (Makino) Hara, *Cotyledon malacophylla* var. *japonica* Franchet & Savatier
COMMON NAME: Iwa-renge.

This species has very large, open rosettes to 20 cm (8 in) across. It is always an annual or biennial, never naturally producing offsets. Fleshy, flat leaves are oblong-spathulate, rounded at apices, and glaucous. Huge pyramids of white flowers in October are spectacular.

HABITAT. *Sedum iwarenge* is thought to be from China, but plants are commonly found on Japanese rooftops.

MAIN POINTS OF DISTINCTION. Rosettes are very large and never offset naturally. Leaves are thin, floppy, and obtuse.

VARIATION. *Sedum iwarenge* 'Fuji' is a beautiful variegated form. *Sedum iwarenge* 'Natsu Fuji' is a spontaneous mutation of *S. iwarenge* 'Fuji' with light median stripes and green margins. Both cultivars have been distributed by the International Succulent Institute and should soon become more widely available.

HORTICULTURE. Ben Zonneveld suggests that the best way to propagate this species is to behead the mother plant before the longest day of the year; this induces offsetting.

SEDUM LIMULOIDES Praeger

SYNONYMS: *Cotyledon fimbriata* Turczaninow, *Umbilicus ramosissimus* Maximowicz, *Sedum ramosissimum* (Maximowicz) Franchet, *Orostachys fimbriatus* (Turczaninow) Berger

Leaves of *Sedum limuloides* are broadly linear, tapering gradually, and tipped with a long, soft, narrow spine that broadens at the base to fuse with a half-moon shaped, dentate cartilage (a hard, white, tough membrane) (Fig. 7.7). A dense spike of white flowers often has secondary spikes. The species is exceptionally rare in cultivation, but was recently distributed by the International Succulent Institute as *Orostachys fimbriata* [sic]. This collection was propagated from cuttings of a plant collected from a tiled rooftop in China.

HABITAT. This species is native to Mongolia, Sichuan Province, China, and adjacent Siberia in the former Soviet Union, on stony soils in open steppe at about 1000 m (3000 ft) elevation.

MAIN POINTS OF DISTINCTION. It is difficult to differentiate this species from some forms of *Sedum erubescens*, but inflorecences are 15 cm (6 in) tall and flowers have long pedicels, especially in the lower part of the inflorescence.

VARIATION. No data available.

HORTICULTURE. Few offsets on short stolons suggest this species will always be in short supply. The plant is highly recommended for the alpine house.

Figure 7.7. *Sedum limuloides* in a 2.5-in (6-cm) pot.

SEDUM SPINOSUM (L.) Willdenow

SYNONYMS: *Sempervivum cuspidatum* Haworth, *Umbilicus spinosus* De Candolle, *Cotyledon minuta* Komarov, *Orostachys spinosus* (L.) Berger

Sedum spinosum, a common plant in succulent collections, has distinctly dimorphic leaves (Fig. 7.8). Outer leaves spread, are banded with a white cartilage, and are tipped with a long, soft, narrow spine. Inner leaves, in contrast, are short and crowded, giving the appearance of a green, shining sunflower. To my knowledge, this species has never flowered in cultivation, but its petals are said to be yellowish.

HABITAT. This stonecrop is indigenous to the Pamir Mountains, Kashmir, through Xizang to Mongolia and north China, on open, stony and gravelly slopes and on rock crevices in steppe grassland. It also grows in glades or on edges of more wooded areas.

MAIN POINTS OF DISTINCTION. Dimorphic, succulent leaves form distinctive flat rosettes on this well-known, easily identified species.

VARIATION. *Sedum spinosum* var. *minutum* comb. nov. (syn. *Orostachys minutus* [Komorov] Berger) is a tiny form across from Korea and China with rosettes never more than 2 cm (0.8 in).

Sedum spinosum var. *thrysiflorum* (Fischer) Fröderström (syn. *Orostachys thrysiflorus* Fischer) is probably in cultivation and appears to be closely related to *S. limuloides* (Fig. 7.9). It is a biennial with light green leaves and long stamens. Native to the former Soviet Union, with suggestions that it may be found as far west as the Urals, it is more likely to be found in southern Siberia and the Altai Mountains.

HORTICULTURE. This species invariably rots if watered from above in late summer, especially if plants are kept indoors or behind glass. A well-ventilated site is needed throughout the year. Because it is generous with offsets on short stolons, it is a popular succulent and a superb alpine specimen plant.

Figure 7.8. *Sedum spinosum* in a 2.5-in (6-cm) pot.

Figure 7.9. *Sedum spinosum* var. *thrysiflorum* coming into bud in September in a 3.5-in (9-cm) pot.

PROMETHEUM GROUP

Prometheum group comprises two hirsute, monocarpic biennials from the southwestern part of the former Soviet Union. Both are the joy of alpine enthusiasts.

SEDUM PILOSUM
Marschall von Bieberstein

PLATE 43

SYNONYMS: *Cotyledon pubescens* Meyer, *Umbilicus pubescens* (Meyer) Ledebour, *Rosularia pilosa* (Marschall von Bieberstein) Borissova, *Prometheum pilosum* (Marschall von Bieberstein) Ohba

Sedum pilosum is a delightful rosetted species, vegetatively not unlike a small, hirsute *Sempervivum* species. Single rosettes are no more than a couple of centimeters (1 in) across in the first year. In the second year, a broad, lax inflorescence carries light pink-violet flowers with petals connate for about 1 mm (0.04 in), and upright in their lower two-thirds.

HABITAT. This species is native to the central and south Caucasus Mountains on stony locations.

MAIN POINTS OF DISTINCTION. Densely hairy rosettes are similar to those of *Sedum tymphaeum*, but the upright petals of *S. pilosum* make identification easy.

VARIATION. Sometimes a rosette offsets and forms several heads, but plants do not perenniate because all rosettes flower the following season. Damage to a growing point can induce dichotomous growth or even multiple heads.

HORTICULTURE. Save seed before it is dispersed and sow it in rough gravel on a coarse compost. Always give plants adequate ventilation. This alpine is very highly prized.

SEDUM SEMPERVIVOIDES Fischer ex Marschall von Bieberstein

PLATE 44

SYNONYMS: *Umbilicus platyphyllus* Ledebour, *Rosularia sempervivoides* (Fischer ex Marschall von Bieberstein) Borissova, *Prometheum sempervivoides* (Fischer ex Marschall von Bieberstein) Ohba

Sedum sempervivoides is a great favorite of alpine enthusiasts, forming flat *Sempervivum*-like, hirsute rosettes to 10 cm (4 in) across. In the second year, tall monocarpic inflorescences to 30 cm (12 in) high carry so many blood-red flowers they often need artificial support. Every part of each plant is hairy except the roots.

HABITAT. This stonecrop is found on dry, stony slopes in the subalpine Caucasus Mountains from 1800 to 2000 m (5900 to 7000 ft), mainly in the Armenian South Transcaucasus Range.

MAIN POINTS OF DISTINCTION. Flat, hairy rosettes are unique. Bright crimson-red petals are vaguely connate, upright in the lower portion, and a superb contrast to light yellow anthers. Carpels, petals, and sepals are hairy.

VARIATION. None noticed except due to situation.

HORTICULTURE. Inflorescences must be picked and stored before carpels dehisce and seeds are lost. Seeds should be planted in an airy place as seedlings damp-off easily. Plants do not enjoy being transplanted, but can self-seed generously in a sharp gravel scree. This is a top-notch alpine.

PSEUDOSEDUM GROUP

The *Pseudosedum* group of perennials has thickened rootstocks with scaly leaves on stem bases and erect, annual flowering stems. Kyphocarpic flowers are produced on dense, hemispherical corymbs. Only one species appears to be in cultivation.

SEDUM MULTICAULE Lindley

SYNONYMS: *S. mekongense* Praeger,
Umbilicus multicaulis Boissier & Buhse,
Pseudosedum multicaule (Lindley) Borisova

From a somewhat thickened rootstock, 15-cm (6-in) long stems rise, and dead stems persist for several seasons. Annual stems of *Sedum multicaule* are densely leafy for the first season with subterete, linear leaves that have broad bases. Kyphocarpic, 6-partite, campanulate, pink flowers with distinctly upright petals fused in the lower half are produced in early summer.

HABITAT. This is a fairly widespread species from northern Iran and central Asia, especially the Kopet Dagh Range from 1500 to 2500 m (4900 to 8200 ft) on mountain steppe, and as far as upper Burma.

MAIN POINTS OF DISTINCTION. Small caudex and upward-pointing, campanulate flowers with kyphocarpic fruit are an unusual combination of features for genus *Sedum*.

VARIATION. With such a large range, variation can be expected. I have only observed a single specimen (Fig. 7.10).

HORTICULTURE. This species needs the protection of a cool alpine house.

Figure 7.10. *Sedum multicaule* in a 5-in (13-cm) terracotta pot. This plant was collected by the Royal Botanic Garden Edinburgh, Himalayan Expedition.

SINOCRASSULA GROUP

Sinocrassula group comprises one or perhaps two variable rosetted species with easily detached leaves and monocarpic inflorescences. A key identifying feature is that all flowers have one whorl of stamens. Several varieties of *Sedum indicum* are in cultivation.

SEDUM INDICUM
(Decaisne) Hamet

PLATE 45

SYNONYMS: *Crassula indica* Decaisne, *Crassula yunnanensis* Franchet, *Sedum ambiguum* Praeger,

Sempervivum multiflorum Jaquemont, *Sinocrassula densirosulata* (Praeger) Berger, *Sinocrassula indica* Berger, *Sinocrassula yunnanensis* (Franchet) Berger

Two distinct forms of *Sedum indicum* are often seen in cultivation as part of mixed bowls of succulents or as unnamed potted plants for a windowsill. A third, which has recently been introduced from Japanese horticulture, appears to be a form of the type species. Apiculate, succulent leaves are very easily detached from rosettes and soon generate new plants.

HABITAT. Found from Nepal to Yunnan and

Sichuan provinces of western China, this species grows at an altitude of 1800 to 3200 m (5900 to 10,500 ft).

MAIN POINTS OF DISTINCTION. Flowers only have a single whorl of stamens, alternate with, and arranged between, petals. Flowers are urceolate (pitcher-shaped). Leaves form relatively dense rosettes at ground level, and terminal inflorescences carry flowers with free petals.

VARIATION. *Sedum indicum* var. *indicum* has flowers tipped pink and light blue-green leaves (Fig. 7.11). The form is very rare in cultivation, except in Japan.

Sedum indicum var. *densirosulatum* Praeger [syn. *S. ambiguum* Praeger, *Sinocrassula densirosulata* (Praeger) Berger] has leaves that are heavily mottled with tiny brown-red intricate markings (Fig. 7.12). Yellow-green petals have a peculiar

Figure 7.11. *Sedum indicum* in bud in August. The longest leaves measure 2.8 cm (1.1 in) long.

Figure 7.12. *Sedum indicum* var. *densirosulatum* is similar in size to the type species.

appendage, and often, because of this feature, this variety is considered a separate species (i.e., *S. ambiguum*). For reasons unknown, this variety was once widely distributed as *Lenophyllum maculatum*. Haplostemonous flowers with odd petals makes differentiation from *Lenophyllum* easy.

Sedum indicum var. *yunnanense* Hamet [syn. *Crassula yunnanensis* Franchet, *Sinocrassula yunnanensis* (Franchet) Berger] has almost-terete, apiculate, felty leaves that turn black in full sun (Plate 45). Flowers are light yellowish, but they can flush orange-red in full sun. The variety is hardy in Mid Northumberland in all but the coldest winters, if given overhead protection from drenching. A nonhardy cristate form is said to be in cultivation.

HORTICULTURE. These plants thrive on neglect. Beautiful specimens can be grown on a shady windowsill, and infrequent water deters the formation of inflorescences, which in turn results in compact plants with delicate markings of picture-perfect rosettes. Given kinder treatment, plants form many inflorescences, and rosettes disintegrate into a pile of leaves, making the remaining plant look rather untidy.

ROSULARIA SPECIES

Rosularia species are rosetted plants very closely related to *Sedum*. I have retained *Rosularia hirsuta* as a *Sedum* species because of its very close relationship to North African forms of *S. dasyphyllum* and its habitat, considerably west of other *Rosularia* species.

Ethel Blatter described two sedums from Kashmir that are often considered synonymous: *Sedum adenotrichum* and *S. rosulatum*. Some plants bearing the former name have stellate flowers and seem to bridge the genera *Rosularia* and *Sedum*. Plants in collections are invariably labelled as belonging to *Sedum* and have flowers very similar to countless species of *Sedum*. Thus, for the sake of integrality, I have decided to include this species with *Sedum*.

SEDUM ADENOTRICHUM
Wallich ex Edgeworth

SYNONYMS: *S. rosulatum* Edgeworth, *Cotyledon papillosa* Aichison & Hemsley, *Umbilicus papillosus* (Aichison) Boissier, *Rosularia adenotricha* (Wallich & Edgeworth) Jansson

One form of *Sedum adenotrichum* from Anapurna, labelled *Rosularia adenotricha* at the Royal Botanic Garden Edinburgh, Scotland, has very large hirsute rosettes and cupped flowers. No one would quarrel about its *Rosularia*-like qualities. A second plant, distributed by the International Succulent Institute(I.S.I.) as *Sedum rosulatum*, is often sold in the United Kingdom as *S. nevii*. It certainly resembles the North American sedums with its thick, creeping stems and compact rosettes, but differs as it is downy and has flowers with slightly connate petals that are erect at the base. The form originally distributed by the I.S.I. as *S. adenotrichum* is an almost-glabrous form with flat rosettes, fine creeping stolons, completely free and spreading white petals, and rosettes that turn bright red in full sun. Such forms of this species will continue to be a bone of contention between taxonomists.

HABITAT. This polymorphic species is from Kashmir province, India to Kumaon Province, China, from 900 m to 2450 m (3000 ft to 8040 ft).

MAIN POINTS OF DISTINCTION. Grown outdoors, low rosettes of flat, petiolate leaves are no more than 3 cm (1 in) across. Lax lateral inflorescences of early summer are spindly and drooped in bud. Petals are erect at first but eventually spread, their bases remaining somewhat erect. Sepals are very pubescent, and fine hairs can be found on inflorescences. Weak, spindly inflorescences separate *Sedum adenotrichum* from similar-looking North American species. Vegetatively *S. adenotrichum* has much in common with the European *S. fragrans*.

VARIATION. Forms of *Sedum*-like plants that are unquestionably referrable to *Rosularia* make up this species. If *Rosularia* is accepted as a genus, and not just a section of *Sedum*, then geographically this species in all its forms is better referred to *Rosularia*.

HORTICULTURE. All forms can withstand very low temperatures, if dry.

CHAPTER 8

African Species of Subgenus Sedum

Only a handful of African *Sedum* species exist. Five species are endemic to the Macronesian Islands (better known as Islands of the Atlantic), in this instance, the Canaries and Madeiran group. A number of ephemerals are indigenous to North Africa, especially the Atlas Mountains area, but only one endemic perennial species is in cultivation and that is *S. multiceps*. Several species have been described from the Great East African Rift Valley, Ethiopian Highlands, and to alpine peaks just south of the equator. Only *S. ruwenzoriense* is in cultivation from East Africa though a plant carrying the label "*Sedum crassularia*" is often seen in the United Kingdom. The latter name is valid, but very old, relating to a form of *Crassula milfordae*, which is hardy and small, forming dense mats of tiny rosettes. Its exceptionally small flowers have only single whorls of stamens, betraying the plants true identity.

The following species are in cultivation:

MACRONESIAN ISLAND SPECIES
Sedum brissemoreti Hamet
Sedum farinosum Lowe
Sedum fusiforme Lowe

Sedum lancerottense ex Murray (see *S. brissemoreti*)

MAINLAND SPECIES
Sedum multiceps Cosson
Sedum nudum Aiton (see *S. brissemoreti*)
Sedum ruwenzoriense Baker

Morphologically and geographically, this small group of sedums is a hotchpotch of species, merely assembled as a tidying-up exercise. The following key will help indentification:

Yellow-flowered species from the Macronesian Islands, with kyphocarpic flowers, carpels fused together in the lower one third, and petals with short mucrones: *S. brissemoreti*, *S. fusiforme*, *S. lancerottense*, *S. nudum*
Yellow-flowered North African species, plants resembling tiny Joshua trees: *S. multiceps*
Yellow-flowered East African species with yellow flowers, upright carpels, and free sepals: *S. ruwenzoriense*
White-flowered Macronesian species: *S. farinosum*

Leaf shape helps distinguish the seven species of this group in cultivation (Fig. 0.1).

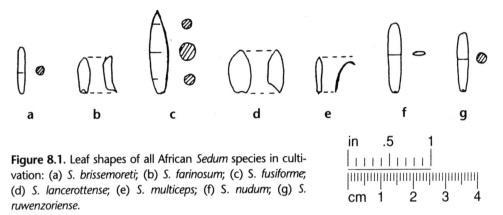

a   b   c   d   e   f   g

Figure 8.1. Leaf shapes of all African *Sedum* species in cultivation: (a) *S. brissemoreti;* (b) *S. farinosum;* (c) *S. fusiforme;* (d) *S. lancerottense;* (e) *S. multiceps;* (f) *S. nudum;* (g) *S. ruwenzoriense.*

in   .5   1

cm   1   2   3   4

MACRONESIAN ISLAND SPECIES

SEDUM BRISSEMORETI Hamet
SEDUM LANCEROTTENSE ex Murray
SEDUM NUDUM Aiton

PLATE 46

These three yellow-flowered Macronesian species are so difficult to separate, I choose to deal with them together (Fig. 8.2). All are glabrous plants with minutely papillose leaves, vegetatively resembling the very common *Sedum album*. Stems become quite woody at the base with age. Yellow flowers immediately separate all three of these Macronesian stonecrops from *S. album* or its close relatives that are almost identical vegetatively. Woody stems that become tortuous with age separate the three species from similar-looking plants of *S. japonicum*, and patent leaves distinguish them from *S. oryzifolium*, another vegetatively similar Oriental species.

All three species have alternate leaves, which are soon lost on lower stems. Flowers are produced in small numbers. *Sedum lancerottense* is the easiest species to identify because of its flatter-topped blue-green leaves, and its unequal, free, noticeably spurred sepals separate it from species outside this group. Out of flower, the three species are just about impossible to separate. A mature plant of *S. brissemoreti* is more

bushy and straggling but, as a young plant, it is a good match for *S. nudum*. In flower, differences are not immediately apparent, but *S. brissemoreti*, with its less-glossy spurred leaves, has large flowers with huge fruit. *Sedum nudum* has blue-green matt leaves and small flowers with petals that narrow at the base. None of these species are particularly common in cultivation.

HABITAT. *Sedum brissemoreti* grows on the north coast of Madeira. *Sedum lancerottense*, as the name suggests, is native to Lanzarote, an island in the Canary group (Plate 46). *Sedum nudum* is indigenous to the south coast of Madeira. All three species are dwellers of steep slopes or semi-shaded cliffs.

MAIN POINTS OF DISTINCTION. All three species have free, unequal sepals and spreading carpels fused in the lower third. *Sedum nudum* has tiny flowers with petals that narrow at the base, but in other respects is indistinguishable from *S. lancerottense*. Together *S. nudum* (Fig. 8.1f) and *S. lancerottense* (Fig. 8.1d) can be differentiated from *S. brissemoreti* by their blue-green papillose leaves that are not terete or club shaped. *Sedum brissemoreti* has green, shiny, oblong leaves (Fig. 8.1a).

VARIATION. None noticed.

HORTICULTURE. All three species require mild winters in which they are best kept fairly

Figure 8.2. (left) *Sedum brissemoreti* seedling; (center) S. *nudum*; (right) S. *lancerottense*.

dry. They often perish in prolonged drought but do well on an indoor windowsill with some winter water. Do not place any plants in a greenhouse in direct sun. None of the three species are particularly beautiful or of horticultural importance, but *Sedum lancerottense* is the neatest.

SEDUM FARINOSUM Lowe

PLATE 47

SYNONYM: *Oreosedum farinosum* (Lowe) Grulich

Dense masses of this pruinose, carpet-forming species from Madeira grow happily outdoors at the Royal Botanic Gardens Edinburgh, Scotland (Plate 47). From its natural habitat (33°N), I assumed this species would not be hardy in Edinburgh (56°N), but obviously this is not so. Edinburgh has a very maritime climate, and the plants referred to above are growing in a steep, south-facing rock garden. Grown outdoors, *Sedum farinosum* attains a height of 15 cm (6 in) or

more, but in pots it is much smaller, making a loose, pruinose mat, topped with quite large (15 mm/0.6 in) white flowers in early summer. This stonecrop is still rare in cultivation.

HABITAT. *Sedum farinosum* is endemic to Madeira and only found at altitudes over 1000 m (3000 ft).

MAIN POINTS OF DISTINCTION. The species is most similar to *Sedum brevifolium* f. *quinquefarium*; both are very chalky in texture. Leaves of S. *farinosum* are much longer, patent, and more loosely arranged (Fig. 8.1b). Flowers have distinct red nectary glands, and carpels tinge winered. Despite Grulich's inclusion of this species within his genus *Oreosedum*, it is without doubt a kyphocarpic species. Deep red carpels only spread a little, but are not much different from those of *Sedum anglicum*, a close relative. They are noticeably gibbous on the ventral side and connate below (fused together for almost half their length). *Sedum farinosum* could easily be mistaken for a white-flowered European species, especially *S. dasyphyllum*, except the latter is never farinose. *Sedum brevifolium* in its five-spiralled form has more spherical leaves whereas those of *S. farinosum* are more like grains of rice. Also, *S. brevifolium* has upright carpels even into fruit, and the basal attachment is minimal.

VARIATION. Because of this species' relatively small habitat, great variation among plants is unlikely, except due to contrasting cultivation methods.

HORTICULTURE. This is a very choice, charming, alpine species. If a gardener can offer a climate that will allow it to grow in an outdoor rock garden, it is very rewarding and cannot get out of hand. Indoors, it loses its stature somewhat, but is a bright, eye-catching specimen plant.

SEDUM FUSIFORME Lowe

Although this species has much in common with the other yellow-flowered Macronesian

Figure 8.3. *Sedum fusiforme* in a 2.5-in (6-cm) pot.

species, it is strikingly different (Fig. 8.3). Leaves are unlike any other species in the genus. Fusiforme, which means swollen in the middle and tapering each way to resemble a spindle, describes the leaves perfectly. In addition, the leaves are just about terete or slightly flattened on the upper surface. Lowe describes them as being without spurs; Fröderström, as with. The apparent contradiction is explained thus: a fresh, live, growing plant has turgid leaves that are tight against the stem, but a plant kept bone-dry in winter has limp leaves. In such a state, the attachment to the stems appears different. A semi-desiccated leaf half-hanging off the stem suggests that leaves are spurred. Fröderström probably only knew the plant from herbarium specimens—hence his statement.

Low, sprawling plants are quite open and become woody, especially at the base. Very large, deep yellow flowers are often streaked with red, and individually they are quite extreme for *Sedum* as bases of petals are fused for about one-fifth their length. *Sedum fusiforme* is rare in cultivation due to its fickle nature and reluctance to propagate vegetatively.

HABITAT. Sea cliffs of the southwest coast of Madeira from about 100 to 200 m (300 to 700 ft) high are the home of this stonecrop.

MAIN POINTS OF DISTINCTION. Leaves as described are distinct (Fig. 8.1c). Sepals are fused at the base and deltoid. Epipetalous stamens are inserted about halfway up petals and are very short.

VARIATION. This is a rare plant both in the wild and in cultivation, but it appears fairly constant.

HORTICULTURE. *Sedum fusiforme* is notoriously difficult to propagate. Cuttings stubbornly refuse to root for many months. Plants can stand a few light frosts if bone-dry, but some heat in winter is recommended. It is a fascinating stonecrop, but only of specialist interest.

MAINLAND SPECIES

SEDUM MULTICEPS Cosson

PLATE 48

Mostly seen as a miniature, indoor potted plant, this delightful species is in fact hardy in many warm, temperate areas. Often likened to a tiny Joshua tree, *Sedum multiceps* can attain a height of 15 cm (6 in) but it is sometimes decumbent. Many-branched stems are quite sturdy, topped with flat-topped tufts of papillose, linear leaves, and shaggy below with dead leaves. A few pale yellow flowers are produced each summer. This species is probably related to, or perhaps should be included with, the European *S. acre* group.

HABITAT. Indigenous to Algeria but cultivated in many Mediterranean areas, *Sedum multiceps* has apparently escaped in Corsica and other islands. It is found from sea level to an elevation of 1500 m (4900 ft).

MAIN POINTS OF DISTINCTION. The habit of this species is very distinct, therefore it is unlikely to be confused with anything else. Kyphocarpic flowers are very similar to those of *Sedum sexangulare*, with pronounced mucronate petals and unspurred sepals, connate at the base. Bases of leaves are somewhat trilobate and leaves are papillate, especially above (Fig. 8.1e).

VARIATION. Flowers can be many-partite: 7-partite is not uncommon. A rather strange, unlabeled little plant from Ron Evans's collection was passed on to me, and for several years I could not identify it. Tufts of leaves at stem tips, with dead leaves below, and bare stems in lower sections remind me very much of *Sedum multiceps*, but in this instance, stems are weaker and decumbent, and leaves are not grouped in flat-topped tufts. Papillation of leaf tips is less pronounced but still visible. Stems are very fine and short, and soon arch; therefore, the general appearance of plants is quite unlike that of *S. multiceps*. I discovered the identity of the oddity in the works of Maire (1977) to be *S. ×battandieri*.

Sedum ×battandieri is described as a natural hybrid of *S. tuberosum* Cosson & Letourneux, a species no longer in cultivation, and *S. multiceps*. *Sedum tuberosum* is a caudiciform stonecrop with a caudex like a potato from which non-perennial stems carry loosely imbricate, papillose leaves. Despite its odd mode of growth, it "seems to be closely allied to *S. multiceps*," according to Fröderström (1932, 70). The hybrid has characteristics of both parents. Unfortunately, in the hybrid, the caudex is missing. Leaves are wider than those of *S. multiceps*, and stems are perennial but weak. Flowers are golden yellow, and, in or out of flower, this is a pretty plant for a tiny pot.

HORTICULTURE. *Sedum ×battandieri* makes a super pseudobonsai plant for a ceramic container. It can become brittle and, if handled roughly, can disintegrate, providing much propagation material. *Sedum multiceps* is charming on a windowsill, superb in a succulent collection, and delightful if grown outside. Plants broken by frosts are easily rerooted.

SEDUM RUWENZORIENSE Baker

Sedum ruwenzoriense is the only true East African *Sedum* in general cultivation, but its fickle nature makes it exceedingly rare. As a high-altitude alpine, it is most difficult to perpetuate in cultivation. Bushy little plants resemble *S. japonicum* in form but can attain 15 cm (6 in) in stature. Lower stems are quite sturdy and bare. Upper halves of stems have light green patent, slightly spurred, long-elliptic leaves in loose spirals. A few pale yellow flowers are produced in spring (Fig. 8.4).

HABITAT. Mount Ruwenzori, Mount Kenya, and adjacent peaks from 2300 to 4000 m (7500 to 13,000 ft) are the home of this equatorial alpine. Often it grows as an epiphyte.

MAIN POINTS OF DISTINCTION. The general appearance of this stonecrop is somewhat distinct. Very large, free, spurred sepals are good proof of identification. Like the leaves, which

Figure 8.4. *Sedum ruwenzoriense*, here growing in a 4-in (10-cm) pot, is most fickle in cultivation.

are flat on both surfaces, sepals are somewhat papillate at their tips (Fig. 8.1g).

VARIATION. Probably the few plants in cultivation have all been propagated from the same stock, but it seems more than feasible that different clones do exist, as there are disjunct sites in the wild.

HORTICULTURE. Unfortunately, hailing from such high-altitude origins, *Sedum ruwenzoriense* detests hot greenhouse conditions. Once part of a plant bakes, the rest of it slowly dies and refuses, in any way, to be propagated. Plants can stand lots of frost if bone-dry but are best kept in a cold frame, which is cool in summer. It is essential to give away as many propagations of this species as possible, so you can beg bits back, if, and when, yours fails.

CHAPTER 9

North American Species of Subgenus Sedum

Robert T. Clausen spent a large part of his life studying *Sedum* in North America. No substitute exists for his magnificent 1975 tome on the subject: nearly 750 pages covering about 30 species. The following species appear to be in cultivation:

Sedum beyrichianum Masters (see *S. glaucophyllum*)
Sedum borschii Clausen
Sedum debile Watson
Sedum divergens Watson
Sedum douglassii Hooker (see *S. stenopetalum*)
Sedum glaucophyllum Clausen
Sedum lanceolatum Torrey
Sedum laxum (Britton) Berger
Sedum leibergii Britton
Sedum moranii Clausen
Sedum niveum Davidson
Sedum nuttallianum Rafinesque
Sedum obtusatum A. Gray
Sedum oreganum Nuttall
Sedum oregonense (S. Watson) M. E. Peck
Sedum pulchellum Michaux
Sedum purdyi Jepson (see *S. spathulifolium*)
Sedum spathulifolium Hooker
Sedum stenopetalum Pursh
Sedum ternatum Michaux

Plants of this group

- Are indigenous to North America.
- Exclude native subgenera *Hylotelephium* and

Rhodiola species, and other species such as *Sedum villosum* and *S. acre*, which are common on the continent. *Sedum villosum* may even be natural to the far northeastern coasts, but it and *S. acre* have spread from Europe. North America has an endemic species of subgenus *Hylotelephium* species and several species of subgenus *Rhodiola*; these will be found under the appropriate sections.
- Exclude several species that grow primarily in Mexico.
- Include species once separated as *Gormania* with distinct flower tubes.
- Comprise both orthocarpic and kyphocarpic species, annuals and perennials.
- Include plants with and without developed rootstocks.
- Comprise species with white, yellow, and purple flowers, and variations on these colors.
- Are mostly rosetted species.

Sedum cockerellii, *S. stelliforme*, and *S. wrightii* grow in the United States, but also grow in Mexico. *Sedum niveum* could easily have been included with Mexican species but, as it was first encountered in the hills behind Los Angeles, I have kept it with the North American group.

The following is not a formal key but an aid to identification:

Plants annual: *S. nuttallianum*

Plants biennial: *S. leibergii*

Rosettes tiny, flowers white or pink: *S. niveum*

Rosettes tiny, flowers yellow: *S. borschii, S. debile*

Leaves small, thick, succulent, shiny, opposite-decussate leaves: *S. divergens*

Leaves small, thick, succulent, shiny, alternate leaves: *S. oreganum*

Leaves large, thick: *S. laxum*

Leaves in elongated tufts: *S. lanceolatum, S. stenopetalum*

Leaves ternate: *S. ternatum*

Inflorescence reflexed, hirsute: *S. moranii*

Petals erect white/yellow: *S. obtusatum, S. oregonense*

Leaves in well-defined rosettes, flowers yellow, stellate: *S. spathulifolium*

Flowers white/pink 4-partite: *S. glaucophyllum, S. pulchellum, S. ternatum*

Figure 9.1 depicts leaf shapes of North American *Sedum* species in cultivation.

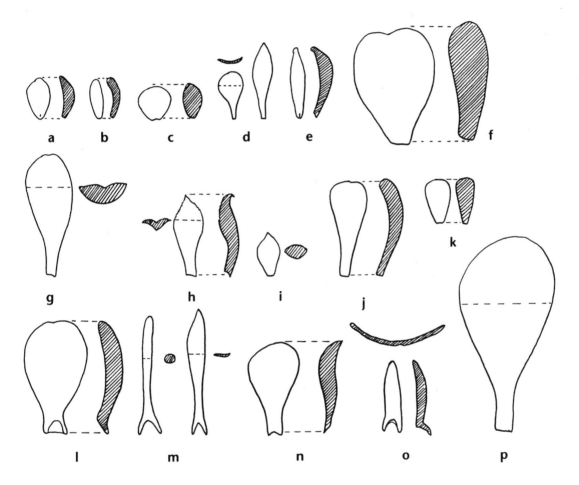

Figure 9.1. Leaf shapes of perennial North American *Sedum* species: (a) *S. borschii*; (b) *S. debile*; (c) *S. divergens*; (d) extreme clones of *S. glaucophyllum*; (e) *S. lanceolatum*; (f) *S. laxum*; (g) *S. laxum* subsp. *heckneri*; (h) *S. moranii*; (i) *S. niveum*; (j) *S. obtusatum*; (k) *S. oreganum*; (l) *S. oregonense*; (m) extreme clones of *S. pulchellum* which sometimes perenniate; (n) *S. spathulifolium*; (o) *S. stenopetalum*; and (p) *S. ternatum*.

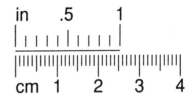

SEDUM BORSCHII Clausen

PLATE 49

Sedum borschii is a delightful miniature stonecrop but, unfortunately, very rare in cultivation (Fig. 9.1a). Tiny rosettes, less than one centimeter (0.4 in) across, are similar to those of the well-known *S. spathulifolium* but much smaller and glabrous. Rosettes form during the first year and elongate to form erect inflorescences 10 cm (4 in) long with two or three branches the following year. In early summer, golden flowers appear.

HABITAT. This species has a very limited habitat on the Idaho Batholith, into Montana, and the adjacent Colombia Plateau, on various rocky cliffs and slopes from 1200 to 2000 m (3900 to 7000 ft). Because of this very limited range, it appears as though *Sedum borschii* is an evolving species or perhaps a natural hybrid.

MAIN POINTS OF DISTINCTION. Tiny rosettes are very similar in size to those of *Sedum debile*, but the latter has opposite-decussate leaves. *Sedum borschii* has pronounced kyphocarpic flowers with carpels spreading fully and subsessile flowers with tiny sepals and mucronate petals. Carpels are papillose at the base becoming fruit with prominent lips. Nectaries of orange-yellow are visible.

VARIATION. Because of disjunct sites, Clausen (1975) believed that, different levels of ploidy existed. Uhl (1977, 102) stated that $2n = 40$ but added that meiosis is irregular, evidence which suggests this stonecrop is of hybrid origin:

> The chromosome number and behavior reported . . . are compatible with origin of *Sedum borschii* as a hybrid between octoploid *S. stenopetalum* ($n = 32$) and diploid *S. leibergii* ($n = 8$). The possibility that this species is a hybrid maintaining itself by asexual means needs further study.

Flowers of more than 5-partite are sometimes produced.

HORTICULTURE. From such altitudes in the Western Cordillera at 46° north, *Sedum borschii* should be hardy for most growers. I find damp, milder winters do not suit the species, so plants reside in a cold frame for the worst three months. The tiny nature of the species makes it ideal for raised beds or as a specimen alpine plant.

SEDUM DEBILE S. Watson

SYNONYMS: *Gormania debilis* (S. Watson) Britton, *Amerosedum debile* (S. Watson) Löve & Löve
COMMON NAME: Great Basin stonecrop

Upon expanding, tiny, pale green, almost-globular rosettes reveal that leaves of *Sedum debile* are opposite-decussate (Fig. 9.1b). Short sterile stems rise from creeping stems. In summer, inflorescences carry yellow flowers with petals that are erect and have slightly connate bases, and the tiny rosettes are often flushed red.

HABITAT. This species hails from the Central Rocky Mountain basin of Nevada, Utah, Idaho, and eastern Oregon in open rocky areas of the forest zone on a variety of rocks at 1600 to 3550 m (5200 to 11,600 ft) altitude.

MAIN POINTS OF DISTINCTION. The diminutive nature of this species with opposite-decussate leaves is the best guide to identification. In addition, connate, upright sepals; yellow, mucronate petals streaked with red; and yellow upright carpels are further reliable points.

VARIATION. Clausen shows that in the wild there is much variation, but the species is very rare in cultivation. A clone propagated from plants originating in the Uinta Mountains east of Salt Lake City, Utah, is particularly diminutive and appears to have much shorter inflorescences than some of the forms depicted by Clausen. Variation on the usual 5-partite flowers is common. $2n = 16$.

HORTICULTURE. A very easily controlled species, it is ideal for raised beds, stone troughs, or as a potted specimen alpine. Wet, milder winters can be fatal as, in the wild, plants are most probably covered with a dry, insulating cover of snow for several months.

SEDUM DIVERGENS S. Watson

SYNONYM: *Amerosedum divergens*
(S. Watson) Löve & Löve

COMMON NAME: Cascade stonecrop

Sedum divergens is a cheerful-looking species with highly succulent, almost spherical, opposite-decussate, shiny, green leaves with lots of red coloring, standing in four columns (Fig. 9.2). In Northumberland it is a relatively shy flowerer, but yellow flowers, produced in summer, are large and contrast with the foliage. Closely packed, glassy leaves are similar in texture and shade to those of *S. oreganum*, but leaf shape and arrangement immediately separate the two species (Fig. 9.1c, k). *Sedum divergens* is available in the trade with a little searching.

HABITAT. This stonecrop is indigenous to highlands and off-shore islands of the Pacific Coast from 43° to 57° north. In the northern part of its range, this species grows near sea level, while in the southern part it is found at over 2250 m (7380 ft) altitude. It grows on a variety of rocky slopes and cliffs throughout its range.

MAIN POINTS OF DISTINCTION. Only one other North American species has opposite-decussate, succulent leaves, namely, *Sedum debile*, which has very light green leaves. Leaves of *S. divergens* are shiny, glassy-green, and turn bright red in full sun. Even in shade, stems are red and leaves blush. Subsessile flowers are stellate with small, upright sepals, mucronate petals, and upright carpels that eventually become widely divergent with age.

VARIATION. Clausen (1975) emphasized the species uniformity, but I have two contrasting clones in cultivation: the first is a miniature, upright form that matches Clausen's drawings very well; the other is a large, rapidly spreading, de-

Figure 9.2. *Sedum divergens.* The stems shown on this larger form are 12 cm (5 in) high.

cumbent form with a propensity for producing 4-partite flowers that I propose to call 'Giant'. Clausen noted 6-partite and 7-partite, in addition to the usual 5-partite flowers, but he did not mention 4-partite flowers. $2n = 16$.

HORTICULTURE. This is a useful and relatively easy-to-obtain species that can be planted in many situations. It is delightful as a rock garden plant. I use the rampant form 'Giant' to cover an unsightly iron inspection hatch, which is lightly covered in grit. Plants grow well in containers and seems tolerant of most soils. *Sedum divergens* is resilient in cold, wet winters as it is indigenous to areas of very high rainfall. The rapid-growing clone makes a beautiful, compact, succulent ground cover that turns bright red in sun. Irrigation may be needed in areas of low summer rainfall.

SEDUM GLAUCOPHYLLUM Clausen

PLATE 50

SYNONYM: *S. beyrichianum* Masters

Not too rare in cultivation, *Sedum glaucophyllum* is nearly always incorrectly labelled "*Sedum nevii.*" Two distinct forms of the species are in cultivation, and they, I believe, are the plants referred to by Praeger as *S. nevii* and *S. nevii* var. *beyrichianum*. *Sedum nevii* is definitely not in cultivation. To my disgrace, I acquired two cuttings of a verified *S. nevii* plant collected by Professor Uhl, and despite careful attention, they failed to root (the parent also passed away). I had cuttings long enough to realize that plants in cultivation purporting to be *S. nevii* were a different species. Uhl's notes (unpublished) to me are most interesting:

We made a trip south earlier in the year and I re-collected a rare *Sedum* there, the true *S. nevii*. This came from bluffs along the Chattahoochee River . . . in west central Georgia. I saw only very few plants. The locality is quite wet with spray . . . lots of Spanish moss there. . . . This species is known from only three oth-

er widely separated localities, two in Alabama, and one in the southeast corner of Tennessee. The much commoner *S. glaucophyllum* is sometimes lumped into *S. nevii*, but it is native mostly to the mountains of western Virginia, with a few outlying populations in adjoining areas of other states. The two are very similar in appearance, but *S. glaucophyllum* has slightly broader, glaucous leaves, and they differ significantly in their chromosomes: $n = 6$ in *S. nevii*, and $n = 14$, $n = 22$, and $n = 28$ in *S. glaucophyllum*. Some nice evolutionary problems in determining the relation here. Some recent specialized work strongly supports the separation of the two into different species. Clausen, years ago, looked closely at the matter and decided that there are two species here, but that [the description of] *S. beyrichianum*, as best he could determine, merely described *S. nevii* again—so Clausen named *S. glaucophyllum*.

Sedum glaucophyllum is a charming, low-growing species with green or waxy, glaucous rosettes of about 12-24 mm diameter (0.5-1 in). Inflorescences of early summer rise to about 10 cm (4 in) high and carry white, 4-partite flowers with patent petals (Plate 50). Petals are very similar to those of *S. ternatum*, which is immediately distinguished by its rounded, ternate (in whorls of three) leaves.

HABITAT. This is a stonecrop of the Eastern Cordillera: northern Appalachians from about 36° to 40° north, on a plethora of steep, semi-shaded rocky surfaces from about 500 to 1200 m (1600 to 3900 ft).

MAIN POINTS OF DISTINCTION. Small, compact rosettes with leaves arranged in spirals, and white, 4-partite, stellate flowers with free petals are the best indicators (Fig. 9.1d). Linear sepals are small, almost terete, unequal, and papillose at their tips. *Sedum nevii* has sepals almost as long as petals. Stamens of *S. glaucophyllum* have broad, flat bases, very flattened filaments, and the epipetalous whorl is fixed at the very base of the petals. Anthers are dull red. White nectaries are wider than long. Carpels are erect at first, but brown fruit are widely spreading.

VARIATION. Clausen (1975) referred to three principal races in the wild, but I believe two contrasting diploids are in general cultivation. One has large rosettes of green, nonglaucous leaves; the name *Sedum beyrichianum* is usually favored by horticulturists rather than *S. glaucophyllum*, an understandable mistake due to the contradiction of glaucous leaves suggested by the latter name. The glabrous form is found at the highest elevations in habitat and has much longer leaves than the other form. Despite its nonglaucous nature, this form should still be labelled *S. glaucophyllum*. Clausen realized that *S. glaucophyllum* was an inappropriate name for the species, as some forms, including plants from the type location, have glabrous, not glaucous leaves. The second, more-common form in cultivation is almost always labelled *S. nevii*. It has smaller, compact, glaucous rosettes, and is most frequent in the wild on calcareous rocks in valleys.

HORTICULTURE. Both forms are extremely pretty plants, ideal for the alpine enthusiast. Neither is particularly hardy, though the green form is more resilient. The smaller, glaucous form is more attractive and grows well in a cold frame. Hot summer sun and over-dry conditions can be as damaging as winter rains, but careful cultivation can be most rewarding.

SEDUM LANCEOLATUM Torrey

Synonyms: *S. shastense* Britton,
Amerosedum lanceolatum (Torrey) Löve & Löve

Sedum lanceolatum is a very rare species in cultivation, though it is now available in the specialist trade (Fig. 9.3). Often it is confused in literature with *S. stenopetalum*, but it is distinct and easily distinguished. *Sedum lanceolatum* and *S. stenopetalum* are tufted species; it is said they resemble the European *Rupestria* group, but I think confusion is highly unlikely. Tufted, brittle, creeping then rooting stems of *S. lanceolatum* are

biennial, but are replaced by offsetting. Spirally arranged leaves are distinct in shape and texture (Fig. 9.1e). They are terete, lanceolate with a short spur, and covered with a minute scaly pattern. Dull, dark gray-green leaves turn maroon in full sun, and 4–10 cm (1.5–4 in) long, short, flat-topped, upright inflorescences of yellow flowers are produced in summer.

HABITAT. This is an exceptionally widespread stonecrop found almost throughout the complete length and breadth of the Western Cordillera: from 35° to 62° north and from near sea level in British Columbia to well over 3700 m (12,100 ft) in alpine tundra in the southern Rockies. Plants even grow on gravel sites in the Great Plains, adjacent to the Western Cordillera. They favor granitic rock, but generally can be found in any rocky situations, although Uhl suggested not on basalt or lava.

MAIN POINTS OF DISTINCTION. Compact rosettes of terete, apiculate leaves elongate in the second season, are very similar to European

Figure 9.3. *Sedum lanceolatum* with a 7-cm (3-in) long inflorescence.

Sedum urvillei. Differentiation is easy, for carpels, except for beaks, and fruit of *S. lanceolatum* remain upright throughout their development. Plants fall to pieces when brushed against. Central flowers are noticeably larger than the others. Upright sepals are small, equal, and narrow, and nectaries, stamens, and anthers are yellow.

VARIATION. I have studied only four forms in cultivation as the species is still exceptionally rare in Europe. A form from Bald Mountain Pass, probably a diploid, does not tinge a great deal with red, but remains dull; its leaves are somewhat glaucous at first but gray-green for most of the year, and its flowers are green-yellow. Another form is somewhat smaller, glabrous, and maroon for most of the year; its flowers are orange-yellow.

Clausen (1975) reported "many" levels of ploidy. Uhl (1977) noted that diploids, tetraploids, and hexaploids with $n = 8$, 16, and 24 are represented at a wide range of elevations with all three, for instance, occuring in Yellowstone National Park. Evans (1983) described an interesting, large variation, *Sedum lanceolatum* subsp. *nesioticum* (G. N. Jones) Clausen, which grows on offshore isles of British Columbia, but, as far as I know, it is lost to cultivation—at least in Europe.

HORTICULTURE. I have never been able to grow this species well. I have tried numerous sites, but plants are dreadfully slow to spread. A recently acquired clone propagated from plants indigenous to Washington State, a high rainfall area, is proving to be much easier. It is not a particularly eye-catching stonecrop, but it is, nevertheless, an interesting variation on a theme with very bright flowers. Light-colored gravel contrasts well with these dark plants.

SEDUM LAXUM (Britton) Berger

SYNONYMS: *Gormania laxa* Rose, *Echeveria gormania* Nelson & MacBride, *Cotyledon brittoniana* Fedde, *Gormania eastwoodiae* Britton, *Sedum jepsonii* Butterfield, *S. heckneri* Peck, *S. eastwoodiae* (Britton) Berger
COMMON NAME: Rose-flowered stonecrop

From the list of synonyms, which is far from being definitive, one can see some of the controversy that this polymorphic species has caused. Fusion of petals for about half their length is not a feature usually associated with *Sedum*. Very rarely seen in Europe, this pink-or white-flowered species is highly succulent with relatively few exceptionally turgid leaves clustering in basal 4-cm (2-in) rosettes (Fig. 9.4). Stems of *S. laxum* rise from a fleshy rootstock. Offsets often have opposite-decussate leaves at first as new rosettes form. Glabrous inflorescences of late summer can be very long, but are usually about 15 cm (6 in) long. Branches of inflorescence are incurved at first, and flowers have erect petals with as much as 3/5 cohesion.

HABITAT. From Josephine County, southern Oregon, to Mendocino and Lake counties of

Figure 9.4. *Sedum laxum* with a 12-cm (5-in) long inflorescence.

northern California, this stonecrop is found on rocky sites in valleys, from less than 200 m (700 ft) elevation in the north to nearly 1800 m (5900 ft) in the south of its range.

MAIN POINTS OF DISTINCTION. Very succulent leaves (Fig. 9.1f), and pink or white flowers with upright petals, connate for about half their length, are the best indicators. Sepals are upright, pressed against flower tubes. Carpels are erect then only spread a little in fruit. Nectaries are broader than long, and almost two-lobed. 2*n* = 30.

VARIATION. This is such a varied species that one school of thought suggests that every distinct, disjunct population deserves its own name. The descriptions that follow are very general and include almost all variations recorded from the wild. According to Clausen (1975), there are four subspecies worthy of note in cultivation, although intermediate forms exist in the wild that often are difficult to assign to a specific subspecies. So many transitional populations exist that specific status for any form is questionable.

Sedum laxum subsp. *laxum* (syn. *S. laxum* subsp. *perplexum* Clausen) has an inflorescence that is not reflexed in bud though branches of the inflorescence are curved in towards each other. Leaves of this subspecies are glabrous, spathulate, and those of the inflorescences are narrow. Flowers are pink, deepening in shade below, with red anthers. This subspecies comes mostly from Rogue River Valley, southern Oregon, and adjacent California from very low altitudes to over 1200 m (3900 ft).

Sedum laxum subsp. *eastwoodiae* (Britton) Clausen has an inflorescence not reflexed in bud, though branches are still curved in towards each other. This subspecies retains its smaller, 1-cm (0.4-in) long, opposite-decussate leaves on offsets for long periods and is usually more glaucous. Leaves of inflorescences are not much smaller or different in shape from those of the rosettes, and are very congested. Flowers, on compact cymes, are deep pink with red anthers

or yellow suffused with red. This subspecies is indigenous to the Northern Californian Coastal Range at high altitudes.

Sedum laxum subsp. *heckneri* (Peck) Clausen has an inflorescence that is reflexed in bud. Leaves of this subspecies are spathulate (Fig. 9.1g), and those of the inflorescence are round, cordate, sessile, and stem-clasping (Fig. 9.5). Pink or white flowers are produced early in summer and have yellow anthers. Petals of this subspecies are very distinct for they spread for the upper third. Of the four subspecies in the group, this one has the greatest range in the wild, and therefore is the most variable: Klamath and Trinity rivers of northern California, over the complete altitudinal range of the species.

Sedum laxum subsp. *latifolium* has an inflorescence that is reflexed in bud. This subspecies has very broad leaves making up rosettes and clothing inflorescence. All leaves are glabrous, green, obcordate or deeply emarginate. Those of the

Figure 9.5. *Sedum laxum* subsp. *heckneri* in a 2-in (5-cm) pot.

inflorescence are rounded but not stem-clasping. Pink flowers with upright petals have red anthers. This subspecies is the most robust of the four and its habitat is restricted to the catchment area of the Smith River, northern California, at low altitudes, on sites not exposed to the south.

Petals of all subspecies are sometimes wavy or even eroded. Out of flower, any can easily be confused with other North American species.

HORTICULTURE. This beautiful, highly succulent species struggles for survival in Northumberland, but thriving outdoor colonies have been established near the east coast of northern Scotland. It should do well in an alpine house or cold frame in most areas, but Clausen reported this was not so in New York State.

SEDUM LEIBERGII Britton

SYNONYMS: *S. divaricatum* Watson non Aiton,
Amerosedum leibergii (Britton) Löve & Löve
COMMON NAME: Leiberg's stonecrop

Sedum leibergii is one of two species in this volume I have never actually grown, but I do know, due to efforts of enthusiastic conservationists in Oregon, that it is in cultivation. Unfortunately, without very specialist horticulture, it is almost impossible to perpetuate this feeble little plant. It is biennial and has spirally arranged, soft, lax leaves that form tiny, flat, open rosettes. Kyphocarpic yellow flowers are produced on long inflorescences and are unusual in that they are generally 6-partite.

HABITAT. The home of this stonecrop is the British Columbian Plateau to Washington, northeastern Oregon, and adjacent Idaho, on cliffs and rocky slopes from about 250 to 1000+ m (820 to 3000+ ft). Sites are wet and mossy in winter and spring, and hot and dry in summer (Fig. 9.6).

MAIN POINTS OF DISTINCTION. Weak, lax rosettes and 6-partite, kyphocarpic flowers are unique in North American sedums. Clausen (1975) described carpels as "warty-papillose." 2*n* = 16.

Figure 9.6. *Sedum leibergii* in habitat. Photograph by Joyce Hoekstra of Oregon.

VARIATION. Flowers can deviate from the frequently encountered 6-partite.

HORTICULTURE. With care, biennial plants can be perpetuated, since rootstocks form underground buds that emerge and form rosettes the next season. Unfortunately, few growers have succeeded. Despite its delicate nature, healthy plants are attractive, and flowers are bright.

SEDUM MORANII Clausen

PLATE 51
SYNONYMS: *Cotyledon glandulifera* L. F. Henderson,
Gormania glandulifera (Henderson) Abrams
COMMON NAME: Glandular stonecrop

Sedum moranii is similar to *S. laxum*, *S. obtusatum*, and *S. oregonense*, but it has huge pendant yellow flowers with erect petals on unique glandular-pubescent inflorescences. Low-growing, compact rosettes are made up of stiff, ascending leaves, which are emarginate or rounded, and which redden at papillose tips (Fig. 9.1h). It is a very rare stonecrop in cultivation.

HABITAT. This species is also very rare in habitat having only a limited distribution in the Canyon of Rogue River, Josephine County, Oregon, in moss on serpentine in steep sites with a southwest or west exposure at just over 200 m (700 ft) above sea level.

MAIN POINTS OF DISTINCTION. Semivertical leaves with scalloped tips in compact rosettes are quite distinct. Hairy inflorescences, drooping in bud, with large, hairy, nodding, yellow flowers, are anomalous for *Sedum*. Like other *Gormania* species, the petals of *Sedum moranii* are upright and connate for a noticeable portion of their length. Anthers are particularly short, and stamens, in essence, are epipetalous in that all are borne on the floral tube. Carpels remain erect, and beaks are on the inner side. Offsets appear from below ground. $2n = 30$.

VARIATION. Some clones have thicker leaves than others.

HORTICULTURE. This is a most pleasing, slow-growing species, which should be hardy in most temperate areas. It is ideal as a specimen alpine despite its low-altitude origins.

SEDUM NIVEUM Davidson

SYNONYM: *Cockerellia nivea* (Davidson) Löve & Löve
COMMON NAME: Davidson's stonecrop

Sedum niveum is difficult to grow. It has never been happy in cultivation in Northumberland, but at least one continental botanic garden grows it. Plants may be in cultivation in the United States, but I know of no enthusiast there who claims to grow the species. Like *S. debile* and *S. borschii*, *S. niveum* is a diminutive alpine, but its white flowers immediately distinguish it from the other two species (Fig. 9.7). From a

Figure 9.7. *Sedum niveum,* an extremely diminutive alpine, produces flat-leaved, glabrous-green rosettes on creeping stems.

fleshy rootstock, tiny rosettes form, each with alternate flat, fairly pointed leaves that elongate, and from creeping stems, short inflorescences rise with rounder leaves (Fig. 9.1i). Plants rarely attain 5 cm (2 in) in height when in flower, and at other times are almost level with the ground. Closely related to, and vegetatively somewhat similar to *S. cockerellii*, *S. niveum* does not die back completely in winter.

HABITAT. This stonecrop is a true alpine from inland ranges of southern California, New York, San Bernadino, and Santa Rosa Mountains. Colonies in Baja California, Mexico, are at elevations of up to almost 3000 m (10,000 ft) on quartz and in fairly moist, north-facing, shady rock ledges.

MAIN POINTS OF DISTINCTION. The extremely diminutive nature of flat-leaved, glabrous-green rosettes rising from creeping stems on tuberous roots makes identification fairly straightforward. Short inflorescences of white flowers with petals splashed red complete a unique combination of features. Orthocarpic flowers are stellate, but petals are slightly fused and erect at the base. Sepals are unequal.

VARIATION. Clausen (1975) reported that freak flowers are commonly encountered with forked or extra petals and stamens. Disjunct sites have cytological variations. Uhl (1985) reported $n = 16$ for U.S. plants, but $n = 64$ (octoploids) for Mexican plants. Despite the 200-km (100-mi) dislocation in the range of this species, Clausen (1981) claimed there were only small genetic differences both within and between populations.

HORTICULTURE. This species dislikes sunny greenhouse conditions and wet summer periods. It appears to need special attention, so it is a real challenge to alpine specialists. Its diminutive nature makes it potentially desirable.

SEDUM NUTTALLIANUM Rafinesque

PLATE 52

SYNONYMS: *S. torryi* G. Don, *S. sparsiflorum* Nuttall

Sedum nuttallianum is the only yellow-flowered, annual North American species in cultivation. Cultivated seed has been widely distributed by Micki Crozier of Kansas to enthusiasts all over the world. It is still rare in cultivation, but hopefully will be successfully perpetuated. Dainty, blue-green plants produce a carpet of yellow flowers in midsummer. Clausen (1975, 329) wrote, "plants vary [in size] from tiny individuals of 5 mm tall [0.2 in] with a single small flower, up to spreading, branched plants with stems 18 cm [7 in] tall and as many as 177 flowers."

HABITAT. This eastern stonecrop grows on the Southern and Western Osark plateaux and on the adjacent Great Plains in shallow soils or bare rock where there is no competition from other plants, usually in sites shaded for part of the day. The clone in cultivation came from seed collected near Sedan, Kansas, which grew in dry moss on sandstone in full sun.

MAIN POINTS OF DISTINCTION. This species is more likely to be confused with a European annual than another North American species. It is a somewhat gangling, floriferous plant, as is the nature of many annual *Sedum* species. Kyphocarpic, sessile, yellow flowers are carried on scorpioid branches. Sepals are free, unequal, and spurred. Petals are mucronate. Stamens and anthers are yellow, and nectaries are just visible.

VARIATION. Environment can cause tremendous variation.

HORTICULTURE. Micki Crozier (pers. com.), who has successfully perpetuated the species for several years, suggests that seed be gathered as leaves wither. This is a delightful unpretentious species for a scree garden where it can self-seed. Glaucous blue-green plants are colorful against a dark background.

SEDUM OBTUSATUM A. Gray

PLATE 53

SYNONYMS: *Cotyledon obtusata* (A. Gray) Fedde,
Echeveria obtusata (A. Gray) Nelson & MacBride,
Gormania obtusata (A. Gray) Britton, *Gormania
burnhami* Britton, *Gormania hallii* Britton,
Sedum rubroglaucum Praeger

COMMON NAME: Sierra stonecrop

The name *Sedum obtusatum* has always used for
other species in the trade. In Europe it is invariably used for *S. oreganum*, which is often labelled
"*S. obtusatum* of gardens.*" To add to the confusion, the plant depicted by Evans as "*S. rubroglaucum*" (syn. *S. obtusatum* subsp. *obtusatum*) is a
form of *S. oregonense*. Evans had a true clone of *S.
obtusatum*—a color photograph verifies this. *Sedum obtusatum* is not in general cultivation nor
has it ever been (at least in Europe), except in perhaps a couple of specialist collections for a brief
period.

Sedum obtusatum is very variable in nature.
Some clones are similar in appearance to *S. laxum* and *S. oregonense*. Small rosettes of southern
forms are less than 2 cm (0.8 in) in diameter, rising from a fleshy rootstock. Small leaves tinge
red in full sun, and inflorescences of about 10
cm (4 in) carry distinctly yellow flowers (Fig.
9.1j). Northern forms are darker, bolder plants
with white flowers.

HABITAT. This species is from the forest zones
of the Californian Sierra Nevada and Klamath
Mountains from below 1500 m (4900 ft) to over
3500 m (11,500 ft) on rocky sites.

MAIN POINTS OF DISTINCTION. Sierra Nevada forms of *Sedum obtusatum* have yellow flowers. Petals are convolute in bud as with *Dudleya*,
connate at the base, erect, and eroded. Stamens
and anthers are yellow, carpels remain erect, and
leaves are amplexicaul. All plants in the United
Kingdom labelled *S. rubroglaucum* are really *S. oregonense*, which is a bolder species with yellow-
white flowers that fade orange-pink. A beautiful
white-flowered northern form of *S. obtusatum*
has just entered the trade, and, like its southern

cousins, can be identified by its huge sepals (Fig.
3.2). Cytologically, *S. obtusatum* is distinct but
vegetatively it is so variable, it is likely to be confused with any of its near relatives. $2n = 30$.

VARIATION. This is an exceptionally variable
species in the wild. Northern forms are fairly robust plants with whitish petals. Southern forms
are much smaller and have yellow petals. These
two forms are now entering cultivation in Europe, but only the latter is sometimes encountered in U.S. collections. Obviously, wild plants
with intermediate features must exist but none
are yet cultivated.

HORTICULTURE. This species should make an
attractive potted plant or a bright subject in a
raised bed or stone trough.

SEDUM OREGANUM Nuttall

JACKET FRONT

SYNONYMS: *Breitungia oregana* (Nuttall) Löve & Löve,
Cotyledon oregana (Nuttall) Fedde,
Echeveria oregana (Nuttall) Nelson & MacBride,
Gormania oregana (Nuttall) Britton

COMMON NAME: Oregon stonecrop

Sedum oreganum is a common stonecrop in cultivation. Unfortunately, it is frequently labelled
"*Sedum obtusatum*." *Sedum oreganum* is a carpet-
forming species with shiny, glassy-green leaves
that tinge cherry-red in full sun. It is similar in
color to *S. divergens*, but leaves are spathulate,
spurred, and carried in spirals that form terminal rosettes on stems 7 cm (3 in) long (Fig. 9.1k).
Bright yellow flowers, an excellent contrast to
foliage, are carried on dichotomously branched
inflorescences about 10 cm (4 in) long. Petals are
exceptionally long and narrow—10 mm (0.4 in)
by 2.5 mm (0.1 in)—and fairly erect, but spread
somewhat with age. They are never patent or
nearly so.

HABITAT. The home of this stonecrop is the
Pacific side of coastal ranges from 43° to 59°
north in areas with cool, moist summers. Rocky,
south-facing and west-facing slopes seem to be

favored, from near sea level to over 1550 m (5090 ft).

MAIN POINTS OF DISTINCTION. This is an easily identified species. There is no fleshy root-stock. Stems, loosely clothed in shiny, green leaves, tinge cherry-red, and are topped with terminal rosettes. Long, narrow, yellow, half-spreading petals are distinct. Sepals are small and upright; short stamens, anthers, nectaries, and carpels are yellowish. Petals are visibly fused at their bases. Both subspecies have $2n = 24$.

VARIATION. Two subspecies are in cultivation. *Sedum oreganum* subsp. *oreganum* is associated with rocky low areas of coastal ranges. *Sedum oreganum* subsp. *tenue* is a low, miniature, creeping form with a greater propensity to turn and remain a very bright, cherry-red throughout (see jacket cover). This form is usually labelled *S. oreganum* 'Procumbens' in cultivation. It is a genuine subspecies, endemic to the Cascade Range, and is a higher-altitude, alpine form.

HORTICULTURE. Both forms seem particularly well-suited to the wet British climate. They are resilient, rewarding plants. The type species is excellent for ground cover, and though it spreads rapidly, it is easy to control, and the carpet produced is dense and always colorful. It is much superior to *Sedum spurium*, which is invariably recommended for ground cover, and which overwinters with a much reduced foliage. *Sedum oreganum* subsp. *tenue* is a delightful, bright subject for almost any site, but its diminutive height of merely a few centimeters makes it an important plant in live pictorial art in parks and gardens (Plate 2).

SEDUM OREGONENSE
(S. Watson) M. E. Peck

PLATE 53

SYNONYMS: *Cotyledon oregonensis* S. Watson, *Echeveria watsoni* (Britton) Nelson & MacBride, *Gormania watsoni* Britton, *Sedum watsoni* (Britton) Tidestrom

Sedum oregonense is common in cultivation and sold under a plethora of names including *S. ob-tusatum*, "*S. rubroglaucum*," and "*S. watsoni*." It has fibrous roots and spreads quite rapidly to form loose, glaucous rosettes of succulent, emarginate leaves that rise from thick, straggling, horizontal stems, and are often clothed with dead leaves. Inflorescences carry creamy flowers with upright petals that often start life green-white, especially dorsally, and fade light orange. Vegetatively *S. oregonense* is very like *S. laxum*, but it is much more likely to be encountered than is the latter.

HABITAT. Not a particularly widespread species from the Cascade Mountains (Mount Hood to Crater Lake, Oregon), and probably Klamath Mountains, this stonecrop prefers rocky, gravel slopes in sunny areas of the forest zone where there is little competition from other plants. Its altitudinal range is from over 1000 m (3000 ft) to under 2500 m (8200 ft).

MAIN POINTS OF DISTINCTION. Emarginate leaves are a feature this stonecrop shares with *Sedum laxum* (Fig. 9.1l). Flowers of *S. oregonense* are never really pink though as they fade they can blush somewhat. Like *S. laxum*, leaves on offsets tend to be opposite-decussate. Sepals are very short and are noticeably fused at the base—a key feature to differentiate this species from other *Sedum* species. Petals are fused below, erect, then spreading a little. They also are somewhat hooded. The long yellow stamens have anthers that sometimes flush with a hint of salmon pink. Small carpels are erect. Differentiating white-flowered forms of *S. laxum* subsp. *heckneri* from *S. oregonense*, its close relative, is most difficult. If a plant grows fairly quickly and spreads quite rapidly, it is most likely *S. oregonense*. Leaves of *S. laxum* tend to be at least 4 mm (0.15 in) thick.

VARIATION. One form, often sold as *Sedum watsoni*, is a very bold form with particularly thick, horizontal stems.

HORTICULTURE. This hardy species has much to offer. It looks good in a rock garden. Planted in a trough, it takes many years before it needs to be cut back. Plants are too slow for ground cover, but, after 10 years, a single plant will cover a square meter (over a square yard) with a dense, blue-green, succulent mat. Plants grow much faster than those of the *Sedum laxum* complex.

SEDUM PULCHELLUM Michaux

PLATE 54

SYNONYMS: *Chetyson pulchellum* (Michaux) Löve & Löve

COMMON NAME: Bird's claw sedum

Once this colorful stonecrop was commonly offered in the trade as a summer bedding plant, but now *Sedum pulchellum* is somewhat difficult to acquire. Large, lilac-pink "cock's combs" of flowers in early summer are a joy to behold, but plants invariably act as annuals. Linear leaves are extremely amplexicaul, and stems rise to about 15 cm (6 in) high when in flower. Inflorescences have large, arching branches, each with many flowers, making the plant very floriferous.

HABITAT. This stonecrop is from the Eastern Cordillera, Appalachians, and adjacent Great Plains as far west as the Mississippi Basin, especially on shallow soils or moss on limestone, and mostly on low plateaus below 400 m (1300 ft).

MAIN POINTS OF DISTINCTION. Amplexicaul leaves with two sharp basal lobes and the very floriferous nature of the plants are the best aids to identification. Flowers are mostly 4-partite, but 5-partite is not unusual. Flower buds are lilac-pink, but, when open, petals are nearly white. Sepals are short and unequal. Anthers are purple. Carpels are erect at first, but flowers become kyphocarpic in fruit.

VARIATION. Clausen claimed that in the wild this species was sometimes confused with *Sedum nevii* as both species can have flat, relatively wide leaves. In cultivation, leaves of *S. pulchellum* are invariably terete. Some forms also have a greater propensity to perenniate themselves; different levels of ploidy have been investigated with $2n = 22, 44$, and 66 ($x = 11$). Diploids tend to be perennial and these sometimes have flat spathulate leaves, but are rarely seen in cultivation (Fig. 9.1m).

HORTICULTURE. This is a difficult plant to perpetuate though several commercial outlets propagate from cuttings in late summer and offer strong, healthy plants each spring. Propagations are kept damp in frost-free grow-tunnels during the winter months. The plant certainly detests full sun, baking conditions, and drought. It seems happier in wetter, shady sites. For many years I have failed to perpetuate it in any particular spot, but by keeping plants in a variety of overwintering sites, at least one usually survives. Unfortunately, the plant that survives tends to be from a different site each year. Growing from seed is perhaps less chancy, but I would recommend a damp, frost-free location with excellent ventilation, as young plants damp-off easily.

SEDUM SPATHULIFOLIUM Hooker

PLATE 55

SYNONYMS: *Cotyledon anomala* (Britton) Fedde, *Gormania anomala* Britton, *Gormania spathulifolia* (Hooker) Löve & Löve, *Sedum anomalum* Britton, *S. californicum* Britton, *S. pruinosum* Britton, *S. purdyi* Jepson, *S. woodii* Britton, *S. yosemitense* Britton

COMMON NAME: Pacific stonecrop

Sedum spathulifolium is probably the most commonly seen North American *Sedum* species in gardens. The form 'Capa Blanca', or more correctly 'Cape Blanco', is deservedly common while others are rather rare. All forms are compact, ground-hugging rosettes of spathulate leaves (hence the name) with patent outer leaves, which form a dense carpet (Fig. 9.1n). Rosettes rise from stout rhizomes or creeping stems and carry stolons that radiate like spokes of wheels and carry new rosettes at their tips. Heavily pruinose forms are popular; they are ideal, trouble-free, multipurpose plants for warm-temperate gardens. Short, compact inflorescences of bright golden-yellow are produced in early summer.

HABITAT. This stonecrop is indigenous to Pacific Coastal ranges of California, Oregon, and Washington from sea level to about 1600 m

(5200 ft) in the Sierra Nevada. Several disjunct sites have been located in British Columbia but all forms are natural to cliffs, rocky slopes, or sandy soils where there is little competition from other plants.

MAIN POINTS OF DISTINCTION. Compact rosettes, with spirally arranged leaves are found at soil level, and straight, terete stolons produce rootless rosettes that grow, and, as their increased weight carries them down, they root or cling onto bare rock. Inflorescences of 3-branched cymes, which fork dichotomously, have 5-partite flowers with widely spreading petals. Petals are separate but erect in the lower quarter. Sepals are narrow and fused at their base, forming a receptacle. Epipetalous stamens are inserted noticeably up from bases of petals. Carpels are erect at first, but flowers are kyphocarpic in fruit. $2n = 30$, and various levels of ploidy exist. $2n = 28$ has also been reported, though Clausen reported (probably quoting Uhl) that it is easy to miscount the tiny chromosomes.

VARIATION. *Sedum spathulifolium* subsp. *spathulifolium* is almost nonexistant in cultivation in Europe. It is native to coastal ranges of California, north to British Columbia, on shady cliffs often in mossy mats. Rosettes are glaucousgreen with few stolons.

Sedum spathulifolium subsp. *pruinosum* (Britton) Clausen, as the name suggests, is a range of lowland, coastal pruinose forms. A tiny, compact, coastal form from Cape Blanco, Oregon, named *S. spathulifolium* subsp. *pruinosum* 'Cape Blanco' rapidly produces exceptionally dense, white, pruinose carpets. It is one of the most well-known stonecrops in cultivation. Unfortunately, it has been over-collected in its habitat.

Clausen (1975, 461) explained the range of forms of *Sedum spathulifolium* thus:

A highly significant difference in average diameter of plants in the Coastal Ranges as compared with the Sierra Nevada may have several explanations. The humid Coast Ranges are a favorable place for growth of seedlings. With more seedlings, competition increases. Likewise, higher humidity favors fungi which cause rot and death of *Sedum*. A result may be smaller plants. In contrast, the drier circumstances in summer of the interior mountains are poor for the survival of seedlings and also for pathogens. Consequences may be that plants of *Sedum* live longer, have less competition, and become larger in the Sierra Nevada, Klamath Mountains, and Transverse Ranges.

Unfortunately, but understandably, larger forms in cultivation usually carry an incorrect tag 'Majus'. *Sedum spathulifolium* var. *majus* was a name erected by Praeger for a large, nonpruinose form of *S. spathulifolium* (perhaps syn. *S. spathulifolium* subsp. *yosemitense*), which I think is no longer in cultivation. Several large forms of *S. spathulifolium* subsp. *pruinosum* are in cultivation; one particularly attractive form has an almost perfect globe of flowers topping each inflorescence (Plate 55), while others have relatively open, flat-topped inflorescences.

Clausen incorrectly equated Praeger's *Sedum spathulifolium* var. *purpureum* with *S. spathulifolium* subsp. *spathulifolium*, as he knew nothing of its habitat or indeed whether this variety had been preserved. It is a very common plant in cultivation originating from sports of *S. spathulifolium* subsp. *pruinosum* 'Cape Blanco'. These large sports are less pruinose than the parent and have rosettes in which the deep purple of the leaves shines through the powdery coating. If removed from the parent plant, these sports never revert and are identical to Praeger's *S. spathulifolium* var. *purpureum*. Perhaps this process also occurs in the wild, but, as Clausen suggests, conditions are not favorable for larger plants near the coast, so they die. Surely this is a good demonstration of how *Sedum* species can, and probably have, adapted to changing conditions. If the climate of the coastal areas of northern California and southern Oregon became hotter and dryer, larger sports would soon outnumber tiny, compact forms. As a foliage-contrast plant, *S. spathulifolium* subsp. *pruinosum* var. *purpureum* is excellent; it is as hardy as 'Cape Blanco'. Other similar cultivars exist and are described below.

Sedum spathulifolium subsp. *pruinosum* 'Carnea' and 'William Pascoe' are very similar. Each has medium-sized rosettes with the reduction of the pruinosity revealing bright red or purple-red leaves (respectively), especially at tips. 'Rosea' is probably similar, but it appears lost to cultivation.

Sedum spathulifolium subsp. *spathulifolium* 'Aureum' is a fascinating cultivar of unknown origin. Its leaf color is outstanding. Unfortunately, plants are not hardy, except in areas with very mild winters. Leaves are glaucous, hardly pruinose, so the plant may be better assigned to the type species. In spring, the overall color is buff-yellow, which is quickly tinged a beautiful rose hue by sunshine. As leaves grow, their bases are green, so the tri-colored effect is quite spectacular. Flowers of this form are very large, nearly 2 cm (0.8 in) across, on an open inflorescence.

Sedum spathulifolium subsp. *purdyi* (Jepson) Clausen grows on the border of California and Oregon in the Klamath Mountains and in the northern Sierra Nevada from about 400 to 1100 m (1300 to 3600 ft). It has glabrous, shiny-green leaves. Stolons are exceptionally long (10 cm/4 in) and slender with flat miniature rosettes at their tips (Fig. 9.8).

Sedum spathulifolium subsp. *yosemitense* (Britton) Clausen is very similar, but apparently has shorter, thick stolons. It is from a disjunct site in the central Sierra Nevada. It is quite tender and appears to have been lost from cultivation in Europe.

Several natural hybrids have been introduced into cultivation by Helen Payne. *Sedum* 'Moonglow' is thought to be *S. laxum* subsp. *heckneri* × *S. spathulifolium* subsp. *spathulifolium*, as it has features midway between both parents. *Sedum* 'Silvermoon' is very similar and from the same location. It is thought to be a backcross.

'Harvest Moon' is probably the most striking of Helen Payne's introductions. It is the least green of the trio, with gray-purple rosebudlike rosettes that have prominent centers resembling centers of *Sempervivum* species. 'Harvest Moon' is a garden hybrid between 'Silvermoon' and

Figure 9.8. *Sedum spathulifolium* subsp. *purdyi*. The main rosette is 3.5 cm (1.4 in) across.

'Moonglow', or, more probably between 'Silvermoon' and 'Carnea'. 'Silvermoon' appears to be most promiscuous and its seedlings show considerable variation.

HORTICULTURE. Some clones of *Sedum spathulifolium* are perfectly suited to the English climate. Clausen found cold-frame cultivation in New York State less than satisfactory. Only 'Aureum', and probably *S. spathulifolium* subsp. *yosemitense*, need winter protection. Other clones appear to withstand wet or dry winters with temperatures falling below freezing frequently, but not for many consecutive days. 'Cape Blanco' is the most rapidly spreading form, so it makes an ideal ground cover. It takes the shape of whatever it is carpeting, so creeping over trough edges, old chimneys, or rocks it is second to none. It never becomes troublesome as it is very easily controlled. It appears to be self-sterile.

The evergreen nature of all forms makes them permanently eye-catching. Mixing forms on the top of a wall or in a stone trough can be most rewarding. Despite their ease of cultivation, plants of this species, because of their appealing nature, invariably catch the eyes of judges in alpine shows where compact, densely white plants seem to stand out.

SEDUM STENOPETALUM Pursh

SYNONYMS: *S. douglassii* Hooker,
Amerosedum stenopetalum (Pursh) Löve & Löve
COMMON NAME: Narrow-petaled stonecrop

Not uncommon in gardens, this bright little stonecrop is upright or creeping with narrow, spirally arranged leaves. Viviparous rosettes form on inflorescences and fall to the ground to propagate new plants as each inflorescence disintegrates. *Sedum stenopetalum*, which has been confused with *S. lanceolatum* in literature, has bright, shiny, green leaves tinged red, without sharp points (Fig. 9.1). Plants often rise to 15 cm (6 in) high or more and produce light yellow flowers in midsummer (Fig. 9.9).

HABITAT. This Western Cordilleran stonecrop is found from 41° to 51° north, on adjacent plains of Montana from very low altitudes to heights in excess of 3000 m (10,000 ft), on scree or in rock-niches in the open pine country of British Columbia, Alberta, Saskatchewan, Nebraska, New Mexico, Nevada, California, Washington, and Oregon. These areas, according to Clausen, have exceptionally dry periods in late summer—hence the adaptation to propagate vegetatively.

MAIN POINTS OF DISTINCTION. The viviparous nature of this plant is unique to *Sedum* in this part of the world. Fresh leaves are semiterete, flattened on upper surfaces. Dead leaves are persistent on stems and also envelope adventitious rosettes, protecting them as they blow around before resting in a favorable spot. Each inflorescence is usually a 3-branched cyme with spurred floral bracts. Sepals are erect and fused to a receptacle. Other flower parts are yellow. Carpels are at first upright but eventually diverge and show distinctly kyphocarpic fruit. $2n = 64$. All forms of *S. stenopetalum* are octoploid.

VARIATION. Two contrasting clones are in general cultivation. One, usually labelled "*Sedum douglassii*," is a more creeping form that vegetatively is very similar to the orthocarpic European *S. montanum*. This form does not produce large numbers of adventitious buds nor does it disintegrate completely in autumn. A second form is taller, and often, as a result of lush green growth in spring, takes on the outline of a miniature Christmas tree. In autumn, this plant disintegrates and only scattered, adventitious propagations remain.

Clausen found intermediate forms in the wild. I have several clones propagated from wild collections, each fairly distinct in size.

HORTICULTURE. *Sedum stenopetalum* is an interesting species that in some forms is not very floriferous, but bright red leaves are attractive in summer. The shedding of propagules never becomes troublesome; on the contrary, some propagules should be nurtured in case one's

Figure 9.9. *Sedum stenopetalum* with an 18-cm (7-in) high inflorescence displaying adventitious buds.

neighbors gain all the propagation material as a result of wind dispersal. This is an excellent species for a scree garden but not dense enough for stone troughs.

SEDUM TERNATUM Michaux

SYNONYM: *Clausenellia ternata*
(Michaux) Löve & Löve

Sedum ternatum favors wetter, shady spots. It is not particularly common in Europe, but is often encountered in the United States in "doorstep or kitchen gardens," according to Joyce Descloux (1989):

In northwestern North Carolina, elevation about 3500 ft [1000 m], one sees it everywhere, planted in stone walls, old crocks and tubs, and often around service stations in old rubber tires filled with gravel or stones. It is supposed to bring good health to the inhabitants of the houses where it grows, and in old days was used as a cure-all for everything from bites and poison-ivy rashes to stomach-ache . . . . [T]he Cherokee . . . almost certainly used *S. ternatum* as one of their herbal cures.

Descloux believes the documented habitat of *S. ternatum* equates too closely with areas travelled by nomadic tribes of the Cherokee nation to be accepted as such. Most probably plants were cultivated by this group of Native Americans and spread beyond the species' true habitat. Stems 8 cm (3 in) long or more carry spathulate, ternate leaves and are topped with compact rosettes of medium green, subpetiolate leaves. Three-branched cymes carry white, 4-partite, slightly fragrant flowers with deeply channeled petals in spring.

HABITAT. This stonecrop is an eastern species from the Appalachians, in coastal valleys, and on to the Great Plains as far as the Mississippi Valley, preferring shady glades or wooded bluffs.

MAIN POINTS OF DISTINCTION. Flat, almost round, ternate leaves and 4-partite spring flowers easily distinguish this species (Figs. 9.1p, 9.10). Sepals are tiny; petals are patent, deeply channeled, carinate below, and very acute. Filaments are flattened, especially at the base. Anthers are dark red. Carpels are erect at first, but fruit are kyphocarpic.

VARIATION. Diploids, triploids, tetraploids, and hexaploids exist in the wild—$2n = 16$, 24, 32, and 48 ($x = 8$)—but visually, plants do not appear distinct. The form *Sedum ternatum* var. *minus* Praeger is probably a diploid, but I do not know of any constantly dwarf form in cultivation.

HORTICULTURE. This species is very important to the *Sedum* enthusiast for it is usually first

Figure 9.10. *Sedum ternatum.* The rosette measures nearly 3 cm (1 in) across

of the hardy species to flower. It must be grown in at least half shade, and it thrives in a dampish spot. It spreads to form a dense carpet, but is very easily controlled. It is hardy in Mid Northumberland, but would be difficult to maintain in much harsher areas. Summer droughts and baking conditions will wipe out a colony.

CHAPTER 10

Latin American Species of Subgenus Sedum

Early botanists described newly discovered Latin American *Sedum* species alongside European species. Today it is generally accepted that, although several Mexican sedums resemble European sedums, they are best treated separately. Some Mexican *Sedum* species are more closely related to other genera of the Crassulaceae than they are to other Mexican sedums. I propose to follow the grouping of Mexican *Sedum* species as suggested by Charles Uhl. His work is the most recent and is the result of detailed cytological studies of all genera of Mexican Crassulaceae. *Sedum* species from areas south of Mexico are rare in habitat, taxonomically questionable, and almost unknown in cultivation. A single South American *Sedum* species in cultivation is kept separate at the end of this chapter.

Latin American *Sedum* species grow over a wide altitudinal range from lowland tropical areas with distinctly seasonal rainfall to true al-pines. Many species favor damp spots on steep canyon walls in partial shade and several grow as epiphytes. The number of species diminishes rapidly south of Mexico. *Sedum guatamalense*, as the name suggests, is a species from Guatemala, but despite the name being encountered in cultivation for *S.* ×*rubrotinctum*, the true epiphyte is not in cultivation. Several Central American sedums have been discovered but none are in cultivation—unless the true home of *S. mexicanum* is here.

Mexican species of *Sedum* can be divided into three groups:

1. *Pachysedum* group: species with perennial, woody stems and terminal inflorescences
2. The group of species with woody stems and lateral inflorescences
3. The group of species without woody stems

PACHYSEDUM GROUP

Section *Pachysedum* was erected by Berger and enlarged and erected as a subgenus by Clausen. Jacobsen added a few more species, and work on chromosomes by Uhl has shown that in addition to vegetative similarities most of the species within *Pachysedum* group have large, thick leaves and lateral inflorescences, and are cytologically similar to each other. Therefore, they form a natural group. This group is perhaps more closely related to Echeverioideae than to other groups of Mexican *Sedum*. *Sedum corynephyllum*, *S. craigii*, and *S. suaveolens* are tentatively placed here because their flowers with upright petals are anomalous. *Sedum corynephyllum* was originally described as the monotypic *Corynephyllum viride* by Rose, and the other two species were transferred to *Graptopetalum* by Clausen (1981), but by and large, these changes appear to have been ignored.

The following species of *Pachysedum* group are in cultivation:

Sedum adolphii Hamet
Sedum ×amecamecanum Praeger
Sedum aoikon Ulbrich (see *S. confusum*)
Sedum batallae Barocio
Sedum clavatum Clausen
Sedum commixtum Moran & Hutchinson
Sedum confusum Hemsley
Sedum corynephyllum Fröderström
Sedum craigii Clausen
Sedum cremnophila Clausen
Sedum 'Crocodile' (see *S. cremnophila*)
Sedum cuspidatum Alexander
Sedum decumbens Clausen (see *S. confusum*)
Sedum dendroideum De Candolle
Sedum hultenii Fröderström
Sedum 'Little Gem' (see *S. cremnophila*)
Sedum lucidum Clausen
Sedum ×luteoviride Clausen
Sedum macdougallii Moran
Sedum nussbaumerianum Bitter
Sedum orbatum Moran & Meyrán
Sedum pachyphyllum Rose
Sedum praealtum T. S. Brandegee
Sedum purpusi Rose (see *S. confusum*)
Sedum ×rubrotinctum Clausen
Sedum suaveolens Kimnach
Sedum treleasei Rose
Sedum 'Vera Higgins' (see *S. ×rubrotinctum*)

Plants of this group

- Are tender Mexican subshrubs with persistent woody stems.
- Have very fleshy, succulent leaves which, if removed cleanly, will root, and produce new plants.
- Have 5-partite white, pink-white, or yellow flowers.
- Can usually be cross-hybridized with each other.

- Can often hybridize with Mexican Crassulaceae other than *Sedum*.
- Flower mostly in early summer.
- Have orthocarpic flowers, but carpels can be somewhat spreading.
- With the exception of the occasional epiphyte, grow in steep, rocky niches.

The following key is intended to enable the reader to narrow down the possibilities when identifying an unnamed species.

Flowers white, stellate: *S. adolphii*, *S. batallae*, *S. clavatum*, *S. cuspidatum*, *S. lucidum*, *S. nussbaumerianum*, *S. orbatum*
Flowers white, petals standing upright for most of their length: *S. craigii*, *S. suaveolens*
Flowers yellow: *S. ×amecamecanum*, *S. confusum*, *S. cremnophila*, *S. decumbens*, *S. dendroideum*, *S. hultenii*, *S. macdougallii*, *S. pachyphyllum*, *S. praealtum*, *S. ×rubrotinctum*, *S. treleasei*
Leaves huge, more than 1 cm (0.4 in) thick: *S. cremnophila*
Leaves tiny: *S. batallae*
Leaves relatively thin, glabrous green: *S. ×amecamecanum*, *S. confusum*, *S. cuspidatum*, *S. decumbens*, *S. dendroideum*, *S. hultenii*, *S. ×luteoviride*, *S. orbatum*, *S. praealtum*
Leaves relatively thin, glaucous: *S. cuspidatum* (sometimes), *S. orbatum* (sometimes), *S. suaveolens*
Leaves very succulent, glabrous: *S. adolphii*, *S. cremnophila*, *S. lucidum*, *S. nussbaumerianum*. *S. ×rubrotinctum*
Leaves very succulent, glaucous: *S. clavatum*, *S. commixtum*, *S. corynephyllum*, *S. craigii*, *S. macdougallii*, *S. pachyphyllum*, *S. treleasei*

SEDUM ADOLPHII Hamet

PLATE 56

Sedum adolphii is one of seven white-flowered species of the *Pachysedum* group in cultivation possessing stellate petals (Plate 56). Clausen thought it could be the same species as *S. nuss-*

baumerianum (Fig. 10.1). Since the former is the older name, perhaps both species should be called *S. adolphii*. Both are widespread in cultivation but easily separated, especially when in flower. I am not contesting Clausen's suggestion, for I have not studied more than a couple of wild plants, and it could be that distinct forms in cultivation are united by intermediates in the wild.

To date, the habitat and range of *Sedum adolphii* remain a mystery. This glabrous-green subshrub grows to about 15 cm (6 in) high before stems start to arch and fall. Eventually stems may excede 35 cm (14 in) in length, and if well-grown, only the very lower stems are bare. Shiny green, patent, keeled leaves almost hide the stem, which is often mottled with deep red. The species is a rather shy flowerer, but when flowers appear they are on exceptionally long inflorescences that are densely covered with green bracts. Bracts are the same shape as the leaves but smaller. White flowers on pink pedicels fade to pink.

HABITAT. Unknown.

Figure 10.1. *Sedum adolphii* (left) and *S. nussbaumerianum* (right).

MAIN POINTS OF DISTINCTION. Vegetatively, this species is very similar to *Sedum nussbaumerianum*, which, if grown in full sun, turns a sickly orange, and to some forms of *S. lucidum*, which has very short pedicels. *Sedum adolphii* has yellow-green leaves that often tinge tan, but newer leaves are always apiculate, carinate, and bright green. Inflorescences are usually more than 15 cm (6 in) long, but can be twice this length, and are densely covered with bracts, terminating in a cluster of pedicels about 2 cm (0.8 in) long. Sepals are unequal and almost free.

VARIATION. Often plants of *Sedum nussbaumerianum* are sold with the label "*S. adolphii*." *Sedum adolphii* was quite rare until recently when Dutch nurseries included it in mixed succulent garden collections (unnamed). It is likely that all plants in cultivation have been vegetatively propagated from the same plant. $2n = 64$.

HORTICULTURE. This is a very easy succulent to grow, ideal for a hanging basket, especially with succulents of different hues. It grows exceptionally well outdoors in terra-cotta urns where few frosts are experienced.

SEDUM ×AMECAMECANUM Praeger

Clausen (1959) first suggested that this low shrub was a natural intergeneric hybrid between *Villadia batesii* and *Sedum praealtum* subsp. *monticola*, and cytological work (Uhl, 1978) confirmed Clausen's suspicions. Pale buff-yellow flowers are normally sterile, and although generally produced on lateral inflorescences, terminal inflorescences are sometimes produced, for hybrids of this nature are variable. Green shiny leaves are not particularly succulent, but flat, spurred, and arranged in loose, terminal clusters (Fig. 10.2). The hybrid is not common in cultivation.

HABITAT. Originally collected on Mount Iztaccihuatl towards Amecameca on the Trans-Mexican Volcanic Belt, this stonecrop is found from 2500 to 4000 m (8200 to 13,000 ft) as a true alpine.

MAIN POINTS OF DISTINCTION. Grass-green, elongated rosettes of thin, oblanceolate leaves are the best indicator. Leaves are very similar to those of *Sedum praealtum*, *S. confusum*, and *S. decumbens* in texture and color, but are much narrower. Blunt sepals are linear, unequal, and patent, and have basal spurs. Ephemeral petals are united, somewhat apiculate, pale yellow, and have broad bases.

VARIATION. All specimens I have seen in cultivation appear to be F$_1$ hybrids, but backcrossing does take place in the wild, and Uhl (1978) suggested that plants from Popocatepetl may have another subspecies of *Sedum praealtum* as a parent.

HORTICULTURE. This hybrid is almost hardy. Due to its high-altitude origin, it dislikes hot summer greenhouse conditions; if baked in this way, it is impossible to revive plants as any cuttings taken from apparently healthy remains languish and die without rooting. If placed outside in summer, especially in a hanging basket, the color of the specimen is far more pleasing to the eye, and there is less chance of loss due to still, hot air. Like many hybrids, it is prone to aphid infestation.

SEDUM BATALLAE Barocio

PLATE 56

The very limited habitat of *Sedum batallae* implies that this tiny member of *Pachysedum* group could be a hybrid. Clausen (1981) suggested *Echeveria secunda* × *Sedum dendroideum* for its parentage, but Uhl (1978) disagreed as the high chromosome count of $n = 34$ is typical of *Pachysedum* group. Tiny, gray imbricate leaves are clustered on tangled stems, which along with aerial roots contribute to the plant's untidy look (Fig. 10.3). The few small, whitish flowers have wine-red carpels and nectary glands.

HABITAT. This stonecrop's habitat is limited to a single cliff near Epazoyucan, Hidalgo, Trans-Mexican Volcanic Belt, and may now be extinct in the wild.

MAIN POINTS OF DISTINCTION. The untidy, decumbent nature of the plant in cultivation, long bare stems, and tiny leaves make it unique in *Pachysedum* group. Sepals are uneven.

VARIATION. To the best of my knowledge, all plants in cultivation are the result of distribution I.S.I. 1496. Grown in sun, leaves can be glaucous blue-green rather than gray. Clausen

Figure 10.2. *Sedum ×amecamecanum* in a 3-in (8-cm) pot.

Figure 10.3. *Sedum batallae* leaves are only about 5 mm (0.2 in) long.

noted that flowers could be red, white, and green. Photographs of plants in the wild show compact specimens with more dead leaves adhering to stems.

HORTICULTURE. This is the ugly duckling of *Pachysedum* group. Specimens look embarrassingly ragged and shabby. Initially the plant is very difficult to establish, but once rooted, it spreads quickly. To disguise its gangling nature, it is best kept in a hanging basket. Like hybrids, the flowering season of *Sedum batallae* is very long.

SEDUM CLAVATUM Clausen

PLATES 56, 57

For a period, *Sedum clavatum* was known as the "*Sedum* species from Tiscalatengo Gorge." Stout, long, bare, creeping stems terminate in glau-

cous, papillose blue-green rosettes of succulent leaves. Compact inflorescences of large white flowers with long pedicels fade pink.

HABITAT. The valley of the Tiscalatengo River, Mexico, in the Trans-Mexican Volcanic Belt is the home of this species.

MAIN POINTS OF DISTINCTION. Long, bare, creeping or falling stems with glaucous papillose leaves in terminal rosettes are good indicators. Long, clavate sepals are unequal, glaucous-green, and tipped with speckles of red.

VARIATION. Two forms of *Sedum clavatum* appear to be in cultivation: one has very long bare stems, few branches, and glaucous-green leaves; the other is smaller and has shorter stems that terminate in smaller, more globular, glaucous-blue rosettes (Plate 57). $n = 33$. Some collected plants, including the type species, have a small extra chromosome; others do not. Perhaps this difference accounts for the two forms in cultivation.

A beautiful hybrid with *Graptopetalum filiferum* has recently been distributed from California. Compact, whitish rosettes of the hybrid have apiculate leaves and appear midway between two very contrasting parents.

HORTICULTURE. This is a very elegant, stately species for hanging baskets.

SEDUM COMMIXTUM
Moran & Hutchison

Young plants of *Sedum commixtum* seem full of promise, as their pruinose, blue foliage is very bright (Fig. 10.4). The tight hummocks of rosettes are stunning when first formed, but even in bright light, stems become very leggy (to 30 cm/12 in), and leaves are soon widely spaced on the equally pruinose stems. Patent leaves turn purple-red at their tips and are cupped at the stem tips. Had the species been discovered in the early 1900s and not 60 years later, Joseph Nelson Rose would probably have created a new genus to accomodate it, as the flowers are unlike any other member of the Mexican Crassulaceae.

This species is an exceptionally shy flowerer.

After 10 years my plant has not bloomed. The excellent drawings in the *Cactus & Succulent Journal* (U.S.) (1980, 52:161) and the photograph by Charles Uhl reproduced in the *Sedum Society Newsletter* (1991, 18:3) show flowers reminiscent in shape to those of *Echeveria* but much smaller and with an urceolate floral tube (i.e., pitcher-shaped, pot-bellied with a narrow rim). The epipetalous stamens are anomalous to *Sedum* and *Echeveria* by being fused to the petals; the free part is exceptionally short and appears more than half way up the green-yellow petals, which are marked heavily with chocolate-brown. It must have been a difficult decision assigning this species to a genus, but the cosmopolitan nature of *Sedum* seemed most fitting. Or, in the words of Professor Uhl (unpub.) "Berger's subfamily Sedoideae is a sort of catch-all for anything that does not fit well into any of the other subfamilies . . . included are the taxa which violate the usual morphological criteria." This is a fairly common species, often unnamed, in mixed succulent collections or bowl gardens.

HABITAT. This stonecrop hails from San Domingo Ozolotepec, Oaxaca, Mexico, at 2600 m (8500 ft), as a true alpine in the Southern Sierra Madre.

MAIN POINTS OF DISTINCTION. Vegetatively, this species is not dissimilar to *Sedum treleasei* and *S. macdougallii*, but is much more chalky-white than either of the yellow-flowered species. If you are lucky enough to study the odd flowers of *S. commixtum*, you will see the significance of its name. Urceolate, distinctly tubed flowers, narrow-based, highly uneven sepals, and brown-mottled petals with stamens inserted at the mouth of the tube are most distinct. $n = 34$.

VARIATION. All plants in cultivation appear to have been propagated from the initial collection.

HORTICULTURE. This is such an attractive species, it is worthwhile beheading it each autumn and pushing stem tips (rosettes) into a

Figure 10.4. *Sedum commixtum*; the tallest stem here is 17 cm (7 in) long.

sandy compost to overwinter. Next spring, the rosettes develop to produce attractive plants for the season. Old plants become very gangling and appear etiolated despite a sunny situation. *Sedum commixtum* is surprisingly cold hardy if kept bone dry, with temperatures of −12°C (10°F) having no ill-effects on the plant. Charles Uhl says that native Mexicans collect ice from the habitat of this species.

SEDUM CONFUSUM Hemsley

PLATE 58

SYNONYMS: *S. aoikon* Ulbrich, *S. purpusi* Rose

SEDUM DECUMBENS Clausen

To clarify the relationships between these frequently confused species, this volume brings them together. The German botanist E. Ulbrich described *Sedum aoikon* in 1917, but his descriptions were based on a plant of unknown origin. Forty-two years later, despite extensive study of plants in the field, Robert T. Clausen knew of no natural habitat for the species. He described *S. aoikon* using two specimens he had grown in Ithaca (Clausen 1959). Propagations of these plants were distributed widely, and plants became common in collections.

Clausen equated *Sedum purpusi* Rose (not Kuntze), which had been collected by Carl Purpus between Esperanza and Orizaba, with *S. aoikon*. Although Clausen was unable to relocate the wild colony, he was confident that the dried specimens of *S. purpusi* were a good match for *S. aoikon*.

A species described by Hemsley in 1878, *Sedum confusum*, proved just as elusive, although Clausen had erroneously keyed differences between *S. confusum* and *S. aoikon* in 1948. In his tome *Sedum of North America* (Clausen 1975, 561-562), which, because of its cost, was never widely available, he reversed decisions he had made earlier: "Additional study of plants in cultivation . . . led to this change in interpretation . . . the opinion now is that the types of both *S. confusum* and *S.*

aoikon apply to the same species." The oldest name, *S. confusum*, had priority, and *S. aoikon* and *S. purpusi* were made synonymous.

A similar but smaller plant in cultivation in the United States was also generally known by the name *Sedum confusum*. This second species had been distributed in the trade as early as 1931. When Clausen encountered it, he realized that this obviously related plant was not *S. aoikon* (i.e., the true *S. confusum*), so he gave the smaller plant a new name: *S. decumbens*. As careful horticulturists are likely to use Clausen's earlier works, these species are unlikely to be correctly identified in collections.

Both species are subshrubs with shiny green leaves. *Sedum decumbens* has much smaller, relatively thicker leaves with wider bases, which tend to cluster at stem tips into tight rosettes. Flowers are light yellow, and inflorescences are open. The name suggests that the plant is more decumbent, but I have not always found this an obvious feature of differentiation. *Sedum confusum* has petiolate leaves up to 2.5 times longer than those of *S. decumbens*, and these usually clothe the top half of stems. Flowers of *S. decumbens* have orange-yellow petals.

HABITAT. Northern Puebla, Trans-Mexican Volcanic Belt, is the home of *Sedum confusum*, but no locality is known for *S. decumbens*.

MAIN POINTS OF DISTINCTION. Both species look like miniature forms of the common *Sedum praealtum*, but can easily be separated by leaf shape and size. For both species, $n = 34$. *Sedum* ×*luteoviride* and *S.* ×*amecamecanum* have similar habits and looks, but leaf shape will also easily distinguish them. Evans depicted *S. decumbens* as *S. confusum*, but Praeger correctly depicted and identified *S. confusum*. Both species have unequal sepals and long stamens.

VARIATION. Plants of the original *"Sedum purpusi"* collection, which have often retained this name in Europe, have longer (but not wider) leaves, and larger sepals than those forms introduced later. It appears as though all the plants of *S. decumbens* in cultivation may have been vegetatively propagated from the same stock. It has been reported that *S. confusum* can produce 6-partite and even 7-partite flowers.

HORTICULTURE. Praeger said that *Sedum confusum* was not in general cultivation in North America, but *S. decumbens* is apparently common, usually carrying the name of the former. In Europe, the names "*S. aoikon,*" *S. confusum, S. decumbens,* and "*S. purpusi*" are all encountered from time to time. True *S. confusum* is sometimes correctly named, but is often referred to as "*S. aoikon*" or "*S. purpusi.*" *Sedum decumbens* mostly carries the label *S. confusum* and is as common as the true *S. confusum.*

Both species are almost hardy. They do not suffer when temperatures plummet below freezing point. In fact, if plants freeze solid for days, they recover well. Repeated thaw-freeze cycles or very wet winters can kill the plants, but, except in extreme areas, it is worthwhile attempting both species outside in a sheltered spot. They are perfect specimens for a cold frame or alpine house. They look exotic when grown in a stone trough.

SEDUM CORYNEPHYLLUM
(Rose) Fröderström

SYNONYM: *Corynephyllum viride* Rose

When Berger moved this species into *Sedum* as *S. viride* (Rose) Berger, the name had been pre-empted by Makino for a species of subgenus *Hylotelephium* and therefore had to be changed to *Sedum corynephyllum.* It is a very rare plant in collections. Juvenile specimens, which resemble the common *S. pachyphyllum,* grow into sturdier plants. This species is a handsome, upright subshrub that develops a thick, gray, woody stem covered with small scalelike tessellations (Fig. 10.5).

Very succulent, upturned, club-shaped leaves are shortly spurred and almost terete. When they fall, leaf scars remain on the stems. Long inflorescences carry only a few peculiar flowers, which are so odd that Rose (Britton & Rose

1905b) felt this species warranted a new genus to itself. Sessile flowers do not open much, but remain cupped, enclosed by huge, free, uneven, spurred sepals that are longer than the green-yellow petals.

HABITAT. This stonecrop is indigenous to vertical cliffs on the Atlantic side of the Eastern Sierra Madre over quite a large area.

MAIN POINTS OF DISTINCTION. Stems 2 cm (0.8 in) thick differentiate this species from *Sedum pachyphyllum* and its hybrids. Green-yellow flowers with huge, upright, free sepals are unique. Epipetalous stamens are inserted some way from the base of the petals. Nectary glands are short and wide.

VARIATION. Both diploids and tetraploids ($n = 34, 68$) are in cultivation. The former appear more sturdy, but I have not observed enough verified clones to comment positively. Diploids are more northerly plants, and, due to the 200-

Figure 10.5. *Sedum corynephyllum* in a 4-in (10-cm) pot.

km (125-mi) range of the species, could be distinct enough to warrant special status.

HORTICULTURE. This species makes a handsome, stately greenhouse stonecrop. It is most attracive as a potted plant in a conservatory, a porch, or on a windowsill.

SEDUM CRAIGII Clausen

PLATE 59

SYNONYM: *Graptopetalum craigii* Clausen

Clausen (1981) expanded *Graptopetalum* to accommodate *Sedum craigii* and *S. suaveolense* because he thought their flowers were anomalous to *Sedum*. Vegetatively, *S. craigii*, which could be a hybrid, is similar to *Graptopetalum amethystenum*, which Clausen suggested could be one parent. Uhl (1978) pointed out that *Echeveria affinis* is a very close relative with exactly the same chromosome count of *n* = 30. *Sedum craigii* is unusual for a member of *Pachysedum* group in that it is in full flower in habitat in autumn. Uhl claimed that few Crassulaceae flower in western Mexico in autumn, but *Echeveria affinis* is indigenous to the area and flowers in autumn.

Whether *Sedum craigii* and the similarly anomalous *S. suaveolens* are hybrids or sports, or whether they should be assigned to *Sedum* or some other genus of Crassulaceae is subject to debate. The outstanding beauty of the plants is not so inapparent. *Sedum craigii* has large, thick glaucous-lilac leaves. Stems are not particularly sturdy, so the upright branches soon tumble and fall with the sheer weight of the succulent leaves. White flowers, which were initially reported to have free petals, have petals somewhat connate at the base. They are upright below and turned out at the tips, as with *Lenophyllum*.

HABITAT. Barranca del Cobre in western Chihuahua in the Western Sierra Madre is the location of this localized species.

MAIN POINTS OF DISTINCTION. Leaf shape and color are distinct for *Sedum*. The only other species with upright petals recurved at the apex is *S. suaveolens*, which is stemless. *n* = 30.

VARIATION. All plants in cultivation have been propagated from a single collected plant.

HORTICULTURE. This is a superb plant for a hanging basket, especially with other plants of contrasting foliage. The bloom on the leaves is easily removed, and therefore it is important that plants are not positioned where they can be rubbed or brushed against. When the glaucous bloom is removed, the purple-lilac color of the leaves shines through.

SEDUM CREMNOPHILA Clausen

PLATES 60, 61

SYNONYMS: *Cremnophila nutans* Rose,
S. nutans Clausen

Sedum cremnophila appears to bridge the genera *Echeveria* and *Sedum*. In recent years, the genus *Cremnophila* has been expanded and redefined (Moran 1978) to act as a buffer between the two large genera *Sedum* and *Echeveria*, so perhaps *Sedum cremnophila* should not be included in this volume. In succulent collections, the species is invariably labelled *Sedum*; individual flowers are just as one would expect for that genus, so I follow Uhl (1978) and include the species with *Pachysedum* group.

Leaves of *Sedum cremnophila* are massive, the largest of any Mexican stonecrop. They are very succulent, somewhat glaucous, papillose, and dull green. Eventually, plants develop a short stem, which is almost completely hidden by leaves. The lateral, many-flowered anomalous spike of pale yellow flowers on short, stout pedicels tends to be almost horizontal, then droops.

HABITAT. Cliffs near Tepoztlán, Morelos, Sierra de Chalchi, adjacent to the Southern Sierra Madre.

MAIN POINTS OF DISTINCTION. The problem is not how to differentiate between this species and other species of *Sedum* (because the sheer nature of the leaves is sufficient evidence), but how to differentiate between this species and other members of Mexican Crassulaceae. I find it impossible to differentiate between *S. cremnophila* and *Echeveria linguifolia* if the plants are not in flower. Several other *Echeveria* and intergeneric hybrids that are relatively common in cultivation help to confuse the situation. When in flower, a distinct spike of stellate, shiny, light yellow flowers separates *Sedum cremnophila* from other species.

VARIATION. *n* = 33. The very limited range of the plant in the wild suggests that little variation exists, though this species hybridizes freely with diverse members of Mexican Crassulaceae. The resulting hybrids are often more common than *Sedum cremnophila* itself, which is not often seen in Europe.

Sedum 'Crocodile' (I.S.I. 1641) has two very contrasting parents—*S. cremnophila* × *S. furfuraceum*. It was distributed as a *Cremnosedum*, but if *Sedum cremnophila* is a member of *Pachysedum* group, the name *Cremnophila* is redundant. Nomenclature aside, this is a handsome hybrid for a hanging basket, whose name comes from the tessellated markings on its stems, which remind one of reptilian leather in both color and texture (Fig. 10.6). Glossy, green leaves turn deep red in full sun, and, in essence, this hybrid and 'Little Gem' are midway between two most unlikely parents. Hybrid sedums often have no set flowering time, or they tend to flower all summer. 'Crocodile' is never a prolific flowerer, but throughout summer, plants produce a few flowers at a time on very small inflorescences. Flowers start very pale yellow and fade to pink-orange. Like *Sedum furfuraceum*, inflorescences can be terminal, but normally they are just discernably lateral.

Like 'Crocodile', 'Little Gem' (I.S.I. 1256), which is *Sedum cremnophila* × *S. humifusum*, is the product of Mr. & Mrs. Robert Grim of California and was distributed by the International Succulent Institute as *Cremnosedum*. The parents of 'Little Gem' contrast even more than do the parents of 'Crocodile'. 'Little Gem' forms a neat, dense, succulent mat of *Sempervivum*-like rosettes, which are shiny green but can tinge red

in full sun. Some enthusiasts report that it is a shy flowerer, but this is certainly not true of my experience, as throughout summer 5-cm (2-in long) inflorescences, carrying a few light yellow flowers, seem to be produced consecutively (Plate 61).

Sedum cremnophila × *Graptopetalum paraguayense* most resembles the latter parent, which is a very common plant often labelled "*Sedum weinbergii*" or "ghost plant." Evans included *Graptopetalum paraguayense* in *Sedum*. If *Graptopetalum* is accepted as a genus, then "*S. weinbergii*" belongs in it. Again, the hybrid appears midway between its parents. Very long inflorescences collapse under their own weight and terminate in large clusters of very pale yellow flowers. Leaves of this hybrid have far more bloom than *S. cremnophila*, but are still green. Leaves of *G. paraguayense* are never green (Fig. 10.7).

Perhaps there are dozens of other hybrids that have appeared in collections. One in my collection has flowered, and my hunch is that it is the

Figure 10.6. *Sedum* 'Crocodile' stems are 11 mm (0.4 in) thick.

Rising to only 15 cm (6 in) high, the plant is relatively dull. Light green leaves are tinged wine-red at the tips and tend to be quite upright—especially in drought conditions. Lower halves of stems are bare with leaf scars. Bare inflorescences carry a terminal cluster with a few large white flowers.

HABITAT. Two disjunct localities in eastern Oaxaca and western Chiapas in the Southern Sierra Madre are the home of this stonecrop.

MAIN POINTS OF DISTINCTION. Small, apiculate, spurred, light green leaves on the upper half of highly textured stems are a good indicator. Petals are erect at the base. *Sedum orbatum*, its nearest relative, has larger leaves.

VARIATION. Both populations have $n = 34$. Most of the plants I have studied probably originated from Dennis Pearson via Ron Evans.

Figure 10.7. *Sedum cremnophila* × *Graptopetalum paraguayense* in a 4-in (10-cm) pot.

result of *Sedum cremnophila* hybridizing with a species of the *S. dendroideum* complex: *S. praealtum, S. confusum,* or *S. dendroideum* itself. A second plant is vegetatively very similar to 'Crocodile', but to date has not flowered, so its parentage is shrouded in mystery.

HORTICULTURE. The true species and all its hybrids are very stately succulents, recommended for lovers of cacti and other exceptionally succulent xerophites. All require good light and are excellent potted plants for windowsills, conservatories, and greenhouses. The type species, in particular, is very susceptible to overwatering in winter.

SEDUM CUSPIDATUM Alexander

PLATE 56

Sedum cuspidatum is an uncommon member of *Pachysedum* group with few exciting qualities.

Figure 10.8. Two clones of *Sedum cuspidatum*. The shorter stem is about 11 cm (4 in) long.

There appear to be two distinct clones in cultivation: one has dull green glabrous leaves, while the other is faintly glaucous, especially at the leaf bases (Fig. 10.8). I am unable to say whether the two forms are evidence of the two disjunct colonies.

HORTICULTURE. This is an easy but slow-growing species, susceptible to mealy-bug infestation. It is best grown in a pot or in an indoor rockery.

SEDUM DENDROIDEUM
De Candolle

An evergreen tree sedum, *Sedum dendroideum* is much rarer than, but often confused with *S. praealtum*. It is very closely related to *S. praealtum*, *S. confusum*, and *S. decumbens*. Its upright trunks can be 60 cm (24 in) high, or much taller in one clone, and spathulate, almost-orbicular, shiny, green leaves cluster at stem tips. In 10 years, this subshrub has never flowered for me, but flowers, when produced, are bright yellow.

HABITAT. This is a widespread species probably native to the Southern Sierra Madre to as far south as Guatemala. It is depicted in Central American art because of its magical (healing) qualities; it must, therefore, have been transported and cultivated.

MAIN POINTS OF DISTINCTION. No other evergreen tree sedum grows to this stature except *Sedum praealtum*, which has been considered synonymous but is distinct. *Sedum dendroideum* has a line of subepidermal glands all along leaf margins, a feature that immediately separates it from its look-alike relatives. These glands can be red in summer, but are clearly visible at all times (Fig. 10.9). *Sedum praealtum* has no such glands and leaves tend to be more yellow-green. Leaf shape is a less reliable aid to identification, as some subspecies of *S. praealtum* have very similar leaves to those of *S. dendroideum*, but the latter has leaves that are always widest in the upper quarter. In addition, the chromosome count of $n = 30$ immediately separates it from *S. praealtum*.

VARIATION. Several clones are in cultivation, though none are common. I.S.I. 1681 is a very tall form, which apparently grows into 3-m (10-ft) trees in habitat in Puebla.

HORTICULTURE. Such a giant stonecrop makes an excellent pseudobonsai subject. It is not as hardy as *Sedum praealtum*, but will withstand mild Northumbrian winters outdoors.

SEDUM HULTENII Fröderström

Not a typical member of this group, *Sedum hultenii* has thin leaves clustered in terminal rosettes on 12-cm (5-in) long, bare stems. The chromosome count of $n = 26$, too, is anomalous. Uhl (1978) recorded that this is the only member of *Pachysedum* group that does not readily hybridize with other species in this group—although it hybridizes with *S. cremnophila*—so perhaps its inclusion in *Pachysedum* group is questionable. Lax, open inflorescences are exceptionally long, often three times as long as stems, very reminiscent of *Aichryson* species, and carry dozens of small pale yellow flowers on slender pedicels (Fig. 10.10). The species is quite rare in cultivation.

HABITAT. This stonecrop has an extensive range throughout Hidalgo into Puebla on the Trans-Mexican Volcanic Belt in damp, shady vertical sites.

MAIN POINTS OF DISTINCTION. Glabrous, not very succulent, medium-green leaves, with short spurs, in terminal rosettes, on short stems, and exceptionally long inflorescences clearly separate this species. Pedicels are long, as are the beaks of carpels. Sepals are united at the base and only slightly uneven. Cytologically the species is distinct.

VARIATION. The large range of this species suggests that variation should be expected, but chromosome counts have been constant. Flowers can sometimes be 6-partite. Grown in shade, leaves can be dark green.

HORTICULTURE. This is a super plant for sunny windowsills, if there is room for the huge, lax inflorescences to tumble.

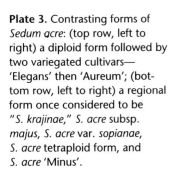

Plate 2. *Sedum* species are ideal plants for pictorial displays in parks and gardens. Pictured here is a scene from Dublin Botanic Gardens, Ireland.

Plate 1. *Sedum album* var. *micranthum* subvar. *chloroticum* is an excellent foliage contrast ground cover. Here it accompanies a conifer in an imitation stone trough.

Plate 3. Contrasting forms of *Sedum acre*: (top row, left to right) a diploid form followed by two variegated cultivars—'Elegans' then 'Aureum'; (bottom row, left to right) a regional form once considered to be "*S. krajinae*," *S. acre* subsp. *majus*, *S. acre* var. *sopianae*, *S. acre* tetraploid form, and *S. acre* 'Minus'.

Plate 4. *Sedum borissovae* in a 6-in (15-cm) terra-cotta pot in early July.

Plate 5. *Sedum grisebachii* tetraploid in a 4-in (10-cm) pot.

Plate 6. *Sedum laconicum* in a 2-in (5-cm) pot, with relatively long inflorescences rising from the cluster of tufts.

Plate 7. *Sedum sexangulare* on a dry whin scree.

Plate 8. *Sedum urvillei* occupying a 6-in (15-cm) pot in August.

Plate 9. Contrasting plants in the *Sedum anglicum* group: (top row, left to right) *S. anglicum* subsp. *arenarium*, *S. anglicum* from the Isle of Man in the Irish Sea, *S. anglicum* var. *hibernicum*; (center left) *S. anglicum* var. *pyrenaicum*; (bottom row) *S. anglicum* var. *pyrenaicum* SF 198/1, *S. anglicum* from Colonsay, Inner Hebrides, and *S. anglicum* subsp. *melanantherum*.

Plate 10. *Sedum anglicum* subsp. *arenarium* in habitat on a granitic outcrop along the Tâmega Valley, north Portugal.

Plate 11. *Sedum gracile* in a 4-in (10-cm) pot.

Plate 12. *Sedum hispanicum* var. *minus*, a deservedly common garden species with 4-partite, 5-partite, and 6-partite flowers, creeping over a concrete paving slab from a whin scree.

Plate 13. *Sedum obtusifolium* var. *listoniae* in August.

Plate 14. *Sedum pallidum* var. *bithynicum* (syn. *S. bithynicum*) just starting to flower in a 6-in (15-cm) pot.

Plate 15. *Sedum rubens* 'Pewter' in a 3-in (8-cm) pot.

Plate 16. *Sedum stellatum* in late May.

Plate 17. *Sedum stoloniferum* growing to perfection in a shady, damp spot where it has almost finished flowering. Note the stellate petals and distinctly kyphocarpic fruit.

Plate 18. *S. forsterianum* 'Welsh Stonecrop', a British form.

Plate 20. *Sedum rupestre* f. *cristatum* in a 6-in (15-cm) pot.

Plate 19. *Sedum pruinatum* in habitat on a cliff on the edge of the Serra de Alvão, northern Portugal.

Plate 21. *Sedum album* subsp. *clusianum* on a rocky outcrop at low altitude in the valley of the Rio Balsemão, northern Portugal.

Plate 22. Four contrasting clones of *Sedum brevifolium* growing together on vertical granite in Serra de Montemuro, northern Portugal, at 1375 m (4511 ft).

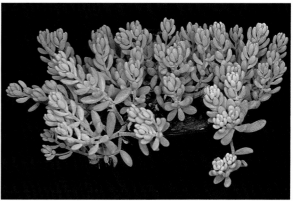

Plate 24. *Sedum dasyphyllum* subsp. *oblongifolium* (or 'Atlas Mountain Form') in a 4-in (10-cm) pot.

Plate 23. *Sedum caeruleum*, the only species of Crassulaceae with blue flowers.

Plate 26. *Sedum hirsutum*, an intermediate form on a schist cliff, lower Douro Valley, Portugal, in late April.

Plate 25. Highly colorful cultivars of *Sedum dasyphyllum*: 'Lilac Mound' and 'Opaline'.

Plate 28. *Sedum tenellum* in a 2½-in (6-cm) pot.

Plate 27. *Sedum spurium* growing on a gate pillar.

Plate 29. *Sedum villosum* in a 6-in (15-cm) pot.

Plate 30. *Sedum aizoon* in July.

Plate 31. *Sedum ellacombianum* in July.

Plate 32. *Sedum kamtschaticum* from the Hikari-Dake Mountains in a 6-in (15-cm) pot in September.

Plate 33. *Sedum middendorffianum* as a bedding plant in the Royal Botanic Garden Edinburgh attains 30 cm (12 in) stature in rich borders.

Plate 34. Range of leaf shapes and leaf arrangements of yellow-flowered Far Eastern species with fibrous roots: (top row, left to right) *Sedum nagasakianum, S. hakonense, S. japonicum, S. linerare* f. *variegatum, S. makinoi*; (middle row) *S. onychopetalum*, three distinct forms of *S. oryzifolium*, two forms of *S. polytrichoides*—the right of the pair 'Yabeanum', *S. rosulatobulbosum*, and *S. rupifragum*; (bottom row) *S. sarmentosum* (two clones), *S. senanense, S.* species RBGE 763791, *S. zentaro-tashiroi, S. subtile, S. tosaense,* and *S. tetractinum.*

Plate 35. *Sedum senanense* turns a rich red in full sun.

Plate 36. *Sedum makinoi* f. *variegatum.*

Plate 37. *Sedum rupifragum* in a mock stone trough.

Plate 38. *Sedum sarmentosum* must be allowed to tumble.

Plate 39. *Sedum mucizonia* showing tubed petals and bristly sepals.

Plate 40. *Sedum boehmeri* 'Keiko'.

Plate 41. *Sedum erubescens* from Tschuchima in a 2½-in (6-cm) pot in September.

Plate 42. *Sedum furusei* in a 2½-in (6-cm) pot.

Plate 43. *Sedum pilosum* in a 3-in (8-cm) pot.

Plate 44. Flowers of *Sedum semper-vivoides* are bright and hirsute.

Plate 45. *Sedum indicum* var. *yunnanense* in a 6-in (15-cm) pot.

Plate 46. *Sedum lancerottense* on a vertical cliff, ridge of Famara, Lanzarote.

Plate 47. *Sedum farinosum* at Royal Botanic Garden Edinburgh, Scotland.

Plate 48. *Sedum multiceps* in a 3-in (8-cm) pot.

Plate 49. *Sedum borschii* in a 2-in (5-cm) pot.

Plate 50. *Sedum glaucophyllum* in a 5-in (13-cm) pot. This glaucous form is nearly always erroneously labelled *S. nevii*.

Plate 51. *Sedum moranii* in a 2-in (5-cm) pot.

Plate 52. *Sedum nuttallianum* in a 3-in (8-cm) pot.

Plate 53. A southern, white-flowered form of *Sedum obtusatum* (foreground) and *S. oregonense* (behind).

Plate 54. *Sedum pulchellum.*

Plate 55. *Sedum spathulifolium* subsp. *pruinosum.*

Plate 56. Seven white-flowered species of *Pachysedum* group: (top row, left to right) *Sedum adolphii*, *S. batallae*, *S. cuspidatum*, two clones of *S. lucidum*, and *S. orbatum*; (below, left to right) *S. clavatum* and *S. nussbaumerianum*.

Plate 57. Two clones of *Sedum clavatum*: the larger rosette is a little over 2 in (5 cm) in diameter.

Plate 58. *Sedum confusum* (left) and *S. decumbens* (right). The taller plant is 17.8 cm (7 in) high.

Plate 60. *Sedum cremnophila* in a 4-in (10-cm) pot. Note the pyramidal inflorescence.

Plate 59. Budding *Sedum craigii* with long, even sepals.

Plate 61. *Sedum* 'Little Gem' in a 3-in (8-cm) pot.

Plate 62. *Sedum lucidum* I.S.I. 1497.

Plate 63. Two plants of *Sedum* ×*luteoviride*: the main plant has been grown outdoors in summer, and is compact and bright red; the green sprawling plant, which was grown in a greenhouse, is draped over the main plant to highlight variation as a result of site.

Plate 64. *Sedum macdougallii* (I.S.I. 1773) in a 4-in (10-cm) pot.

Plate 65. *Sedum nussbaumerianum* in a bed of black volcanic ash, at Pajares, Fuerteventura, Canary Islands, forming a mound 36 cm (14 in) across.

Plate 66. *Sedum pachyphyllum*, a popular plant for a windowsill.

Plate 67. *Sedeveria hummellii* bedded in the arid house of the Royal Botanic Garden Edinburgh.

Plate 68. *Sedum praealtum* flowering on a gatepost in northern Portugal.

Plate 70. This rosette of *Sedum suaveolens* measures 3 in (8 cm) across and carries fragrant white flowers with upright petals reflexed at the tips.

Plate 69. Two forms of *Sedum* ×*rubrotinctum*: (right) the original cherry-red form; (left) 'Aurora', a pearl pink chimera.

Plate 71. Two forms of *Sedum treleasei*: (left) the typical form; (right) 'Haren', which appears midway between *S. trealeasei* and *S. pachyphyllum*.

Plate 72. *Sedum allantoides*, the typical form with leaves shaped like sausages.

Plate 73. *Sedum allantoides* 'Goldii' has flat, succulent, spathulate leaves 2.5 cm (1 in) long.

Plate 74. Three burro's tails: (left) *Sedum morganianum*; (middle) *Sedeveria* 'Harry Butterfield'; (right) *Sedum burrito*.

Plate 75. A mature *Sedum frutescens* in Mexico City University Botanic Gardens. Photograph by Professor Mavis Doyle O.B.E.

Plate 76. *Sedum furfuraceum* in a 6-in (15-cm) pot.

Plate 77. *Sedum griseum* in a 4-in (10-cm) pot.

Plate 78. *Sedum obcordatum* in a 6-in (15-cm) pot.

Plate 79. *Sedum oxycoccoides* flower color is most unusual for a Mexican Crassulaceae.

Plate 80. *Sedum oxypetalum* flowers are fragrant.

Plate 81. *Sedum palmeri* flowers are harbingers of spring. This plant is a tetraploid (syn. *S. compressum*).

Plate 83. *Sedum compactum*, a tiny carpeting species.

Plate 82. *Sedum bellum* has flat, spathulate, imbricate leaves.

Plate 84. *Sedum ebracteatum* in a 4-in (10-cm) pot.

Plate 85. *Sedum greggii* in December in a 4-in (10-cm) pot.

Plate 86. *Sedum hintonii* in springtime in a 5-in (13-cm) porous clay pot.

Plate 87. *Sedum humifusum* is perhaps the lowest-growing species.

Plate 88. Similar white-flowered Mexican non-woody species: the large central plant is *Sedum* 'Spiral Staircase'; to the left of it are three contrasting clones of *S. moranense*; the right side comprises (top row, left to right) *Sedum* species from Hidalgo and *S. diffusum* 'Potosinum'; (below) *S. liebmannianum* and *S. diffusum*.

Plate 89. *Sedum nanifolium* in a 12-in (31-cm) pan (saucer) is half-hardy.

Plate 90. *Sedum oaxacanum* in a handmade terra-cotta pot 4 in (10 cm) wide with a flat back so it can be mounted on a wall.

Plate 91. Three distinct clones of *Sedum reptans*: (left) a 36-cm (14-in) bowl containing I.S.I. 1222; (top right) Lau 081; and (bottom right) the type collection.

Plate 92. *Sedum versadense* f. *chontalense.*

Plate 93. *Sedum spectabile* attracts butterflies in October.

Plate 94. *Sedum tatarinowii*, a miniature upright species.

Plate 95 (far right). *Sedum telephium* 'Autumn Joy' lives up to its name.

Plate 96. A mature plant of *Sedum sieboldii* in a hanging basket; the whole plant measures 60 cm (24 in) across.

Plate 97. *Sedum anacampseros*, a shy flowerer, is worthy of the wait.

Plate 98. *Sedum cauticola* 'Lidakense' growing from a mock stone trough in late September.

Plate 99. *Sedum ewersii* var. *ewersii* becomes a stunted and tortuous but interesting specimen when grown in a dry spot. The terra-cotta wall pot is 9 in (23 cm) wide.

Plate 100. *Sedum ewersii* var. *homophyllum,* is a common stonecrop often confused with other species.

Plate 101. *Sedum pluricaule.*

Plate 102. Female flowers of *Sedum bupleuroides* displaying large black nectaries.

Plate 103. *Sedum integrifolium* subsp. *procerum*—female flowers in fruit.

Plate 104. *Sedum kirilowii* inflorescence of male flowers with distinct bracts.

Plate 105. *Sedum rosea* with fasciated inflorescence of male 4-partite flowers.

Plate 106. *Sedum rhodanthum* inflorescence.

Plate 107. *Sedum semenovii* from Siberia.

Plate 108. *Sedum amabile* in a 6-in (15-cm) pot.

Plate 109. *Sedum trollii* outdoors at the Royal Botanic Gardens, Kew, in November.

Plate 110. *Sedum hobsonii* in a 6-in (15-cm) pot.

Figure 10.9. *Sedum dendroideum* showing the subepidermal glands in a single row along leaf margins.

Figure 10.10. *Sedum hultenii* in a 4-in (10-cm) pot.

SEDUM LUCIDUM Clausen

PLATES 56, 62

Several very distinct clones of *Sedum lucidum* are quite commonly grown. Extreme forms are so contrasting that they appear only distantly related. Thick, shiny, green leaves tend to be present along much of the length of stems, which are about 24 cm (9 in) long. Inflorescences appear to develop from or near stem tips, but by the time they are mature, they are unquestionably lateral. White flowers are produced in a terminal cluster and soon look pink because of light green carpels that turn orange then wine-red.

HABITAT. Veracruz is the home of this stonecrop, adjacent to the Rio Blanco in the Southern Sierra Madre, on mossy calcareous or granitic cliffs to 2000 m (7000 ft).

MAIN POINTS OF DISTINCTION. Lustrous, glabrous leaves (rather than drab, glaucous leaves) along with fully leafy stems and white flowers are good indicators. Pedicels thicken upwardly. $n = 34$.

VARIATION. *Sedum lucidum* is a highly variable stonecrop despite its relatively limited habitat. The form depicted by Evans is a short, little branched, slow-growing lighter green plant: it is rare in cultivation and the lack of gloss on leaves suggests it may be of hybrid origin. The common form in cultivation is darker, very glossy, more open, and has open inflorescences. It is fast growing and has many branches. The most extreme form was collected by Alfred Lau and distributed as I.S.I. 1497. It is often labelled *S. lucidum* 'Obesum', which describes it very well (Plate 62). Leaves have very rounded apices, and plants turns bright red if underwatered.

A rather quick-growing, bright green fasciated form is becoming more widely available.

HORTICULTURE. *Sedum lucidum* is an outstanding plant for a hanging basket. In all its forms, it needs a sunny spot to avoid etiolation.

SEDUM ×LUTEOVIRIDE Clausen

PLATE 63

Originally described as a true species, *Sedum ×luteoviride* is a natural hybrid between two contrasting parents: *S. praealtum* subsp. *parvifolium* and *S. greggii*. It is a very bright green, eye-catching subshrub with patent leaves clustered on the upper third of the 10-cm (4-in) high stems. In time, plants form dense mounds of green and red. Flowers can be lateral or terminal and are bright yellow.

HABITAT. This stonecrop grows near San Vicente, Hidalgo, on the edge of the Trans-Mexican Volcanic Belt, but probably in other areas where the parents grow together.

MAIN POINTS OF DISTINCTION. Small, bright yellow-green leaves, which turn cherry red with full exposure, distinguish this species from *Sedum decumbens*, its nearest look-alike (Plate 63). In many respects it resembles 'Little Gem', which shares a parent. Stems of *S. ×luteoviride* are often 12 cm (5 in) long, much longer than those of 'Little Gem'. Meiosis is irregular.

VARIATION. Perhaps backcrossing in the wild will produce a host of intermediate forms, but I guess all plants in cultivation have derived from a collection made by Moran and Kimnach.

HORTICULTURE. Almost fully hardy, this stonecrop grows outdoors in southwest England. It is an excellent foliage-contrast plant for bowl gardens, and a very bright ground cover for a potted bay tree or other half-hardy shrub.

SEDUM MACDOUGALLII Moran

PLATE 64

Sedum macdougallii is a recently described species that comes nearest to *S. treleasei*. Attractive glaucous, blue-gray leaves are packed on upright stems to about 50 cm (20 in) long. Old plants have long bare stems below. Flowers are tiny and pale yellow with bright red nectaries.

HABITAT. This stonecrop is from a very limited range in Oaxaca, northeast of Tehuantepec, at 1500 m (4900 ft) in the Southern Sierra Madre on south-facing slopes.

MAIN POINTS OF DISTINCTION. Leaves are smaller than those of the quite common *Sedum treleasei* and are much less uniform up the stem. They resemble the leaves of *S. clavatum*, which has white flowers. Inflorescences carry small pale yellow flowers with carpels that start red on the dorsal side and eventually become red fruit. $n = 34$.

VARIATION. The most common clone in cultivation was distributed as clonotype I.S.I. 1773. I have a topotype U2683 which is a bolder plant with keeled leaves concave above. Photographs in the *Cactus & Succculent Journal* (U.S.) (1977, 49:40) show leaves on the upper third of stems that are bare below. Moran stated that lower leaves can persist, but that they fall irregularly.

HORTICULTURE. This species looks good among other Mexican Crassulaceae. It is very slow, loses its roots easily, and unfortunately becomes gangling with age.

SEDUM NUSSBAUMERIANUM Bitter

PLATES 56, 65

In a garden in Garachico on Tenerife, *Sedum nussbaumerianum* has been planted in black tephra (volcanic ash), and the sight is quite stunning due to the vibrant orange-tan color of the subshrub. In full sun the plant is always a bright, almost luminous shade, and even if grown in shadow, it is a bright sickly yellow-green. White flowers, carried on long, slender pedicels, are slightly fragrant.

HABITAT. The habitat of this stonecrop was something of a mystery until plants were recently recollected in Vera Cruz at fairly low altitudes not far from the Gulf Coast.

MAIN POINTS OF DISTINCTION. This species is very similar to *Sedum adolphii* and *S. lucidum* both of which have green leaves, though *S. adolphii* can have a tan hue. The keel and apicu-

lation at the apex of young leaves of *S. adolphii* are far more pronounced than in *S. nussbaumerianum*, and leaves themselves are incurved and green. Leaves of *S. nussbaumerianum* are flatter, wider, and larger than those of *S. adolphii*, widest in the middle rather than in the upper third, and are not apiculate. Anthers and nectary glands are pink. $n = 64$.

VARIATION. Some clones in cultivation appear nearer to *Sedum adolphii*, suggesting that perhaps they are the same species or that hybrids have been created.

HORTICULTURE. Because of its bold color, this stonecrop is worth planting in a rock garden for summer, especially against a dark background (Plate 65). It is not frost hardy, though a few dry frosty nights do not seem to worry it. It is also excellent for hanging baskets and window boxes, or as a potted plant for home, porch, or conservatory.

SEDUM ORBATUM
Moran & Meyrán

PLATE 56

Sedum orbatum is a newly described species, resembling a giant *S. cuspidatum*. Large, dull green leaves tinge red in summer, especially on margins. Stout stems rise to 25 cm (10 in), and large, succulent, spathulate-ovate leaves form clusters at stem tips, with the largest leaves cupping smaller ones (Fig. 10.11a). The 10-cm (4-in) high inflorescence is glaucous and violet-gray, carrying a cluster of white 6-partite flowers with very keeled petals (Fig. 10.11b), tinged purple dorsally.

HABITAT. No locality is known for this stonecrop, but it was obtained by Felipe Otero from a nursery at Tenengo de las Flores, Puebla, suggesting it is native to the Trans-Mexican Volcanic Belt.

MAIN POINTS OF DISTINCTION. Large, subglaucous, medium green leaves are a good indicator; 6-partite flowers are very unusual in this group, and wide-spreading, green-yellow carpels, narrow sepals, and bright orange nectary glands are all additional points of verification. Uhl (unpub.) is convinced it is a good species with $n = 34$ and normal meiosis.

VARIATION. Petals appear free to me, but Moran and Meyrán described them as connate for 0.5 mm (about 0.02 in). Undoubtedly all plants in cultivation must have spread from the initial source. Inflorescences appear longer on photographs taken by Uhl than on my plants.

HORTICULTURE. This is an interesting variation for succulent collections or bowl gardens, vegetatively resembling an *Echeveria* species. Beware, it seems particularly susceptible to mealybug infestations.

SEDUM PACHYPHYLLUM Rose

PLATES 66, 67

Probably the most common member of *Pachysedum* group in cultivation, *Sedum pachyphyllum* has glaucous, light green, terete leaves, often tipped with red. Plants of this species are a common sight on windowsills or in general collec-

tions of succulents. Upright stems can reach to 50 cm (20 in) long, collapsing under their own weight, but generally they are half this length and are bare in the lower half. In time of drought, stems carry a terminal cluster of leaves. Yellow flowers are produced freely.

HABITAT. Sierra Mixteca, San Luis, Oaxaca, is the home of this species, but most plants in cultivation have been propagated from original introductions over a period of generations as no material of known origin appears to have been introduced until recent times.

MAIN POINTS OF DISTINCTION. Unfortunately, Evans depicted a hybrid of the species, *Sedeveria hummellii*, as the true species. Once seen, *Sedum pachyphyllum* is easy to recognize, for it is very distinct with club-shaped, glaucous, light green leaves, and small, pure yellow petals. Sepals are free, spurred, club-shaped, and very uneven. Stamens are long, and carpel beaks are short and stout. $n = 34$.

VARIATION. Several distinct forms appear to be in cultivation. The most attractive form is one with yellow-green leaves that cluster dense-

Figure 10.11. *Sedum orbatum*: (a) a rosette, measuring 12 cm (5 in) across, with the longest leaves nearly 6 cm (2 in) long; (b) 6-partite flowers measure about 11 mm (0.4 in) across.

ly at stem tips and have distinctly redder leaf tips (Fig. 10.12). This form has been in cultivation for a century or more. Another form is taller, more glaucous, blue-green with leaves having only a hint of red on their tips or none at all. More leaves adhere to less woody stems in this second form, sometimes baring only the lower quarter of stems (Fig. 10.12). Recently, this second form was distributed under the erroneous label *Sedum platyphyllum*, a species with wide flat leaves and a pyramidal terminal inflorescence.

Sedeveria hummellii Walther (Plate 67) is a cross with *Echeveria derenbergii*. It is a very common plant, but not usually named. Flowers of this hybrid are large and fade red; those of *Sedum pachyphyllum* are tiny and do not noticeably turn red.

Ron Evans acquired a similar plant that pro-duced enormously long inflorescences. An exceptionally shy flowerer, it has not repeated its surprising debut performance. Evans was unfamiliar with *"Sedum viride"* (syn. *S. corynephyllum*) at that time, but knew it should have club-shaped leaves and long inflorescences. He had much correspondence with Keith Powell and Charles Uhl, and upon receiving true plants of *S. corynephyllum*, he realized that his plant was quite different. Unfortunately, by this time his book was in an advanced state so this oddity appeared as *S. viride*, an error that was corrected in the second edition. To give the plant in question a handle, Keith Powell (1990) proposed that it be known as *Sedum* 'Ron Evans'. Vegetatively, it is very similar to *S. pachyphyllum*, but stems are not as tall before they collapse, and leaves are more upturned, slightly flattened above, and more glaucous-blue, without red tinges.

Figure 10.12. Two distinct clones of *Sedum pachyphyllum*; the width of the widest rosette is 7 cm (3 in).

HORTICULTURE. This stonecrop will thrive on neglect in a porch or conservatory, or on a windowsill. When it becomes too leggy, top-cuts root easily. It is very resilient, and plants can withstand frosts if dry. The hybrid with *Echeveria derenbergii* is equally useful.

SEDUM PRAEALTUM De Candolle

PLATE 68

A very common, almost hardy, evergreen tree sedum, *Sedum praealtum* has escaped in many warm temperate areas. Previously treated as a subspecies of *S. dendroideum*, this light green, coarse, fast-growing plant grows into a dense bush, perhaps a meter (3 ft) high. Like *S. dendroideum*, it was grown in Central America for its medicinal qualities. Stout trunks can be 2 cm (0.8 in) in diameter but are generally seared by frosts at ground level in bitter winters. Grown outdoors, the plant can be severely checked by cold, but I have never known it not to reroot of its own accord and grow again the following spring.

HABITAT. The habitat is difficult to define due to its cultivation for centuries, but tropical lowlands of Vera Cruz in the Rio Blanco Valley seem a good possibility.

MAIN POINTS OF DISTINCTION. Apart from *Sedum dendroideum*, no other evergreen, yellow-flowered *Sedum* of such stature exists. Large leaves have a distinct shape but margins, without subepidermal glands, are the best way to differentiate this species from *S. dendroideum* (Fig. 10.9). Yellow flowers have particularly long narrow petals.

VARIATION. If grown indoors, the plant is more pallid and not as tall. To some, the cristate form is bizarre; for others, it is an artist's delight. A contrasting subspecies is rare in cultivation. My initial encounter with the subspecies was in an Irish garden, where I took it to be a money tree, *Crassula argenta*. Further inspection made me think it was a beautiful spherical mound of

S. dendroideum, but it was the lack of subepidermal glands that finally made me realize the plant in question was *S. praealtum* subsp. *parvifolium* (De Candolle) Clausen. As the name suggests, leaves are much smaller than those of the type species. They are wider and more rounded, and therefore are very difficult to separate from those of *S. dendroideum* by shape alone.

Sedum praealtum subsp. *parvifolium* is much neater, more compact, and has a better overall shape compared to that of *S. praealtum* subsp. *praealtum*. The habitat of the former appears to be the southern end of the Eastern Sierra Madre, the Trans-Mexican Volcanic Plateau, and southeast of the Central Mexican Plateau at around 3000 m (10,000 ft).

The type species has $n = 34$; *Sedum praealtum* subsp. *parvifolium* has $n = 34$, 35, or 36.

HORTICULTURE. It is worth attempting to grow these shrubby sedums outdoors in large containers, as border plants, or in a big rock garden. Along the Mediterranean, the type species has become as common as *Aeonium arboreum*. It has escaped in Madeira and can be seen growing particularly well in a Jersey (Channel Isles) quarry. In all my years of growing several plants, not one has flowered for me, though only a few miles from where I live, the type species bloomed after the hot summer of 1990.

SEDUM ×RUBROTINCTUM Clausen

PLATE 69
COMMON NAMES: Christmas cheer, Jelly bean plant

For several decades, *Sedum ×rubrotinctum* was confused with *S. guatemalense* for it was misidentified by Walther. The latter species, a tropical epiphyte, is definitely not in cultivation and was thought to be extinct until it was rediscovered by Kimnach in 1991. *Sedum ×rubrotinctum* is a very common plant with such rich colors that it is a favorite for succulent bowl gardens. Bottle-green, only if overwatered or in heavy shade, the whole plant turns cherry-red in sun or drought. It flowers from time to time, when yellow petals can be a stark contrast to red foliage. It appears to be a cross of *S. pachyphyllum* and *S. stahlii*.

HABITAT. The hybrid is of horticultural origin.

MAIN POINTS OF DISTINCTION. Terete, cherry-red, spirally arranged leaves are unique.

VARIATION. A minor, unnamed form in cultivation is rare. 'Aurora', a pearl-pink chimera is as common as the original form, but is a very shy flowerer (Plate 69). Foliage is a dynamic color due to a chlorophyl-deficient epidermis. Together with the cherry-red form, the two common forms are very eye-catching.

A plant that entered Britain in the 1950s via a California nursery was referred to as *Sedum rubrum* Hort., not *S. rubrum* (L.) Thellung, in the little booklet *Sedums* (Hart and Wrigley 1971). By the time the booklet was published, the plant had flowered in the United Kingdom, and flowers had been discussed by Messrs. Pearson, Wrigley, and Ginns. Plants resemble small forms of highly colored *Graptopetalum paraguayense*, but flowers are yellow. Glaucous-gray leaves turn deep mauve in full sun and are crowded into elongated rosettes at stem tips. Stems are bare below. The plant is a shy flowerer, but, when produced, flowers are stellate and shiny yellow. Dennis Pearson (in Hart and Wrigley 1971) noticed that petals show signs of red markings in full sun, thus betraying *Graptopetalum* blood. Pearson claimed flowers were terminal, but this is not my experience. The red markings on the petals add to the evidence that this plant is of hybrid origin and not a species picked up by a traveller crossing Mexico. In recent years in the United Kingdom, the plant has been sold under a host of names, most frequently as a *Sedeveria* or *Graptoveria*, followed by a cultivar name generally referring to the nursery propagating it. In the United States, the name 'Vera Higgins' has been used frequently. I do not know if the name is a valid one, but it appears to be the only name used with any consistency. Vera Higgins did

much to promote the growing of succulent plants.

Graptosedum 'Vera Higgins' could be a hybrid between *Sedum ×rubrotinctum* or *S. stahlii* and *Graptopetalum paraguayense*, but this is merely assumption. Vegetatively, it resembles a red-colored, small form of *S. nussbaumerianum*. Planted against *S. nussbaumerianum* or *Graptopetalum paraguayense*, 'Vera Higgins' is a good foliage contrast. Clausen (1948) used a photograph by W. R. Fisher to show a plant thought to be *G. paraguayense* × *Sedum rubrotinctum*; it appears a very good match for 'Vera Higgins'.

Graptosedum 'Francesco Baldi' is a common potted plant in continental Europe. It probably has a member of *Pachysedum* group as a parent, and *Graptopetalum paraguayense* as the other parent.

HORTICULTURE. Haphazard cultivars of this sort are generally of such easy cultivation, they become exceptionally common house plants. When they are entered in succulent shows, their dubious parentage often makes the judges' job a difficult one, especially where classes are strictly defined.

Because of its reliable foliage color, *Sedum ×rubrotinctum* is used extensively for floral clocks and for living pictures in parks and gardens. It is not fully hardy, but it will withstand an outdoor winter in mild areas. *Sedum ×rubrotinctum* and its chimera 'Aurora' make excellent potted plants for windowsill, porch, or conservatory and thrive on neglect.

SEDUM SUAVEOLENS Kimnach

PLATE 70

SYNONYM: *Graptopetalum suaveolens*
(Kimnach) Clausen

If *Sedum suaveolens* is indeed a *Sedum* species, it is a very anomalous one. Nomenclature aside, it is a remarkably beautiful, stemless plant, impossible to separate from *Echeveria* when not in flower. Glaucous, blue-green to pure white ro-

settes up to 15 cm (6 in) across send out stolons, until, after a number of years, a tightly
packed mound is formed. Relatively short inflorescences carry whitish flowers with petals
erect in the lower two thirds, then spreading at
the tips. As the name suggests, flowers are
sweetly smelling.

When it was discovered and described in
1978, this species created a stir in the scientific
world because it had the largest number of
chromosomes of any living thing on planet
earth: n = circa 320. Like many oddities and rar-
ities, its distribution by the International Succulent Institute has meant that it now is probably
the most common *Sedum* species in specialist
collections of succulents, where others are perhaps considered too easy or too mundane. It
saddens me to see a class of *Sedum* in British succulent shows with this species dominating the
scene to the exclusion of all other species—
though it is no surprise it is revered by succulent specialists.

HABITAT. Topia, northwestern Durango in
the Western Sierra Madre, is the home of this delightful stonecrop.

MAIN POINTS OF DISTINCTION. *Sedum suaveolens* can not be confused with any other
Sedum species: large glaucous rosettes of flat, up-
curving leaves, and lateral inflorescences bearing flowers with white, free petals, erect at the
base, then spreading at tips, are unique.

VARIATION. All plants in cultivation are derived from the same collection. *Sedum suaveolens*
has been successfully crossed with *Tacitus bellus*
and is sure to be a parent of many future hybrids.

HORTICULTURE. This is an outstandingly
striking specimen succulent. Keep it on the dry
side at all times, but especially in winter.

SEDUM TRELEASEI Rose

PLATE 71

Sedum treleasei is a common plant with tall,
straight, unbranched stems carrying very succulent, glaucous-green leaves that are flattened
and have a broad spur. Leaves are crowded, uniform in size, and cover much of the stems. Only
in drought conditions are lower leaves lost. This
is a neat plant often sold as part of a bowl garden. If the roots are given room, the plant can
spread rapidly, and 55-cm (22-in) long stems
tumble under their own weight. Short inflorescences with long pedicels carrying yellow flowers, are compact, and individual flowers are
large.

HABITAT. Southeast Puebla in the Eastern Sierra Madre is the habitat of this tall stonecrop.

MAIN POINTS OF DISTINCTION. Tall upright
stems, branching only from the base, unless
damaged, and carrying short, very thick, glaucous-green homogenous leaves, are good indicators. Sepals are free and uneven. Petals are bright
yellow, mucronate, and stamens are long.

VARIATION. Quite a variety of forms exist in
cultivation suggesting that some may be of hybrid origin. A whiter form with narrower leaves
is commonly seen in mainland Europe and appears midway between the true species and *Sedum pachyphyllum*. It was first brought to my attention by Daan Vergunst of Holland. As it
grows particularly well at Haren Botanic Gardens, Netherlands, and appears to be without a
name, I propose to call it 'Haren'.

HORTICULTURE. This is an easily propagated
plant, attractive on a windowsill or as part of a
mixed dispay of succulents. It is fairly cold hardy, though it could not survive cold, wet winters
outdoors.

MEXICAN WOODY SPECIES

This group of Latin American *Sedum* species is not such an entity as *Pachysedum* group, but rather a diverse aglomeration of plants classified by Berger into his sections *Dendrosedum, Leptosedum,* and *Fruticisedum,* and Alexander's group *Centripetalia,* plus a few species with terminal inflorescences that are very closely related to *Pachysedum* group.

The following woody species with terminal inflorescences appear to be in cultivation:

Sedum allantoides Rose
Sedum bourgaei Hemsley
Sedum burrito Moran
Sedum calcicola Robinson & Greenman
Sedum compressum Rose (see *S. palmeri*)
Sedum frutescens Rose
Sedum furfuraceum Moran
Sedum 'Green Rose' (see *S. palmeri*)
Sedum griseum Praeger
Sedum guadalajaranum S. Watson
Sedum hernandezii Méyran
Sedum morganianum Walther
Sedum obcordatum Clausen
Sedum oxycoccoides Rose
Sedum oxypetalum Humboldt, Bonpland & Kunth
Sedum palmeri S. Watson
Sedum pulvinatum Clausen
Sedum quevae Hamet
Sedum retusum Hemsley
Sedum stahlii Solms
Sedum torulosum Clausen

Plants of this group

- Are tender Mexican subshrubs with persistent woody stems.
- Have terminal inflorescences.
- Have 5-partite flowers, but on rare occasions produce a few 4-partite or 6-partite ones.

The following is not a formal key, but merely a guide to identification.

Tree deciduous with stout trunk: *S. frutescens, S. oxypetalum, S. torulosum*
Tree deciduous with feeble trunk: *S. quevae*
Inflorescence is a panicle with the outline of a cone: *S. allantoides*
Leaves very narrow, linear, densely arranged on stems like pine needles: *S. bourgaei, S. griseum, S. guadalajaranum, S. oxycoccoides, S. pulvinatum* (to some extent)
Leaves terete or subterete, fleshy, plants pendant: *S. burrito, S. morganianum, S. stahlii*
Leaves terete or subterete, fleshy, plants upright (or at least upturned): *S. allantoides, S. furfuraceum, S. hernandezii, S. stahlii* (at first)
Stems continue to grow to one side of the terminal inflorescence with yellow flowers—leaves flat, relatively thin: *S. compressum, S. obcordatum, S. palmeri*
Leaves scaly, terete: *S. furfuraceum, S. hernandezii*
Leaves flat, retuse: *S. retusum*
Leaves flat, obcordate: *S. obcordatum*
Stems densely hairy: *S. hernandezii*

SEDUM ALLANTOIDES Rose

PLATES 72, 73

Sedum allantoides and *S. platyphyllum,* a species not yet available for cultivation, make up Alexander's section *Centripetala.* Both species share unusual inflorescences for Mexican Crassulaceae—a loosely branched panicle with the outline of a cone (Plate 72). Almost-white glaucous leaves are terete, very blunt, and not dissimilar to those of the common *Sedum pachyphyllum. Sedum allantoides* has very pale leaves, which are progressively smaller up the stem and do not cluster at stem tips. White flowers are produced in early summer. Plants are seldom seen in cultivation.

HABITAT. This stonecrop is indigenous to the Southern Sierra Madre, Puebla, Oaxaca, on cliffs from 1900 to 2100 m (6200 to 6900 ft).

MAIN POINTS OF DISTINCTION. The sausage-shaped leaves (origin of its name) of this stonecrop are fairly distinct, and, when in flower, the species cannot be mistaken for another. Flowers have long pedicels and almost equal sepals which are two-thirds as large as petals. Flowers have a somewhat unpleasant smell. $n = 29$, and $n = 58$.

VARIATION. A collection of plants made by Dudley Gold near Ixmiquilpan were described as *Graptopetalum goldii* Matuda and distributed under this name. Vegetatively and geographically they are midway between *Sedum allantoides* and *S. platyphyllum*. Moran reduced the species to synonymy with *S. allantoides* in 1966, but the name *Graptopetalum goldii* persists. To differentiate between the two quite different forms of *Sedum allantoides* in cultivation, the form with wide, flat leaves is referred to as *S. allantoides* 'Goldii' (Plate 73). 'Goldii' is perhaps even more beautiful than the relatively more common terete-leaved form. Inflorescences and individual flowers appear identical in the two forms. Uhl (1980) reported that *S. platyphyllum* and *S. allantoides* are interfertile and that hybrids are an excellent match for 'Goldii', suggesting they are extreme clones of one species. 'Goldii' is very rare in Europe, but more often encountered in the United States, especially in California.

HORTICULTURE. Personally I have found this to be the least hardy of any *Sedum* species I have ever grown. Plants are unable to recover from slight frosts and are extinguished by cold, damp weather when temperatures are no lower than 4°C (39°F). Both forms are wonderful windowsill specimens or beautiful in a mixed succulent garden.

SEDUM BOURGAEI Hemsley

A much-branched green subshrub, *Sedum bourgaei* has shiny, rich brown stems about 35 cm (14 in) high, with thin, crowded, sessile, linear leaves present along most of their length. The plant is very similar to the green form of *S. griseum*, but more upright. Alternate leaves are narrow, terete, only 1 cm (0.4 in) long, and usually at right angles to the branch. A few subsessile, white flowers are arranged on one side of the branches of the inflorescences.

HABITAT. This stonecrop grows near Mexico City, west into Michoacán and Querétaro, at 2200 m (7200 ft) altitude, on the Trans-Mexican Volcanic Belt.

MAIN POINTS OF DISTINCTION. *Sedum bourgaei* could only be confused with the nonglaucous form of *S. griseum*, which has gray stems with peeling bark. *Sedum bourgaei* is more upright and its smooth red-brown stems do not peel. Sepals are minutely spurred, linear, and unequal. Petals are mucronate, and anthers usually purple. Dark purple nectaries are spathulate. Out of flower, it is somewhat difficult to differentiate between young plants of this species and the tall, green form of *S. griseum*, but with mature specimens, *S. griseum* has a tendancy to collapse. *Sedum bourgaei* has only fibrous roots, and no rootstock. $n = 29$.

VARIATION. None noticed.

HORTICULTURE. *Sedum bourgaei* is an interesting plant for the succulent fancier. Stems are very brittle, so pots should be placed where they will not be brushed against.

SEDUM BURRITO Moran

PLATE 74

COMMON NAME: Baby burro's tail

Appearing like a smaller, more compact variation of the well-known *Sedum morganianum*, pendulous branches of *S. burrito* are completely hidden by spirals of imbricate, glaucous-gray, very blunt 2.5-cm (1-in) long leaves. Wine-red flowers appear in spring and hang on long pedicels from stem tips. Petals are upright (though they are generally upside-down) and pink on the outside. This has become an exceptionally popular plant for hanging baskets, especially on the European mainland where it is often labelled 'Baby Burro's Tail'. Not described until 1977, this compact, highly attractive species has rapidly become common on both sides of the Atlantic.

HABITAT. No locality is known.

MAIN POINTS OF DISTINCTION. This stonecrop could only be confused with *Sedum morganianum* and its hybrids, which are green and have sharply pointed leaves. *Sedum burrito* has very blunt leaves, and only in a very shady spot can it sometimes appear somewhat green. Sepals are even and deltoid. $n = 34 + 1$.

VARIATION. Sometimes inflorescences are just discernably lateral, so perhaps this is a hybrid, or perhaps it should be assigned to *Pachysedum* group.

HORTICULTURE. This is the best *Sedum* for a hanging basket, even better than *S. morganianum* as it has more compact "tails," which if knocked, do not discard leaves. *Sedum morganianum* has a nasty habit of shedding hundreds of leaves if disturbed. *Sedum burrito* is a perfect subject for a window box or anywhere where delicately colored tails can hang. It is happy outside in summer and does not seem to disapprove of heavy rains as long as it is well drained. A single plant is slow to fill a hanging basket but mature specimens attract much attention.

SEDUM CALCICOLA
Robinson & Greenman

SYNONYM: *Altamiranoa calcicola* Rose,
Sedum lenophylloides (Rose) Clausen

Very rare in cultivation, *Sedum calcicola* is usually labeled *S. lenophylloides*. The latter was once considered a distinct species but now is considered a regional variant of *S. calcicola*. Lanky, woody stems are clearly evident in the marked gaps between short patent leaves which should remind one of the inflorescences of *Lenophyllum* species, although I am reminded more of *Villadia*. Wiry stems rise to about 30 cm (12 in) and then sprawl to form a tangled mass—not the most desirable mode of growth. Short, terminal, fastigiate panicles carry inconspicuous, green-white flowers.

HABITAT. This stonecrop is indigenous to the Eastern Sierra Madre, from near Monterrey to the state of Hidalgo including San Luis Potosí.

MAIN POINTS OF DISTINCTION. Turgid 1.5-cm (0.6-in) long elliptic leaves have a small point of attachment, so are often removed by accident. Subsessile flowers have very short, equal, free sepals with suggestions of spurs. Epipetalous stamens are inserted noticeably above the bases of the petals. Nectary glands are large and orange. Carpels, with long beaks, are erect but spread somewhat.

VARIATION. Leaves can be papillose, especially on the southern forms (first form to be labelled *Sedum calcicola*), but although different levels of ploidy exist, they do not help to separate *S. calcicola* from the more northerly forms (once known as *S. lenophylloides*); on the contrary, plants of the most northerly forms and some of the most southerly forms have $n = 64$, 32, and 48. Uhl (1980) showed that the different levels of ploidy do not seem to match geographical or morphological patterns. The only plant I know in cultivation, an octoploid with $n = 64$, was collected near Cañada Verde on the south side of the Rio Verde in San Luis Potosí.

HORTICULTURE. Interesting to the enthusiast, *Sedum calcicola* is difficult to maintain in a greenhouse unless it is broken up and restarted every couple of seasons.

SEDUM FRUTESCENS Rose

PLATE 75

One of the deciduous tree sedums, *Sedum frutescens* develops a bole 10 cm (4 in) across and nearly a meter (3 ft) high, with paperlike, peeling bark. Flat, nonsucculent leaves are small and fall in autumn. Most branches produce terminal dichasiums, that carry white flowers.

HABITAT. This stonecrop grows on lava fields of the southern slopes of the Trans-Mexican Volcanic Belt in the State of Mexico.

MAIN POINTS OF DISTINCTION. When dormant, it is impossible to differentiate between this species and *Sedum oxypetalum*, but in growth, leaf shapes of the two species differ considerably. *Sedum frutescens* has acute, lanceolate leathery leaves with median grooves; *S. oxypetalum* has thin, flat, spathulate leaves. In addition, flowers of *S. oxypetalum* are pink while *S. frutescens* has white flowers, and fruiting branches of *S. oxypetalum* are deciduous, while those of *S. frutescens* persist. The chromosome counts of the two similar species are also different: $n = 30$ for this species, $n = 29$ for *S. oxypetalum*. Sepals are free, even, and slightly spurred. Carpels are very divergent, and stamens are as long as mucronate petals. Nectaries are large and cream colored. *Sedum frutescens* is vegetatively similar to *Crassula sarcocaulis*, which has cupped flowers with only 5 stamens and no peeling bark.

VARIATION. If grown in shade, branches can become overdrooping and thin, giving the plant a gangling appearance.

HORTICULTURE. This stonecrop makes a superb bonsai specimen and actually performs better if plants are underpotted. Propagation can be disappointing as cuttings invariably fail to root. Take softwood cuttings in spring, lightly bind a dozen, then stand the bundle on a sandy compost with a little heat from below. Cuttings usually strike after a few weeks, when the binding can be removed, and the cuttings potted up separately.

SEDUM FURFURACEUM Moran

PLATE 76

Although *Sedum furfuraceum* was not discovered until 1961, it is a common species in succulent collections. This stonecrop is a low-growing plant with thick, tortuous stems and very succulent, scaly, waxy, purple leaves crowded on stem tips. It will form a fleshy mat if allowed. The few flowers are pink-white, and several are produced in early summer. Clausen (1981) suspected that this stonecrop could be an intergeneric hybrid between *S. moranense* and *Pachyphytum hookeri* because of several facts: (1) *Sedum furfuraceum* has

an extremely limited range; (2) petals are somewhat bulged on either side of the attachment of the epipetalous stamen, where one would expect to find appendages on *Pachyphytum*; (3) *Sedum moranense* and *Pachyphytum hookeri* occur on the same site. Uhl disagreed (unpub.) and wrote (1980, 398) that "[i]ts chromosome count is common in Mexican *Sedum* though it seems not closely related to any others."

HABITAT. The localized habitat of this stonecrop is above El Ranchito, San Luis Potosí, on the Mexican Plateau.

MAIN POINTS OF DISTINCTION. This species cannot be mistaken for any other, for the dark-colored, scaly, wavy, mealy, egg-shaped leaves tightly packed on short, thick, tortuous stems are unique. Nectaries are large and pink, sepals are equal and very succulent, and stamens are almost as long as petals. $n = 34$.

VARIATION. I would think that all plants in cultivation have been vegatatively propagated from I.S.I. 428, which was distributed in 1963. In shade, plants may turn very dark green and have pure white flowers. If underwatered, thick, bare stems are revealed as leaves fall. In full sun, leaves turn almost black, and petals become pink.

At the time of going to press, a larger, greener plant labelled *Sedum hernandezii* has entered cultivation. In many respects it resembles *S. furfuraceum*, but its oblong leaves in columns of four are produced on very hairy stems.

HORTICULTURE. *Sedum furfuraceum* looks delightful in a shallow pottery bowl as tortuous stems creep over the edge. Keep plants on the dry side to produce compact specimens.

SEDUM GRISEUM Praeger

PLATE 77

Two very different clones of *Sedum griseum* appear in cultivation: the common one is a glaucous, almost pruinose, gray-green, fairly low-growing, many-branched subshrub. The other, relatively rare in Europe, has green, glabrous leaves. Uhl (1980) stated that perhaps these clones warrant subspecies status. Leaves of *S. griseum* are linear and patent. They are particularly densely arranged in the upper parts, hiding narrow, gray-brown stems that in maturity have peeling bark. White flowers are produced on cymes in late winter.

HABITAT. The glaucous form is from Guanajuanto, while the green form is from further south in Jalisco and Michoacán, all on the Trans-Mexican Volcanic Belt.

MAIN POINTS OF DISTINCTION. The glaucous form is vegetatively almost identical to *Sedum guadalajaranum*, which has tuberous roots, and to *S. oxycoccioides*, which has deep purple-red flowers. The green form of *S. griseum* is vegetatively similar to *S. bourgaei*, but is less upright and has less brittle, peeling stems. In flower, *S. griseum* has yellow or white nectaries. The glaucous form has $n = 26$, while the green form has $n = 30$.

VARIATION. Two distinct clones appear in cultivation.

HORTICULTURE. These are interesting plants for the succulent enthusiast. Because eventually they become rather untidy and leggy, they are best restarted every 4 years or so.

SEDUM GUADALAJARANUM
S. Watson

Sedum guadalajaranum is a glaucous-gray subshrub with thin, wiry stems from Guadalajara. It is similar to *S. griseum*. Growing to about 25 cm (10 in) high, its leaves are narrow, closely packed, especially in the upper two-thirds, linear, and very soft and flexible to touch (Fig. 10.13). Rootstocks are thickened and tuberous. Inflorescences usually comprise a two-branched cyme that produces whitish flowers on very short pedicels in winter. This stonecrop is still very rare in cultivation.

HABITAT. Rio Blanco area, Jalisco, on the southwestern part of the Mexican Plateau, and the western part of the Trans-Mexican Volcanic Belt is the home of this stonecrop.

MAIN POINTS OF DISTINCTION. A delicate stonecrop, *Sedum guadalajaranum* has summer flowers with white petals that flush rose at the base. Scarcely spurred sepals are nearly as long as petals, slightly uneven, and widespreading. Nectaries are pink, and anthers are dark red. $n = 29$.

VARIATION. In the wild, contrasting forms have been discovered and described. A green-leaved form, *S. guadalajaranum* subsp. *viridifolium*, from the southern part of the Western Sierra Madre, is not in cultivation.

HORTICULTURE. Such a dainty shrub grows well in a hanging basket.

Figure 10.13. *Sedum guadalajaranum* has soft, short (10-mm/0.4-in), glaucous leaves and two-branched inflorescences.

SEDUM HERNANDEZII Meyrán

This stonecrop became available in a very limited way when this volume was in its final stages of assembly. Resembling *Sedum furfuraceum*, *S. hernandezii* has longer terete leaves organized in four columns. The stems are stout and hirsute and flowers are yellow.

HABITAT. Felipe Otero discovered this stonecrop in Sierra Negra near Coxcatlán, Puebla, in 1988.

MAIN POINTS OF DISTINCTION. *Sedum stahlii* has terete leaves arranged in four columns, but has glabrous weak stems. *Sedum hernandezii* has stout stems 10 mm (0.4 in) in diameter covered with long hairs. Upturned, blunt, succulent leaves are mealy like those of *S. furfuraceum* but at least four times the length of that species (to 3.8 cm/1.5 in). Yellow flowers immediately separate it from *S. furfuraceum* but not from *S. stahlii*. Inflorescences, like those of *S. furfuraceum*, are simple and sessile.

VARIATION. The few plants in cultivation have derived from M5120.

HORTICULTURE. Perhaps by the year 2000 there will be some bold, mature specimens on the show bench.

SEDUM MORGANIANUM Walther

PLATE 74

COMMON NAME: Burro's tail

Sedum morganianum is a deservedly popular plant for hanging baskets. Pendant stems are covered with spirals of fleshy, imbricate, glaucous, apple-green leaves. On mature plants, stems can be a meter (over a yard) long, but are generally about 30 cm (12 in). Flowers on long pedicels only appear at stem tips when drooping stems have reached 25 cm (10 in). Petal color in the original description is given as begonia-rose. Flowers do not open fully.

HABITAT. The habitat of this stonecrop is still unknown despite the fact it has been in cultivation since 1935. It is commonly cultivated, and has frequently escaped in Mexico. It is assumed it may be wild near the peak of Orizaba.

MAIN POINTS OF DISTINCTION. Only *Sedum burrito* bears any resemblance to *S. morganianum*, and it seems as though they have both evolved from the same ancestral stock. Readily detached, thick, turgid, subterete, curved leaves of *S. morga-*

nianum with fairly acute apices are distinct. *Sedum burrito* has blunt leaf apices. $n = 35$.

VARIATION. I would think all plants in cultivation have been cloned from the same collection. An exceptionally striking hybrid *Sedum morganianum* × *Echeveria derenbergii* (i.e., *Sedeveria* 'Harry Butterfield') is often called super burro's tail in the United States (Plate 74)). It has the advantage of leaves that are not easily detached and the disadvantage of less striking flowers, which start pale pink-yellow and fade to orange-pink. Giant burro's tail, apparently a hybrid with *S. treleasii*, is now available in North America, sometimes bearing the name *Sedum* 'E. O. Orpet'.

HORTICULTURE. There are few specimens in any genus that are better for a hanging basket. In warm temperate areas, plants benefit when hung from a pergola or under a wrap-around porch. I do not water at all in winter, and there is no loss of leaf.

SEDUM OBCORDATUM Clausen

PLATE 78

Sedum obcordatum as its name suggests has obcordate leaves that are opposite-decussate, but in other respects the species resembles *S. palmeri* (syn *S. compressum*). Long, bare, 15-cm (6-in) long, arching stems are topped with rosettes comprising a few pairs of glaucous, obcordate leaves. the species is a shy flowerer, but yellow flowers are huge for *Sedum* and are carried on short pedicels from terminal cymes. Petals are erect, mucronate, and over 1 cm (0.4 in) long.

HABITAT. This true alpine or subalpine grows on the border of Puebla and Veracruz on the Trans-Mexican Volcanic Belt up to 4225 m (13,860 ft).

MAIN POINTS OF DISTINCTION. This is one of three Mexican *Sedum* species that has opposite-decussate leaves. The other species are *S. hernandezii* and *S. stahlii*, which, with their terete, dark leaves, bear no resemblance to *S. obcorda-*

tum. Carpels are divergent and somewhat sticky. Sepals are unequal, upright, sometimes spurred, and two-thirds the length of petals. $n = 34$.

VARIATION. Very mature plants can produce hanging, bare stems of considerable length, but this species is quite constant.

HORTICULTURE. This is one of my favorite Mexican species. It is ideal for a hanging basket or window box. Glaucous rosettes are most eye-catching, and because the species is native to high altitudes in the wild, it is half-hardy, surviving mild winters unprotected.

SEDUM OXYCOCCOIDES Rose

PLATE 79

Out of flower, *Sedum oxycoccoides* is indistinguishable from *S. guadalajaranum*, and very similar to, but frailer than, *S. griseum*. Stems are narrow, and, like *S. guadalajaranum*, leaves are gray-glaucous, narrow-linear, and soft and flexible to touch. Very deep purple-red flowers in autumn or early winter are most unusual for *Sedum*.

HABITAT. Indigenous to the Western Sierra Madre, *Sedum oxycoccoides* is found in the state of Nayarit, and probably into Zacatecas, in deep shady ravines.

MAIN POINTS OF DISTINCTION. It is difficult to differentiate between this species and *Sedum guadalajaranum* when they are not in flower. As both species flower freely, one must only wait a season to confirm identity. Flowers are produced in small numbers per branch tip, but the very deep color of the mucronate petals distinguishes this stonecrop from any other Mexican species. Linear, terete, free, spurred sepals are nearly as long as petals. Roots are fleshy and somewhat tuberous.

VARIATION. This species is exceptionally rare in cultivation, and probably all plants are propagations of Ron Evans's plant.

HORTICULTURE. I grow this plant in a hanging basket where it is elegant, but not as upright as I had expected.

SEDUM OXYPETALUM
Humboldt, Bonpland & Kunth

PLATE 80

Sedum oxypetalum is one of the deciduous tree sedums, which produces a hefty trunk with peeling, paperlike bark. It is very similar to *S. frutescens*, but leaves are a different shape, and flowers have pinkish petals, deepening in color towards their bases. Flowers are fragrant—some people describe them as musty, but they remind me of hawthorn blossom.

HABITAT. Often growing on solid lava, this stonecrop is indigenous to the state of Mexico, across to central Michoacán on the Trans- Mexican Volcanic Belt.

MAIN POINTS OF DISTINCTION. Only *Sedum frutescens* has such a stout trunk. Leaves and flowers of each species are distinct. *Sedum oxypetalum*, unlike its close relative, flowers in the wild in the dry season and retains its fruiting branches. Sepals are unequal and shortly spurred. Petals are mucronate, and carpels are widely divergent.

VARIATION. Clausen (1959) noted significant variation in the wild among different colonies. Plants are rare in cultivation; all I have studied appear alike. $n = 29$.

HORTICULTURE. Such a magnificent bonsai specimen plant deserves a special terra-cotta container. The species can be propagated in the same way as *Sedum frutescens* is propagated.

SEDUM PALMERI S. Watson

PLATE 81

SYNONYM: *S. compressum* Rose

Clausen (1981) united *Sedum palmeri* and *S. compressum*. When I had only one plant of each, I found them quite distinct, but since then I have acquired a whole range of intermediates and even a specimen purporting to be a hybrid of the two extremes. Thus it appears there is a single polymorphic species.

Relatively thin, glaucous, light green leaves are alternate and cluster at tips of bare, arching, 20-cm (8-in) long stems. Because plants give the impression they have lateral inflorescences, it appears they should be included in *Pachysedum* group. Uhl (1980, 393) pointed out:

> Vegetative axes in species of the *Sedum palmeri* group are continued beyond the terminal inflorescences by branches which develop from the axils of leaves a few nodes below the inflorescence. Sometimes, after flowering, growth of the axillary vegetative axis pushes aside the terminal inflorescence so that the latter superficially appears to be lateral.

Yellow flowers are very welcome in late winter as harbingers of spring (Plate 81).

HABITAT. *Sedum palmeri* subsp. *palmeri*, with *n* = 34, has rounded leaf apices and grows in the north of the Eastern Sierra Madre, north of Guayalejo River in Tamaulipas, Nuevo León, and Coahuila. *Sedum palmeri* subsp. *palmeri*, with *n* = 68 (i.e., "*S. compressum*"), has more acute leaf apices and comes from near Guajuca in Nuevo León. Both species are found at 800 m (2600 ft).

MAIN POINTS OF DISTINCTION. Rising, then arching bare stems, topped with glaucous, thin, spirally arranged leaves, and lateral inflorescences are distinct. Sepals, almost as long as petals, are unequal. Bright orange-yellow petals are mucronate and taper to acute apices.

VARIATION. Clausen (1981, 9) erected two subspecies. *Sedum palmeri* subsp. *emarginatum* from the Eastern Sierra Madre in Hidalgo has as its diagnostic features:

> pale leaves [that] are concave dorsally and so recurved apically that they will not lie flat on a plane surface. Also they are emarginate [shallowly notched] . . . plants . . . in cultivation for 33 years have retained their distinctive features.

Sedum palmeri subsp. *rubromarginatum* which is midway between *S. palmeri* subsp. *palmeri* and *S.*

palmeri subsp. *emarginatum*, has leaves that are broadly rounded and abruptly short-mucronate. Clausen (1981) reported that only mature leaves in some populations are prominently red-margined. The clone in cultivation is only tinged red if grown outdoors.

A miniature form has stems no more than 10 cm (4 in) long and emarginate leaves that are very glaucous and without any hint of green. The plant is slow growing and completely at home in a small, 3 in (8 cm) pot.

A plant Gordon Rowley received originally labeled as a member of subgenus *Rhodiola* looks like a robust, thick-stemmed tetraploid *Sedum palmeri* (i.e., "*S. compressum*"). It took several years to trace it in the trade, and when located in a Devon nursery, it bore the label *S.* 'Green Rose' which originated from a continental nursery (Fig. 10.14). The horticulturist who first distributed this plant claims to have received it from the International Succulent Institute. The I.S.I. has no record of distributing it, so the origin of the name 'Green Rose' is still a mystery.

For several winters I kept this plant outdoors, hoping it was hardy; despite drenching and freezing, it is still alive. Yellow flowers with upright petals are huge for *Sedum*. One of its parents could be *S. obcordatum*, which also has large flowers and is quite hardy. However, the plant's succulent leaves are not opposite, as are those of *S. obcordatum*, but occur in spirals, so I have tentatively placed this plant alongside *S. palmeri*. Either it is a cross between *S. obcordatum* and an *Echeveria* similar to *E. derenbergii*, or more likely a similar hybrid with *Sedum palmeri* as a parent.

HORTICULTURE. This species is ideal for a cold conservatory, porch, or windowsill. I prefer to grow it in hanging baskets to accomodate spreading, falling inflorescences. All forms are half-hardy and make excellent subjects for window boxes, stone troughs, and terra-cotta containers. This species is not as tolerant as *Sedum obcordatum*, a very similar species. *Sedum palmeri* thrives on neglect in a porch or conservatory and can survive low temperatures if kept dry.

Figure 10.14. *Sedum* 'Green Rose' in a 6-in (15-cm) pot.

SEDUM PULVINATUM Clausen

Sedum pulvinatum is a shrubby species, resembling a small, thinly stemmed tree with bare stems below, rising to about 28 cm (11 in) long. Distinctly spurred, bright green leaves the size and shape of grains of rice are arranged in spirals. White flowers are produced singly (Fig. 10.15).

HABITAT. Central Oaxaca is the home of this stonecrop, which grows in mountains east of Ayutla.

MAIN POINTS OF DISTINCTION. Only *Sedum quevae* in cultivation is similar, but it has flat, deciduous leaves. *Sedum pulvinatum* is evergreen, has white flowers produced singly in early winter, and has uneven, free, spurred sepals. n = circa 54.

VARIATION. *Sedum pulvinatum* is very rare in cultivation. All plants have probably been cloned from the original collection.

Figure 10.15. *Sedum pulvinatum* in a 4-in (10-cm) pot.

HORTICULTURE. This is not a very popular species—perhaps because it has no stout bole or stems tortuous enough to make it a good bonsai specimen, though it is easy to cultivate and quite rewarding.

SEDUM QUEVAE Hamet

Sedum quevae is a deciduous subshrub that rises to about 30 cm (12 in) from subterranean tubers. Thin stems are brittle and can snap cleanly. Very thin, 2-cm (0.8-in) long spathulate leaves, resembling those of *S. oxypetalum*, are not succulent at all. White flowers, which appear in early winter, have red anthers.

HABITAT. This species grows in two disjunct colonies: one in the Trans-Mexican Volcanic Belt, and the other in part of the Southern Sierra Madre, Oaxaca, in very well drained ravines.

MAIN POINTS OF DISTINCTION. Only more robust tree sedums share the deciduous nature of *Sedum quevae*. Inflorescences are terminal cymes carrying white flowers on very short pedicels. Sepals are spurred and speckled with red. Anthers are red. Plants I received from Ron Evans labeled *S. quevae* turned out to be *S. oxypetalum*, which may account for his "[a] stout tree-like *Sedum*." Stems, with peeling paperlike bark, only reach about 7 mm (<0.3 in) in girth. $n = 20$.

VARIATION. Clausen (1959) noted more variation within neighboring plants than between the two populations. He also recorded natural intergenetic hybrids with two species of *Villadia* in the wild.

HORTICULTURE. *Sedum quevae* is not compact enough to be eye-catching, but is happy on a sunny windowsill and undemanding.

SEDUM RETUSUM Hemsley

A rare subshrub in cultivation, *Sedum retusum* attains a height of about 15 cm (6 in), with bare stems below, except for aerial roots. It is topped with glabrous, grooved, spathulate leaves with distinctly retuse apices (Fig. 10.16). Loose rosettes of medium green leaves often flush red in full sun. In many respects, leaves, and flowers with petals which have rose bases, are similar to those of *S. oxypetalum*, but stems of *S. retusum* are never massive.

HABITAT. This stonecrop is native to San Luis Potosí, southern Tamaulipas, and Hidalgo in the Eastern Sierra Madre.

MAIN POINTS OF DISTINCTION. The only other species with such rounded and shallowly notched apices to the leaves is *Sedum obcordatum*, but *S. obcordatum* has glaucous, opposite-decussate, and obcordate (heart-shaped) rather than retuse leaves. The inflorescence of *S. retusum* is usually composed of two short, scorpioid branches, each with a few flowers, produced in summer. Sepals are free, erect, narrowed in the middle, and uneven. Petals are erect in the lower half. $n = 27$, $n = 28 + 1$, $n = 29$, and $n = 31$.

VARIATION. Despite the variety of chromosome counts, the morphology is fairly constant.

HORTICULTURE. This is a neat plant for pot culture. It is particularly slow; perhaps development of aerial roots on my plant are an indica-

Figure 10.16. *Sedum retusum* in a 3.5-in (9-cm) pot.

tion I am underwatering, but having had plants rot at the base on several occasions, I tend to water sparingly.

SEDUM STAHLII Solms

Sedum stahlii is one of the most common Mexican sedums in cultivation. Its small jelly bean-shaped leaves fall at the slightest opportunity, each one rooting and growing. Opposite-decussate, hairy but lustrous leaves are always brown-red unless the plant is kept in total shade and heavily misted daily. Rising to about 18 cm (7 in) tall before arching and falling, pendulous stems, often with aerial roots, can grow in excess of a meter (3 ft) if allowed (Fig. 10.17). In summer (in cultivation), bright yellow flowers are produced on terminal, usually three-branched cymes.

HABITAT. This stonecrop originates from Puebla, Veracruz, on limestone in the northeastern Southern Sierra Madre, and on adjacent slopes of the Trans-Mexican Volcanic Belt.

MAIN POINTS OF DISTINCTION. Opposite-decussate, terete, brown-red, hairy leaves are unique. Flowers on short pedicels have greenish, unequal, hairy sepals, and orange nectaries. Petals have a subapical, mucronate appendage. $n = 29$.

VARIATION. A recently collected form in my collection is more open, and young growth is quite green at the base of the leaf. Grown in an outdoor rock garden, it is so compact that stems are just visible.

HORTICULTURE. Surprisingly, this stonecrop is hardy in Northumberland in a sheltered spot. It is an excellent plant for hanging baskets, window boxes, and edges of stone troughs. Unfortunately, its very dull, dark color means it needs to be accompanied by lighter-colored plants.

Figure 10.17. *Sedum stahlii* leaves are less than 2 cm (0.8 in) long.

SEDUM TORULOSUM Clausen

A very rare, but highly attractive deciduous tree sedum, *Sedum torulosum* has waxy, pruinose stems that vary considerably in thickness—eventually reaching a meter or so (3 ft) high (Fig. 10.18). It is an exceptionally shy flowerer in Europe, with leaves falling unseasonally to no apparent pattern, though it appears to prefer to grow in winter. Leaves are leathery, and, like the stems, are covered in a white cuticle. Growing points are covered with a white powder that can be blown off, reminiscent of pruinose *Dudleya* species.

HABITAT. Northwest Oaxaca is the home of this stately stonecrop.

MAIN POINTS OF DISTINCTION. *Sedum torulosum* is a very distinct tree sedum. Knobbly stems (the reason for its name) and a white, waxy cuticle covering the whole plant make identification easy. Apparently, flowers resemble those of the *S. palmeri* group with red nectaries and divergent, linear sepals that soon wither. *n* = 34.

VARIATION. I have only observed plants from one clone.

HORTICULTURE. This is an immensely stunning species as a "frosted" bonsai. Unfortunately, it is extremely difficult to propagate, with cuttings remaining unrooted for more than a

Figure 10.18. *Sedum torulosum*; this plant is 30 cm (12 in) tall.

year. It is very prone to rotting at the base if overwatered. I am looking forward to the day that the bole on my specimen attains 10 cm (4 in) in diameter.

MEXICAN NONWOODY SPECIES

This group of Mexican species is made up of low-growing, sometimes creeping plants often referred to as "typical *Sedum*" species. These species have been drawn together for convenience rather than because they represent some taxonomic entity. In reality, within this group there are distantly related plants with perhaps more affinity to other groups than to each other.

The following species appear to be in cultivation:

Sedum alamosanum S. Watson

Sedum bellum Rose ex Praeger
Sedum caducum Clausen
Sedum chontalense Alexander (see *S. versadense*)
Sedum cockerellii Britton
Sedum compactum Rose
Sedum diffusum S. Watson
Sedum diversifolium Rose (see *S. greggii*)
Sedum ebracteatum Moçiño & Sessé ap. De Candolle
Sedum glabrum (Rose) Praeger
Sedum grandipetalum Fröderström
Sedum greggii Hemsley

Sedum hemsleyanum Rose
Sedum hintonii Clausen
Sedum humifusum Rose
Sedum liebmannianum Hemsley
Sedum longipes Rose
Sedum mellitulum Rose
Sedum mexicanum Britton
Sedum moranense Humboldt, Bonpland & Kunth
Sedum multiflorum Clausen
Sedum muscoideum Rose
Sedum nanifolium Fröderström
Sedum oaxacanum Rose
Sedum pachucense (Thompson) Praeger (see *S. hemsleyanum*)
Sedum parvum Hemsley
Sedum potosinum Rose (see *S. diffusum*)
Sedum reptans Clausen
Sedum rhodocarpum subsp. *edwardsii* (Rose) Clausen
Sedum species Lau 081 (see *S. reptans*)
Sedum 'Spiral Staircase' (see *S. moranense*)
Sedum stelliforme S. Watson
Sedum trichromum Clausen
Sedum versadense C. H. Thompson
Sedum wrightii A. Gray

Plants of this group

- Are low growing chamaephytes.
- Are native to Mexico and also perhaps to the southern states of the United States.
- Are perennial.

The following is not a formal key, but merely a guide to help pinpoint unidentified species.

Flowers whitish, roots fibrous, leaves very narrow, terete or almost-terete (at least six times longer than wide): *S. alamosanum*, *S. diffusum*, *S. liebmannianum*, *S. mellitulum*, *S. multiflorum*

Flowers whitish, roots fibrous, leaves somewhat flattened: *S. bellum*, *S. caducum*, *S. compactum*, *S. longipes*, *S. moranense*, *S. muscoideum*, *S. versadense*, *S. stelliforme* (leaves almost-globular)

Flowers whitish, rootstock succulent, leaves somewhat flattened: *S. cockerellii*, *S. glabrum*, *S.hintonii* (to some extent), *S. trichromum*, *S. wrightii*

Flowers yellowish, leaves very narrow, terete or almost-terete (at least six times longer than wide): *S. mexicanum*, *S. reptans*

Flowers yellowish, leaves somewhat flattened, roots fibrous: *S. grandipetalum*, *S. greggii*, *S. humifusum*, *S. nanifolium*, *S. oaxacanum*, *S. parvum*, *S. rhodocarpum*

SEDUM ALAMOSANUM S. Watson

Similar to *Sedum mellitulum*, *S. alamosanum* is a low, creeping stonecrop with tight tufts of leaves. Plants form low hummocks and stems elongate next season. Blue-green, erect, tightly clustered leaves are linear, completely hiding stems, and they appear glaucous due to a covering of tiny white papillae. The previous season's leaves turn a lilac shade in good light. Plants are similar in appearance to the Eurasian *S. hispanicum*. Several whitish flowers are produced in simple clusters in spring. *Sedum alamosanum* is rare in cultivation.

HABITAT. Growing in disjunct sites divided by the Gulf of California, this stonecrop is native to Baja California and the Eastern Sierra Madre of Sonora (especially the Alamos Mountains), Chihuahua, and Coahuila.

MAIN POINTS OF DISTINCTION. A magnifying glass is needed to observe the white papillae of leaves, which otherwise appear very similar to those of *Sedum mellitulum*. Pink-white spring flowers are carried on stout pecidels. Sepals are free, equal, and spurred. *Sedum mellitulum* does not have spurred sepals. Stamens are almost as long as petals, which have little pink dots. Carpels remain erect.

VARIATION. This species is very variable in the wild with several levels of ploidy. A diploid clone ($n = 18$) in my collection is much whiter than the plant photographed by Evans. Clausen (1981, 12) summarized variation in this species in this way: "Although plants from the populations . . . are not the same in all respects, similarities outweigh differences." No subspecies have been erected for different levels of ploidy: $n = 17 + 1$, $n = 18$, $n = 36$, $n = 54$ (Fig. 10.19).

HORTICULTURE. *Sedum alamosanum* is a neat, compact, creeping species—probably best in an indoor rock garden or outdoors in areas only very rarely experiencing frosts. Plants look delightful in a shallow bowl or pot.

SEDUM BELLUM Rose ex Praeger

PLATE 82

SYNONYM: *S. farinosum* Rose (non Lowe)

Flowering plants of *Sedum bellum* are so delightful, they certainly live up to their name. After flowering, specimens are reduced to dead stems with globular buds of farinose, imbricate leaves at ground level, from where next year's growth will take place. Flat, spathulate, white-green leaves almost cover the pruinose stems as they elongate and arch. Large terminal flat-topped cymes carry numerous large, white flowers in spring.

HABITAT. This stonecrop is indigenous to Western Durango in the Western Sierra Madre on rocky, mossy cliffs at 2000 m (7000 ft).

MAIN POINTS OF DISTINCTION. Alternate, spathulate, flat leaves with emarginate edges, followed by a glorious show of white flowers with mamillate sepals, and widely spreading carpels are a unique combination.

VARIATION. Two distinct forms are in cultivation: the true species ($n = 36$), and a far more common impostor, which is similar but altogether larger including the flowers. The impostor appears to be a triploid with 17 to 18 paired elements and 18 to 22 univalents. Clausen (1959) thought the impostor to be a cross between *Sedum bellum* and a species of *Echeveria*, but Uhl's (1985) cytological work suggested that the other parent appeared to be a diploid *Sedum* species.

HORTICULTURE. This is a superb plant for the

Figure 10.19. Two pots of *Sedum alamosanum*; the larger 4.5-in (11-cm) pot contains a hexaploid ($n = 54$) plant from Chihuahua; the smaller pot contains a plant, probably a diploid ($n = 18$), from Sonora (near the type locality).

hanging basket, but it dislikes being baked in sun. Although it demands exceptional drainage, it likes frequent watering. As a result, it is fickle and easily lost.

SEDUM CADUCUM Clausen

Made up of stemless, red-green, low, few-leaved, perenniating, monocarpic rosettes, *Sedum caducum* very much resembles *Lenophyllum* species (Fig. 10.20). Rosettes elongate to produce inflorescences in midwinter, which can be 15 cm (6 in) tall, carrying a simple terminal cyme often with a few stray white flowers. Petals are erect at the base, but do not recurve as do those of *Lenophyllum*.

HABITAT. Low areas of the Eastern Sierra Madre in southern Tamaulipas in the catchment areas of Purification and San Marcos rivers are the home of this monocarpic stonecrop.

MAIN POINTS OF DISTINCTION. Dark green, succulent, pocked leaves, heavily spotted with red are very easily detached, and, like bracts of the inflorescence, are able to root and grow. Plants very much resemble *Lenophyllum acutifolium* and *Sinocrassula* species, but white, stellate flowers are proof of identity. *n* = 64, 96.

VARIATION. Clausen thought he had collected a *Lenophyllum* species until it flowered. Since *Sedum caducum* resembles species of *Lenophyllum*, Clausen suggested that it could be an intergeneric hybrid. Cytological work by Uhl (1985) showed this is most unlikely. I cannot differentiate between plants of the type species (*n* = 96) and a plant from a higher elevation, some 70 km (40 mi) to the north.

HORTICULTURE. This stonecrop is an exceptionally low grower, and has a dull color. It could make a reasonable ground cover accompanying a larger plant. Although capable of propagating itself from easily detached vegetative material, *Sedum caducum* never becomes troublesome.

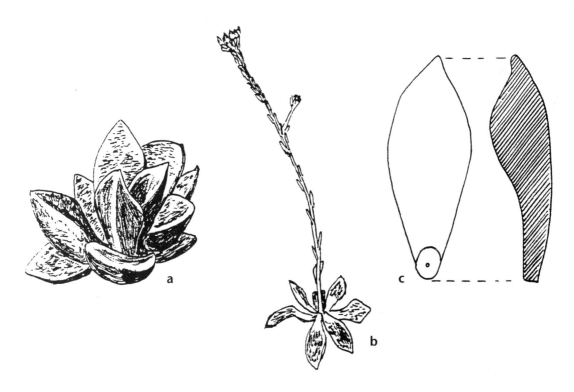

Figure 10.20. *Sedum caducum* (a) rosette; (b) inflorescences are usually about 14 cm (5 in) tall; (c) longest leaves are about 2.5 cm (1 in) long.

SEDUM COCKERELLII Britton

SYNONYMS: *S. griffithsii* Britton,
Cockerellia cockerellii (Britton) Löve & Löve

In their second season, tiny rosettes of *Sedum cockerellii* elongate from a fleshy rootstock to about 18 cm (7 in). Scattered, flat, spathulate-to-lanceolate, spurred, smooth leaves are light green. In autumn, cymes of white, campanulate flowers are produced.

HABITAT. This is a widespread stonecrop from Arizona, through New Mexico into Texas, and from Sonora into Chihuahua, Mexico at about 2700 m (8900 ft).

MAIN POINTS OF DISTINCTION. Small, loose buds overwinter at soil level on a chunky rootstock, and dead stems and inflorescences resemble dry grass. Long, broad, slightly unequal sepals are free and spurred.

VARIATION. Cytologically, this species is exceptionally varied with $n = 14$, 15, 16, 29, 30, and 32. I find plants from distant locations similar, but *Sedum puberulum* Watson from Chihuahua, which has been equated with *S. cockerellii*, according to Clausen (1981), is marginally a candidate for subspecies status. Flowers can be somewhat pink.

HORTICULTURE. This species propagates slowly. Stems appear difficult to strike, but division of rootstock is usually successful. The plant is pleasant for pot culture and almost hardy, so it should survive in a sheltered spot in warm temperate areas.

SEDUM COMPACTUM Rose

PLATE 83

Superficially, *Sedum compactum* is similar to the well-known *S. humifusum* in that it produces an exceptionally tight mat of short stems clothed with tufts of leaves. Said to resemble moss in the wild, *S. compactum* has papillose leaves, which are clustered into compact rosettes no more than a centimeter (0.4 in) across. White flowers, which are produced singly or a few at a time, are unusual in that they are globular. This species is rare in cultivation.

HABITAT. This stonecrop is native to Oaxaca, Cerro de Sentile, in the Southern Sierra Madre at 2100 to 2400 m (6900 to 7900 ft), most probably on solid rock, for in anything more friable, plants may be lifted without effort, as fibrous roots are feeble.

MAIN POINTS OF DISTINCTION. This species could only be confused with *Sedum humifusum*, which has hairy leaves and yellow flowers. Globular flowers of *S. compactum* never fully open, but have a faint, sweet smell.

VARIATION. None noticed.

HORTICULTURE. Plants are easily split for propagation, which I recommend doing frequently as overhead watering can kill plants. Plants frequently remain with no signs of growth for months before perishing—often without apparent reason. This is a very special plant because of its low, very compact growth. Large specimen plants in a shallow pan are a joy to behold, but a challenge to the grower. Plants are not at all hardy, so in some countries this stonecrop could not be considered for alpine shows as the grower would have to keep frosts away from the greenhouse by artificially heating it.

SEDUM DIFFUSUM S. Watson
S. POTOSINUM Rose

PLATE 88

Like Clausen who wrote (1981, 17), "I am unaware of a good means of separation," I, too, find these two species very similar. In fact, there are far more dramatic differences between the two clones of *Sedum diffusum* that I have studied than between *S. potosinum* and one of the forms of *S. diffusum*. Both species form lax, glaucous mats, very similar to the Eurasian *S. hispanicum* var. *minus* and the longer-leaved forms of *S. dasyphyllum*, but the Mexican plants are generally taller. Glaucous-blue leaves are imbricate at first, then more spreading. Old leaves turn a pink shade, then ashy-white. Dead leaves clothe the lower stems. White flowers on scorpioid branches are attractive and are produced in summer.

HABITAT. *Sedum diffusum* is found mainly on calcareous rocks on eastern slopes of the Eastern Sierra Madre with outlying colonies to the northwest. As the name suggests, *S. potosinum* is a native of San Luis Potosí.

MAIN POINTS OF DISTINCTION. Glaucous-blue, rather than papillose, spurred leaves, distinguish these species from *Sedum alamosanum*, which they can resemble and to which they are obviously closely related. Flowers are noticeably kyphocarpic, a feature that immediately separates the species from *S. dasyphyllum*. *Sedum hispanicum* is kyphocarpic, but has hairy carpels. Sepals of the Mexican pair are about half the length of the petals.

VARIATION. Three distinct forms appear in cultivation. *Sedum diffusum* 'Potosinum' is the tallest form with stems up to 25 cm (10 in) tall that tend to fall and rise to support themselves. A second form of *S. diffusum* is so similar that until fully grown, it cannot be distinguished, and even then the difference is merely in size. This form is a little shorter in stature than plants from San Luis Potosí and perhaps more compact. A third form, the most rewarding of the three, is a minor, very floriferous plant with compact carpets completely covered with flowers. Leaves of this minor form tend to be gray. Diploids, tetraploids, and hexaploids exist: $n = 19, 38,$ or 57.

HORTICULTURE. None of the forms are quite hardy for me, but all grow outdoors for most of the year. One form has apparently escaped in France, where it is often believed to be a form of *Sedum hispanicum*. All forms hate baking conditions under glass and seldom recover from such an experience. Good ventilation seems to be a requisite in hot weather. This species would make a fine carpet-forming plant in warm temperate areas that experience few frosts. It makes excellent ground cover to accompany potted shrubs, looks attractive in a window box, and is bright in a rock garden.

SEDUM EBRACTEATUM
Moçiño & Sessé ap. De Candolle

PLATE 84

SYNONYMS: *S. chapalense* S. Watson, *S. incertum* Hemsley, *Sedastrum rubricaule* Rose

Sedum ebracteatum is a member of the *S. glabrum* complex. The true *S. ebracteatum*, a pubescent species, was unfortunately not depicted by Evans who drew and described a regional variation of *S. glabrum*.

HABITAT. *Sedum ebracteatum* is from the southern part of the Central Mexican Plateau plus a few locations on the Mexican Volcanic Belt and Eastern Sierra Madre, to San Marcos River near Ciudad Victoria, Tamaulipas.

MAIN POINTS OF DISTINCTION. Plants are covered with short erect hairs, but in most other respects resemble other *Sedastrum* plants (i.e., plants of the *Sedum glabrum* complex). They are especially similar in having spurred leaves on inflorescences, but in this case they are amplexicaul and more rounded (Fig. 10.21).

Clausen used width of leaves on floriferous stems as the key feature to distinguish *Sedum ebracteatum* and *S. hemsleyanum:* the former has wide, rounded leaves; the latter has narrower linear-lanceolate leaves. With this in mind, he equated *S. pachucense* (syn. *S. painteri*) with *S. hemsleyanum*, for leaves of the inflorescences are narrow (Clausen 1959). Later Clausen (1981, 14) changed his mind and said these plants from Pa-

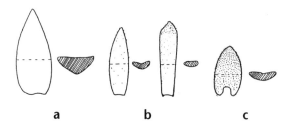

Figure 10.21. Shapes and textures of leaves of the inflorescences of some *Sedastrum* in cultivation: (a) *Sedum glabrum*; (b) *S. hemsleyanum* (left) and *S. hemsleyanum* FO 54 from Pachuca (right); (c) *S. ebracteatum*.

chuca "may not be *S. hemsleyanum* as I once supposed, but [are] better identified with *S. ebracteatum*." This is most confusing. Figure 10.21 shows differences clearly, but the group is in great need of clarification.

SEDUM GLABRUM (Rose) Praeger

SYNONYMS: *Sedastrum glabrum* Rose, *Sedastrum palmeri* Rose, *Sedastrum turgidum* Rose

The *Sedum glabrum* complex includes several closely related stonecrops: *S. ebractearum*, *S. glabrum*, and *S. hemsleyanum*. Rose erected a new genus, *Sedastrum*, to contain these commonly confused plants.

> Caespitose perennials with dense *Sempervivum*-like basal rosettes, usually pubescent. Floriferous stems usually long and weak, dying down to the base after flowering, their leaves flattened and fleshy . . . carpels erect, concave under the scales (Rose 1905, 58).

Sedastrum species have very fleshy rootstocks on which rosettes form at the bases of old inflorescences. Inflorescences are stout stems which rise or are tortuous. They carry white, sessile flowers with thin, broad petals and erect sepals. Epipetalous stamens are inserted noticeably above the base. All parts of the plants may be streaked or splashed with purple. Rose thought the hollows under the nectaries to be of taxonomic importance.

The species *Sedum glabrum* differs from other species in the *S. glabrum* complex for, as the name suggests, it is glabrous. Clausen (1981, 14) suggested that it is really only a subspecies of *S. ebracteatum*.

HABITAT. *Sedum glabrum* hails from the northern Mexican Plateau in Coahuila, Saltillo, and San Luis Potosí states at about 2000 m (6561 ft).

MAIN POINTS OF DISTINCTION. This stonecrop has glabrous leaves that are papillose on margins, and, although variable, they differ in shape from leaves of the other *Sedastrum* species. Leaves of inflorescences are spurred, blunt-lanceolate, and not amplexicaul (Fig. 10.21). Carpels are densely papillose, streaked, and dotted purple. Petals are eroded. *Sedum glabrum* is the easiest member of this group to distinguish as it flowers in late summer; all other *Sedastrum* species flower around Christmas.

VARIATION. Further exploration in habitat may reveal evidence to support uniting *Sedum glabrum* with its near relatives. Several contrasting clones appear to be in cultivation, and position plays an important part in the overall size plants attain.

HORTICULTURE. Plants dislike overwatering, and large rootstocks rot easily, but with care they can be split for propagation purposes. Once split, they must be allowed to dry fully before replanting. Half-shade seems preferable. This group is only really suited to pot culture.

SEDUM GRANDIPETALUM Fröderström

Very similar in habit to the well-known *Sedum greggii*, *S. grandipetalum* produces small conelike buds of fairly flat, imbricate leaves on stems after flowering (Fig. 10.22). The buds overwinter in this state and elongate next season to arch and then fall. Leaves have trilobate spurs and are glaucous-green with papillose margins. They resemble fish scales. Flowers on tumbling inflorescences are, as the species name suggests, large and produced in quantity. Petals are light yellow. A plant in flower is most graceful though rarely seen in cultivation.

HABITAT. Southwest Jalisco on the Western Sierra Madre on mossy cliffs at about 2500 m (8200 ft) is the home of this stonecrop.

MAIN POINTS OF DISTINCTION. Differentiating this species from *Sedum greggii* is difficult, though the latter is bright glabrous yellow-green rather than glaucous blue-green. Sepals of *S. grandipetalum* are free, small, spurred, and uneven, while those of *S. greggii* are even. $n = 34$

VARIATION. The species appears to be constant.

HORTICULTURE. Small propagules form near the ends of inflorescences making propagation easy. Avoid baking plants under glass. Athough perfect drainage is recommended, plants appreciate regular watering in summer. A better show is produced if specimens are grown in hanging baskets, to display the beauty of the pendulous stems and inflorescences.

Figure 10.22. Conelike buds of *Sedum grandipetalum* measure about 5 cm (2 in) long.

SEDUM GREGGII Hemsley

PLATE 85

SYNONYM: *S. diversifolium* Rose

After yellow flowers are spent in midsummer, tightly packed, imbricate leaves of *Sedum greggii* form conelike rosettes at bases of stems (Plate 85). These buds elongate the following winter. By spring, stems are seen for the first time as simple, terminal inflorescences of several flowers rise above still relatively tightly packed, elongated tufts. This delightful species is quite common in collections as it propagates easily and is not very demanding.

HABITAT. Found in the western section of the Trans-Mexican Volcanic Belt from Puebla to southern Jalisco and northern San Luis Potosí, this stonecrop prefers shady cliffs.

MAIN POINTS OF DISTINCTION. Evans describes leaves as light green, but in my experience they are a very intense, bright color, especially in the bud stage. This species is similar in habit to *Sedum grandipetalum*, and although quite variable, the two could hardly be confused. *Sedum greggii* is a much smaller plant with floriferous branches only about 6 cm (2 in) long, while branches of *S. grandipetalum* are often four times this length. Leaves of buds and inflorescences are papillose. Pedicellate flowers, carried on small cymes, have sepals which may or may not be spurred. Sepals, like leaves, are papillose and often are speckled with tiny pin-spots of deep red. Sulphur-yellow petals frequently have red markings, especially on the underside.

VARIATION. Cytologically, much variation has been observed by Uhl (1985): $n = 18 + 6B$, $24 + 1$, 26, 30, 33, $33 + 6$, and 34. An oddity with $n = 74 \pm 4$ has been erected as a subspecies by Clausen (i.e., *Sedum greggii* subsp. *angustifolium*). The visible distinguishing characteristic of this subspecies is its linear leaves on inflorescences. It grows on Volcán de Tequila in Jalisco. Regional variations show a wide contrast in leaf size, leaf width, and petal color (ranging from light to deep yellow). I have only observed three obviously different clones, one of which was bluer green with lighter colored petals, but many more variations could be in cultivation.

HORTICULTURE. This is a delightful, bright, low-growing species that is easy to propagate. Not only can conelike buds be easily removed from stem bases, but more are formed on inflorescences and these begin to push out roots before inflorescences disintegrate. In addition, plants seem to be spontaneous from inflorescence litter, so one is never short of propagation material. Having said this, *Sedum greggii* can never become a pest. It is a bright subject for a mixed bowl garden.

SEDUM HEMSLEYANUM Rose

SYNONYM: *S. pachucense* (C. H. Thompson) Praeger

Sedum hemsleyanum is a member of the *S. glabrum* complex. It and *S. pachucense* are disjunct and easily separated, although very closely related, clones.

HABITAT. *Sedum hemsleyanum* grows on the southeastern edge of the Trans-Mexican Volcanic Belt and adjacent Southern Sierra Madre. *Sedum pachucense* hails from Pachuca in Hidalgo, and in this volume is assumed to be a disjunct form of *S. hemsleyanum*.

MAIN POINTS OF DISTINCTION. *Sedum hemsleyanum* has narrow, pale nonamplexicaul leaves on the inflorescence. *Sedum hemsleyanum* subsp. *pachucense* comb. nov.(?) has slightly more amplexicaul, strap-shaped leaves, widest in the upper third. Together, both subspecies can be best distinguished from other *Sedastrum* species by studying leaf shape on inflorescences.

VARIATION. Two contrasting forms described above are in cultivation. *Sedum hemsleyanum* subsp. *pachucense* is encountered more frequently.

SEDUM HINTONII Clausen

PLATE 86

This remarkably beautiful stonecrop is quite a challenge to the succulent enthusiast. Dense rosettes of *Sedum hintonii* are so covered with short, stiff, white hairs that the color of the leaves is masked. In intense light, a white hairy mound is formed. Drawings of the type species show that the clone in cultivation (I.S.I. 174), from which all plants in cultivation (prior to 1991) have been derived, is quite different from the type species. The unusual inflorescences on stout stems are produced in winter, during which time plants must be kept bone dry. White flowers with red anthers are large, and, like the rosettes, are most charming.

HABITAT. This species is associated with the gorge of the Ventana River in the Western Sierra Madre, Durango; the Trans-Mexican Volcanic Belt in western Jalisco; and the Southern Sierra Madre. Although the initial International Succulent Institute distribution was offered without collection data, it would appear it was collected in western Jalisco. Clausen (1981) suggested this plant was a subspecies or an intergeneric hybrid between *Sedum ebracteatum* and a hairy *Echeveria*.

MAIN POINTS OF DISTINCTION. No other Mexican *Sedum* species has such bristly leaves. The rootstock is quite fleshy. The inflorescence is almost a spike of sessile flowers with free, bristly sepals, and huge anthers, which are red before they spill out their pollen. Petals of the type species are much smaller, and leaves are longer. $n = 25$.

VARIATION. All plants in cultivation before 1991 were derived from a 1959 distribution. Another clone was distributed in 1991 from Canoas, Durango, but it is too early to comment on it.

HORTICULTURE. Perhaps this is the most prized *Sedum* species in succulent collections. Is this only because of its sheer beauty? Perhaps it is partly a demonstration of the skill of the grower. Watering this species overhead at any time can be fatal for plants. Although I hose all my sedums due to the sheer number of plants, I do not water *S. hintonii* from September until its inflorescences have turned papery-white and are starting to shrivel, which can be as late as May or June, by which time inflorescences should be cut and removed. These cuttings can generate new plants if potted in a sandy mixture. I recommend growing this special stonecrop in a porous, terra-cotta pot so it can be generously watered in summer months without fear that botrytis could rush through a plant and kill it in a matter of days. This species seems to tolerate cold conditions and even a few frosts, if dry. Rosettes become leggy if grown in shade, but pleasing specimens can be produced on a sunny windowsill.

SEDUM HUMIFUSUM Rose

PLATE 87

Sedum humifusum is popular with alpine enthusiasts due to its exceptionally low-growing habit. Often referred to as "catkinlike," tufted stems carry tightly packed, imbricate leaves with a fringe of white hair on margins. Mosslike mats are very dense, and stems produce single, bright yellow flowers in summer.

HABITAT. This species is native to eastern Guanajuato, across Querétaro to western Hidalgo on the north of the Trans-Mexican Volcanic Belt, in relatively dry spots at about 2000 m (7000 ft).

MAIN POINTS OF DISTINCTION. Only *Sedum compactum* has a similar habit of growth, but it has white, globular flowers. Leaves of *S. humifusum* are distinctly ciliate. Fleshy, free sepals are like the leaves in shape and have a line of cilia on the upper margins. Spreading, bright yellow petals, which become erect and white with age, are mucronate, and nectary glands are orange-yellow.

VARIATION. Uhl (1985) has documented plants with *n* = 34, 35, and 68, but I have not observed any major variation of clones in cultivation except due to situation.

HORTICULTURE. This species really needs to be watered from below as it rots very quickly when damp. The root system is feeble, and the plant resents being broken up and transplanted, often sulking for months. Grown in a very shallow terra-cotta saucer, it spreads to form a delightful 1-cm (0.4-in) high mat. It is not completely cold hardy, but will withstand several brief frosts if completely dry.

SEDUM LIEBMANNIANUM Hemsley

PLATE 88

Similar in appearance and closely related to *Sedum moranense*, *S. liebmannianum* is much less frequently encountered in cultivation. Stems 7 cm (3 in) long have their lower sections covered with a shaggy tangle of white, dead leaves. Stems creep, then rise, and eventually can be twice this length. They dry in summer, become very brittle, and often the whole plant disintegrates, producing propagules which fall and root. Gray-green leaves, which are imbricate at first, have spurs and tinge with pink in full sun. White flowers are produced in compact clusters in summer.

HABITAT. This species grows over a large range from Oaxaca to Puebla on calcareous rocks at about 2500 m (8200 ft), but is also reported from San Luis Potosí and the Chisos Mountains in western Texas.

MAIN POINTS OF DISTINCTION. Kyphocarpic flowers immediately separate this stonecrop from *Sedum alamosanum* and *S. mellitulum*, but not from *S. diffusum*, *S. potosinum* or *S. moranense*. *Sedum diffusum*, including *S. potosinum*, has leaves with the upper face distinctly convex and the cross section almost terete, while *S. liebmannianum* has leaves with the upper face flat or even slightly concave and the section much flatter. *Sedum moranense* is a more upright plant that does not disintegrate in early winter, nor does it have lower stems shaggy with white, dead leaves. *Sedum liebmannianum* has long, narrow, slightly unequal, free, spurred sepals. Petals are white and mucronate. Stamens are almost as long as petals, and anthers are pale yellow.

VARIATION. Leaves can be smooth or papillose. Uhl (1985) showed that odd levels of ploidy exist. Many collections have a large range of elements, which are very irregular at meiosis, but *n* = 34 is commonly encountered. I have only grown one clone of *Sedum liebmannianum*, but it is reasonable to assume that variation exists in cultivation.

HORTICULTURE. This species is as pretty as its near relatives and is very easy to grow and propagate in a greenhouse. Its biggest failing is that it is never very compact. Do not worry about plants disintegrating completely in winter. Keep them perfectly dry during this period: when watered again in spring, rapid growth quickly follows.

SEDUM LONGIPES Rose

Sedum longipes is a peculiar creeping or pendant plant. It looks etiolated even in full sun, for there are long gaps on the stems between tiny scattered, rounded leaves. Plants are very light green throughout with finely papillose stems that are speckled red. Spurred leaves cluster more at stem tips, but the whole plant is very open with literally hundreds of fine, hanging stems. Lax, terminal cymes carry flowers, reminding one more of *Monanthes* than *Sedum*. Flowers, carried on threadlike pedicels, are unusual in having huge two-horned, deep red nectary glands. Rose thought these flowers so unique he erected a new genus *Keratolepis* to contain this species.

HABITAT. This stonecrop is native from Michoacán to Morelos along the Trans-Mexican Volcanic Belt. It grows on damp, shady, vertical canyon walls.

MAIN POINTS OF DISTINCTION. Only *Sedum pentastamineum*, also with a single whorl of stamens, has any similarity to this species, but it has leaves only a few millimeters (0.1 in) across and is not in general cultivation. Vegetatively, *S. longipes* is more similar to Far Eastern species than to other Mexican species, but Far Eastern species tend to have yellow flowers. Whitish flowers of *S. longipes* have speckled, spurred sepals, which are papillose at tips. Large, deep red, horned nectaries are toothed and speckled pale green-yellow. Pale green mucronate petals are speckled with red, especially near apices. Stamens are orange.

Variation. Two clones appear in cultivation. *Sedum longipes* subsp. *rosulare*, which has a tendency to produce rosettes, especially when in flower, and which also has shorter petals, similar in length to or slightly shorter, than sepals. Its location in the wild is unknown. *Sedum longipes* subsp. *longipes* has petals longer than sepals.

HORTICULTURE. Such unusual species are treasured by the specialist, but will not attract a casual observer. Grown as ground cover in a pot containing a large succulent such as a *Euphorbia*, it looks delightful and soon hangs over the container's edge. Both subspecies do well in hanging baskets and give much pleasure when they flower in midwinter.

SEDUM MELLITULUM Rose

As the name suggests, this species is a "little darling." It resembles *Sedum alamosanum*, but in winter is reduced to tiny tufts of linear leaves rising from a short rootstock. Slightly rough, procumbent stems lengthen to about 8 cm (3 in), carrying linear, spurred, very papillose, almost-white leaves. White flowers are produced in autumn on fairly long, nodding inflorescences. The winter rosettes are very reminiscent of the hardy European yellow-flowered *S. laconicum*.

HABITAT. This stonecrop is indigenous to Chihuahua, the northern section of the Western Sierra Madre, and areas into Sonora, at about 2400 m (7900 ft). Similar plants have been collected from much further south in Michoacán and Guerrero; they may be in cultivation but probably are a different and as yet unnamed species with divergent carpels.

MAIN POINTS OF DISTINCTION. This species flowers in autumn and by December is reduced to papillose basal tufts. This feature, plus erect carpels, separates this species from *Sedum alomosanum* and *S. stelliforme*. Unequal sepals are without spurs. White petals have a broad mucron.

VARIATION. Recently collected clones have orange-red rather than yellow nectaries. Uhl (1985, 397) reported that "the species is very diverse cytologically and includes some high polyploids" and that $n = 18, 19$, circa 50, circa 66, 80–84, and 95.

HORTICULTURE. *Sedum mellitulum* is a delicate species with upright, arching, then falling stems; it forms a compact mound of frosty blue-green. It is delightful in a small container or perhaps even better in an indoor rock garden. It should be virtually hardy in warm temperate, maritime margins.

SEDUM MEXICANUM Britton

It is possible that *Sedum mexicanum* originated from the Far East for it has no close relatives in Mexico and it has more affinity with Chinese species than anything indigenous to Central America. Historians are beginning to realize that ancient trade links between the Far East and Central and South America help explain anomalies, such as jade of Chinese origin being found in Ecuadorian burial chambers. Ancient charts show that the Chinese knew of the string of volcanic isles from the Kuriles, along the Aleutians to North America, and that ancient craft could travel to the Americas for long periods without losing sight of land. Perhaps *S. mexicanum* was brought to Mexico from the Orient in this way, but I think not.

The precise habitat of *Sedum mexicanum* is unknown though it is commonly grown and has escaped in several Central American countries. It has also, more recently, escaped in Florida. Praeger (1921) encountered it as a cottage window-sill plant in the heart of Ireland. In Berlin, it was labeled as a European species even before the initial collection of the type species. At Kew, years before it was first named, specimens bore the label of a different Oriental species. Whether this is an Orieintial species is highly debatable, and whether it was introduced to Mexico directly from the Far East or via Europe is also open to speculation. Clausen's suggestion (1959, 308) of El Salvador possibly being the origin of the species cannot be dismissed. A Madeiran Botanic Garden erroneously labels it as being indigenous.

Sedum mexicanum is a very bright green plant with shiny, linear, sessile, nearly terete leaves in whorls of 3, 4 or 5, particularly below. Bright yellow kyphocarpic flowers are produced on a huge flat cyme of 4 very long scorpioid branches in early summer. Morphologically it is very similar to two Oriental species, *S. sarmentosum* and *S. lineare*, both less upright and with flatter leaves, but similarly whorled. It is interesting to note that these Oriental stonecrops have also escaped

in Central America and elsewhere. Plants distributed in California in recent years purporting to be *S. mexicanum* have white flowers and are probably 'Spiral Staircase' (Plate 88).

HABITAT. The origin of this species is unknown, but possibly it is not Central America.

MAIN POINTS OF DISTINCTION. The very bright green upright nature of the plant and the subterete leaves, mostly in whorls of 4, make positive identification easy. Peduncles gain girth upwards. Free, unequal sepals are spurred, and the longest is almost as long as the petals. Epipetalous stamens are inserted noticeably above the base of golden-yellow petals. Anthers are orange-red and yellow nectaries are visible. $n = 18$.

VARIATION. None.

HORTICULTURE. Half hardy, *Sedum mexicanum* survives mild winters in Northumberland. It is certainly hardy 485 km (300 miles) south in Cornwall, England. It is such a bright species, it is worthwhile to bed it out in spring in more extreme areas. It will survive on a dry greenhouse floor for longer frosty periods. This stonecrop is a good subject for window boxes and containers. In areas of mild winter it is a good ground cover but may need to be contained. It likes damp, shady spots and dislikes dry, hot, stony areas.

SEDUM MORANENSE
Humboldt, Bonpland & Kunth

PLATE 88

Fully hardy in some of its forms, *Sedum moranense* is normally grown as an outdoor rock garden plant alongside European *Sedum* species with which it is frequently confused. Many names have been erected for forms of *S. moranense*, but Uhl (1983, 243) pointed out that "it has the greatest cytological diversity of all the Mexican Crassulaceae which as a group are distinguished for their great variety of chromosomes." It is very similar in appearance to the full range of *S. acre* and *S. sexangulare*, but is usually a little taller. Flowers of *S. moranense* are white, so plants in flower can be differentiated from the yellow-flowering European species. Ovate-to-lanceolate leaves are closely arranged in 5 or 6 spirals on the upper half of 10-cm (4-in) stems. Lower stems are bare with perhaps a few scalelike dead leaves and aerial roots. Kyphocarpic flowers are produced on one or two branched cymes in summer.

HABITAT. Uhl (1983, 244) devoted a whole section of his series titled *Chromosomes of Mexican Sedum* to this species, delimiting the habitat thus:

> *Sedum moranense* is one of the commonest and widest ranging species of the Crassulaceae in Mexico. It occurs as disjunct populations, most often on volcanic rock above 2000 metres [7000 ft] from the southern Sierra Madre Oriental in the state of Hidalgo, Puebla and Veracruz west to the vicinity of Mexico City and Toluca and northwest to the Sierra de Guanajuato and to the interior mountains of San Luis Potosí; it is especially common in the state of Hidalgo . . . . The species also is common in cultivation in Mexico.

It can be a very high altitude species as it is found above 3500 m (11,500 ft). It is more than possible that some recorded sites are the result of plants escaping from cultivation.

MAIN POINTS OF DISTINCTION. Leaves on the upper parts of the stems spiral. The hardy nature of plants and kyphocarpic white flowers are the best indicators. The species is very similar in many respects to the European *Sedum anglicum*, but the latter rarely attains 6 cm (2 in) in stature. *Sedum moranense* is generally very upright and twice this height. Its sepals are almost equal, free, and spurred. Stamens have red or purple anthers, and nectary glands are white or creamy. Out of flower the plant is similar to yellow-flowered *S. nanifolium*, but *S. nanifolium*, too, is less erect.

VARIATION. *Sedum moranense* is an exception-

ally variable species. Despite the futility of naming countless variations on a theme, *S. moranense* subsp. *grandiflorum* (Humboldt, Bonpland & Kunth) Clausen, with $n = 140$, is a name that horticulturists will wish to retain because of the larger nature of the flowers. $n = 21, 24, 38, 40, 50, 52, 54, 57, 60, 63, 72, 77, 100, 140$, and 153, plus numerous odd-ploids were recorded by Uhl (1983). Other variety names are pointless due to the extreme polymorphic nature of the species.

Two oddities have been in cultivation in the United Kingdom for decades. The first appears to be a very vigorous form of *Sedum moranense*, but its leaves are larger and more patent. This plant usually carries the label "*Sedum* species from Hidalgo," certainly an area in which *S. moranense* is common (Plate 88). Clausen (1959, 274–275) depicted a plant found not far from the border of Hidalgo, which he suggested could be *S. moranense* × *Villadia batesii*, but

> the plant from Nevado de Toluca has large leaves and more flowers per inflorescence than either *S. moranense* or *V. batesii*, and it also produces flowers over a long period of time. Since I did not see anything like it on my visits to the Nevado de Toluca, I lack data from the field to substantiate the idea that it might be a hybrid. Obviously its proper status requires more attention.

Uhl (1983, 250) concluded: "Clausen's plant appears clearly to be a hybrid, but its chromosomes, and its location make it very doubtful that *Sedum moranense* could have been one of its parents." It is only speculation that the plant in cultivation was propagated from Clausen's hybrid. Therefore, at present it may be prudent to keep the label "*Sedum* species from Hidalgo."

The second plant has been a bone of contention for many years. Commonly grown in the United Kingdom, it nearly always comes with label "*Villadia batesii*." When the bright green plant I received with this label first flowered, I was surprised to see stellate flowers without much (if any) connation of petals. Those with more experience than me, including Ron Evans, identified this plant as *V. batesii*, yet Fröderström (1935, 146) clearly depicted *V. batesii* flowers with petal connation that one would expect for a *Villadia* species. Plants grown in the United Kingdom with this label definitely belong to *Sedum*. Charles Uhl (unpub.) confirms that this plant is not a *Villadia*: "It has a very Mexican look about it, but I do not recognize it."

Probably this plant was introduced by a traveller passing through Mexico, and it has entered the trade incorrectly identified. Until it can be relocated in the wild, I propose to give this plant a cultivar handle so that there is no more perpetuation of the confusion that it is a *Villadia* species. *Sedum* 'Spiral Staircase' was a name suggested by Dr. David Jackson, and it seems most fitting as the 10-mm (0.4-in) long lanceolate leaves form attractive neat spirals (Plate 88). I now grow true clones of *Villadia batesii*, which confirm my suspicions. The flowers of 'Spiral Staircase' are very like those of *Sedum moranense* but are nearly twice the size.

HORTICULTURE. Severe frosts after repeated drenchings can decapitate an outdoor population of *Sedum moranense*, but fallen shoots soon root in spring to regenerate. This is a very useful hardy plant for a rock garden or raised bed. It does not spread at the rate of its European counterparts. The species from Hidalgo and 'Spiral Staircase' are less hardy.

SEDUM MULTIFLORUM Clausen

Sedum multiflorum is a relatively new species to be discovered and introduced to cultivation. Densely leaved basal stems appear each year from a thickened rootstock and gradually elongate to 30 cm (12 in) or more, forming arching inflorescences with white flowers. Of similar habit and closely related to *S. wrightii*, *S. multiflorum* has linear, sessile leaves. Red, fairly brittle stems are a contrast to green glabrous leaves. White stellate flowers are produced in large numbers.

HABITAT. This stonecrop has a very limited range, confined to a small area near Cuidad Guzman, Jalisco, in the western section of the Trans-Mexican Volcanic Belt, on shaded hillsides of a canyon.

MAIN POINTS OF DISTINCTION. Red, elongating, arching stems with back-arching, downward-pointing leaves terminating in flowers in spring are fairly distinct. *Sedum wrightii* has petals that are obviously upright in the lower portion while those of *S. multiflorum* are spreading. Sepals are free, patent, equal, and somewhat papillose. Petals are eroded, mucronate, and topped with wine-red. Anthers are red.

VARIATION. Most plants in cultivation have been propagated from I.S.I. 1411.

HORTICULTURE. Easily detached leaves root and produce new plants. Viviparous tufts also form on inflorescences, making propagation easy. This species is very easily rotted if overwatered. I have never been able to produce pretty specimens, but do know that very beautiful plants have been cultivated in hanging baskets. It can withstand a few frosts.

SEDUM MUSCOIDEUM Rose

Sedum muscoideum is not an uncommon stonecrop in cultivation but it is almost always labelled *S. cupressoides* Hemsley. The latter is a pink-white-flowered species not in cultivation. The confusion, I think, appears to have started with Rose (1905) who described petals of *S. cupressoides* as "yellow (but described as rose-colored)." Rose (1903) offered a correct description of *S. muscoideum*: "[c]losely resembling *Sedum cupressoides*, but with yellow flowers. Mr. Hemsley has compared the material with his type of the latter species and agrees with me that it is different." Praeger obviously missed the earlier version in the *Bulletin of the New York Botanical Garden* and depicted *S. muscoideum* beautifully but with the label *S. cupressoides*. This error was perpetuated by Fröderström (for petal color of herbaria is often faded), and then Evans. Uhl (1985) pointed out that the true *S. cupressoides* is similar to *S. liebmannianum*, and that plants have invariably been confused.

Sedum muscoideum is a distinct plant with tiny, imbricate leaves, tightly appressed to 8-cm (3-in) long, upright stems, and large yellow flowers that are produced in small numbers in summer (Fig. 10.23).

HABITAT. This stonecrop is native to Peotitlán, Oaxaca, the Southern Sierra Madre, at about 3000 m (10,000 ft).

MAIN POINTS OF DISTINCTION. This is an easy plant to identify, but very similar to tiny forms of European *Sedum acre*. *Sedum muscoideum* resembles a tiny whipcord hebe and is much taller than *S. acre* var. *minus*. The Mexican species has no real inflorescences: sessile, kyphocarpic flowers appear at stem tips, with leaves clustered right up to the sepals. Sepals are free, somewhat unequal, and only one-third the length of long, lanceolate petals.

VARIATION. Plants in cultivation appear to be propagations of those introduced at the beginning of the twentieth century. Until very recently, no newly collected clones have been introduced to cultivation. F.O.166, distributed by the Echeveria Society, was collected on the Sierra Negra near Coxcatlán Pue at 2400 m (7900 ft), and appears more quickly growing, but vegetatively identical to the common clone. *n* = 34.

HORTICULTURE. Due to its high-altitude habitat, *Sedum muscoideum* is fairly hardy and should be fine in a cold frame in most areas. It is fully hardy in cool, wet, temperate areas. As with most alpines, it dislikes hot summer greenhouse conditions.

SEDUM NANIFOLIUM Fröderström

PLATE 89

SYNONYM: *Villadia parva* (Hemsley) Jacobsen (in part)

Lost to cultivation for decades, *Sedum nanifolium* was redistributed, but it is still rare. It very much

Figure 10.23. *Sedum muscoideum* carries large flowers with respect to the width of the stems and tightly packed leaves.

resembles diploid *S. acre*, except that it turns deep red in full sun, is less upright, and has bare lower stems that eventually become long and creeping. Tightly packed leaves in spirals have an almost triangular, truncate appendage at each tip and are amplexicaul. Stellate, kyphocarpic, yellow flowers are produced in summer and remind me very much of those of the *S. acre* group. I cannot understand why Jacobsen transferred this species to *Villadia*, for petals are just about free and patent.

HABITAT. This stonecrop is native to drier western slopes of the Eastern Sierra Madre in southeastern Coahuila, southeast of Saltillo, in southern Nuevo León, and perhaps in southwestern Tamaulipas at high altitudes to 2400 m (7900 ft).

MAIN POINTS OF DISTINCTION. Clausen submerged this species with *Sedum parvum*, but *S. nanifolium* is a much bolder plant. Uhl (1985) showed the two are cytologically distinct. Turgid, compactly arranged leaf spirals tinging red in full sun are quite unlike those of *S. parvum*. The problem with juvenile plants will be to distinguish them from European species rather than from other Mexican species. Distinct leaf appendages will help. In addition, long, very unequal sepals are free and spurred, petals are mucronate, and nectary glands are very inconspicuous.

VARIATION. A clone with $n = 26$ collected by Clausen from Cañada Zacatosa, north of La Escondida in Nuevo León, has always struggled in my greenhouse. Another collected north of La Ascensión in Nuevo León and believed to be a tetraploid with $n = 52$ is much more vigorous. The latter clone was foolishly overlooked on an outside bench, but fortunately it happily overwintered a relatively mild season. Perhaps it preferred outdoor cultivation or is a faster growing, healthier clone. Different levels of ploidy could account for this apparent difference.

HORTICULTURE. This stonecrop produces a good, dense ground cover and should be hardy in warm temperate areas. It is a bright subject for a rock garden, raised bed, or container.

SEDUM OAXACANUM Rose

PLATE 90

Sedum oaxacanum is a fairly common species in succulent collections, often bearing the label *S. australe*, which is a similar species (not in cultivation) with terete leaves. Alternate leaves, which cluster into rosettes on tips of 8-cm (3-in) long stems, are pruinose, especially when new. Purple, trailing stems are rough-papillose with tips erect. The overall effect is quite charming. Yellow flowers are produced sparsely in early summer.

HABITAT. Central Oaxaca on Cerro de San Felipe at 3500 m (11,500 ft) is the main home of this stonecrop, but it is also reported from southern Puebla.

MAIN POINTS OF DISTINCTION. Scurfy-white flattish, papillose, spurred leaves are quite distinct. Yellow kyphocarpic flowers have equal sepals, and petals with stamens inserted 2 mm (0.08 in) from the base. $n = 34$. This stonecrop resembles, and is often seen masquerading as, one of several South African *Crassula* species, especially *C. dasyphylla*, a plant with tiny flowers and a single whorl of stamens.

VARIATION. Most plants in cultivation have been propagated vegetatively over a couple of generations, but a new distribution from a lower altitude in San Miguel Aztatla, Sierra Mixteca, appears identical.

HORTICULTURE. This is a delightful species for a small earthenware container where it can creep over the edge. Being from such a high altitude, it is half-hardy and worth trying outdoors in warmer areas.

SEDUM PARVUM Hemsley

SYNONYM: *Altamiranoa parva* (Hemsley) Rose, *Villadia parva* (Hemsley) Jacobsen

A diminutive species, rare in cultivation, *Sedum parvum* resembles *S. moranense* except it has yellow flowers. Papillose leaves are short and crowded on wiry stems that are bare in the lower half. Plants become untidy with age. Flowers of late summer are produced singly.

HABITAT. This species is native to mountains of southwest San Luis Potosí.

MAIN POINTS OF DISTINCTION. Tiny, spurred leaves are more patent than those of *Sedum moranense*, and the plant is much less tidy in appearance. Together, the 5-cm (2-in) long stems with the leaves are very narrow. Blunt, papillose sepals are not spurred, but are united for one-quarter their length. Mucronate petals are just united, and nectaries are spathulate. *Sedum nanifolium* is very closely related and regarded by Clausen to be a subspecies of *S. parvum*. Although the latter has a very similar habit of growth, leaves of *S. nanifolium* are longer and more patent.

VARIATION. *Sedum parvum* subsp. *diminutum* (Hemsley) Clausen is, as the name suggests, an even more feeble form. It has a chromosome count of $n = 34$. *Sedum parvum* subsp. *parvum* has $n = 32$, $32 + 2B$, circa 60, and 64 (Uhl 1985).

HORTICULTURE. This stonecrop is interesting to the specialist, but of little horticultural use.

SEDUM REPTANS Clausen

PLATE 91

Sedum reptans is a recently distributed but not yet well-known stonecrop. At Huntington Botanic Gardens, California, it grows outdoors all year and has spread over a large area for which it is a profusely flowering ground cover. Myron Kymnach (1989 unpub.) commented, "Oddly, despite its prominence at our entrance, *S. reptans* has never been commercialized by the ground cover nurseries (a big business in California), although they do carry other sedums."

It forms a low, lax, tangled, creeping (hence the name) mat of vibrant green. Some would say it was a sickly shade of green, but, at flowering time in particular, the color is exceptionally intense. Upright tufts of terete leaves produce only tiny inflorescences of single or several flowers in Northumberland rather than the "brilliant sheet of yellow" produced in California.

HABITAT. This species is indigenous to Sierra Equiteria, San Luis Potosí, and to the south in Querétaro on felsite rock, though some plants grow on oak trunks and branches as epiphytes up to 4 m (13 ft) above ground level at 1700 m (5600 ft).

MAIN POINTS OF DISTINCTION. Terete, upright, elliptic-lanceolate leaves, and yellow flowers are fairly distinct. The creeping and rooting nature of the plant with spring flowers on slender pedicels are further evidence. Sepals are succulent, equal, blunt, and free. Anthers, stamens, and carpels are yellow.

VARIATION. The most frequent clone in cultivation is I.S.I. 1222 (or Moran 13381 from Cerro Agujón, Sierra La Equiteria, southwest of Rioverde, which is a tetraploid with $n = 72$). The type species from the same location shares the same chromosome count, but is not identical vegetatively. Two other diverse clones are in cultivation.

Sedum reptans subsp. *carinatifolium* Clausen from Sierra Gorda, Querétaro at 2165 m (7100 ft) is even more creeping and an exceptionally low-growing, open species with lots of aerial roots. Shorter leaves are said to be keeled (hence the name). Only in drought conditions are leaves carinate. Flowers of this subspecies are large, but are produced sparsely late in summer, at least a month after the type species. Uhl (1985) questioned the inclusion of this subspecies with *S. reptans* because of its different appearance and its anomalous chromosome count of $n = 60$.

The other clone in cultivation is Lau 081 from near Vizarron, the same locality as *Sedum reptans* subsp. *carinatifolium*. I find little similarity between this clone and *S. reptans* subsp. *reptans* or *S. reptans* subsp. *carinatifolium*, although Kimnach believes it is close to the latter. Lau 081 is a large, upright, robust plant with glaucous, white leaves on scabrid stems. Leaves have an odd papillose appendage, not dissimilar to that found on leaf apices of *S. nanifolium*. Flowers are very small, one-quarter the size (area) of the type species, with light yellow petals. Inflorescences, which are unlike those of the other subspecies, comprise a long branch on which new flowers take the place of earlier ones; over a period of a month or more, branches of the inflorescences expand until they are 7 cm (3 in) or more long. This is by far the most eye-catching clone of *S. reptans*, if indeed it is not an entirely new species. $n = 34$.

HORTICULTURE. Here we have three relatively overlooked gems that are just about hardy. *Sedum reptans* subsp. *carinatifolium* is fully hardy for me but slow-growing, and it only forms a very open carpet. The type species and I.S.I. 1222 are very similar, each forming very dense bright carpets, flowering in spring, and turning an odd buff shade in very cold, wet weather. I have grown them outside for a number of years with very minimum of protection. Lau 081 is said to be cold hardy, but I have not yet experimented with it outdoors in winter. It is likely to be almost as hardy as *S. moranense*.

SEDUM RHODOCARPUM SUBSP. EDWARDSII (Rose) Clausen

The type species appears lost to cultivation, but *Sedum rhodocarpum* subsp. *edwardsii* now in cultivation is still exceptionally rare and a real oddity (Fig. 10.24). Rising, then arching from basal buds, this hirsute herb reaches to 18 cm (7 in) high and has flat ternate leaves. Brownish flowers are produced in midwinter, but if petals are examined closely, they are red on the underside and greenish gold on the upperside. Petals are strongly recurved between very hairy sepals. The whole plant, including the flowers, is often indiscriminately splashed with red.

HABITAT. This subspecies was found in Tamaulipas, near Villa Hidalgo, on mossy, north-facing cliffs from 1400 to 1800 m (4600 to 5900 ft), and near Dulces Nombres mines, Nuevo Leon, in the Eastern Sierra Madre.

MAIN POINTS OF DISTINCTION. This is the only Mexican *Sedum* species with wide leaves in whorls of three. In addition, leaves are densely hirsute on stems that resemble bamboo because

of their leaf scars. Flowers of a very odd shade have a musty aroma. The type species has glabrous leaves in threes on stems that are triangular in section.

VARIATION. The plant I grow is a tetraploid and has $n = 64$.

HORTICULTURE. This strange but delightful stonecrop is at its best in midwinter. I grow it in a hanging basket near the apex of the greenhouse for maximum light. It is a pleasant windowsill plant, but will become leggy and more likely to collapse unless given a bright spot.

SEDUM STELLIFORME S. Watson

Sedum stelliforme, a tiny, glabrous, creeping stonecrop from both sides of the U.S.–Mexican border, turns red in full sun. Blunt, shortly spurred leaves are semiterete, and dead leaves remain attached to stems. Kyphocarpic flowers are produced in summer with white mucronate petals that tinge with purple. Plants are exceptionally rare in cultivation and almost unknown in Europe.

HABITAT. U.S. habitats include southern Arizona in the Huachuca Mountains and New Mexico near Fort Wingate, to 3260 m (10,700 ft). Mexican habitats include Chihuahua on the Western Sierra Madre near Colonia Garcia, at much lower altitudes.

MAIN POINTS OF DISTINCTION. The diminutive nature of this plant with shiny, spurred leaves and white kyphocarpic flowers with free, spurred, just-about-equal sepals is a good guide to its identity. Stamens are very long with epipetalous stamens inserted above the petal bases. Nectaries are spathulate and obcordate.

VARIATION. I only know of a single collection made in Arizona, but Uhl (1985, 407) wrote that as a species "it is very diverse cytologically . . . with $n = 11, 13 + 3, 14, 22, 24, 26$, circa 54, and circa 60." Flowers are often 6-partite.

HORTICULTURE. Rather an insignificant stonecrop and difficult to cultivate successfully in Northumberland, *Sedum stelliforme* is not fully hardy.

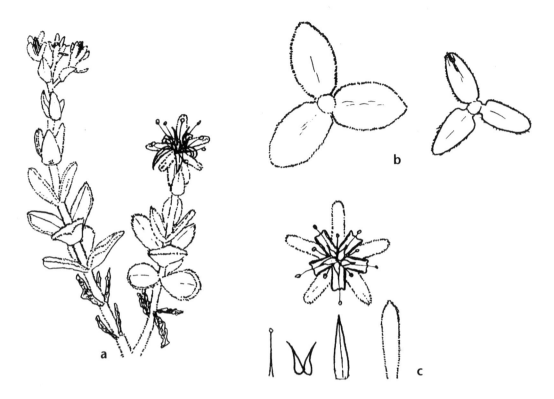

Figure 10.24. *Sedum rhodocarpum* subsp. *edwardsii*: (a) the tallest stem pictured is 17 cm (7 in); (b) leaves are ternate, densely hirsute; (c) flowers have reflexed petals, short stamens, upright carpels, and hirsute sepals.

SEDUM TRICHROMUM Clausen

Exceptionally rare and a most difficult species to maintain, perhaps *Sedum trichromum* is lost to cultivation. From a fleshy rootstock, basal, over-wintering buds rise the following spring to 18 cm (7 in) high. Stout, rising, then arching purple stems soon lose their leaves. Drooping inflorescences carry flowers with petals of three colors (hence the name) and only a single whorl of stamens.

HABITAT. The species has a very limited distribution, localized to a few areas in the Western Sierra Madre in western Durango at over 2000 m (7000 ft). Clausen (1981) suggested that because of its limited distribution and the lack of pollen produced, *Sedum trichromum* could possibly be an intergeneric hybrid of *Echeveria* and *Sedum*. Uhl (1985) disagreed as the species displays normal meiosis.

MAIN POINTS OF DISTINCTION. The growth habit of this stonecrop is not particularly distinct, but resembles *Sedastrum* species somewhat. Large flowers are unusual, as petals with green bases are white and heavily tinged red at their tips. There are no epipetalous stamens. Five stamens between the petals are arched over the carpels like a cage, sticking together by the anther tips when the flowers first open. Eventually stamens spread and arch back as one would expect for *Graptopetalum* species. *n* = 19.

VARIATION. Clausen (1981) noted that sepals on plants in cultivation became longer than petals, but this is not my experience. Petals can become quite translucent.

HORTICULTURE. Not too difficult to propagate as bracts root easily, *Sedum trichromum* is exceptionally difficult to perpetuate because it is very susceptible to overwatering. In addition, it languishes in drought and is favored by sciara, blackfly, and greenfly.

SEDUM VERSADENSE
C. H. Thompson

PLATE 92

SYNONYM: *S. chontalense* Alexander

My clones of *Sedum versadense* and *S. chontalense* are distinct and easily separated when in flower. Inflorescences of the latter are two or three gracefully arched branches while leaves appear more truncate. The former has compact inflorescences and more-apiculate leaves. Thus I was sceptical when Clausen united the two species, but he had studied a whole range of forms in the wild, and those in cultivation were only samples from within that range. Hirsute, tufted leaves are most charming, the undersides of which often tinge deep purple. Spring flowers are pink-white.

HABITAT. Found over quite a large range in three areas, *Sedum chontalense* forms come from summits of cliffs above San Miguel, in mountains west of Tehuantepec, Oaxaca. *Sedum versadense* proper is found in two locations: in the gorge of River Tenancingo on the southern edge of the Trans-Mexican Volcanic Belt and in the Southern Sierra Madre under 2000 m (7000 ft).

MAIN POINTS OF DISTINCTION. Imbricate, hirsute leaves edged in purple or with purple undersides are unique (Plate 92). Very unequal sepals are glabrous. Petals are noticeably mucronate. Carpels are erect and white like the nectaries.

VARIATION. I now have a number of forms and can see why they have been reduced to synonomy. *Sedum versadense* f. *chontalense* is a robust tetraploid with $n = 64$—so enthusiasts are almost certain to maintain its status in their collections. The other clones appear to have $n = 32$.

Another collection with $n = 32$ was introduced to cultivation as I.S.I. 1683. It is distinct vegetatively and should be labelled *Sedum versadense* subsp. *villadioides* (C. H. Thomson) Kimnach. It has narrower, almost-terete leaves, and, as the name suggests, resembles *Villadia* species. Inflorescence and individual flowers are a good match for the diploid *S. versadense*, I.S.I. 1683 collected northeast of Teotitlan del Camino at 2135 m (7005 ft). It is probably the only clone of this subspecies in cultivation.

HORTICULTURE. I grow all subspecies and forms in hanging baskets, but they look superb in small bowls or ceramic dishes. They need a lot of light and are delightful on a sunny windowsill. *Sedum versadense* subsp. *villadioides* is more arching than the other forms.

SEDUM WRIGHTII A. Gray

From a thick, fleshy rootstock, sessile rosettes of yellow-green succulent rosettes overwinter and elongate the following spring into erect, rigid stems of about 11 cm (4 in). Inflorescences of two-branched cymes appear in autumn and carry white, pleasantly aromatic flowers with distinct petals that open around Christmas. Petals are erect in their lower half then spreading. This stonecrop is not very commonly encountered in cultivation.

HABITAT. *Sedum wrightii* and its subspecies are native to the Eastern Sierra Madre in Tamaulipas and Nuevo León, and to the adjacent Mexican Plateau of Coahuila and San Luis Potosí. They grow as far north as Texas and New Mexico, especially in arid areas and usually on rocky ledges from very low altitudes to above 2000 m (7000 ft). Generally the colonies are associated with semishade provided by other vegetation, or with north-facing slopes on rocks of very diverse natures.

MAIN POINTS OF DISTINCTION. This stonecrop has a similar habit to *Sedum cockerellii*, but the latter has thin, papillose leaves and stellate flowers lacking a strong smell. Upright bases of the petals of *S. wrightii* are very distinct. All stamens are upright, as are carpels. Anthers are red, and to find the white nectaries, petals need to be removed.

VARIATION. This plant is found over a wide range so is very varied in the wild. Three subspecies have been described, two of which are in cultivation.

Sedum wrightii subsp. *wrightii* is the form most likely to be encountered. It has a variety of levels of ploidy: *n* = 12, 24, 36, 48, 60, and 72. Plants vary in size and color.

Sedum wrightii subsp. *densiflorum* Clausen is greener than the type species, and, as the name suggests, more floriferous. Leaves of the inflorescences are almost terete, and inflorescences are twice the length of those of the type species—reaching 20 cm (8 in) before collapsing under their own weight. Sepals of this subspecies are narrow, and carpels are pink along a ventral groove. Sometimes the type species flowers in late summer in cultivation. *Sedum wrightii* subsp. *priscum* Clausen may have entered collections. It is a diploid from New Mexico, vegetatively midway between the other two subspecies, with noticeable pedicels.

HORTICULTURE. The flowers of winter are very welcome. Leaves and bracts of the inflorescences fall and root easily, making propagation no problem. I grow plants in hanging baskets, but a dense hummock of rosettes looks good in a shallow container. All forms are very prone to rot if overwatered.

SOUTH AMERICAN SPECIES

There is a great deal of confusion and misunderstanding when the subject of *Sedum* species from south of Mexico is broached. When *S. andinum* was described by Ball in 1887, it was the first stonecrop to be described from South America. Ball had discovered the species near Chica at 4000 m (13,000 ft) in the Peruvian Andes five years earlier. In his group *Andinum*, Fröderström (1935, 82) described four additional species: *S. berillonanum* Hamet, *S. dyvrandae* Hamet, and *S. grandyi* Hamet—all from Peru—and *S. cymatopetalum* Fröderström from Bolivia. He pre-empted the descriptions with "probably most of these species do not belong to *Sedum* but to *Altamiranoa*, or to some new genus."

Altamiranoa was proposed by Rose (Britton and Rose 1905b, 31) for "[c]ertain anomalous species which have heretofore been resting in *Cotyledon*, but with the habit of *Sedum* or [others which have hereforeto been resting] in *Sedum* but with united petals." Baehni in 1937 united *Altamiranoa* with *Villadia* under the latter, older name. Clausen in 1959, using only the measurement of petal fusion (greater than 1.2 mm is *Villadia*, less than 1 mm is *Sedum*), transferred several species one way or the other. Petals of these South American species are somewhat fused so they are at the center of debate. *A Handbook of Succulent Plants* by Hermann Jacobsen (1960) is a widely available set of books that lists all the then-known succulent plants. In it the author briefly describes *S. backebergii* Poellnitz from Peru. Several *Sedum*-like plants have been discovered in South America, which have generally been considered to be *Altamiranoa* (syn. *Villadia*), but others remain in *Sedum*. At the time the present volume is going to press, this situation is being reassessed by Moran and Uhl, but there is one relatively newly described species in cultivation—*Sedum jujuyensis* Zardini from Argentina, which has only ever been described as a *Sedum* species.

In his enumeration of *Sedum* species of Argentina, Zardini (1971) listed *S. acre*; a European escape, *S. cymatopetalum*, which has somehow avoided being transferred to *Villadia* by Jacobsen or Clausen; and a new species which he, with some reservation, placed in *Sedum*—*S. jujuyensis*.

True species of *Sedum* exist south of Mexico in Central America, but none are in cultivation as far as I know. The only South American species in cultivation is *S. jujuyensis*.

SEDUM JUJUYENSIS Zardini

Not described until 1971, this geographical oddity looks like a very lax, etiolated *Sedum album*. It is a sprawling, hanging, open species with blunt, linear, well-spaced, alternate leaves. White flowers have fairly erect connate petals. Only a few plants exist in cultivation, but oddly not in Argentina. Hopefully it will soon be distributed.

HABITAT. This species grows in a pendulous fashion on cliffs, which break humid forest, and on higher meadow near Volcán in Northern Argentina—sometimes as an epiphyte.

MAIN POINTS OF DISTINCTION. Vegetatively this stonecrop is not very distinct. Flowers are very extreme for *Sedum*, having upright petals connate for 2 mm (0.075 in), free, very spurred sepals—more than half as long as petals, and carpels with distinct beaks. Carpels arch and spread, petals are wavy, and nectaries are large.

VARIATION. I have observed no more than a tiny established cutting.

HORTICULTURE. I have been so careful with this oddity that I have not subjected it to freezing temperatures, but on one occasion it suffered 0°C (32°F) without harm.

CHAPTER 11

Subgenus Hylotelephium

Some members of the subgenus *Hylotelephium* have been closely associated with Homo sapiens for millennia. Perhaps early humans considered these species to hold magical powers since flower stems stay alive for weeks after picking. Apothecaries believed these plants had powerful medicinal qualities. In any case, early migratory tribes regularly collected and transported some members of this plant group, whose wide distribution is considered proof of early social osmosis. As a result, natural habitats are confused and species often misidentified.

Once considered to be species of the genus *Anacampseros* by Haworth, Jordan, Fourreau, and others, it became apparent that flower structure of these herbaceous plants was very much like that of flowers of the genus *Sedum*, which in the early nineteenth century only included evergreen, succulent, tufted species like *S. acre*. Therefore section *Telephium* S. F. Gray was erected to accommodate these tall herbaceous species. Most modern florae consider the group to be a section of *Sedum* after Gray, Ledebour, and Boissier.

By the mid-nineteenth century, root structure was considered the key character to separate section *Telephium* from other *Sedum* species (Fig. 3.10). Unfortunately, fleshy root systems associated with the first species to be described in the section are not characteristic of all species in the section. Gardeners who grow a variety of these plants realize that several commonly grown plants do not possess the carrotlike rootstock once considered to be a prescriptive feature of this group (e.g., *Sedum ewersii* Fig. 3.10d). *Sedum populifolium*, too, has only a meager woody rootstock and for this reason has been repeatedly included and excluded from section *Telephium* as the group has been reviewed in subsequent books on the subject.

Index Kewensis shows that 25 species of *Anacampseros* and 34 species of *Sedum* are now considered merely to be forms of *S. telephium*. Opinion has always varied as to whether this group of plants should be described as scores of regional species or whether Fröderström's (1930) amalgamation of most of the tall forms into one species was more sensible. Baldwin (1937) and others showed that Fröderström's grouping of the numerous species of section *Telephium* into one species with lots of subspecies, although convenient, cannot be substantiated from cytological evidence. Studies of chromosome behavior, number, and morphology have often supported conclusions reached by systematists other than Fröderström and show that several distinct species do exist.

The most recent treatise on the group is "The Taxonomic Status of *Sedum telephium* and Its Allied Species (Crassulaceae)" published in 1977 by Hideaki Ohba of the Department of Botany, University Museum, University of Tokyo. In addition to Ohba's work, which grew out of many years of study of wild species and herbarium specimens, this study also takes into account cytological findings of Baldwin, Sigiura, Toyohuka, and others. Like Fröderström, Ohba viewed floral features to be of principal importance. His concern with floral differences led him to remove section *Telephium* from the genus *Sedum* and to establish a new genus *Hylotelephium*. I propose to use his name to differentiate this natural grouping of plants, for, although not exactly identical to Gray's section *Telephium* or Berger's section 3 *Telephiastrum*, Ohba's work is the most recent. However, I retain *Sedum* names for each species as I believe the name *Hylotelephium* will soon not be generally accepted as a genus in its own right but merely as a revised subgenus of *Sedum*. In this volume then, *Hylotelephium* is treated as a subgenus of *Sedum*.

Plants included in subgenus *Hylotelephium* must possess characteristics common to Crassulaceae plus the following:

- Rootstock fleshy or woody, often partly above ground (caudex).
- Herbaceous, although remnants of leaves sometimes persist throughout the winter from where buds of next year's growth often emerge in autumn and persist in favorable conditions.
- Stem deciduous to the fleshy caudex or persistent woody, lower part.
- Rootstocks without thin, scalelike leaves.
- Leaves, flat, spurless, (some newly discovered forms of *Sedum pluricaule* have almost terete leaves but this is unusual), arranged along stems.

- Inflorescences with compact, terminal, purple, pink, white, green, or creamy flowers, never true yellow.
- Flowers 5-partite or rarely 4-partite, with usually short sepals, always without spurs, which are free or almost free.
- Bisexual flowers with free petals without mucrons.
- Carpels free, stalked, waisted or tapered at the base (Fig. 3.4f, g, h).
- Carpels never swollen on the inner side, remaining erect at maturity.
- Carpels never existing in any part below the line of petals.
- Epipetalous stamens, inserted above the base of the petals.
- Seeds somewhat winged.

According to Uhl and Moran (1972, 60), $n = 12$ for members of the subgenus *Hylotelephium* with several exceptions: $n = 10$ for *Sedum tatarinowii* and $n = 11$ for *S. ewersii* and *S. pluricaule*. Several polyploids occur in this group. The species of subgenus *Hylotelephium* can be arranged in a number of ways. I intend to follow Ohba (1977), though placing species of this subgenus into groups is very tenuous:

1. *Hylotelephium* group has erect to ascending stems and well-developed rootstocks.
2. *Sieboldii* group has decumbent to pendulous stems and well-developed rootstocks.
3. *Populisedum* group lacks well-developed underground rootstocks, and flowering stems rise only from persistent nodes on the bases of the remains of last year's flowering stems.

HYLOTELEPHIUM GROUP

Species of this group have stems that are erect to ascending and well-developed rootstocks. *Hylotelephium* group comprises the following species in cultivation:

Sedum alboroseum Baker (see *S. erythrosticum*)
Sedum caucasicum (Grossheim) Borissova
Sedum erythrostycum Miquel
Sedum fabaria Koch (see *S. telephium*)

Sedum maximum (Suter) Praeger (see *S. telephium*)

Sedum purpureum Link (see *S. telephium*)

Sedum ruprechtii Jalas (see *S. telephium*)

Sedum sordidum Maximowicz

Sedum spectabile Boreau

Sedum tatarinowii Maximowicz

Sedum telephioides Michaux

Sedum telephium subsp. *fabaria* (Koch) Kirschleger

Sedum telephium subsp. *maximum* (L.) Krocker

Sedum telephium subsp. *ruprechtii* (L.) Jalas

Sedum telephium subsp. *telephium* L.

Sedum telephium 'Autumn Joy'

Sedum verticillatum L.

Sedum viride Makino

Sedum viridescens Nakai

Sedum viviparum Maximowicz

The following is not a formal key but will help to isolate species within this group:

Leaves amplexicaul: *S. caucasicum, S. telephium* subsp. *ruprechtii*

Leaves extremely petiolate: *S. viride, S. viviparum*

Leaves somewhat petiolate, stems <20 cm (8 in): *S. sordidum, S. tatarinowii, S. telephioides*

Leaves somewhat petiolate, stems >20 cm (8 in): *S. erythrosticum, S. spectabile, S. telephium, S. viridescens, S. verticillatum*

Figures 11.1 and 11.2 show leaf shapes of species in subgenus *Hylotelephium*.

SEDUM CAUCASICUM (Grossheim) Borissova

Sedum caucasicum is an almost unknown member of *Hylotelephium* group in cultivation, with 40-cm (16-in) long, suberect stems, carrying well-spaced, deeply cupped leaves. Creamy-white flowers, wine red on the outside, are not as showy as those of many other species in this group, and plants are less robust, tending to lean or collapse when flowering.

HABITAT. Indigenous to Russian Caucasus and perhaps just into Turkey from 1000 to 2500 m (3000 to 8200 ft), *Sedum caucasicum* is found in meadows, and on forest margins.

MAIN POINTS OF DISTINCTION. Almost round, deeply concave, amplexicaul leaves are the best means of identification (Fig. 11.1a). Unfortunately, some otherwise reputable nurseries have distributed a particular *Sedum maximum* hybrid with opposite, semi-cupped leaves as the true species. The imposter has dark, almost bronze leaves that are nearly twice as long as wide.

VARIATION. So few clones exist in cultivation, it is difficult to comment, but considering the limited range in the field, it is unlikely much variation exists. It is suspected that where the habitats of this species and *S. maximum* meet in northern Turkey, natural hybrids are more than a mere possibility, especially when *S. maximum* appears to hybridize freely with most of the other species in subgenus *Hylotelephium* in cultivation.

HORTICULTURE. Anyone lucky enough to acquire a plant of this species should propagate additional plants as soon as possible and take extra precautions to keep one specimen under cover in winter just in case the main plant rots in a wet period—a frequent problem. This species is one of the earliest in its group to flower, often just after midsummer. Plants are unsuitable for rock gardens (except for the very largest) or raised beds due to their sprawling, gangling nature. They are best grown as border plants in a dry or well-drained spot or in a chimney-pot.

SEDUM ERYTHROSTICUM Miquel

SYNONYM: *S. alboroseum* Baker
COMMON NAME: Benkei-sō

Enthusiasts and gardeners alike may be unwilling to break their habit of referring to this species by the name *"Sedum alboroseum"*—the name most generally known. Regardless of personal preferences, *S. erythrosticum* is an older and therefore valid name.

This species is very similar to the common ice

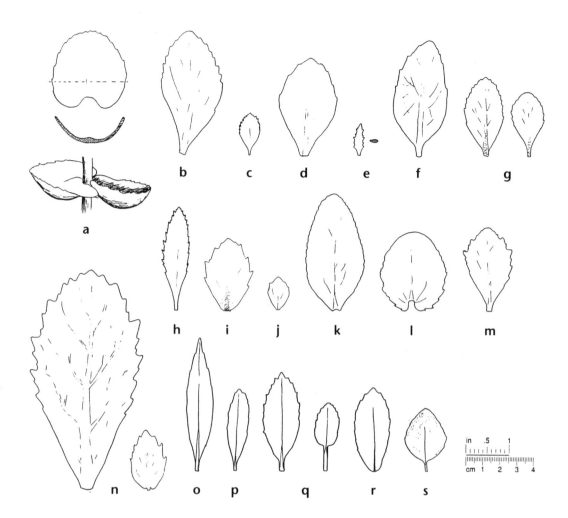

Figure 11.1. Leaf shapes of subgenus *Hylotelephium*: (a) *Sedum causasicum* has amplexicaul, cupped leaves in opposite pairs; (b) *S. erythrosticum*; (c) *S. sordidum*; (d) *S. spectabile* leaf of a potted plant—leaves of plants in a rich border can be twice this size (area); (e) *S. tatarinowii*; (f) *S. telephioides*; (g) *S. telephium* subsp. *fabaria*; (h) *Sedum telephium* subsp. *fabaria* var. *borderi*; (i) 'Ruby Glow'; (j) 'Vera Jameson'; (k) *S. telephium* subsp. *maximum*; (l) *S. telephium* subsp. *ruprechtii*; (m) *S. telephium* subsp. *telephium*; (n) 'Autumn Joy' possesses the largest of all *Sedum* leaves but its upper leaves are much smaller than and rather different in shape from the large lower ones; (o) *Sedum verticillatum* mainland form; (p) *S. verticillatum* var. *nipponicum*; (q) *S. viride*; (r) *Sedum viridescens* leaf; (s) *Sedum viviparum* leaves are not succulent.

plant *Sedum spectabile* and often is difficult to differentiate from it, especially in spring. Like *S. spectabile*, *S. erythrosticum* reaches 30–60 cm (12–24 in) high and is pale glaucous-green. These two very closely related species can be plants with alternate, ternate, opposite or scattered leaves. Very showy flowers in September separate them: *S. erythrosticum* has white petals and rosy carpels (another reason why the name "*S.*

alboroseum" will be perpetuated) while all the flower parts of *S. spectabile* tend to be the same color. A third reason why the more commonly used name will be perpetuated is that it is so much easier to pronounce.

HABITAT. Central, northern, and eastern China, Korea, and Japan are the homes of this relatively widespread species (?), which prefers low altitudes.

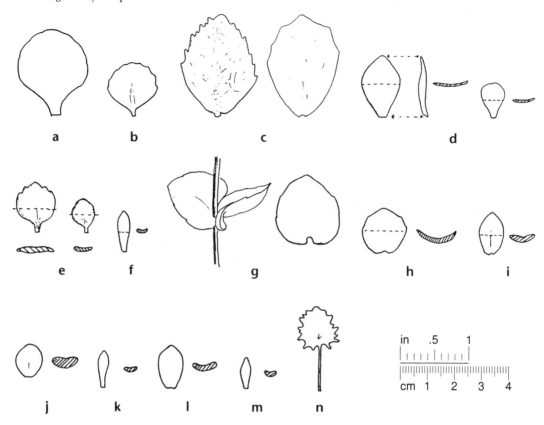

Figure 11.2. Leaves of subgenus *Hylotelephium*: (a) *Sedum ettyuense*; (b) *S. sieboldii*; (c) *S. tsugaruense* (left) typical leaf (and right) extreme form; (d) *S. anacampseros* leaves are very varied in shape but usually are clustered in terminal rosettes; (e) *S. cauticola* (left) form from Mount Apoi, Japan (and right) 'Lidakense'; (f) *S. cyaneum*; (g) *S. ewersii* subsp. *ewersii* (left) pairs of leaves are well spaced on long stems and (right) leaves are amplexicaul; (h) *S. ewersii* var. *cyclophyllum*, (i) *S. ewersii* var. *homophyllum*; (j) *S. pluricaule* var. *pluricaule*; (k) *S. pluricaule* var. *ezawe*; (l) *S. pluricaule* var. *yezoense*; (m) *S. pluricaule* var. *yezoense* from Rebun; (n) *S. populifolium* leaves can be much larger than this but are always just as anomalous.

MAIN POINTS OF DISTINCTION. It is likely that confusion could arise between this species and *Sedum spectabile* or its cultivated forms. Earlier monographs make the disposition of the leaves an important issue when distinguishing the two. Unfortunately, each species is too variable. Baker (1868, table 33) said that the leaves of *S. erythrosticum* are never opposite, Praeger (1921) that they are usually opposite, Ohwi (1965) that they are opposite or alternate, and Evans (1943) that they are opposite-decussate. I have just examined a dozen or so plants and none fit exactly any of the above descriptions, so leaf arrangement as a point of differentiation is a poor indicator.

The best time to differentiate these very similar species is before they flower when *Sedum erythrosticum* has very distinct leaflike bracts that half enclose the inflorescence (Fig. 11.3). It is taller and more slender than *S. spectabile*, which has pure pink flowers, or, in certain cultivated forms, white flowers. *Sedum spectabile* always has exceptionally long stamens, while stamens of *S. erythrosticum* (Fig. 11.1b) are about equal in length to its petals. Leaves of *S. erythrosticum* are more upright than those of *S. spectabile*, which are spreading. Because of irregular meiosis and aborting pollen, it is probable that *S. erythrosticum* is a plant of hybrid origin; n = circa 48. I am only speculating, but *S. spectabile* and *S. viri-*

descens seem likely parents both geographically and vegetatively.

VARIATION. A particularly splendid variegated form *Sedum erythrosticum* f. *variegatum* [syn. *S. alboroseum* f. *foliis medio-variegatis* (Baker) Regel], is quite common in collections, but often reverts to normal.

HORTICULTURE. This is an easy specimen for the border, but it is not as common or showy as *Sedum spectabile*. Remove all normal shoots from the variegated form as they are much more rapid growing and will soon overtake the plant.

SEDUM SORDIDUM Maximowicz

COMMON NAMES: Chichippa-benkei-sō, Titippabenkei

Sedum sordidum is a little known Japanese member of *Hylotelephium* group that could easily be mistaken for one of the countless garden hy-brids of *Sedum maximum*. However, because the species is likely to be available only from an enthusiast or botanic garden, plants will be accompanied by the correct name. In cultivation this stonecrop grows to only 20 cm (8 in) high, but in the wild it can grow twice as tall. The alternate or rarely opposite leaves are suffused dark brown-purple. Flowers are not true yellow, but are pale yellow-green. The species is closely related to *S. viride*, another rarity in cultivation.

HABITAT. Endemic to mountains of Honshu, this stonecrop is rare in the wild.

MAIN POINTS OF DISTINCTION. Leaves have a very short petiole and are remotely undulate-toothed (Fig. 11.1c). European garden hybrids approach the color of this species, but their leaves tend to be much larger than those of *Sedum sordidum*. *Sedum viride*, which is similar, has much longer petioles, and its leaves tend to be opposite. *n* = 12.

Figure 11.3. Differentiating *Sedum erythrosticum* from *S. spectabile*: (left) *S. erythrosticum* f. *foliis medio-variegatis*; (center) *S. spectabile* with less obvious, more patent bracts; (right) *S. erythrosticum* with bracts half enclosing the flower buds.

VARIATION. Few plants are in cultivation, so that it is hard to comment on variation. Because the species has such a limited range in the wild, variation is likely to be minor.

HORTICULTURE. Anyone lucky enough to acquire a plant should carefully tend it and give away propagations to friends. Otherwise this rarity could disappear. It is a collector's plant which, because of its deep shade, needs to be grown against a very light background. The flowers, too, are rather dull compared to those of other species in this group, but nevertheless plants are an interesting variation on a theme.

SEDUM SPECTABILE Boreau

PLATE 93

COMMON NAME: Ō-benkei-sō

This species, known as the common ice plant of cottage gardens, is usually 45 cm (18 in) high, very light glaucous green, and a bright subject for the border. Perhaps *Sedum spectabile* is still more common in its true form than in the plethora of cultivars now available. Large, flat-topped, pink-purple inflorescences of autumn are a great attraction to nectar-feeding insects, especially butterflies and hoverflies (Plate 93).

HABITAT. This stonecrop is native to Korea and northern China at low altitudes.

MAIN POINTS OF DISTINCTION. The species could be confused with any of the other common species in *Hylotelephium* group (e.g., *Sedum erythrosticum*, *S. telephium* and its subspecies and varieties including 'Autumn Joy'). Exceptionally light green foliage of *S. spectabile* immediately separates it from all *S. telephium* subspecies and cultivars except 'Autumn Joy', which is similar in color. However, the latter is blue-green and generally a larger plant with huge, very dentate leaves, unlike the sparsely toothed leaves of *S. spectabile* (Fig. 11.1d). The very long stamens of *S. spectabile* are the best identifying feature to set the species apart from other species. Flower parts of *S. spectabile* are generally of the same color, in contrast to *S. erythrosticum* with its distinctly bicolored flowers.

VARIATION. As this stonecrop has been in cultivation for centuries, it has many cultivated forms. The actual wild plant is usually no more than 35 cm (14 in) in height, but in developing new, deeper flower colors and a greater variety of hues, sturdier strains with double chromosomes have been developed. $n = 25$, and, in some cultivated forms, $n = 50$.

The following cultivars are commonly seen and offer alternative flower colors:

'Brilliant' is a North American cultivar that dates back to before the First World War. Its bright pink anthers and carpels are an improvement on the type species, but it often sports light colored flowers.
'Carmen' and 'Meteor' have darker, rich purple flowers.
'Rosenteller' is a European cultivar similar to 'Brilliant'
'Septemberglut', originating on mainland Europe, is perhaps the most spectacular form as it has the darkest umbels. Although the inflorescences are large, individual flowers are slighly smaller than those of the other cultivars.
'Snow Queen' and 'Stardust' have white flowers.

Vegetatively, cultivars appear to be quite similar to the true species. In a well-manured border, tall spectacular plants can be grown, but the same clones confined to clay pots are pallid and stunted, though still pleasing.

HORTICULTURE. Division of the rootstock is the usual method of propagation, though cuttings in spring will also grow. Avoid peat-based composts at all costs. The plants themselves do not dislike this medium, but peat attracts and harbors their most harmful enemies.

SEDUM TATARINOWII Maximowicz

PLATE 94

Sedum tatarinowii is a most attractive, though relatively unknown, miniature member of *Hylotelephium* group with suberect, arching stems to 13 cm (5 in) long, topped with dainty white flowers bearing large purple anthers. It is an early flowerer—from July to August—and does not spread, but instead develops a very large rootstock for its diminutive size.

HABITAT. Native to North China and central Mongolia, this stonecrop inhabits rocky zones from 1400 to 3000 m (4600 to 10,000 ft).

MAIN POINTS OF DISTINCTION. Narrow, deeply dentate leaves are the best indicator (Fig. 11.1e), though very young leaves in spring are almost entire. By flowering time it would be difficult to mistake the species for any other. Fairly crowded, scattered leaves are largest in the upper third of the plant, and then light glaucous green contrasts with the darker purple-brown stems. Flowers are carried on long slender pedicels and have long stamens. $n = 10$.

VARIATION. The type species is pretty constant, but several hybrids of this species have been made: the most well known, especially in the United States, is 'Sunset Cloud', a hybrid with a taller, darker species of *Hylotelephium* group, probably *Sedum maximum*. I have inadvertently hybridized *S. sieboldii* with this species, and the offspring are sterile with freak flowers. It has also been reported that crosses have been made with *S. populifolium*.

HORTICULTURE. This stonecrop requires good drainage. Because of its diminutive size, it is an ideal plant for raised beds and stone troughs. As the rootstock is so large, division is quite easy, but allow broken roots to dry thoroughly before watering. This is such a charming plant, it is well worth searching hard to acquire it. Like *Sedum sieboldii*, it makes a pleasant potted plant for a windowsill, but, as such, is less robust.

SEDUM TELEPHIOIDES Michaux

Sedum telephioides is the only species in *Hylotelephium* group that is indigenous to the Americas, though several Old World species have escaped there and have become quite common (but not in the habitat of this species). Much shorter than its Eurasian counterparts—20 cm (8 in) long in cultivation—it has white flowers and a distinct leaf-shape (Fig 11.1f). This stonecrop is almost unknown in cultivation outside the United States.

HABITAT. The species is a native of the Eastern Cordillera, found in the Appalachians and neighboring low plateaux from Georgia to Pennsylvania, often in rocky woodland glades where it can attain a greater stature of 70 cm (28 in).

MAIN POINTS OF DISTINCTION. *Sedum telephioides* in cultivation is short in stature with white petals, red anthers, and green, glabrous leaves each with a few large teeth. It is very possible for this plant to be taken for its Old World counterpart *S. telephium* or one of its numerous subspecies and forms, but *S. telephioides* has petiolate leaves with larger flowers—over 11 mm (0.4 in) in diameter—in contrast to flowers of Eurasian cousins less than 8 mm (0.3 in) across. In addition, roots of the North American member of *Hylotelephium* group are not jointed or so carrotlike as those of *S. telephium*.

VARIATION. Leaf shape varies considerably, even on a single plant. In shady conditions, the species can become taller than suggested, and variation occurs in chromosome counts as well as in pigmentation. Clausen (1975) concluded that the greatest cause of variation is site, and the degree of sunlight exposure is the main factor determining overall variation. He also suggested that the species is unlikely to flower in areas not experiencing at least 14 hours of sunshine in summer. $n = 12, 24$.

HORTICULTURE. This stonecrop is not at all common in cultivation on either side of the Atlantic, which is surprising, as it is a less vigorous plant than the common *Sedum telephium* and therefore more desirable since it is less difficult to control. It is suitable for both borders and large rock gardens, as well as old chimney pots, sinks, and large tubs.

SEDUM TELEPHIUM SUBSP. FABARIA (Koch) Kirschleger

COMMON NAMES: Orpine, livelong, midsummer men

Long known in cottage gardens, the English *Sedum telephium* is often, even in serious florae, confused with garden escapes of more easterly subspecies. It is not a spectacular plant, but one worthy of a place in any border. It becomes a 40-cm (16-in) high, fresh green herb crowded with upward pointing medium-sized leaves and topped with glaucous-violet buds and purple flowers.

HABITAT. Widespread throughout west and central Europe, this stonecrop is usually a plant of hedgerows.

MAIN POINTS OF DISTINCTION. Dark purple flowers immediately distinguish this subspecies from *Sedum telephium* subsp. *maximum* and *S. telephium* subsp. *ruprechtii*, but the more easterly *S. telephium* subsp. *telephium* (syn. *S. purpurascens*) is virtually identical. The cytologist can distinguish the two by chromosome counts: *S. telephium* subsp. *fabaria* has only $2n = 24$, while the more easterly subspecies has counts of $2n = 36$ and $2n = 48$. The best indicators for the English subspecies are the completely glabrous leaves, which are cuneate below, and the shortly petiolate lower leaves (Fig. 11.1g). Carpels have no grooves on the outer side, and leaves are regularly dentate.

VARIATION. Unless this subspecies has been propagated vegetatively from wild stock, it is likely that hybridization has occurred. Literally dozens of cultivars have been produced, and enthusiastic horticulturists sell seeded offspring, which can be of sharp contrast to the one known parent. 'Munstead Dark Red' is a good example; it has bright red stems and a generous amount of red suffusion throughout, but its seedlings are any color from green to red.

Only one wild form is worthy of mention due to its consistent, distinctive characteristics—*Sedum telephium* subsp. *fabaria* var. *borderi* Rouy & Camus—which is unfortunately now quite a rare variation. It seems to have been replaced in cultivation by *S. telephium* 'Autumn Joy', though once it was a relatively common tall plant of the cottage garden, carrying distinct narrow leaves with cuneate bases (Fig. 11.1h). In other respects it is identical to *S. telephium* subsp. *fabaria*. It ap-

pears to be susceptible to fungal infection.

Sedum telephium subsp. *fabaria* 'Roseo-variegatum' appears very close to the subspecies, except in spring when young shoots are light rose-colored. Later in the year it is indistinguishable from the subspecies.

Sedum telephium hybrids are frequently encountered in gardens. *Sedum telephium* 'Ruby Glow' is eventually a decumbent, dark hybrid with fairly succulent, dull green leaves which are ternate below, and turn purple in full sun, especially on the underside (Fig. 11.1i). This sprawling stonecrop is one of the most common clones of the subgenus *Hylotelephium* in the United Kingdom. If restricted by pot cultivation, it remains upright. It appeared on mainland Europe in 1960 from a cross between *Sedum telephium* and *S. cauticola*.

Sedum telephium 'Vera Jameson' appeared in the garden of the lady of the same name around 1970 as a hybrid of a dark form of *S. telephium* subsp. *maximum* and 'Ruby Glow'. Plants have suberect stems 25 cm (10 in) high carrying small leaves (Fig. 11.1j) which together with the stems turn very deep purple in full sun. It is not an easy hybrid to perpetuate.

In response to demand for new plants with attractive, easily remembered names, nurseries, bombard the market with new cultivars. Unfortunately, many cultivars with distinct names are not necessarily of a distinct or desirable nature. 'Pink Jewel', 'Evening Cloud', and 'Munstead Red' have become commonly used names, but careless distribution of seeded offspring has meant that plants bearing such labels are variable. Hybrids tend to be prolific, easy to grow, and colorful or floriferous (or both), but cultivars are more susceptible to infestation and fungal infection.

HORTICULTURE. For centuries orpine was considered to be a lucky plant with suggestions that it promoted longevity. Its medicinal qualities have made it a feature of herbals since they were first produced. It is a very easy species to grow, but needs shade and preferably a damp spot in latitudes less than 50°, unless altitude modifies temperatures.

SEDUM TELEPHIUM SUBSP. MAXIMUM (L.) Krocker

SYNONYM: *S. maximum* (Suter) Praeger, *Hylotelephium jullianum* (Boreau) Grulich

As the name suggests, *Sedum telephium* subsp. *maximum* is a giant stonecrop. It is quite common in gardens in its multitude of forms or as a parent of a cultivar, but is duller than many of the other members of this group: opposite-decussate leaves are drab green to brown-maroon, and flowers are an inconspicuous cream color. Plants can reach 80 cm (32 in) high, but 40 cm (16 in) is more usual. Plants are sparingly leafy with long gaps between the leaf pairs which diminish in size up the stem.

HABITAT. Native to mainland Europe, this *Hylotelephium* group species grows usually in forest glades and rich soils of alluvial meadows.

MAIN POINTS OF DISTINCTION. Bluntly dentate, opposite-decussate, well-spaced leaves (Fig. 11.1k), and creamy flowers are an important combination of characteristics that separates this stonecrop from *Sedum telephium* subsp. *fabaria*, which has more upright leaves and purple flowers, and from *S. telephium* subsp. *ruprechtii*, which has identical flowers but cordate, stemclasping leaves. $2n = 48$.

VARIATION. Unfortunately, this subspecies is exceptionally varied, and, because it seems more willing than any other species of *Sedum* to hybridize with near relatives, its range is fogged by intermediates with other species. For example, leaves of *S. telephium* subsp. *maximum* can be alternate, whorled, or sometimes glaucous, and in rare reports, flowers of the true species are purple. These factors make identification very difficult, but fortunately not all these contrary features occur in one regional race.

The variation of greatest horticultural importance is usually referred to as *Sedum maximum* var. *atropurpureum* and is suffused purple

throughout. In my experience *S. telephium* subsp. *maximum* 'Atropurpureum' (syn. *S. maximum* var. *haematodes* Miller) is not true from seed, as it seeds readily with mixed progeny. It is a major element in a great multitude of cultivars, including 'Arthur Branch' and 'Philip Holbrook'. Against a light background, these dark red to violet forms can be useful herbs for formal floral displays.

HORTICULTURE. As this species comes in every shade between dull green and deep violet, it is important to choose the right plant for the desired spot. I only recommend this species for a herbaceous border or for hybridizing to create new cultivars.

SEDUM TELEPHIUM SUBSP. RUPRECHTII (L.) Jalas

Only available in recent years, *Sedum telephium* subsp. *ruprechtii* is still a rare plant in cultivation and perhaps not yet available outside Europe. Rising, arching, then falling, stems, to about 30 cm (12 in) long, carry opposite-decussate, almost round leaves, which are lobed like the shape of a heart (cordate) and wrapped around the stem (amplexicaul). Glaucous blue-green leaves are tinged red on the margins, which range from almost entire to quite deeply toothed on the same plant.

HABITAT. Northeast Europe is the home of this stonecrop—chiefly in the Russian commonwealth on riverbanks and in meadows.

MAIN POINTS OF DISTINCTION. Cordate, amplexicaul, suborbicular leaves are the best indicator though, as this plant is only available from specialized growers, it is likely to be correctly named (Fig. 11.1l). It is surprisingly similar vegetatively to *Sedum caucasicum*, another Russian member of *Hylotelephium* group that has more-cupped leaves and short, reflexed carpel beaks. Beaks of *Sedum ruprechtii* are long, straight, and hard. Perhaps it is only a matter of time before hybrids between this and promiscuous *S. maximum* confuse the situation. $2n = 48$.

VARIATION. Plants in cultivation probably

have been vegetatively propagated from the same group of herbs and therefore will be pretty constant. Upper, smaller leaves tend to be sharply serrated while lower leaves tend towards being entire. Translucent, vaguely carinate, creamy-white petals in full sun can show pink edging (color of the buds).

HORTICULTURE. This is a pleasing subject for the front of a border or large rock garden. I expect it will become a plant for hanging baskets or urns, as the long, tumbling stems, carrying delightfully colored leaves, are most attractive.

SEDUM TELEPHIUM SUBSP. TELEPHIUM L.

SYNONYMS: *S. purpureum* Link, *S. purpurascens* Koch

Sedum telephium subsp. *telephium* is almost indistinguishable from the English *Sedum telephium* subsp. *fabaria*, and, except for a few minor differences, has the same appearance and can be used in the same situations. It is very rare in its true natural form in Britain, but is commonly grown in Japan.

HABITAT. This is an exceptionally widespread stonecrop native to lowland meadow margins from central Europe to Japan.

MAIN POINTS OF DISTINCTION. Carpels are distinctly grooved on the outer side, and lower leaves (Fig. 11.1), which are not particularly glaucous, are not cuneate (tapered below).

HORTICULTURE. See *Sedum telephium* subsp. *fabaria* for suggestions.

SEDUM TELEPHIUM 'AUTUMN JOY'

PLATE 95

SYNONYMS: *Sedum* 'Herbstfreude',
Sedum 'Indian Chief' (?)

'Autumn Joy' is the most common tall clone in subgenus *Hylotelephium* in parks and gardens in Europe and the United States. Growing to 60 cm (24 in) high or more, it throughly deserves its popularity. Renowned for its huge convex cymes of purple flowers late in the year, which attract butterflies in profusion at a time of the year when little else is flowering, it soon forms a glaucous, almost spherical, herbaceous mound. It is a hybrid between *Sedum telephium* and *S. spectabile* as the pollen parent.

HABITAT. This hybrid is of garden origin, appearing in Europe in 1955. Perhaps it is more correct to refer to it as 'Herbstfreude', but in English speaking countries 'Autumn Joy' is well known and widely used.

MAIN POINTS OF DISTINCTION. Flowers have no male parts (i.e., no stamens or anthers). Petals are light pink, but the flower color is dominated by fleshy, dark pink-purple carpels compacted on flat-topped umbels. Vegetatively this cultivar could be (and often is) confused with *Sedum spectabile*, but the latter has less-dentate, light green leaves and is usually much shorter in stature. 'Autumn Joy' leaves are blue-green, the largest of any stonecrop, and extremely dentate (Fig. 11.1n). Upper leaves are much smaller than lower leaves and have a different shape. Flowers are distinct and a stark contrast to those of *S. spectabile* with its very long stamens.

VARIATION. As plants are always cloned from vegetative propagations, every plant in cultivation should be identical, but growing conditions do make some difference: in a well-manured border, plants can be a meter (3 ft) high and a meter (3 ft) across, but in poorer soil, the show is less impressive.

HORTICULTURE. Perhaps this is one of the easiest stonecrops to grow—hence its wide distribution in parks and gardens. Generally, roots are divided in spring and allowed to dry out thoroughly under a bench (perhaps in a greenhouse) before replanting. It is just as easy for cuttings to be rooted up in spring from new stems (on which it only takes a few weeks for the carrotlike roots to develop), although such cuttings may not flower in their first year.

Drying stems produce heads of rust-colored fruit in early winter, and these can be taken and dried artificially for use in flower arrangements. This has become a very important plant for flower arranging on both sides of the Atlantic. Heads can be dyed or painted, and the dried stems and inflorescences are long-lasting and tend not to break up because they are sterile.

SEDUM VERTICILLATUM L.

COMMON NAME: Mitsuba-benkei-sō

Sedum verticillatum is a Far Eastern stonecrop, one of the tall species of *Hylotelephium* group of about 50 cm (20 in) high. It has petiolate leaves in distinct whorls of 3, 4, or 5—hence its name. More common in Japanese gardens than elsewhere, the species is rarely seen in European or American gardens. Pale, dull green leaves are irregularly dentate. Like *Sedum viviparum*, this species too, can be viviparous (i.e., small adventitious buds develop in the leaf axils in autumn, and fall to the ground), and in this way plants propagate themselves. Flowers are light yellow-green.

HABITAT. Native to Hokkaido, Honshu, Shikoku and Kyushu islands of Japan, Sakhalin Island in the former Soviet Union (and perhaps mainland Siberia), the Kurile Islands, and Korea, this stonecrop favors riverbanks or alluvial meadows.

MAIN POINTS OF DISTINCTION. Green, glabrous, verticillate leaves, (Fig. 11.1o) and large heads of greenish flowers are the best indicators. Leaves are pocked with tiny purple-black dots. A chromosome count of $2n = 96$ is distinct.

VARIATION. A west Japanese form is a slighter plant, flowering when only just over 30 cm (12 in). It may be more common in cultivation, but this is relative, as both forms are exceptionally rare. Praeger (1921) named this minor form with frequently opposite leaves *Sedum verticillatum* var. *nipponicum* (Fig. 11.1p). Leaves can be in 3s and even 2s on the same plant. If encountered, the species is likely to be correctly named, as it is as yet only in collections of specialists.

HORTICULTURE. As this stonecrop is indigenous to areas of very high rainfall, perhaps it should be recommended to those growers whose gardens suffer in this respect. Rich soil appears to be the best medium, and hopefully the plant will be more easily obtained in the near future.

SEDUM VIRIDE Makino

COMMON NAME: Ao-Benkei-sō

This stonecrop should not be confused with the Mexican stonecrop once named *Sedum viride* Rose but now known as *S. corynephyllum* (Rose) Berger. The Oriental *S. viride* is a short, upright species, only 20 cm (8 in) or so high with opposite, green (hence its name), bluntly, regularly dentate leaves with distinct petioles (Fig. 11.1q). Leaves decrease in size up the stems. This is an exceptionally rare plant outside Japan.

HABITAT. Native to Honshu, Shikoku, and Kyushu islands of Japan, this stonecrop sometimes grows as an epiphyte.

MAIN POINTS OF DISTINCTION. The only other species in *Hylotelephium* group with such long petioles are *Sedum populifolium* (Fig. 11.2n) and *S. viviparum* (Fig 11.1s). The former has extremely dentate, bright green leaves rather than elliptic, dark green, glaucous leaves, and the latter is a real oddity with very spindly, deep red stems and viviparous bulbils.

Flowers of *Sedum viride* are whitish with long stamens, at least as long as the petals, each with large dark pink to yellow anthers. *Sedum sordidum*, the nearest relative, is similarly rare in cultivation, but it has alternate leaves or leaves that are very loosely arranged. *Sedum viride* has opposite-decussate leaves. $n = 12$.

VARIATION. So few clones are in cultivation, it is difficult to comment, but it is not unlikely that the three Japanese islands have clones that differ slightly. I have grown quite contrasing forms.

HORTICULTURE. This medium-sized member

of *Hylotelephium* group prefers damp and shade. It is a tidy plant and, although not pretentious, is a worthwhile miniature for raised bed, stone trough, or rock garden.

SEDUM VIRIDESCENS Nakai

SYNONYM: *S. taquetii* Praeger

Very much resembling *Sedum telephium* subsp. *maximum*, *S. viridescens* grows into a 40-cm (16-in) long, not very flamboyant herb with usually opposite-decussate, deep green, sessile leaves. Flowers are green and purple, petals are pale green, and huge carpels are green streaked with purple—especially on their divergent beaks.

HABITAT. This stonecrop is indigenous to Korea and adjacent islands at low altitudes.

MAIN POINTS OF DISTINCTION. Large carpels, at least as long as petals (i.e., about 8 mm/0.3 in) with spreading beaks, dark green leaves, and relatively large flowers are the best means of differentiating the species from *Sedum telephium* subsp. *maximum*, but this is not an easy task. The decisive point of verification is the known geography of the clone, though the chromosome count of $n = 23$ is most distinct. Only a well-documented plant can be considered authentic.

VARIATION. In the wild where plants grow intermingled with *Sedum spectabile*, it is often difficult to identify plants not in flower. In cultivation, *S. spectabile* is always a much lighter green than is *S. viridescens*. Leaves are often scattered or ternate (Fig. 11.1r). Like *S. telephium* subsp. *maximum*, if plants of *S. viridescens* are grown in full sun, they can develop a purple hue, and, if grown in complete shade, flowers can be wholly green.

HORTICULTURE. The rarity of this species reflects how difficult it is to cultivate. It is more appropriate for the true enthusiast than as a distinct specimen plant and is only suitable for a very large rock garden or a herbaceous border.

SEDUM VIVIPARUM Maximowicz

Sedum viviparum is a real oddity. It is not particularly succulent and has frail, slender, shiny, purple stems carrying fresh green, opposite-decussate or ternate, widely spaced leaves that decrease in size up the stems. Often a whole plant disintegrates before flowering, with vegetative material being cast to the wind. Each autumn, adventitious buds are formed in the upper leaf-axils (hence the name of the species), and many of these buds fall to the base of the parent. If conditions are suitable, a colony of spindly plants rises next season. Flowers are insignificant, greenish, and unusual in that they are campanulate.

HABITAT. This stonecrop is native to northern China, North Korea, and Siberia (Ussuri Province), preferring forested areas.

MAIN POINTS OF DISTINCTION. Plants look more like mesophytes than like xerophytes, reminding me of the common weed "fat hen" (*Chenopodium album*). Weak, red-purple stems and ternate (especially in the lower section), thin leaves (Fig. 11.1s) are good indicators, but the viviparous nature of the plant is almost unique in *Sedum*. The only other species in *Hylotelephium* group to produce viviparous bulbils is *Sedum verticillatum*, but it is a much more robust plant with stems 10 mm (0.4 in) thick, in contrast to stems of *S. viviparum*, which (for me) struggle to attain a girth of 2 mm (0.08 in). $2n = 36$.

VARIATION. Leaves are in whorls of 2, 3, or 4, often all on the same colony of plants. Given a damp, cool summer, individuals can attain 35 cm (14 in).

HORTICULTURE. Only interesting because of its odd nature, this stonecrop is certainly a talking point, but has little horticulturally to recommend it.

SIEBOLDII GROUP

Species of *Sieboldii* group of subgenus *Hyloteleph-ium* have decumbent to pendulous stems and well-developed rootstocks. *Sieboldii* group comprises the following species in cultivation:

Sedum ettyuense Tomida
Sedum sieboldii Sweet ex Hooker
Sedum tsugaruense Hara

The following key differentiates these three species:

Leaves rounded, ternate below, opposite
  above, several inflorescences per stem, pink
  flowers: *S. ettyuense*
Leaves rounded, ternate, on arching stems,
  pink flowers: *S. sieboldii*
Leaves distinctly toothed, flowers whitish:
  S. tsugaruense

Figure 11.1 shows leaf shapes of these species.

SEDUM ETTYUENSE Tomida

SYNONYM: *S. kagamontanum* Maximowicz
COMMON NAME: Kaga-no-benkei-sō

This stonecrop is very rare in cultivation. I find it surprising that taxonomists consider it a distinct species. In appearance it resembles a giant form of *Sedum sieboldii*. Lower leaves, like those of *S. sieboldii*, are ternate, but above, they tend to be opposite. Leaves are much larger than those of *S. sieboldii*, and red margins are even more pronounced.

HABITAT. Endemic to Kaga Province, Honshu island, Japan.

MAIN POINTS OF DISTINCTION. Stout, suberect branches carry leaves that are ternate below and opposite above. Leaves are petiolate, remotely toothed, almost round, fleshy, and glaucous (Fig. 12.2a). The only plant that could be mistaken for this one is a very well-grown

specimen of *Sedum sieboldii*, but its leaves are ternate throughout and stems can be well over 30 cm (12 in) long, by which time they arch down. Stems of *S. ettyuense* are suberect or arching to perhaps 20 cm (8 in) long. *Sedum ettyuense* has additional axillary inflorescences not found in *S. sieboldii*. If *S. sieboldii* is grown in very poor soil or is underwatered (or both), it can regress to produce opposite leaves, but as such it is stunted and could not be mistaken for *S. ettyuense*.

VARIATION. None.

HORTICULTURE. This stonecrop is much slower growing than is *Sedum sieboldii*, but is an even more delightful plant. Cuttings do strike, but, despite a hefty rootstock, vegetative material is sparse, so propagation material may take many years to get into the trade.

SEDUM SIEBOLDII
Sweet ex Hooker

PLATE 96
COMMON NAME: Misebaya

A dual-purpose stonecrop, *Sedum sieboldii* is popular as a rock garden plant and as a potted house plant. It is commonly seen in hanging baskets in the home, porch, or conservatory from where it sends out 30-cm (12-in) long, arching stems that carry progressively smaller, not particularly succulent, gray-glaucous, almost round, ternate leaves, which are toothed in the upper half (Fig. 11.2b). Outdoors, stems are shorter and leaves more succulent and colorful, with red leaf margins becoming much more pronounced. Pink flowers appear in October, after which the plant disintegrates leaving straight, dead, leafless stems. Indoor specimens at this stage almost immediately form tiny rosettes at the bases of dried stems and thus overwinter in preparation for next year's growth. Outdoor plants make no surface growth until spring. *n* = 25.

HABITAT. As this species has been cultivated

in Japan for so long, its true origin in the wild is fogged by a plethora of garden escapes. It is believed that Shikoku Island is its real home.

MAIN POINTS OF DISTINCTION. The distinct shape of the leaves, and the fact that they are produced in 3s are the main distinguishing features of this species.

VARIATION. In addition to variation between outdoor and indoor specimens, *Sedum sieboldii* f. *variegatum*, is a delightful variegated form (Fig. 11.4). Its leaves tend to be green, often with little powdery coating, and some clones have shiny dark green leaves splashed with pale yellow or chrome-yellow markings. It is said that the variegated form is less hardy than the species, but as plants die back completely in winter, this is questionable. I have grown the variegated form outdoors for many winters without loss. Variegated clones grown outdoors have the additional feature of blushing with red in summer, giving a tri-colored effect as the chrome-yellow splashes are superimposed with wine-red. Non-

Figure 11.4. *Sedum sieboldii* f. *variegatum*.

variegated shoots should be removed from the parent variegated plant, otherwise ordinary growth becomes so vigorous that soon the whole plant reverts. $n = 25, 50$.

HORTICULTURE. This stonecrop is a most useful hardy plant in both its forms. It needs good drainage outdoors and is best seen on a trough edge so it can arch over. Beware—mollusks love it.

SEDUM TSUGARUENSE Hara

COMMON NAME: Tsugaru-misebaya

Sedum tsugaruense, relatively new to cultivation, rises then arches as stems grow to about 20 cm (8 in). Leaves are loosely ternate to irregularly arranged, glaucous, gray-green, irregularly bluntly dentate, and without median grooves or keels. Creamy flowers are carried in large numbers for such a small plant, which is similar to *S. ewersii* var. *cyclophyllum*, *S. sieboldii*, and *S. tatarinowii* in size and form.

HABITAT. This species is endemic to Mutsu Province, Honshu Island, Japan.

MAIN POINTS OF DISTINCTION. Leaves are quite distinct, and their loose arrangement on all plants is a good key to identification (Fig. 11.2c). Ternate leaves on the lower stem, almost opposite leaves in the upper stem, and scattered leaves between seems the most common arrangement. Creamy (or very light yellow-green) flowers with brick-red anthers are carried on long pedicels and have exceptionally tiny sepals.

VARIATION. A recently acquired propagation from the Sashauchi River valley of Aomori Prefecture has lower leaves that are barely crenate, and upper ones that are very stem-clasping. In this clone, the leaf veining is more pronounced throughout.

HORTICULTURE. *Sedum tsugaruense* is an exceptionally useful species for the edge of a raised bed, stone trough, or rock niche. Despite being indigenous to relatively high rainfall areas, plants rot in wet winters even with perfect drainage, so extra precautions are advised. The species is cold hardy and probably covered with snow for part of the winter in habitat, which explains how it remains dry during the worst of winter.

POPULISEDUM GROUP

Species of *Populisedum* group lack well-developed underground rootstocks, and flowering stems rise only from persistent nodes on the bases of last year's flowering stem remains. *Populisedum* group comprises the following species in cultivation:

Sedum anacampseros L.
Sedum cauticola Praeger
Sedum cyaneum Rudolph
Sedum ewersii Ledebour
Sedum pluricaule Kudo
Sedum populifolium Pallas
Sedum yezoense Kudo (see *S. pluricaule*)

The following is not a formal key, but will help in the identification of unnamed plants:

Leaves clustered at the ends of bare stems:
  S. anacampseros
Bracts large, rounded, petiolate half-enclosing
  the inflorescence: *S. cauticola*
Leaves amplexicaul, opposite-decussate, well-
  spaced on long decumbent stems: *S. ewersii*
Growth low, fleshy, compact: *S. cyaneum*
  S. ewersii var. *homophyllum*, *S. pluricaule*
Leaves petiolate, dentate, on twiggy stems:
  S. populifolium

SEDUM ANACAMPSEROS L.

PLATE 97

COMMON NAME: Lover come back

Sedum anacampseros is a sprawling, tangled plant that uses rocks and other plants for support. Stem tips are topped with rosettes of leaves, which elongate in summer, leaving the lower stems bare or crowded with smaller leaves. Stems are generally about 20 cm (8 in) long. Specimens are commonly found in cultivation in Europe. Although this species has striking lilac buds followed by flowers of a unique deep red-purple, it is, unfortunately, a shy flowerer.

HABITAT. This delightful stonecrop is apparently native to Spain, France (Pyrenees), and Italy (southwest Alps and Apennines) on alpine meadows and moraine, as a calcifuge.

MAIN POINTS OF DISTINCTION. The orbicular to obovate, or sometimes obcordate, leaves crowded into terminal rosettes are an immediate pointer to its identification (Fig. 11.1d). The only species of subgenus *Hylotelephium* likely to be confused with *Sedum anacampseros* is its nearest relative, *S. ewersii*, from the Himalayas. The latter has opposite-decussate leaves spaced throughout the full length of its stems.

Vegetatively, *Sedum anacampseros* is remarkably similar to Mexican stonecrops of the *S. palmeri* complex, which are not fully hardy, not deciduous, and have yellow flowers. $2n = 36$.

VARIATION. Praeger (1921) described and depicted a form he named *Sedum anacampseros* f. *majus*, which is more upright and bolder than the typical plant. If planted in a rich border, the species will respond in this way and become an attractive herb. In poorer, more rocky situations, it will revert to being a more decumbent plant. Leaves can be almost perfectly orbicular and entire. Flowers are rarely 4-partite rather than 5-partite. Otherwise the stonecrop is without much variation.

HORTICULTURE. Surprisingly *Sedum anacampseros* does not appreciate a bone-dry spot, but prefers to have its roots below a damp stone. Beware, it dislikes calcareous rocks. Planted in a clay pot, growth is very stunted, therefore it is best planted between large stones in a sunny spot in a rock garden without limestone, so it can tumble. Plants look most attractive in raised beds, stone troughs, or on top of a wall in soil. This is a very easily controlled species that will never become a pest, but will give years of pleasure with a minimum of attention. Plants take a very long while to become established and will only perform well if the situation is ideal. Seen at its best, little can surpass the beauty of the foliage and the almost spherical violet inflorescences.

SEDUM CAUTICOLA Praeger

PLATE 98

COMMON NAME: Hidaka-misebaya

In its multitude of forms, *Sedum cauticola* is probably the most common of the miniature species in subgenus *Hylotelephium* (Fig. 11.5). Plants form a loose carpet of suberect stems, each about 12 cm (5 in) long, carrying mainly opposite, glaucous-gray leaves heavily spotted with purple. Plants appear to be stoloniferous since rootstocks send out slender white shoots that appear as new plants perhaps more than 10 cm (4 in) from the parent. The carpet formed, topped with purple flowers in September–October, is very eye-catching.

HABITAT. Hokkaido Island, Japan.

MAIN POINTS OF DISTINCTION. Opposite, almost circular, fleshy, flat-to-cupped leaves with obscure teeth are the best pointer, but in recent years the trade has propagated and distributed several hybrids and several dubious names (Fig. 11.2e). In England the most commonly used name for this species is 'Lidakense', which is a valid name for a small regional variation. Unfortunately, this is often misquoted as 'Hidakense'.

Sedum cauticola could possibly be confused with *S. ewersii* var. *homophyllum* or *S. pluricaule*, but neither of these species have obscure teeth on the leaf margins. *Sedum sieboldii* has such teeth, but its leaves are ternate rather than oppo-

site. *Sedum cauticola* has large, ovate, entire cupped, petiolate bracts that partially enclose the flower buds. *n* = 24.

VARIATION. Often true plants produce scattered rather than opposite leaves, but this is no indication of hybridization. Many plants offered in the trade are of hybrid origin and often have pseudo-scientific suffixes. 'Robustum' and 'Hidakense' appear to be hybrids of *Sedum cauticola* and a taller species of subgenus *Hylotelephium*—perhaps *Sedum telephium* subsp. *maximum*. 'Ruby King' is a similar form found in Japanese horticulture. In recent years, a more upright, very branched cultivar hybrid, 'Bertram Anderson', has become popular in the United Kingdom. The true species has a rather distinctive leaf shape and is exceptionally rare in cultivation. 'Lidakense' is the most common form in cultivation with small, almost-entire, ovate leaves (Fig. 11.2e). It is probably just a minor regional Japanese form, not a form spontaneous in cultivation. It is a better soil coverer than the type species.

HORTICULTURE. In all its forms, *Sedum cauticola* is a must for the alpine grower. Plants are at their best in a well-drained scree, but look most attractive in a rock garden, especially at the end of a hot summer, when most other plants are past their prime. *Sedum cauticola* is ideal for raised beds and containers and is seen to great advantage against light-colored rocks as its leaves and stems turn dark glaucous-gray suffused with purple.

SEDUM CYANEUM Rudolph (Not S. CYANEUM Hort.)

Sedum cyaneum is one of the most charming miniature stonecrops, but it also is one of the most difficult to acquire (Fig. 11.6). Praeger and later Evans described and depicted the species well, but nonetheless plants acquired with this label are invariably creeping *S. ewersii* var. *homophyllum*. To irritate the situation further, *Plantfinder* (1990/1st edition) and several other publications equate these two distinct species.

Figure 11.5. Wild forms and hybrids of *Sedum cauticola*: (left to right) 'Hidakense'; two clones of *S. cauticola* collected in Hokkaido; two plants of 'Lidakense' grown in contrasting sites; 'Robustum'; 'Ruby King'.

Sedum cyaneum should never be confused with *S. ewersii* var. *homophyllum* as it is a delightful, gray-glaucous, mostly upright gem with lilac-purple flowers that rise from a many-leafed rosette of spirally arranged leaves.

HABITAT. This stonecrop is indigenous to eastern Siberia, including the Kamchatka Peninsula and Sakhalin Island, and prefers scree.

MAIN POINTS OF DISTINCTION. Leaves are at least three times as long as they are wide, densely crowded, and arranged in compact spirals (Fig. 11.2f). They are soft to the touch, never green or even vaguely green, and not opposite-decussate. The many stems, which are not twiggy, rise and arch from a single spot, then disin-

tegrate completely in winter, except for embryo rosette-buds that overwinter at soil level.

In winter and into spring *Sedum ewersii* var. *homophyllum* has a mat of tangled, twiggy stems, and later opposite-decussate, light glaucous-green leaves. *Sedum pluricaule* var. *yezoense* from Rebun Island is visually the closest form to *S. cyaneum*, but has white flowers and is firm to touch.

VARIATION. Few plants are in cultivation, so it is difficult to comment. For years I was over cautious with my slow-growing plant, not realizing that if given a richer compost and more water this species can grow into a 10-cm (4-in) high plant. For many years my original healthy

Figure 11.6. *Sedum cyaneum* at one of the few British nurseries to offer the correct, choice species.

specimen in a clay pot with perfect drainage grew to no more than 2 cm (0.8 in) high. Kinder treatment obviously is more risky, as, in the wild, drainage is perfect; *Sedum cyaneum* is indigenous to stony slopes.

HORTICULTURE. A very well-drained site is essential for successful cultivation. A raised site is preferable, as plants are so diminutive that much of their beauty would be lost without close inspection. This stonecrop is ideal for a stone trough as long as it has a good drainage system. It is perfectly cold hardy, but needs protection in winters with high rainfall. It is well worth searching long and hard for the genuine species—it is a gem.

SEDUM EWERSII Ledebour

PLATES 99, 100

Sedum ewersii is a tumbling, crawling, creeping, sprawling species of subgenus *Hylotelephium* with thin but wiry stems, which do not have the strength to support opposite-decussate leaves. Each pair of glaucous-green, sessile leaves is several centimeters from the next pair, so the shiny, brown stems show. Literally hundreds of stems rise, then tumble, on a mature plant, each terminating in a cyme of purple flowers. The plant is common and useful, and normally correctly labelled.

HABITAT. Widespread from Altai Mountains of Mongolia to western Himalayan ranges, this stonecrop is found as a true alpine on stony slopes, up to 3500 m (11,500 ft).

MAIN POINTS OF DISTINCTION. Decumbent stems, 40 cm (16 in) long, and longer with opposite-decussate, amplexicaul leaves are the best indicators (Fig. 11.2g, h, i). *Sedum sieboldii* has a similar habit, but stems are much shorter, and its leaves are smaller and ternate. $2n = 22$.

VARIATION. If grown in a clay pot, the plant is stunted, and stems become very woody and tortuous (Plate 99). A network of woody stems becomes a permanent feature of a mature plant, and new growth appears from different points on this basketwork. If roots are given room to spread, preferably near a large flat stone, stems cascade a meter (3 ft) or more. *Sedum ewersii* is an excellent feature plant in a large rock garden. Two very distinct varieties exist in cultivation. They are so different from the type species, one would be forgiven for thinking them to be entirely different species.

Sedum ewersii var. *cyclophyllum* (Ledebour) S. Pritszer is a recently introduced variety not a great deal different in form from the type species but much its miniature. Stems 15 cm (6 in) long are much shorter than those of the type species and, as a result, tend to be more erect. Plants are paler throughout, leaves are smaller and pale green, and petals are pale pink. I recommend this variety for sinks, stone troughs, and raised beds as it is less rampant. It appears to be identical to 'Nanum', described by Clausen in 1978.

Sedum ewersii var. *homophyllum* (Ledebour) Praeger is a commonly encountered miniature, carpet-forming species, often masquerading as *Sedum pluricaule* or *S. cyaneum* (Plate 100). A network of dried stems is left on the surface in winter, from which short, erect branches arise, carrying light green, opposite-decussate, crowded leaves. Even in full sun, leaves remain light glaucous-green, a bright patch of color for any scree. Unfortunately, the true form is a shy flowerer and not as succulent or compact as *S. pluricaule*, which turns purple in sun and is very floriferous. Flowers and chromosomes are indistinguishable from the type species.

Sedum ewersii var. *homophyllum* 'Rose Carpet' ('Rosenteppich') is sometimes referred to as 'Pink Carpet'. It is recommended because it is much more floriferous than the true variety, it grows a little more lushly, and it is taller (10 cm/ 4 in), but entire leaves and other features match the true form. Like the variety, a few leaves or buds usually remain on this cultivar's twisted stems in winter, and this feature plus the always light-glaucous-green leaves are the best means of distinguishing this stonecrop from *S. pluricaule*, which like this cultivar, has few sterile shoots (i.e., nearly all branches flower).

HORTICULTURE. *Sedum ewersii* var. *ewersii* is too big for a small rock garden unless one stunts a plant by growing it in a clay pot sunk high in the rock garden. The species is too sprawling for a herbaceous border and a stone trough because of its rapid growth in the summer months that smothers dwarf plants. Plants are superb for hanging baskets, wall urns (Plate 99), and old chimney pots, or for planting on the top of a stone wall (in soil). It is an easy plant to grow and second to none in the right spot. It does not seem prone to damping-off and is fully frost hardy. Miniature forms are excellent ground cover and suitable for a rock or scree garden.

SEDUM PLURICAULE Kudo

PLATE 101

COMMON NAME: Ezo-misebaya

Sedum pluricaule is one of the best miniature species in the subgenus *Hylotelephium* as it is highly succulent and reaches only a few centimeters above ground level. Very crowded, entire, opposite-decussate leaves and pink flowers are highly colorful. In full sun, stems are only a few centimeters long and leaves are flushed glaucous-purple. The species is most desirable in any of its varieties and forms but difficult to acquire.

HABITAT. This stonecrop is native to the far east of Siberia (Amur Region) on bald mountains, rock clefts, steep seashore cliffs, and sometimes among dwarf conifers.

MAIN POINTS OF DISTINCTION. General descriptions of this species and *Sedum ewersii* var. *homophyllum* match quite well, but seen together the plants are very contrasting, except in early growth when they are about identical. In bright sites, stems of *S. pluricaule* do not elongate much, and therefore the leaves remain very crowded. Moreover, leaves are highly succulent and pearl-pink to purple-gray (Plate 101). On the other hand, *S. ewersii* var. *homophyllum* stays light glaucous-green throughout the season, and its stems root as they spread. *Sedum pluricaule* tends to rise from the same rootstock year after year. Other species with similar forms are unlikely to be confused because leaves of *S. pluricaule* are entire (not remotely crenate or toothed) (Fig. 11.2j, k, l, m). *n* = 11. 'Rosenteppich' is a cultivar of *S. ewersii* var. *homophyllum* not *S. pluricaule*.

VARIATION. Some clones in cultivation appear to color-up much quicker than other clones and turn a deeper shade, but in my experience plants of *Sedum pluricaule* do not remain green in a sunny summer (except sometimes for the Japanese variety *S. pluricaule* var. *yezoense*). All forms of *S. pluricaule* produce a dense mound. Three very distinct variations now exist in cultivation, all as interesting as the type species.

Sedum pluricaule var. *ezawe* (Ledebour) Nosaka is a recently introduced variety, more widely available in the United States than elsewhere. This regional variation is beautifully flushed glaucous-purple throught the year. Stems are more elongated and leaves are less crowded than the type species so this variety is similar in form to *S. sieboldii*, except that leaves of *S. pluricaule* var. *ezawe* are entire and oppposite-decussate (Fig. 11.2k). In the United States, *S. pluricaule* var. *ezawe* is usually labeled "*S. pluricaule* from Sakhalin."

Sedum pluricaule var. *yezoense* is a Japanese variation with *n* = 11. It has much narrower leaves (Fig. 11.2l) and remains very light green (almost white) throughout the season, except in very hot, dry conditions, when it may be flushed slightly with pink.

Sedum pluricaule var. *yezoense* from Rebun Island is vegetatively very similar to *S. pluricaule* var. *yezoense* but more succulent and upright. Oddly the Rebun form has pure white flowers and may yet be described as a separate subspecies or even an entirely new species. It is a most eye-catching variation; against a dark background it is an exceptionally bright little plant. I recommend alpine specialists grow this form as a specimen plant: it is a showstopper in and out of flower, forming a dense 5-cm (2-in) high mound. It will grow well in an alpine house, but due to its herbaceous nature seems to tolerate wet, cold winters if well drained.

HORTICULTURE. *Sedum pluricaule* in all its forms is ideal for a raised bed, natural stone trough, or niche in a rock garden. It needs good drainage as rootstocks can rot if waterlogged in any season. It is completely cold hardy if well drained, and much superior to *S. ewersii* var. *homophyllum*, which is generally supplied in error. *Sedum pluricaule* is the very last herbaceous *Sedum* species to surface—there could be justification for concern when other herbaceous stonecrops do not surface by midsummer—not showing itself until July.

SEDUM POPULIFOLIUM Pallas

In a number of works, *Sedum populifolium* is not included with subgenus *Hylotelephium* because of its more woody rootstock and peculiar (for *Sedum*) leaves. Baldwin (1937, 132) remarked,

> Cytological and genetical data demonstrate a close affinity between *S. populifolium* and the members of the Section *Telephium* and furnish additional basis for the permanent inclusion of the species in this section.

Wherever it is placed, this plant is an oddity (Fig. 11.7): woody stems rise to about 25 cm (10 in) high, carrying petiolate, glabrous, shiny, green leaves reminiscent of leaves on a poplar tree—hence its name. Leaves are not particularly succulent but leathery. Pink-white flowers are attractive and appear in July, which is early for this subgenus.

HABITAT. This very odd Russian stonecrop is found near Lake Baikal (Siberia) to nearly 4000 m (13,000 ft) and is apparently dying out in the wild.

MAIN POINTS OF DISTINCTION. *Sedum popu-*

Figure 11.7. *Sedum populifolium* in late July.

lifolium is quite unlike any other *Sedum* species. It is a bone of contention among taxonomists. Leaves are unique (Fig. 11.2n), stems are unusually brittle for *Sedum*, and flowers have a light aroma—another unusual feature for the genus. No other *Sedum* species has such petiolate leaves. $2n = 22$.

VARIATION. In some soils, flowers appear pink rather than white, but purple-red anthers and pink-tipped petals always give flowers a suggestion of pink. In addition, transpiration causes flowers to fade pink, especially the carpels, but generally plants in cultivation are very similar.

There are reports of hybrids of this species with other members of subgenus *Hylotelephium* and *Aizoon* group, but most plants I have examined appear no different from the true species. Baldwin proved the existence of hybrids of *Sedum populifolium* and *S. spectabile* in the 1930s, but many sold with this label are merely *S. populifolium*. I have examined plants said to be *S. populifolium* × *S. tatartinowii* and vegetatively they appear midway between the parents.

HORTICULTURE. As a border plant, this is a most useful stonecrop, forming small bushes with dense flower clusters. Broken brittle stems can root easily, so in a rich bed, plants may need controlling. As a rock garden plant, *Sedum populifolium* is both unusual and trouble-free.

CHAPTER 12

Subgenus Rhodiola

Since Ron Evans published *Handbook of Cultivated Sedums* in 1983, much investigation has taken place in the field, especially in the Himalayas, with regard to subgenus *Rhodiola*. As a result, more species have been introduced into cultivation, and some familiar names are disappearing as relationships between species are reviewed. Many subgenus *Rhodiola* names were published for what appeared at the time to be distinct plants encountered in the wild, but further investigation has shown that many species vary slightly over a vast range. New information from the field has shed light on the distribution and variability of subgenus *Rhodiola* species and has meant that several have been united under the oldest of the published names, which are not always the best-known names. Gardeners and stonecrop enthusiasts must therefore expect that plants with identical labels may not be identical in every respect and that some familar names have disappeared.

Throughout this chapter I have followed Hideaki Ohba's system (1975, 1978, 1981a, 1981b), this work being the most recent and the result of much study in the field. Species of this subgenus of plants are notoriously difficult to identify— even professional botanists cannot seem to agree. In botanic gardens throughout the world, species of subgenus *Rhodiola* are often unnamed, but identified by a field number (e.g., Chadwick 284, a label which accompanies a particular plant

grown from seed collected in the Himalayas, progeny of which have refused to flower to make their identity known). Subgenus *Rhodiola* species are often reluctant to flower, or plants sometimes abort flowers before they develop properly. This coupled with the fact that male flowers of a species invariably contrast sharply with female flowers of the same species makes identification exceptionally difficult. With further exploration of Siberia now a real possibility and better understanding of the subgenus as a whole more probable, we can expect further changes of nomenclature as relationships between published species become more fully understood.

In one way it is fortunate that subgenus *Rhodiola* species are not in general cultivation, as plants from specialist sources are more likely to be correctly named. Apart from *Sedum rosea* and *S. heterodontum*, species tend to be rare, though *S. pachyclados* made a remarkable impact on horticulture in the late 1980s and early 1990s. Because of its great resilience and outstanding beauty, it has been propagated in large numbers and distributed widely in the trade. Few books make reference to *S. pachyclados* even though it is the most common species of subgenus *Rhodiola* in the trade. As a direct result, we are already suffering from variations of the true name due to careless labeling.

Plants of subgenus *Rhodiola* in cultivation are more likely to resemble each other than are plants in the wild because the majority of subgenus *Rhodiola* species are propagated vegetatively by division of the rootstock, and because seed-grown plants likely come from several plants in the same colony.

Subgenus *Rhodiola* species offer a real challenge to the amateur gardener because high alpines and plants of subarctic wastelands are difficult to cultivate successfully. In return for masterful horticulture, rewards are great. Perfect drainage is essential for the majority of plants in this subgenus and they do not welcome high temperatures. They are basically spring growers, and by midsummer are past their best. Dry winter conditions mean that low and freezing temperatures are not harmful, but repeated freeze-thaw cycles are fatal.

Plants of subgenus *Rhodiola*

- Have thin scaly leaves on a fleshy rootstock that protect overwintering buds.
- Have free petals.
- Have orthocarpic flowers, which are frequently unisexual and very rarely monoecious, on terminal inflorescences.
- Have a main stem that ceases after seedlings form cotyledons.

In addition, stems are often simple and annual, rising from sturdy rootstocks. Inflorescences are usually cymose. Flowers are mostly 4-partite or 5-partite but rarely 6-partite. Sepals are equal and united, and sometimes carpels are partially below the line of petals.

Except for a few species, plants of subgenus *Rhodiola* are dreadfully difficult to acquire, almost impossible to propagate, and a task to keep alive. Figures 12.1 and 12.2 show leaf shapes of subgenus *Rhodiola* species.

Subgenus *Rhodiola* is broken into six groups:

1. Species of *Rhodiola* group can be recognized by their unisexual flowers with strongly united sepals on dioecious plants. Carpels are sometimes partly below the line of petals. Stems are deciduous.
2. Species of *Chamaerhodiola* group can also be recognized by their unisexual flowers, strongly united sepals on dioecious plants, and somewhat embedded carpels. In addition, they possess a tangle of persistent dead stems from previous seasons.
3. Species of *Clementsia* group have bisexual flowers clustered on elongated inflorescences with the outline of a short tube (racemous spike).
4. Species of *Crassipedes* group have large bisexual flowers and inflorescences with the outline of a hemisphere.
5. Species of *Primuloida* group have narrow creeping rhizomes that bury themselves, surface, and then produce rosettes of foliage that sometimes remain evergreen. Inflorescences are very simple: from a single flower to a diachasial cyme. Bisexual flowers are large.
6. The single species of *Hobsonia* group has bisexual flowers and stamens with dorsifixed anthers. Annual stems rise from a sturdy caudex and spread out on the land's surface like spokes of a wheel.

RHODIOLA GROUP

The following species are in cultivation:

Sedum atropurpureum Turczaninow (see *S. integrifolium*)
Sedum bupleuroides Wallich
Sedum heterodontum Hooker & Thomson

Sedum imbricatum (Edgeworth) Walpers
Sedum integrifolium (Rafinesque) Nelson
Sedum ishidae Myabe & Kudo
Sedum kirilowii Regel
Sedum pamiroalaicum (Borissova) Jansson (see *S. imbricatum*)

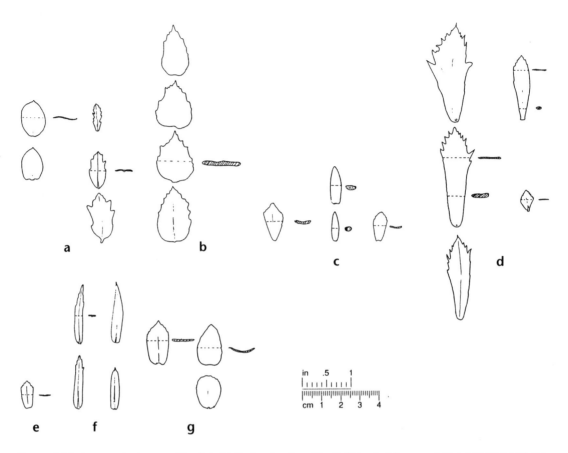

Figure 12.1. Leaves of subgenus *Rhodiola* (a) *Sedum bupleuroides* (left) typical form and (right) Yu104437; (b) a selection of leaves from one specimen of *S. heterodontum*; (c) *S. imbricatum* (left) f. *imbricatum*, (center) f. *pamiroalaicum*, and (right) f. *recticaule*; (d) *S. integrifolium* (left) var. *atropurpureum* and (right) var. *integrifolium*; (e) leaves of *S. ishidae* are never glaucous; (f) a selection of *S. kirilowii* leaves; (g) leaves of commonly encountered forms of *S. rosea*.

Sedum recticaule (Borissova) Wendelbo (see *S. imbricatum*)

Sedum rosea Scopoli

The following is not a formal key but an aid to help isolate species:

Flower stems massive, leaves glaucous, individual flowers small: *S. rosea, S. heterodontum*

Flower stems slender, leaves glabrous, shining, individual flowers small, not red: *S. imbricatum, S. ishidae*

Flower stems slender, leaves glaucous, individual flowers large and white: *S. kirilowii*

Flowers red/reddish: *S. bupleuroides, S. integrifolium, S. heterodontum*

SEDUM BUPLEUROIDES Wallich

PLATE 102

Synonym: *Rhodiola bupleuroides* Wallich ex Hooker & Thomson

Sedum bupleuroides is one of natures oddities. Some forms are of such a weird nature, they would not look out of place on the set of a science fiction film. From a massive, gnarled, mossy caudex, which is partly above ground, sparse narrow stems with well-spaced, very thin, nonsucculent leaves rise each spring. Grown in pots, red or chestnut stems tend to be no more than 10 cm (4 in) high, but wild plants are often much taller. Several odd-looking crimson flowers are produced in early summer.

HABITAT. This stonecrop is particularly widespread across Nepal, Sikkim, Bhutan, Himalayan China, and northwest Burma on exposed rocky banks from 2200 to 5200 m (7200 to 17,100 ft).

MAIN POINTS OF DISTINCTION. This species is exceptionally varied in the wild. The best pointers are sparse stems rising from a huge caudex, sparsely clothed in scattered, thin, flat leaves (Fig. 12.1a) and topped with a few crim-son flowers. Female flowers have very tiny beaks and black nectaries.

VARIATION. I have two contrasting clones that are so different it is difficult to believe they are the same species. Yu104437 has leaves 4 cm (2 in) long, four times the length of its neighbor. Both have red stems.

HORTICULTURE. Perfect drainage is essential.

SEDUM HETERODONTUM
Hooker & Thomson

SYNONYM: *Rhodiola heterodonta*
(Hooker & Thomson) Borissova

After *Sedum rosea*, *S. heterodontum* is the most easily obtained species of *Rhodiola* group, but it is by no means common. Huge carrot-shaped

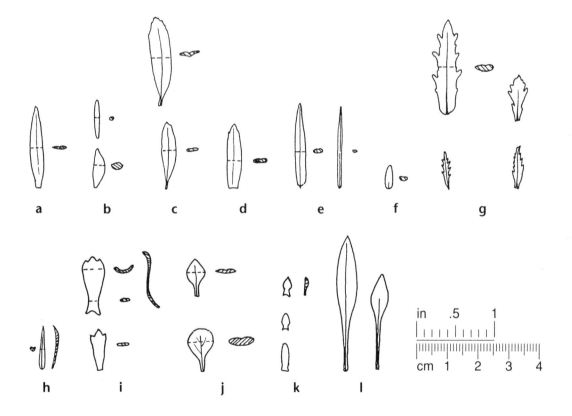

Figure 12.2. Leaves of subgenus *Rhodiola*: (a) *S. alsium* is not particularly succulent; (b) *S. fastigiatum*; (c) *S. himalense*; (d) *S. rhodanthum*; (e) *S. semenovii*; (f) *S. amabile*; (g) *S. crassipes* is very variable; (h) *S. dumulosum*; (i) *S. pachyclados*; (j) *S. primuloides*; (k) leaves of *S. trollii* can be up to twice this length if grown lushly; (l) *S. hobsonii*.

roots are topped with hemispherical buds that grow into 40-cm (16-in) long stout stems with well-spaced succulent, glaucous blue-green leaves. Stems are topped with exceptionally compact dense corymbs—so dense, it is nearly impossible to distinguish individual diplostemonous flowers. Flowers range from brick red to lilac. I have observed no female flowers outside of botanic gardens.

HABITAT. This stonecrop is widespread across Kashmir, Nepal, and China from 1820 to 5080 m (5980 to 16,670 ft).

MAIN POINTS OF DISTINCTION. Between bases of annual stems, bulbous, bulging, hemispherical buds covered with scaly leaves are the embryos of next year's stems (Fig. 12.3). Leaves are more succulent than those of similar forms of *Sedum rosea*.

VARIATION. *Sedum heterodontum* is very variable in habitat. Few clones are available in cultivation, and those that are have been vegetative-ly cloned. Flower color varies somewhat, and leaves on a single plant vary in shape considerably (Fig. 12.1b).

HORTICULTURE. Not as difficult to grow as most subgenus *Rhodiola* species, *Sedum heterodontum* prospers in a rich border as long as it does not become waterlogged. The nursery trade offers plants for several reasons: (1) a caudex becomes so huge, it is easy to split, (2) plants can withstand wet winters, and (3) plants can survive reasonably hot summers as they are past their best by the longest day and therefore dormant during the hottest part of summer.

SEDUM IMBRICATUM
(Edgeworth) Walpers

SYNONYMS: *Rhodiola imbricata* Edgeworth, which includes *Sedum recticaule* (Borissova) Wendelbo, and *S. pamiroalaicum* (Borissova) Jansson

Despite the name *Sedum imbricatum*, plants of

Figure 12.3. Bulging hemispherical buds of *Sedum heterodontum* in late summer already forming next year's growth. Stems here are 1 cm (0.4 in) thick at the base.

this species do not have imbricate leaves—they are only imbricate in bud. This small member of *Rhodiola* group is found over a vast range in habitat, and plants from distant areas are highly contrasting vegetatively. Recently distributed forms in cultivation from distant stations include Chadwick 315 from Himalayan Nepal (i.e., *Sedum imbricatum* in the strict sense) with dentate leaves, one from Pamir with entire leaves (i.e., *"S. pamiroalaicum"*), and a third form (i.e., *"S. recticaule"*), which is vegetatively midway between *S. imbricatum* and *"S. pamiroalaicum."* Ohba united all three under the oldest name because they appear interlinked across a large geographical range.

In cultivation, plants grow to no more than 20 cm (8 in) high, which is smaller than many wild plants. Leaves are tiny, fairly succulent, and well spaced, and some dead stems from the previous season persist. Flowers are usually 5-partite, small, and creamy.

HABITAT. Exceptionally widespread from Iran and northern Pakistan to Nepal and beyond into the Altai Mountains in alpine meadows and stony alpine soils, this stonecrop is found at 3300 to 5650 m (10,800 to 18,540 ft).

MAIN POINTS OF DISTINCTION. Thin stems topped with 4-partite or 5-partite, pale yellow dioecious flowers with huge yellow nectaries, short beaks, and very long stamens, are a good guide. Leaves are generally not much more than 1 cm (0.4 in) long (Fig. 12.1c).

VARIATION. *Sedum imbricatum* in the strict sense has trapezoidal, dentate leaves and is upright in cultivation. *"Sedum pamiroalaicum"* has entire, succulent leaves. *"Sedum recticaule"* has leaves somewhat intermediate (Fig. 12.1c). Flowers of all forms are indistinguishable.

HORTICULTURE. Of three dozen seed-grown plants distributed in the 1980s, only one was female. Ohba (1981), in contrast, stated that flowers are hermaphrodite or male only. This species is very susceptible to wet winters and appears impossible to propagate vegetatively.

SEDUM INTEGRIFOLIUM
(Rafinesque) Nelson

PLATE 103

SYNONYMS: *Rhodiola integrifolia* Rafinesque, *Sedum atropurpureum* Turczaninow, *Rhodiola atropurpurea* (Turczaninow) Trauvtvetter
COMMON NAMES: Entire-leaved rosewort, king's crown

Until very recently, it was uncertain whether the vast number of polymorphic forms of *Sedum integrifolium* from hundreds of disjunct sites in North American and northeast Asia could be circumscribed as a natural entity, or, if delimitation proved impractical, whether they should be included with the even more polymorphic *S. rosea*. Cytological research has shown that *S. integrifolium* and *S. rosea* are distinct.

At least three forms of *Sedum integrifolium* are in general cultivation, but none are common. Purple-red flowers are the best indicator, as vegetatively the three forms are highly contrasting.

HABITAT. This stonecrop is indigenous to the U.S. Rocky Mountains, British Columbia and its offshore islands, Alaska, the Aleutian Island chain, Okhotsk, Sakhalin, Kamchatka, and Arctic Siberia. (North American members of subgenus *Rhodiola* from northeastern shorelines are *Sedum rosea*). The species is found at all altitudes, but is an alpine in lower latitudes.

MAIN POINTS OF DISTINCTION. The main identifying feature of *Sedum integrifolium* is its chromosome number, $n = 18$. Gardeners, however, can use flower color: purple-red as opposed to yellow-green flowers are a good but not infallible guide. Male flowers have narrow, spathulate petals.

VARIATION. *Sedum atropurpureum* is a tall, sturdy, Asian form with very dentate leaves that once was considered a separate species (Fig. 12.1d). Probably across the Aleutian islands, intermediate forms exist between this and the North American mainland forms, but as the Asian form in cultivation is a strongly growing plant compared to its North American cousins, I believe the correct name should be *S. integrifolium* var. *atropurpureum*. This variety grows to 40 cm (16 in) high and produces an elegant display of purple 4-partite (or sometimes 3-partite) hermaphrodite flowers.

Sedum integrifolium from the Rockies is difficult to cultivate as it dislikes hot summers. Four-partite flowers are dioecious but sometimes yellow, so without geographical knowledge of the origin of the plant, there is no way it can be differentiated (out of the laboratory) from *S. rosea*. Plants are generally low, rising no more than 15 cm (6 in) high, with small glaucous leaves (Fig. 12.1d).

Sedum integrifolium subsp. *procerum* Clausen (Plate 103) is taller, and has longer, narrow leaves, devoid of much dentation (Fig. 12.1d). It is from the southern Rockies at about 4000 m (13,000 ft) and appears a little happier in cultivation than other North American forms.

HORTICULTURE. No forms enjoy hot summers. The Asiatic form is the least fickle and makes a good plant for a border as it flowers considerably later than other forms, often into August.

SEDUM ISHIDAE Myabe & Kudo

SYNONYM: *Rhodiola ishidae* (Myabe & Kudo) Hara

From small rhizomes, 25-cm (10-in) long stems rise with glabrous green, alternate leaves. In most other respects *Sedum ishidae* resembles *S. rosea*. Dioecious flowers with yellow-green petals are produced on dense cymes.

HABITAT. This stonecrop is endemic to Hokkaido and central and north Honshu as an alpine.

MAIN POINTS OF DISTINCTION. Except for glabrous green leaves (Fig. 12.1e), I am unable to distinguish this species from *Sedum rosea*, but Japanese plants never become large. Stamens are long, and square nectaries are deep yellow.

VARIATION. Many names have been erected for Japanese species of *Rhodiola* group, but most are now considered synonymous with *Sedum ishidae* or *S. rosea*. This suggests tremendous vari-

ation in the wild due to numerous disjunct sites, but few clones are in cultivation.

HORTICULTURE. This species is very difficult to perpetuate in hot summers. Its wet alpine origin means it needs careful treatment in cultivation.

SEDUM KIRILOWII Regel

PLATE 104

SYNONYM: *Rhodiola kirilowii*
(Regel) Regel & Maximowicz

Two color variations of *Sedum kirilowii* are infrequently encountered in cultivation. The type species has golden-brown flowers and often carries the pseudoscientific 'Aureum' tag in the trade. Praeger (1921) erected the name *S. kirilowii* var. *rubrum* for dark-flowered forms. All forms have densely arranged, linear leaves on 30-cm (12-in) long, narrow stems, which are twice this height in the wild. Three or four flowering stems arise from each branch of the caudex, and large leaflike bracts are very pronounced.

HABITAT. This stonecrop is from near the headwaters of the Mekong River, across Yunnan and Sichuan provinces to the Hwang-ho Gorge, around 3500 m (11,500 ft).

MAIN POINTS OF DISTINCTION. Leafy bracts partially enclosing dense inflorescences are most distinct (Plate 104). Linear-lanceolate, entire leaves are fairly distinct, but often have remote teeth (Fig. 12.1f). All plants in cultivation appear to be male.

VARIATION. Two color variations are in cultivation.

HORTICULTURE. *Sedum kirilowii* is not as difficult to grow successfully as are many species of subgenus *Rhodiola*, but because it is such an early flowerer, plants are often spent by May.

SEDUM ROSEA (L.) Scopoli

PLATE 105

Synonym: *Rhodiola rosea* L., *R. arctica* Borissova

Ohba (1981b) recognized 15 taxa proposed as distinct to be this species. The range of *Sedum ro-*

sea is so great, and there are so many disjunct sites, a whole page could literally be filled with synonyms; in general cultivation, however, there are only two forms. The North European form is indigenous to the highlands and islands of Scotland as well as to the fjelds of Norway. It can be coaxed to grow into a magnificent, glaucous, bushlike sphere a meter (3 ft) high and wide (generally it is less than half this size). The other form in general cultivation is a miniature, highly glaucous, succulent-leaved arctic form (syn. *Rhodiola arctica*).

Plants die down to gnarled visible rootstocks in winter. Both male and female plants are in cultivation, and more rarely, hermaphrodites are encountered. Pale yellow, 4-partite flowers with brighter yellow nectaries are produced in fairly dense clusters. This is a stately plant and the most common subgenus *Rhodiola* species in cultivation. Any tiny forms are usually referred to as 'Arcticum', though the Russian plant (*R. arctica*) has almost-round, only slightly dentate, succulent glaucous leaves (Fig. 12.1g). I am not suggesting it is distinct enough to warrant specific status, but alpine specialists wanting a blue-green, miniature specimen plant will need to acquire the true subarctic form. *Sedum rosea* f. *arcticum* comb. nov. is an outstandingly beautiful plant.

HABITAT. This circumpolar stonecrop is found right across northern Eurasia and in central European mountain ranges as far south as Italy. There are literally thousands of disjunct colonies with some as distant as Central Asia, Korea, Japan, northeast United States, Labrador, and Greenland, at all altitudes, but tending to be alpine in lower latitudes and coastal in very high latitudes.

MAIN POINTS OF DISTINCTION. In cultivation, glaucous stems with glaucous leaves (Fig. 12.1g) rising from massive gnarled rootstocks and 4-partite yellow flowers in late spring are a good guide. $n = 11$.

VARIATION. A collection of nothing but different forms of *S. rosea* would be large and make a terrific sight, but in cultivation, generally only two forms are found. Forms from the Alps of Europe have very narrow leaves and reddish flowers, but are not in general cultivation.

HORTICULTURE. Large plants grow well in a rich well-drained partially shaded border. I doubt they would grow in areas where temperatures exceed 20°C (67°F) for more than three consecutive months without administering careful treatment. *Sedum rosea* f. *arcticum* is even less likely to survive a summer baking. As plants are dormant in winter, they can take a great deal of rain if well drained. Beware, vine weevil can reduce a 25-year-old plant to little more than waste in a season.

CHAMAERHODIOLA GROUP

Species of *Chamaerhodiola* group have a tangle of twiggy persistent stems left over from previous seasons. Unisexual flowers sometimes have carpels somewhat below the line of petals. Only three species are in general cultivation, although *Sedum quadrifidum* Pallas has been collected in recent years and may soon be available:

Sedum algidum Fischer (see *S. alsium*)
Sedum alsium Fröderström
Sedum fastigiatum Hooker & Thomson
Sedum himalense Don

SEDUM ALSIUM Fröderström

SYNONYMS: *Rhodiola alsia* (Fröderström) Fu,
S. algidum Ledebour,
Chamaerhodiola algida (Ledebour) Nakai

It is unusual for a subgenus *Rhodiola* species to have large attractive flowers. It is true that clusters of small flowers are often pleasing, but single china-white, bisexual flowers of *Sedum alsium* are almost 2 cm (0.8 in) across. Growing no more than 20 cm (8 in) high, this is a useful and worthwhile species. Unfortunately, it is almost unknown in cultivation at present.

HABITAT. This stonecrop is indigenous to Yunnan Province around 3200 m (10,500 ft) and to Sichuan Province around 4900 m (16,000 ft), growing on alpine, rocky, stony slopes usually near glaciers on ancient moraines. In addition, plants grow on pebbly lichen tundra near streams in western Siberia from Mongolia to the Altai Mountains.

MAIN POINTS OF DISTINCTION. A relatively tall scaly cylindrical caudex with 18-cm (7-in) long stems carrying large white flowers, all enclosed with a nest of dead stems from previous years, are good clues to identification. Leaves are lanceolate, entire, or have faint hints of notching (Fig. 12.2a).

VARIATION. Flowers are sometimes female, and stems are often sterile.

HORTICULTURE. Such a species is ideal for raised pots or pot culture, but is difficult to perpetuate.

SEDUM FASTIGIATUM
Hooker & Thomson

SYNONYMS: *Chamaerhodiola fastigiata* (Hooker & Thomson) Nakai, *Rhodiola fastigiata* (Hooker & Thomson) Fu

From tall, terete, elongated rhizomes, sparsely papillate stems of *Sedum fastigiatum* rise to about 30 cm (12 in). Leaves are small, linear, glabrous, shiny green, and almost terete (Fig. 12.2b). The type species has creamy-white flowers with dull wine-red blotches on the outer sides of petals, is exceptionally rare in cultivation, and possibly not grown outside botanic gardens. Wild plants across their enormous range have flowers in all shades from almost white, through cerise, to very dark red. A beautiful red-flowered form is offered by the specialist trade. Praeger (1921) claimed this startling form originated from Yunnan Province, so to avoid confusion I propose to refer to it as 'Yunnan Red'.

HABITAT. Kashmir, Nepal, Sikkim, Himalayan China, and Yunnan are the homes of this widespread species, at 3700 to 5650 m (12,100 to 18,540 ft).

MAIN POINTS OF DISTINCTION. Densely arranged, short linear, almost terete leaves have minute spurs, and, in age, become imbricate by deflexing. Petals of female flowers are very short.

VARIATION. 'Yunnan Red' grows no more than 25 cm (10 in) tall and has deep red flowers in contrast to the type species, which has a much taller aerial caudex and pale cream flowers. A spontaneous hybrid of 'Yunnan Red' and *Sedum kirilowii* (two species not considered closely related) appeared recently at Greenslacks Nursery, England. The hybrid is midway between the parents and appears fertile.

HORTICULTURE. This little gem is not too difficult to perpetuate. It is best on a raised bed or in a stone trough, though the type species grows very well in a rich loam border at the Royal Botanic Garden Edinburgh.

SEDUM HIMALENSE Don

SYNONYM: *Rhodiola himalensis* (Don) Fu

From a tall, narrow, conical caudex, which is mostly above ground and covered with scaly leaves, red papillose stems of *Sedum himalense* push their way through a tangle of spent stems and carry flat, grooved, scattered leaves that are lighter in color underneath. My verified plant has flowered but widely distributed plants bearing this name that lack a conical caudex have not. Flowers are dioecious, purple-red, and 4-partite or 5-partite.

HABITAT. This widespread stonecrop is from Nepal, Sikkim, Bhutan, Himalyan China, and Yunnan, from 4000 to 5000 m (13,000 to 16,000 ft) among *Rhododendron* species near streams.

MAIN POINTS OF DISTINCTION. The conical caudex is a good indicator. Leaves are flat and not succulent (Fig. 12.2c). Flowers have purple-black nectaries.

VARIATION. *Sedum himalense* is exceptionally

rare in cultivation. I have only studied a single verified specimen from Nepal. In nature the species is very variable.

HORTICULTURE. This stonecrop can take a lot of rain in winter as long as it is in a well-drained site.

CLEMENTSIA GROUP

The two species of this group come from exceptionally disjunct sites, but vegetatively they are remarkably similar. Inflorescences are elongated somewhat into a raceme. *Clementsia* group comprises

Sedum rhodanthum Gray
Sedum semenovii Regel & Herder

SEDUM RHODANTHUM Gray

PLATE 106

SYNONYMS: *Clementsia rhodantha* (Gray) Rose,
Rhodiola rhodantha (Gray) Jacobsen
COMMON NAME: Rose crown

Stout rootstocks of *Sedum rhodanthum* with brown scaly leaves bear 14-cm (5-in) long stems (though they are often taller than this in the wild) topped with pink flowers (Plate 106). Erect rose-colored petals and red carpels are most pleasing.

HABITAT. This Rocky Mountain stonecrop is endemic to peaks in Arizona, Nevada, Utah, and Colorado from a little under 2000 m (7000 ft) to over 4100 m (13,500 ft). Clausen (1975, 485) said of the habitat that it is "generally poorly drained."

MAIN POINTS OF DISTINCTION. Narrow-leaved forms with whiter petals are almost impossible to distinguish from their Asian counterparts. Glabrous leaves have a median furrow above and are densely arranged (Fig. 12.2d). Petals remain erect. $n = 7$.

VARIATION. Often inflorescences do not elongate much, and leaves vary considerably in size and shape.

HORTICULTURE. Seed is often offered by alpine societies on both sides of the Atlantic, but without specialist treatment, plants are baked in hot summers. This is a most striking plant for a raised bed or a stone trough. Despite Clausen's comment, the species requires perfect drainage in winter if the soil is not frozen solid.

SEDUM SEMENOVII Masters

PLATE 107

SYNONYMS: *Clementsia semenovii* (Masters) Rose,
Rhodiola semenovii (Regel & Herder) Borissova

Rootstocks of *Sedum semenovii* are very branched, and linear leaves are crowded on 30-cm (12-in) long stems, as they are on stems of *S. rhodanthum*. Praeger (1921) likened the inflorescence of this species to a bottle brush (Plate 107). White petals are somewhat spreading, and carpels flush red.

HABITAT. This widespread central Asian stonecrop grows in the Altai Mountains on moist, stony river banks, mountain forests, mossy alpine meadows, and even in boggy areas to 3500 m (11,500 ft).

MAIN POINTS OF DISTINCTION. Very narrow leaves increase in size up the stem (Fig. 12.2c). Carpels are as long as petals, which are somewhat spreading. Leaves are grooved above.

VARIATION. Plants are rare in cultivation; for many years I only studied two plants that have minor differences in flower color and leaf size. Newer clones to cultivation appear shorter in stature, but it is too early to comment on them.

HORTICULTURE. This is another stonecrop that can withstand wet winters if well drained. It is an untidy plant in late summer, but striking in spring. It is too large for a stone trough, but should perform well in a rock garden if kept cool in summer.

CRASSIPEDES GROUP

Plants of *Crassipedes* group can be recognized by their large bisexual flowers and their inflorescences that are topped with hemispherical flower clusters. Three species appear to be in cultivation:

Sedum amabile Ohba
Sedum asiaticum (Don) De Candolle (see *S. crassipes*)
Sedum crassipes Wallich ex Hooker & Thomson
Sedum dumulosum Franchet
Sedum stephanii Chamisso (see *S. crassipes*)
Sedum wallichianum Hooker (see *S. crassipes*)

SEDUM AMABILE Ohba

PLATE 108
SYNONYM: *Rhodiola amabilis* (Ohba) Ohba
COMMON NAME: *Sedum* species from Lahul

Sedum amabile is one of the most attractive *Sedum* species. A low, compact bright green hummock is peppered with large white flowers in midsummer. Rhizomes are rather narrow, and flowers are produced in small numbers on ends of short arching stems no more than 8 cm (3 in) high. The spectacle in early summer is most showy.

HABITAT. This outstanding stonecrop is indigenous to Nepal and Kashmir (Lahul is near the border of Kashmir) on moss covered rocks from 250 to 5200 m (820 to 17,100 ft).

MAIN POINTS OF DISTINCTION. A bright green hummock of small fleshy leaves topped with large white stellate flowers is unique (Fig. 12.2f).

VARIATION. Only one form has been distributed. It originated from Dennis Pearson's collection and was distributed by Ron Evans and the Sedum Society as "Species from Lahul" or *S. linearifolium*. Five-partite, 6-partite, or 7-partite flowers are 14 mm (0.6 in) across.

HORTICULTURE. Compact, neat growth, large flowers, and pleasing colors make this species outstanding. It is a perfect alpine specimen plant for pot cultivation, but is equally pleasing in a stone trough. It is too small for a rock garden though it is a bright subject.

SEDUM CRASSIPES
Wallich ex Hooker & Thomson

SYNONYMS: *Rhodiola crassipes* (Wallich ex Hooker & Thomas) Borissova, including *Sedum asiaticum* (Don) De Candolle, *S. stephanii* Chamisso, and *S. wallichianum* Hooker

For many years I grew plants labeled *Sedum crassipes*, *S. asiaticum*, and *S. stephanii*, and, apart from size and slight differences in petal color, I was unaware of a good way to separate them. The much stronger plants growing in rich beds in botanic gardens confused me even more, for the largest of my plants was dwarfed by plants in botanic gardens that should have been the smallest forms. Study of wild plants has shown that *S. crassipes*, "*S. asiaticum*," and "*S. stephanii*," once considered distinct species, along with others which grow over a vast area of upland Asia, are all interconnected.

Leaves are bright green, sharply toothed, and very variable in size. Hermaphrodite flowers are mostly 5-partite and creamy-white to light yellow with orange-yellow nectaries.

HABITAT. The range of this stonecrop is vast: Kashmir, Nepal, Sikkim, and Xizang, from 3400 to 5500 m (11,200 to 18,000 ft) and beyond to moist forests, river valleys, and seashores of Okhotsk.

MAIN POINTS OF DISTINCTION. Heavily serrated, densely arranged leaves, hooded straw-colored petals, and orange-yellow nectaries help to distinguish this species.

VARIATION. The type species is a tall form with light flowers and creeping rhizomes that act as stolons and surface some distance from a parent plant, producing offspring. *Sedum crassipes* 'Asiaticum' is a neat miniature form. *Sedum crassipes* var. *stephanii* (Chamisso) Jacobsen often has single sex flowers—female flowers have reduced stamens, and male flowers have reduced ovaries. It has petals of a deeper hue and smaller leaves than the type species (Fig. 12.2g). This very floriferous variety comes from the far eastern end of the range and is a coastal plant.

HORTICULTURE. The type species is more often offered than the others because of its ability to produce offspring. It can reach 50 cm (20 in) high in a rich border. Smaller forms are better for a rock garden, raised bed, or stone trough.

SEDUM DUMULOSUM Franchet

SYNONYM: *Rhodiola dumulosa* (Franchet) Fu

Sedum dumulosum is a small delightful stonecrop that rises from a relatively large rootstock. Stems 13 cm (5 in) long are quite densely clothed with loosely arranged glabrous, linear leaves and topped with large white, campanulate flowers. Unfortunately, the floriferous species is not readily available.

HABITAT. This eastern Himalayan stonecrop grows on mountain chains from Bhutan through northern Burma, China, and beyond to Mongolia and North Korea. It has an altitudinal range of 2000 to 4300 m (7000 to 14,100 ft).

MAIN POINTS OF DISTINCTION. Large white, hermaphrodite flowers with succulent, mucronate petals, upright at the base, recurved at their tips, and stems crowded with ascending, linear leaves make a unique combination of features (Fig. 12.2h).

VARIATION. Some stems are sterile.

HORTICULTURE. The small nature of this plant makes it ideal for a stone trough or raised bed. Its neat nature makes it suitable for pot culture, but clay pots must not be allowed to overheat in sunny summers.

PRIMULOIDA GROUP

One would be forgiven for thinking this group of plants was not part of subgenus *Rhodiola* but of subgenus *Sedum*. Very narrow rhizomes creep, bury themselves, and then surface, producing neat rosettes of leaves which, in several instances, are evergreen. Large hermaphrodite flowers are produced on very short inflorescences in small numbers. Three species are in cultivation:

Sedum pachyclados Aichison & Hemsley
Sedum primuloides Franchet
Sedum trollii Werdermann

SEDUM PACHYCLADOS
Aichison & Hemsley

JACKET BACK

I can think of no other stonecrop which, in a single decade, has become so widespread in cultivation. In the 1970s the name was only found in scientific journals. Today hundreds of plants are being propagated, and the demand is greater than the supply. This species has a combination of qualities found nowhere else in subgenus *Rhodiola*. Glaucous blue-green evergreen rosettes form such compact hummocks that it often seems even a blade of grass cannot squeeze through. *Sedum pachyclados* withstands, indeed, enjoys wet winters.

The hummocks of succulent foliage take on the shape of whatever they engulf (see jacket back). Large, white, stellate flowers, although produced in small numbers, appear twice a year—once in spring and again in fall.

HABITAT. This stonecrop hails from Afghanistan and Pakistan between 2400 and 3400 m (7900 to 11,200 ft).

MAIN POINTS OF DISTINCTION. Three-toothed, glaucous leaves forming cupped rosettes are very distinct (Fig. 12.2i). Rhizomes are stoloniferous and surface some distance from the parent.

VARIATION. I have noticed no variation, but it is reported that two clones are available in the United States.

HORTICULTURE. In 5 years, a dense hummock 45 cm (18 in) across is formed. Creeping plants enjoy engulfing rocks. Eventually they engulf weaker plants, but the invader is so spectacular, I suggest making way for its advance. I was surprised to find this species loved cold, wet English winters. An Ohio commercial grower indicates that plants kept dry under cover in winter perform badly compared to those that have weathered the elements.

SEDUM PRIMULOIDES Franchet

SYNONYM: *Rhodiola primuloides* (Franchet) Fu

Sedum primuloides is a delicate stonecrop and a real beauty, but it is not easy to perpetuate. Glabrous rosettes are not usually evergreen. Leathery, petiolate leaves form quite dense hummocks, and campanulate flowers with erect petals are produced in late summer.

HABITAT. This eastern Himalayan stonecrop is indigenous to Yunnan Province from 2500 to 4600 m (8200 to 15,100 ft) altitude.

MAIN POINTS OF DISTINCTION. Flowers never fully open and have eroded petals. Rosettes

dry up, old leaves persist, and stems regenerate next spring from growing tips. Leaves are distinctly petiolate (Fig. 12.2j).

VARIATION. Two forms appear to be in cultivation: a light-colored form with pure white flowers on short pedicels spreads faster than a darker form with longer pedicels, hanging flowers, and petals tipped red.

HORTICULTURE. Once established, this is a fairly resilient species, but it languishes when small unless conditions are just right. A cool spot for summer is essential. Because it is dormant in winter, as long as it is well drained it will take some heavy rain without distress. Twiggy stems are not easy to root if removed from a parent plant for cuttings. Softer spring cuttings have a much better chance of striking.

SEDUM TROLLII Werdermann

PLATE 109

Sedum trollii appears to be a miniature form of *S. primuloides*, but its flowers are more like those of *S. pachyclados*. Evergreen rosettes no more than 2 cm (0.8 in) across sit on top of stems that are very shaggy with old leaves. Stems bury themselves and become rhizomes, which surface elsewhere to become stems. Eventually stems and rhizomes are so tangled it is impossible to differentiate between them. Large, white, stellate flowers often have green tips. This very shy flowerer is cold and wet hardy. Oddly, *S. trollii* seems to have been ignored in modern monographs—perhaps due to destruction of herbaria in the Second World War. Plants are becoming available in the trade and should be fairly easy to propagate.

HABITAT. This stonecrop was first collected at Nangar Parbat in Lichar Valley on the Kashmir border at 3200 m (10,500 ft).

MAIN POINTS OF DISTINCTION. Small, fleshy, green, distinctly waisted leaves forming evergreen rosettes on stems shaggy with dead leaves are good pointers to identification (Fig. 12.2k). If one is lucky enough to flower a plant, the solitary or group of white, stellate flowers are large and very distinct.

VARIATION. I grow two clones with minimal differences. Petals can be green in the upper third, and late flowers of October/November often tinge pink.

HORTICULTURE. I hope this species becomes more widely distributed in the near future as it is much more resilient than *Sedum primuloides*. It also has the advantage of winter color. It needs room to spread. At the Royal Botanic Garden Edinburgh, a specimen grew under a path by sending stoloniferous rhizomes to the other side of the walkway. The carpet produced is very dense and never more than a few centimeters high. Perhaps this stonecrop is too slow for ground cover, but in 10 years it will carpet a square meter (about 10 square feet).

HOBSONIA GROUP

This group contains only one very extreme *Sedum* species with dorsifixed anthers:

Sedum hobsonii Prain ex Raymond-Hamet

SEDUM HOBSONII
Prain ex Raymond-Hamet

PLATE 110

SYNONYM: *Sedum praegerianum* W. W. Smith

Had I planned to end my book on a "high" I could have chosen no better species. Unfortunately, *Sedum hobsonii* is almost impossible to keep alive in cultivation. At the crown of a tuberlike caudex, glabrous, petiolate, deciduous leaves spread, and helicoid cymes, like spokes of a wheel, spread across the ground to produce pink bisexual flowers with upright petals.

HABITAT. Mainly from the Xizang Plateau, this stonecrop is found from Sikkim, through Nepal, to Afghanistan, at 2800 to 3650 m (9200 to 11,980 ft).

MAIN POINTS OF DISTINCTION. This species is quite unlike any other member of Crassulaceae. In summer, a crown of leaves is produced with particularly long petioles (Fig. 12.2l). Arrangement of prostrate stems is unique. Pink, campanulate flowers with tips just spreading are very beautiful.

VARIATION. As the range in habitat is so great, there is considerable variation, but plants in cultivation are exceptionally rare.

HORTICULTURE. In botanic gardens, a caudex is often planted above ground as a preventive measure against rot. Plants can be grown from seed, but this species requires more intensive husbandry than any others in any of the families I have ever attempted to grow.

Sedum Species Not in Cultivation

EUROPEAN SPECIES OF SUBGENUS SEDUM

There are a score or so European species not in general cultivation, but the majority of these are tiny annuals. Several interesting biennial, rosette-forming species from Cyprus, perhaps closely related to *Rosularia*, have been in cultivation in the past, but appear no longer to be. The name *Sedum creticum* is sometimes used in the United States, but for reasons unknown to me, it often accompanies a species of Japanese origin. Other ephemerals are indigenous to the Middle East, but few have many horticultural qualities.

The following species appear not to be in cultivation:

Sedum aetnense Tineo
Sedum alsinifolium Allioni
Sedum assyriacum Boissier
Sedum campanulatum (Willkomm) Fernándes & Cantó
Sedum candollei Hamet
Sedum caricum Carlström
Sedum caroli-henrici Kit Tan
Sedum confertiflorum Boissier
Sedum creticum Presl
Sedum cyprium A. K. Jackson & Turrill
Sedum cyrenaicum Brullo & Furnari
Sedum delicum (Vierh.) Carlström
Sedum ekimianum Metzger & Duman
Sedum hewittii Chamberlain
Sedum hierapetrae Rech.
Sedum inconspicuum Handel-Mazzett
Sedum lagascae Pau
Sedum lampusae (Kotschy) Boissier
Sedum longibracteatum Fröderström
Sedum louisii (J. Thiébaut & Gombault) Fröderström

Sedum microstachyum (Kotschy) Boissier

Sedum nevadense Cosson

Sedum pedicellatum Boissier & Reuter

Sedum polystriatum Clausen

Sedum porphyreum Kotschy

Sedum rivasgodayi Segura

Sedum schizolepis Fröderström

Sedum sorgerae Kit Tan & Chamberlain

Sedum steudelii Boissier

Sedum tetramerum Trautvetter

Sedum tristriatum Boissier

Sedum zollikoferi F. Hermann & Stefanov

Additionally, others like *S. idaeum* D. A. Webb and *S. horakii* Rohlena are considered by some as good species.

FAR EASTERN SPECIES OF SUBGENUS SEDUM

The list of Oriental *Sedum* species not in cultivation is long, but as most of these plants were described in the distant past and few are likely to be collected in the near future, listing these plants seems a pointless excercise.

AFRICAN SPECIES OF SUBGENUS SEDUM

Sedum baleensis Gilbert

Sedum bracteatum Viviana non Diels

Sedum churchillianum Robyns & Boutique

Sedum crassularia Raymond-Hamet

Sedum epidendrum Hochstetter

Sedum gattefossei Battandier

Sedum glomerifolium Gilbert

Sedum jaccardianum Maire & Wilczek

Sedum jahandiezii Battandier

Sedum maurum Humboldt & Maire

Sedum meyeri-johannis Engler

Sedum modestum Ball

Sedum mooneyi Gilbert

Sedum pubescens Vahl

Sedum surculosum Cosson [syn. *S. atlanticum* (Ball) Maire]

Sedum tuberosum Letourneux ex Pomel

Sedum versicolor Cosson ex Maire

NORTH AMERICAN SPECIES OF SUBGENUS SEDUM

Sedum albomarginatum Clausen

Sedum oblanceolatum Clausen

Sedum pusillum Michaux

Sedum radiatum Watson

Sedum rupicolum G. N. Jones

LATIN AMERICAN SPECIES OF SUBGENUS SEDUM

All *Pachysedum* species are in cultivation except for *Sedum oteroi* Moran, although some are difficult to acquire.

The following Mexican woody species appear not to be in cultivation:

Sedum botteri Hemsley
Sedum chloropetalum Clausen
Sedum platyphyllum Alexander
Sedum tortuosum Hemsley (recently available in specialist circles)
Sedum tuberculatum Rose

The following Mexican nonwoody species appear not to be in cultivation:

Sedum australe Rose
Sedum batesii Hemsley
Sedum chihuahuense S. Watson
Sedum clavifolium Rose
Sedum cormiferum Clausen
Sedum cupressoides Hemsley
Sedum flaccidum Rose
Sedum forreri Greene
Sedum globuliferum Clausen
Sedum havardii Rose
Sedum jaliscanum S. Watson (syn. *S. navicularum* Rose)
Sedum latifilamentum Clausen
Sedum lumholtzii Robinson & Fernald
Sedum madrense S. Watson
Sedum millspaughii Hamet
Sedum minimum Rose
Sedum napiferum Peyritsch
Sedum oteroi Moran
Sedum pentastamineum Clausen (recently available in specialist circles)
Sedum robertsianum E. J. Alexander (may soon be distributed)
Sedum semiteres Rose
Sedum vinicolor S. Watson

Finally, the South American species *Sedum cymatopetalum* Fröderström is not in cultivation.

SUBGENUS HYLOTELEPHIUM SPECIES

Sedum angustum Maximowicz
Sedum bonnafousi Raymond-Hamet
Sedum callichroum Ohba comb. nov.
Sedum eupatorioides Komarov
Sedum mingjinianum Fu
Sedum pallescens Freyn

Sedum subcapitatum Hayata
Sedum ussuriense Komarov

SUBGENUS RHODIOLA SPECIES

Scores of synonyms exist, but the following species appear not to be in general cultivation.

Rhodiola Group

Sedum callianthum Ohba
Sedum crenulatum Hooker & Thomson
Sedum cretinii Raymond-Hamet
Sedum discolor Franchet
Sedum linearifolium Royle
Sedum ovatisepalum (Raymond-Hamet) Ohba
Sedum sacrum (Raymond-Hamet) Ohba

Chamaerhodiola Group

Sedum bouvieri Raymond-Hamet
Sedum quadrifidum Pallas

Primuloida Group

Sedum handelli Ohba (comb. nov.)
Sedum humile Hooker & Thomson
Sedum saxifragoides Fröderström
Sedum smithii Raymond-Hamet

Crassipedes Group

Sedum chrysanthemifolium Léveillé (syn. *S. trifidum*)
Sedum liciae Raymond-Hamet
Sedum nepalicum Ohba
Sedum sinuatum Royle & Edgeworth

Several other groups of subgenus *Rhodiola* beyond the scope of this volume have no species in cultivation.

Selected Lists of Sedums

The species recommended below are neither difficult to grow nor impossible to acquire, although several could be elusive.

LARGE MUNICIPAL SITES, FACTORIES & HOSPITALS

Sedum acre, especially tetraploids

Sedum album

Sedum ellacombianum

Sedum forsterianum (but in areas with hot dry summers substitute with *S. sediforme*)

Sedum hispanicum var. *minus*

Sedum kamtschaticum var. *floriferum*

Sedum oreganum

Sedum spurium (all forms except 'Tricolor')

Sedum ternatum (if shaded with some trees)

SMALL ROCK GARDENS

Sedum aggregeatum

Sedum cauticola

Sedum dasyphyllum

Sedum divergens

Sedum ewersii var. *homophyllum*

Sedum hybridum

Sedum kamtschaticum

Sedum lydium

Sedum montanum

Sedum moranense

Sedum oreganum subsp. *tenue*

Sedum oryzifolium (not where heavy frosts are experienced)

Sedum pachyclados

Sedum pluricaule

Sedum senanense

Sedum spathulifolium 'Cape Blanco'

Sedum stefco

Sedum urvillei

OUTDOOR CONTAINERS IN AREAS WITH FEW FROSTS & HOT SUMMERS

Graptosedum 'Francesco Baldi'

Graptosedum 'Vera Higgins'

Sedum adolphii

Sedum burrito (especially for hanging containers or windowboxes)

Sedum commixtum

Sedum confusum or *S. decumbens*

Sedum dendroideum

Sedum 'Green Rose'

Sedum morganianum (especially for hanging containers or window boxes)

Sedum nussbaumerianum

Sedum obcordatum

Sedum pachyphyllum

Sedum palmeri

Sedum praealtum
Sedum ×rubrotinctum
Sedum stahlii

OUTDOOR CONTAINERS IN AREAS WITH FROSTY WINTERS

Sedum acre 'Minus' and diploids
Sedum album (especially small colorful subspecies, varieties, or forms)
Sedum anacampseros
Sedum cauticola
Sedum dasyphyllum
Sedum divergens
Sedum 'Harvest Moon'
Sedum middendorffianum
Sedum ochroleucum
Sedum oregonense
Sedum rosea
Sedum rupestre
Sedum rupifragum
Sedum sieboldii
Sedum spathulifolium 'Cape Blanco'
Sedum spathulifolium var. *purpureum*
Sedum tatarinowii
Sedum trollii

INDOOR WINDOWSILLS

Sedum allantoides
Sedum clavatum
Sedum frutescens
Sedum hintonii
Sedum hultenii
Sedum lineare f. *variegatum*
Sedum 'Little Gem'
Sedum lucidum
Sedum oaxacanum
Sedum oxypetalum
Sedum pachyphyllum
Sedum ×rubrotinctum
Sedum ×rubrotinctum 'Aurora'
Sedum suaveolens
Sedum treleasei
Sedum versadense

BORDERS

Back of border
Sedum aizoon
Sedum telephium 'Autumn Joy'
Sedum telephium subsp. *maximum*

Middle of border
Sedum aizoon
Sedum cepaea
Sedum litorale
Sedum rosea
Sedum spectabile and all its cultivars
Sedum telephium subsp. *fabaria* and its associated cultivars
Sedum telephium subsp. *maximum*

Front of border
Sedum acre 'Elegans'
Sedum cepaea
Sedum forsterianum f. *purpureum*
Sedum kamtschaticum f. *variegatum*
Sedum makinoi (but not in areas with severe winters)
Sedum spurium 'Schorbuser Blut'
Sedum spurium 'Tricolor'

LIVING PICTURES, FLORAL CLOCKS & FLORAL MODELS

Blue-green species
Sedum dasyphyllum
Sedum hispanicum 'Minus'

Dark brown, black or deep purple species
Sedum album 'Murale'
Sedum gypsicola

Red species
Sedum album 'Coral Carpet'
Sedum oreganum ssp. *tenue*
Sedum ×rubrotinctum
Sedum spathulifolium 'William Pascoe'

White species
Sedum dasyphyllum 'Lloyd Praeger'
Sedum spathulifolium 'Cape Blanco'

Yellow-green species

Sedum album subsp. *micranthum* var. *chloroticum*

Sedum makino f. *variegatum*

GROUND COVER

* = *for areas with mild winters (occasional frosts) only*

Sedum acre—most forms

Sedum album—most forms

Sedum ellacombianum

Sedum forsterianum (some shade beneficial)

Sedum kamtschaticum var. *floriferum*

*Sedum makinoi (some shade beneficial)

Sedum oreganum

*Sedum reptans

**Sedum sarmentosum*

Sedum sexangulare

Sedum spurium—all forms except 'Tricolor'

SPECIMEN ALPINE PLANTS

Sedum boehmeri

Sedum brevifolium—all forms

Sedum chanetii

Sedum dasyphyllum var. *mesatlanticum*

Sedum dasyphyllum subsp. *oblongifolium*

Sedum diffusum

Sedum farinosum

Sedum glaucophyllum

Sedum hirsutum

Sedum humifusum

Sedum luteoviride

Sedum multiceps

Sedum muscoideum

Sedum pilosum

Sedum pluricaule

Sedum sempervivoides

Sedum spathulifolium 'Aureum'

Sedum spinosum

GREENHOUSE CULTIVATION

Sedum allantoides 'Goldii'

Sedum bourgaei

Sedum clavatum

Sedum compactum

Sedum craigii

Sedum cremnophila

Sedum 'Crocodile'

Sedum ebracteatum

Sedum furfuraceum

Sedum grandipetalum

Sedum greggii

Sedum griseum

Sedum lucidum

Sedum 'Spiral Staircase'

I.S.I. Distributions

Prior to 1988, the International Succulent Institute did not include the year in its numbering system. Thereafter, the first two numbers refer to a year in which a plant was offered. I am deeply indebted to Roy Mottram of Whitestone Gardens for providing much of the information here.

Year	I.S.I. No.	Species
1959	I.S.I. 105	*Sedum greggii*
	I.S.I. 174	*Sedum* affin. *hintonii* (originally thought to be *S. hintonii*)
1960	I.S.I. 204	*Sedum humifusum*
1961	I.S.I. 205	*Sedum spathulifolium*
	I.S.I. 221	*Sedum moranii*
1959	I.S.I. 240	*Sedum erubescens* var. *japonicum* (as *Orostachys japonicus*)
	I.S.I. 241	*Sedum aggregeatum*
	I.S.I. 295	*Sedum nanifolium* (originally thought to be *S. moranense*)
1960	I.S.I. 387	*Sedum lineare*
1963	I.S.I. 428	*Sedum furfuraceum*
1966	I.S.I. 509	*Sedum rubrotinctum* 'Aurora'
1968	I.S.I. 532	*Sedum frutescens*
1976	I.S.I. 985	*Sedum burrito* (offered as a variant of *S. morganianum*)
1977	I.S.I. 1037	*Sedum adenotrichum* (referred to *Rosularia* at a later date)
1978	I.S.I. 1100	*Sedum suaveolens*
1979	I.S.I. 1161	*Sedum clavatum*
1980	I.S.I. 1222	*Sedum reptans*
	I.S.I. 1223	*Sedum rosulatum* (referred to *Rosularia adenotricha* at a later date)
1983	I.S.I. 1411	*Sedum multiflorum*
1984	I.S.I. 1496	*Sedum batallae*
	I.S.I. 1497	*Sedum lucidum* (the form now known as 'Obesum')
1986	I.S.I. 1681	*Sedum* affin. *dendroideum*
	I.S.I. 1682	*Sedum nussbaumerianum*
	I.S.I. 1683	*Sedum versadense* var. *villadioides*

Year	I.S.I. No.	Species
1987	I.S.I. 1772	*Sedum dasyphyllum* subsp. *oblongifolium* (originally distributed as a variant of *S. album*)
1987	I.S.I. 1773	*Sedum macdougallii*
	I.S.I. 89-66	*Sedum limuloides* as *Orostachys fimbriata*
	I.S.I. 89-67	*Sedum sarmentosum* (originally distributed as *S. acutifolium*)
	I.S.I. 90-71	*Sedum iwarenge* 'Fuji'
	I.S.I. 91-54	*Sedum iwarenge* 'Natsu Fuji'
	I.S.I. 91-60	*Sedum hintonii*
	I.S.I. 91-61	*Sedum kamtschaticum*
	I.S.I. 92-61	*Sedum indicum* var. *yunnanense* (as *Sinocrassula yunnanensis*)
	I.S.I. 93-52	*Sedum hernandezii*
	I.S.I. 93-53	*Sedum* sp. Lau 081 (as *Sedum* cf. *reptans*)
	I.S.I. 94-44	*Sedum* sp. (*S. dasyphyllum* form)

APPENDIX 4

Useful Addresses

United States
American Rock Garden Society
15 Fairmead Road
Darien, CT 06820 U.S.A.

Cactus and Succulent Society of
    America
810 East St
Box 1897
Lawrence, KS 66044-8897 U.S.A.

Hardy Perennials
RFD #3, Box 445
Augusta, ME 04330 U.S.A.

I.S.I.
Huntington Botanical Gardens
1151 Oxford Road
San Marino CA 91108 U.S.A.

Sedum Society
10502 N 135th W.
Sedgwick, KS 67135 U.S.A.

Squaw Mountain Gardens
36212 SE Squaw Mountain Road
Estacada, OR 97023 U.S.A.

Europe
Abbey Dore Gardens
(National Collection of *Sedum*)
Abbey Dore Court
Hereford HR2 0AD
England

Alpine Garden Society
Lye End Link
St. John's
Woking
Surrey GU21 1SW
England

British Cactus and Succulent Society
23 Linden Leas
West Wickham
Kent BR4 0SE
England

Greenslacks Nurseries
Ocot Lane
Scammonden
Huddersfield HD3 3FR
England

International Succulent Institute
Woodsleigh
Moss Lane
St. Michaels on Wyre
Preston PR3 0TY
England

N.C.C.P.G.
The Pines
Wisley Garden
Woking
Surrey GU23 6QB
England

The Scottish Rock Garden Club
The Linns
Sheriffmuir
Dunblane
Perthshire FK15 0LP
Scotland

Sedum Society
12 Langdale Road
Gateshead
Tyne and Wear NE9 5RN
England

Whitestone Gardens Ltd.
The Cactus Houses
Sutton-under-Whitestonecliffe
Thirsk
North Yorkshire YO7 2PZ
England

Glossary

ACTINOMORPHIC: Radiating out from a central point or circle like the rays of the sun.

ACUMINATE: Tapering from inwardly curved sides to a narrow point.

ACUTE: Pointed.

ADVENTITIOUS BUD: A casual bulbil.

AERIAL ROOTS: Roots sent out from stems above ground level.

ALTERNIPETALOUS: Alternating with the petals, between the petals.

AMPLEXICAUL: Clasping the stem; see Figure 3.8b.

ANDROECIUM: The stamens taken collectively.

ANEUPLOIDY: The loss or gain of a chromosome.

ANTHER: The part of the stamen containing pollen, see Figure 3.3.

APICULATE: Ending abruptly in a sharp point.

APPRESSED: Lying against.

AQUATIC: Used of a plant that lives in water.

BASIFIXED: Joined at the base.

BEAK: A stigma lobe, the appendage at the top of a carpel.

BRACT: A leaflike appendage on the inflorescence.

BULBIL: An easily detached rosette of a potential new plant.

CALCIFUGE: A plant that hates calcareous (limestone family) rocks.

CALYX: The sepals collectively.

CAM: Crassulacean Acidic Metabolism. Used of plants that survive arid conditions by depending on temperature change (rather than light) to trigger photosynthesis.

CAMPANULATE: Bell-shaped.

CARINATE: Keeled, having a ridge down the middle of the lower face.

CARPELS: The female part of a flower; pistil cells; fruit; see Figure 3.4.

CARTILAGE: Firm gristly tissue.

CAUDEX: A massive rootstock.

CHAMAEPHYTE: A creeping plant.

CHIMERA: One form enveloped by another.

CHROMOSOME: A rodlike structure found within the nucleus of a cell.

CILIA: Eyelashlike fringes of hair.

CLONOTYPE: A vegetatively propagated descendant of the actual plant designated as the type by the first author of the species.

CONNATE PETALS: Petals that are united at the base.

CORDATE: Heart-shaped.

COROLLA: The petals collectively.

CORYMB: A compact inflorescence; see Figure 3.5d.

CRENATE: Edged with rounded teeth.

CRISTATE: Crested, comblike tuft when a freak plant develops growth from a line rather than a point. Such oddities are often considered very beautiful and are usually propagated vegetatively.

CULTIVAR, Cv.: Cultivated variety; a garden form that sometimes is an improvement on the wild species due to selection or controlled hybridization.

CUNEATE: Wedge-shaped.

CUTICLE: Superficial film or skin.

CYME: A compact inflorescence; see Figure 3.5c.

CYTOLOGY: The study of cells.

DECUMBENT: Creeping then rising.

DEFLEXED: Bent aside.

DEHISCE: To burst open; said of seed vessels.

DELTOID: Triangular.

DENTATE: Notched, toothed.

DICHASIUM: A simple inflorescence in which two stems arise below a terminal flower; see Figure 3.5a.

DICHOTOMOUS: Divided in two, repeated bifurcation.

DICOTYLEDON: Any plant producing an initial pair of seedling leaves, from the center of which emerge true leaves and stem; see Figure 4.1.

DIGITATE: Fingerlike.

DIOECIOUS: Having male flowers on one plant and female flowers on another.

DIPLOID: Having two sets of chromosomes.

DIPLOSTEMONOUS: Having two whorls of stamens, the outer whorl opposite the sepals and the inner whorl opposite the petals.

DISJUNCT: Separate, disjoined.

DORSAL: Belonging to the back or outer face, as opposed to the ventral (belly) or inner face.

DORSIFIXED: Joined on the back; see Figure 3.3g.

DYSPLOIDY: Having unrelated chromosome counts.

EMARGINATE: Having a notch at the end as though a piece has been taken out.

ENTIRE: Having a smooth, unbroken margin devoid of indentation of any sort.

EPHEMERAL: Short-lived.

EPIPETALOUS: Used of stamens inserted at the base of the petals.

EPIPHYTIC: Used of a plant growing on another plant.

ERODED: Uneven, fringed, or toothed; not entire.

ETIOLATED: Spindly, drawn, pale plants usually resulting from a lack of light.

FASCIATION: Freak growth such as cristate or monstrous.

FASTIGIATE: Conical in outline.

FILAMENT: The lower part of a stamen; see Figure 3.3.

FJELD: An ice-scraped plateau between fjords.

FOLD MOUNTAINS: Chains of uplifted sedimentary layers, cordilleras.

FREE: Unattached; used of sepals that are not united at the base; see Figure 3.2.

FRIT: A mixture of materials.

GAMETE: A sexual photoplasmic body that unites with another for reproduction.

GIBBOUS: Protruberant, humped, bulging.

GLABROUS: Bald, naked, without cilia.

GLANDULAR-PAPILLOSE: Having tiny nipplelike protuberances covering the surface.

GLAUCOUS: Having a powdery bloom like a grape or cabbage.

GYNOECIUM: The carpels collectively.

HAPLOSTEMONOUS: Having only a single whorl of stamens.

HELICOID: Spiralling out.

HERBACEOUS: A plant whose stems do not persist from season to season.

HERMAPHRODITE: A flower with both male and female organs.

HEPTAPLOID: Having seven sets of chromosomes

HETEROPLOIDY: the existence of different levels of ploidy.

HEXAPLOID: Having six sets of chromosomes.

HIRSUTE: Hairy.

HOLOTYPE: The specimen designated as the type by the author first publishing a species.

HYALINE PAPILLAE: Clear, glassy nipplelike protruberances; usually used of leaf or sepal ornamentation.

HYPOGYNOUS SCALES: Nectaries, which are sweet fuid producing glands, see Figure 3.1.

IMBRICATE: Overlapping and appressed to the stem; used of leaves arranged like tiles on a roof or like scales on a fish; see Figure 3.7e.

INFERIOR OVARY: Sunken fruit that sit below the line made by the petals; see Figure 4.1.

INFLORESCENCE: The collective arrangement of flowers on a stem.

I.S.I.: International Succulent Institute, Huntington Botanical Gardens, San Marino, California.

ISOMEROUS: Having an equal number of flower parts (e.g., stamens, petals, carpels).

KYPHOCARPIC: Having bulged carpels that arch outwards and spread flat when flowers fruit; see Figure 3.4.

LANCEOLATE: Shaped like the head of a lance (i.e., broader at the base and narrower at the apex).

LATERAL: From the side.

LAX: Open, loose, not compact.

LINEAR: Long and narrow with parallel sides.

LITHOPHYTE: A plant that lives on rock.

MARGINAL: Used of a plant that grows on the edge of a vegetation belt.

MEIOSIS: A phase of change in cells wherein the number of chromosomes is halved.

MERISTEM: The growing tip.

MESOPHYTE: A regular, ordinary plant that requires a normal amount of water—neither xerophytic or aquatic.

MITOSIS: The process of cell division.

MONOCARPIC: Used of a rosette or plant that produces a single inflorescence before expiring.

MONOCHASIUM: An inflorescence with only one main stem; half a dichasium.

MONOCOTYLEDON: Any plant producing initial seedling leaf; see Figure 4.1.

MONOECIOUS: Having male and female flowers on the same plant.

MONOTYPIC: Used of a genus having only one species.

MONSTROUS: A freak plant in which the growing tip has split into lots of small ones.

MORAINE: Stones and clay deposited by a glacier.

MUCRO (mucrones): A pointed tip.

MUCRONATE: Apiculate or sharply tipped.

N.C.C.P.G.: National Council for the Conservation of Plants and Gardens, Surrey, England.

NECTARIES/NECTARY GLANDS: Flower organs that secrete honeylike liquid, see Figure 3.1.

OBCORDATE: Inverse heart-shaped.

OBDIPLOSTEMONOUS: Having two whorls of stamens—an inner whorl fixed to the petals and an outer whorl fixed between the petals.

OBOVATE: Inverse egg-shaped.

OBTUSE: Blunt.

OCTOPLOID: Having eight sets of chromosomes.

OPPOSITE-DECUSSATE: Leaves in pairs, each pair at right angles to the next; see Figure 3.7b.

OPPOSITIPETALOUS: Said of stamens when they are directly opposite a petal.

ORBICULAR: Round.

ORTHOCARPIC: Having carpels that do not bulge and remain upright even after they burst open to reveal seed; see Figure 3.4.

OVARY/OVARIES: The carpels collectively.

OVATE/OVOID: Egg-shaped.

PANICLE: A loose, irregular, compound inflorescence.

PAPILLOSE (papillate): Having minute warty ornamentation.

PARTITE: Having parts; used of a flower.

PATENT: Spreading at right angles from the base.

PEDICEL: A flower stalk.

PEDICELLATE: Having well-defined pedicels.

PEDUNCLE: The main stalk of the inflorescence.

PENDULOUS: Hanging.

PENTAPLOID: Having five sets of chromosomes.

PETAL: Any part of the corolla.

PETIOLATE: Stalked.

PHOTOSYNTHESIS: The process by which the energy of sunlight is trapped by the chlorophyll in green plants and used to build up complex materials from carbon dioxide and water.

PISTIL: Carpel beak.

PLOIDY: Sets of chromosomes.

POLYMORPHIC: Used of a plant that takes on numerous forms.

POLYPLOID: A plant in which the chromosomes have doubled several times.

PROCUMBENT: Prostrate.

PROPAGULE: Shoot that can be propagated.

PRUINOSE: Heavily frosted with a white powdery substance.

PUBESCENT: Downy, covered with hairs.

QUADRATE: Square-shaped.

RACEME: A flower cluster.

R.B.G.E.: Royal Botanic Garden Edinburgh.

RECEPTACLE TUBE: The point at which sepals are fused partly into a cylinder.

RECURVED: Bent backwards.

REFLEXED: Recurved.

RETUSE: Having a rounded apex with a shallow notch.

RHIZOME: A prostrate rootlike stem, emitting roots.

ROSETTE: An arrangement of leaves resembling the petals on a rose.

ROSULATE: Like a rosebud with leaves packed over each other.

SCABROUS/SCABRID: Having a rough or scurfy surface.

SCORPIOID INFLORESCENCE: Having zigzag branching that resembles the shape of a scorpion; see Figure 3.5e.

SENSU LATO: In the widest sense.

SENSU STRICTO: In the strictest sense.

SEPAL: A leaflike bract enclosing a petal; see Figure 3.1.

SERPENTINE: Soft greenish metamorphic rock consisting of hydrous magnesium silicate.

SERRATE: Having lopsided teeth like those of a saw.

SESSILE: Stalkless.

SPATHULATE: Spoon shaped; see Figure 3.8d.

SPIKE: An elongated inflorescence shaped like a cylinder or a cone; see Figure 3.5f.

SPURRED: Said of leaves and sepals having a projection on the heel; see Figure 3.8b.

SQUAMAE: Nectaries.

STAMEN: The male part of a flower made up of a filament and an anther; see Figure 3.3.

STELLATE: Star-shaped.

STEPPE: A prairie, temperate Eurasian grassland.

STERILE SHOOTS (of stems): Those without inflorescences.

STIPITATE: With a little stalk, waisted.

STOLON: A prostrate branch which develops into a new plant.

STOMATA: Pores through which plants breathe.

SUBEPIDERMAL: Just below the surface.

SUBSESSILE: Having very short pedicels.

SUBULATE: Tapering from a broad base to a sharp point, awl-shaped.

SUPERIOR OVARY: An ovary that sits above the line made by the petals; see Figure 4.1.

SYMPATRIC: Occupying the same terrain.

TAXONOMIST: One who classifies and orders plants.

TERETE: Round in cross section.

TERMINAL: Used of inflorescences that originate from the growing tip as opposed to lateral inflorescences that originate from the side of a stem.

TERNATE: In groups (whorls) of three.

TETRAPLOID: Having four sets of chromosomes.

TOPOTYPE: A plant from the same locality as the type species.

TORTUOUS: Full of twists and turns.

TRANSPIRATION: The plant world equivalent of perspiration.

TRILOBATE: With three lobes.

TRIPLOID: Having three sets of chromosomes.

TRUNCATE: Appearing as if chopped off.

TUFT: A bunch of leaves growing close together at the base.

TURGID: Swollen, inflated.

TYPE: The specimen from which a species was first described.

URCEOLATE: Urn shaped.

VENTRAL: Belonging to the inner face.

VERTICILLATE: Having leaves in whorls.

VIVIPAROUS: Producing miniature plants while still attached to the parent plant.

WHORL: A ringlike arrangement around the stem; stamens are produced in rings around the carpels and leaves are sometimes grouped in whorls of 3 or 4.

XEROPHYTIC: Drought resistant.

Bibliography

Abrams, L. 1944. "Crassulaceae." In *Illustrated Flora of the Pacific States*. 2: 342–346. California: Stanford University Press.

Baehni, C. 1937. "*Villadia* et *Altamiranoa*: etude sur la fusion de deux genres de Crassulacées." *Candollea* 7: 283–286.

Baker, J. G. 1868. "*S. alboroseum.*" *Refugium Botanicum*, t. 33.

Baldwin, J. T. 1937. "The Cytotaxonomy of the *Telephium* section of *Sedum.*" *American Journal of Botany* 24: 126–132.

Barocio, I. 1973. "Una especie nueva de *Sedum* (Crassulaceae) encontrada Cerca de Epazoyucan, Hidalgo (México)." *Cactáceas y Succulentas Mexicanas* 18: 96–100.

Berger, A. 1930. "*Sedum.*" In *Die Natürlichen Pflanzenfamilien*. 2nd ed. Eds. A. Engler and K. Prantl. Leipzig: Verlag von Wilhelm Englemann. 18a: 436–462. Translation by R. L. Evans. Indexed by R. Stephenson. R. L. Evans. London: 1985.

Borissov, A. G. 1939. "Crassulaceae." In *Flora SSSR*. Eds. V. L. Komarov et al. Moscow and Leningrad: Izdatel'stvo Akademi Nauk SSSR. 9: 8–134. Translation by L. Behrman. 1971. Jerusalem: Israel Program for Scientific Translations. 8–105.

Britton, N. L., and J. N. Rose. 1903. "New or noteworthy North American Crassulaceae." *Bulletin of the New York Botanic Gardens* 3: 1–45.

_____. 1905. "Crassulaceae." In *North American Flora*. Eds. N. L. Britton et al. New York: New York Botanical Garden. 22(1): 7–74.

Carlström, A. L. 1985. "Two new species of *Sedum.*" *Willdenowia* 15: 108–113.

Cavender, R. 1991. "From members letters." *Sedum Society Newsletter* 17: 17.

Chamberlain, D. F. 1972. "*Sedum L.*" In *Flora of Turkey*. Ed. P. H. Davis. Edinburgh: Edinburgh University Press. 4: 224–243.

Chŏng, T'aeyŏn. 1956. *Han'guk Singmul Togam*. Seoul: Synji Sa. 2: 281–291.

Clausen, R. T. 1940. "Studies in the Crassulaceae: *Villadia, Altamiranoa*, and *Thompsonella.*" *Bulletin of the Torrey Botanic Club* 67: 195–198.

_____. 1946. "Nomenclatural changes and innovations in the Crassulaceae." *Cactus and Succulent Journal (U.S.)* 18: 60–61.

_____. 1948. "A name for *Sedum guatelmalense* of horticulturists." *Cactus and Succulent Journal (U.S.)* 20: 82.

_____. 1959. Sedum *of the Trans-Mexican Volcanic Belt: an Exposition of Taxonomic Methods*. Ithaca, NY: Cornell University Press.

_____. 1975. Sedum *of North America North of the Mexican Plateau*. Ithaca, NY: Cornell University Press.

_____. 1978. "*Sedum*—Seven Mexican perennial species." *Bulletin of the Torrey Botanic Club* 105(3): 214–223.

_____. 1979. "*Sedum* in six areas of the Mexican Cordilleran Plateau." *Bulletin of the Torrey Botanic Club* 106(3): 205–216.

_____. 1981. *Variations of Species of* Sedum *of the Mexican Cordilleran Plateau*. Ithaca, NY: R. T. Clausen.

Clausen, R. T., and C. H. Uhl. 1943. "Revision of *Sedum cockerellii* and related species." *Brittonia* 5(1): 33–46.

Coste, H. 1937. "Crassulacées." In *Flore de la France*. Paris: Librairie des Sciences et des Arts. 2: 109–114.

Coutiñho, A. 1913. "Crassulaceas." In *A Flora de Portugal*. Paris, Lisbon: Alves & Cia. 227–280.

Crozier, M. 1991. "*Sedum nuttallianum*." *Sedum Society Newsletter* 16: 17.

Davis, P. H., see Chamberlain, D. F.

Descloux, J. 1989. "*Sedum ternatum* and the Cherokee nation." *Sedum Society Newsletter* 10: 13.

Eggli, U. 1988. "A monographic study of the genus *Rosularia* (Crassulaceae)." *Bradleya* 6 supplement.

Evans, R. L. 1983. *Handbook of cultivated sedums*. London: Science Reviews.

_____. 1988a. "*Sedum* from Taiwan." *Sedum Society Newsletter* 4: 4–5.

_____. 1988b. "*Sedum serpentini* Janchen." *Sedum Society Newsletter* 5: 4–5.

Fournier, P. 1936. "Crassulacées." In *Les quatre flores de la France, Corse comprise*. Rev. ed. Paris: Éditions Lechevalier S.A.R.L. 457–467.

Fröderström, H. 1930, 1931, 1932, 1935, "The genus *Sedum:* a systematic essay." In *Acta horti Gothoburgensis* 5, 6, 7, 10: Appendices.

Gilbert, M. G. 1985. "The genus *Sedum* in Ethiopia." *Bradleya* 3: 48–52.

Greuter, W., H. M. Burdet, and G. Long. 1981. "*Sedum*." In *Med—checklist* 3. Geneva: Conservatoire et Jardin Botanique.

Grulich, V. 1984. "Generic division of *Sedoideae* in Europe and the adjacent regions." *Preslia* 56: 29–45.

Hageman, I., and H. 't Hart. 1986. "*Sedum* L." In *Mountain flora of Greece*. Ed. A. Strid. Cambridge, UK: Cambridge University Press. 1: 341–359.

't Hart, H. 1971. "Cytological and morphological variation in *Sedum acre* L. in Western Europe." *Acta Botanica Neerlandica* 20(3): 282–290.

_____. 1972. "Chromosome numbers in the series *Rupestria* Berger of the genus *Sedum* L.." *Acta Botanica Neerlandica* 21(4): 428–435.

_____. 1974. "*Sedum tenuifolium* (Sibth. & Sm.) Strobl. subsp. *ibericum* nov. ssp." *Acta Botanica Neerlandica* 23(4): 549–554.

_____. 1978. *Biosystematic Studies in the* acre *Group and the Series* Rupestria *Berger of the genus* Sedum *L. (Crassulaceae)*. Utrecht: Drukkerij Elinkurijk BV-Utrecht.

_____. 1982a. "Systematic position of *Sedum tuberosum* Coss. & Let. (Crassulaceae)." *Proceedings Koninklijke Nederlandse Akademie van Wetenschappen, Series C,* 85(4): 497–508.

_____. 1982b. "The white-flowered European *Sedum* species. 1. Principles of a phylogenetic classification of the Sedoideae (Crassulaceae) and the position of the white-flowered *Sedum* species." *Proceedings Koninklijke Nederlandse Akademie van Wetenschappen, Series C,* 85(4): 663–675.

_____. 1983a. "Micro-endemism in *Sedum* (Crassulaceae): the sibling species *S. alsinefolium* All. and *S. fragrans* spec nov. from the French-Italian Alps." *Botanica Helvetica* 93: 269–280.

_____. 1983b. "*Sedum apoleipon*, a new species of the *Sedum acre* group (Crassulaceae) from Central Greece." *Willdenowia* 13: 309–319.

_____. 1983c. "A reappraisal of *Sedum grisebachii* (Crassulaceae). Typification and infraspecific variation." *Willdenowia* 13: 295–307.

_____. 1987. "Natural hybrids in *Sedum* (Crassulaceae) 1. Two new hybrids of *S.* series *Rupestria* and a new locality of *S.* × *brevierei.*" *Botanische Jahrbücher für Systematik, Pflangeschichte und Pflanzengeographie* 109(1): 1–16.

_____. 1990. "*Sedum ursi* (Crassulaceae), a new species from Sandras Daği (Turkey)." *Acta Botanica Neerlandica* 39(2): 203–206.

_____. 1991. "Evolution and classification of the European *Sedum* species (Crassulaceae)." *Flora Mediterranea* 1: 31–61.

't Hart, H., and K. Alpinar. 1990. "The *Sedum* flora of Turkey, part 1." *Sedum Society Newsletter* 15: 10–15.

't Hart, H., and A. J. J. van den Berg. 1982. "White-flowered European *Sedum* species. 2. Cytotaxonomic notes on *S. album* and *S. gypsicolum* Boiss & Reut." *Proceedings Koninkjke Nederlandske Akademie van Wetenschappen, Series C,* 85(4): 677–691.

Hart, J. A., and T. C. Wrigley, eds. 1971. *Sedums.* Morden, Surrey: The Succulent Plant Institute, Succulent Plant Trust.

Hébert, L. P. 1983. "Analyse d'un complexe chromosomique en Méditerranée: *Sedum* ser. *Rupestria* Berger emend." *Revue de Cytologie et de Biologie Végétales—Le Botaniste* 6: 179–224.

Hensen, K. J. W., and N. Groendijk-Wilders. 1986. "An account of some sedums cultivated in Europe." *Plantsman* 8(1): 1–20.

Hoekstra, J. 1990. "*Sedum leibergii.*" *Sedum Society Newsletter* 15: 7.

Hulme, F. E. 1902. *Familiar Wild Flowers.* London: Cassell.

Jacobsen, H. 1960. *A Handbook of Succulent Plants* 2. Poole, UK: Blandford Press.

Jankalski, S. 1991. "Tale of a burro's tail." *Sedum Society Newsletter* 16: 13.

Kimnach, M. 1978. "*Sedum suaveolens*, a remarkable new species from Durango, Mexico." *Cactus and Succulent Journal (U.S.)* 50: 3–7.

Liu, Tang-shui, and Niang-june Chung. 1976. "*Sedum* L." In *Flora of Taiwan.* Eds. Hiu-liu Li et al. Taipei: Epoch Publ. Co. 2: 14–24.

Löve, Á., and D. Löve. 1985a. "Chromosome number reports LXXXVI." *Taxon* 34(1): 159–164.

_____. 1985b. "Chromosome number reports LXXXVI." *Taxon* 34(2): 346–351.

Makino, T. 1891. *Illustrations of The Flora of Japan, to Serve as an Atlas to the Nippon-Shikubutsushi* 1. Photocopy of the Linnean Society of London.

Maire, R. 1977. "Crassulaceae" In *Flore de L'Afrique du Nord*. Paris: Éditions Lechevalier S.A.R.L. 14: 239–393.

Meyrán, J. 1963. "The generic classification of the Mexican Crassulaceae." *Cactus and Succulent Journal (U.S.)* 63: 115–121.

Moran, R. "*Sedum spectabile* in South Korea." *Cactus and Succulent Journal (U.S.)* 36: 140–144.

_____. 1965. "*Sedum viridescens* Nakai." *Cactus and Succulent Journal (U.S.)* 37: 5–8.

_____. 1971. "*Sedum sikokianum*—a neglected Japanese species." *Cactus and Succulent Journal (U.S.)* 43: 147–149.

_____. 1976. "The section *Centripetalia* of *Sedum*." *Cactus and Succulent Journal (U.S.)* 48: 75–80.

_____. 1977. "*Sedum macdougallii*, a new species from Oaxaca, Mexico." *Cactus and Succulent Journal (U.S.)* 49: 39–41.

_____. 1978. "Resurrection of *Cremnophila*." *Cactus and Succulent Journal (U.S.)* 50: 139–146.

_____. 1990. "*Villadia aristata*, a new species from northeast Mexico." *Cactus and Succulent Journal (U.S.)* 62: 177–182.

Moran, R., and P. C. Hutchinson. 1980. "*Sedum commixtum*, a fairly new species from Oaxaca, Mexico." *Cactus and Succulent Journal (U.S.)* 52: 159–163.

Moran, R., and J. Meyrán. 1974. "*Tacitus bellus*, un nuevo género y especie de Crassulaceae de Chihuahua, México." *Cactaceas y Succulentas Mexicanas* 19: 75–84.

Murata, G., and H. Yuasa. 1975. "*Sedum yabeanum* v. *setouchiense*." *Acta Phytotaxanomica et Geobotanica* 27(1–2): 37–38.

Nosaka, Shirô. 1971. "*Sedum pluricaule* ssp. *ezawae*." *Journal of Japanese Botany* 46(6): 167–172.

Ohba, H. 1975. "A revision of the Eastern Himalayan species of the subgenus *Rhodiola* of the genus *Sedum*." *Flora of Eastern Himalaya, 3rd. report*. Ed. H. Ohashi. Tokyo: University of Tokyo Press. 283–362.

_____. 1976. "Notes on Himalayan *Sedum* 5. *Sedum* subgen. *Rhodiola*" *Journal of Japanese Botany* 51(5): 385–387.

_____. 1977 "The taxonomic status of *Sedum telephium* and its allied species (Crassulaceae)." *Botanic Magazine* (Tokyo) 90: 41–56.

_____. 1978. "Generic and infrageneric classification of the Old World Sedoideae." *Journal of the Faculty of Science, Tokyo University, Section 3*, 12: 139–197.

_____. 1980. "A revision of the Asiatic species of Sedoideae (Crassulaceae). Part 1." *Journal of the Faculty of Science, Tokyo University, Section 3*, 12: 337–405.

_____. 1981a. "A revision of the Asiatic species of Sedoideae (Crassulaceae). Part 2." *Journal of the Faculty of Science, Tokyo University, Section 3*, 13: 65–119.

_____. 1981b. "Nomenclatural changes and notes on Japanese Sedoideae." *Journal of Japanese Botany* 56(6): 181–187.

Ohwi, J. 1965. "*Sedum*." In *Flora of Japan*. Washington, DC: Smithsonian Institution. 493–496.

Pearson D., see Hart, J. A.

Philip, C. 1987, 1988, 1989, 1990, 1991. *The Plant Finder*. Whitbourne, UK: Hardy Plant Society.

Pignatti, S. 1982. "*Sedum* L." In *Flora d'Italia*. Bologna: Edagricole. 1: 494–504.

Pilon-Smits, L. 1991. *Variation and Evolution of Crassulacean Acid Metabolism in* Se-dum *and* Aeonium *(Crassulaceae)*. Utrecht, Netherlands: Faculteit Biologie R.U.U.

Pires de Lima, A. 1946. *Crassuláceae*. In *Flora Portuguesa*. Imprensa Moderno, ed. 2 of *Manual da Flora Portuguesa*, 1909–1914. Porto: Ferreira Sampaio. 370–375

Powell, K. 1990. "Ron's *S. viride*." *Sedum Society Newsletter* 12: 12–14.

Praeger, R. L. 1921. "Account of the genus *Sedum* as found in cultivation." *Journal of the Royal Horticultural Society* 46.

Priszter, S. 1975. "Über einige pflanzen des Westlichen Tienschan. 1." *Acta Botanica Academiae Scientiarum Hungaricae* 21(3–4): 381–385.

Raymond-Hamet, M. 1929. "Contribution a l'étude phytographique du genre *Sedum*." *Candollea* 4: 1–52.

_____. 1932. *Crassulacearum icones selectae*. 1. Paris.

Rowley, G. 1980. *Name that succulent*. Cheltenham, UK: Stanley Thornes.

Runemark, H., and W. Greuter, 1981. "Notes on Cardaegean plants 1. The *Sedum litoreum* group." *Willdenowia* 11: 13–21.

Rzedowski, G. C. 1974. "Las Crasuláceas del Valle de México." *Cactáceas y Succulentas Mexicanas* 19: 51–63.

Sampaio, G., see Pires de Lima, A.

Sanchez-Mejorada, H. 1975 "Un interesante *Sedum* de Chamela, Jalisco. *Cactáceas y Succulentas Mexicanas* 20: 84–89.

Soeda, T. 1944. "A cytological study on the genus *Sedum*, with remarks on the chromosome numbers of some related plants." *Journal of the Faculty of Science of the Hokkaido Imperial University, Series 5, botany*, 5(3): 221–231.

Stephenson, R. 1989. "Anyone for *Sinocrassula*." *British Cactus and Succulent Journal* 7(3): 82.

_____. 1990. "*S. caespitosum* (Cav.) DC. and *S. andegavense* (DC.) Desv." *Sedum Society Newsletter* 15: 18–21.

Stearn, W. T. 1983. *Botanical Latin*. 3rd. rev. ed. London: David & Charles.

Tomida, M. 1973. "*Sedum ettyuense*." *Journal of Japanese Botany* 48(5): 140–141.

Uhl, C. H. 1952. "Heteroploidy in *Sedum rosea*." *Evolution* 6: 81–86.

_____. 1961. "Some cytotaxonomic problems in the Crassulaceae." *Evolution* 15: 357–377.

_____. 1963. "Chromosomes and phylogeny of the Crassulaceae." *Cactus and Succulent Journal (U.S.)* 35: 80–84.

_____. 1970. "Heteroploidy in *Sedum glaucophyllum*." *Rhodora* 72(792): 460–479.

_____. 1972. "Intraspecific variation in chromosomes of *Sedum* in the southwestern United States." *Rhodora* 74(799): 301–320.

_____. 1976. "Chromosomes, hybrids and ploidy of *Sedum cremnophila* and *Echeveria linguifolia* (Crassulaceae)." *American Journal of Botany* 63(6): 806–20.

_____. 1977. "Cytogeography of *Sedum lanceolatum* and its relatives." *Rhodora* 79: 95–114.

_____. 1978. "Chromosomes of Mexican *Sedum* II. Section *Pachysedum*." *Rhodora* 80(824): 491–512.

_____. 1980. "Chromosomes of Mexican *Sedum* III. Sections *Centripetalia, Fruci-tisedum* and other woody species." *Rhodora* 82(830): 377–402.

_____. 1983. "Chromosomes of Mexican *Sedum* IV. Heteroploidy in *Sedum moran-ense*." *Rhodora* 85(842): 243–252.

_____. 1985. "Chromosomes of Mexican *Sedum* V. Section *Sedum* and subgenus *Sulcus*." *Rhodora* 87(851): 381–423.

_____. 1992. "The San Andreas fault plate boundary and a natural boundary with-in the genera of the American Crassulaceae." *Sedum Society Newsletter* 21: 13–15.

Uhl, C. H., and R. Moran. 1972. "Chromosomes of Crassulaceae from Japan and South Korea." *Cytologia* 37: 59–81.

Webb, D. A. 1964. "*Sedum*." In *Flora Europaea*. Eds. T. G. Tutin et al. Cambridge, UK: Cambridge Press. 356–363.

Werdermann, E. 1939. "*Sedum trollii*." *Notizblatt des Botanischen Gartens und Muse-ums zu Berlin–Dahlem* 14: 349–350.

Woroshilov, W. N., and S. D. Sholthauer. 1984. "Additional seven new taxa of the Fareast flora." *Byull. Moskovskogo obshchestva ispyatelei prirody. Otdel biolog-icheskii* 89(4): 117–119.

Zardini, E. M. 1971. "Las especies del genero *Sedum* (Crassulaceae) espontaneas en la Republica Argentina." *Boletín de la Sociedad Argentina de Botánica* 14(1–2): 95–106.

Zohary, M., C. C Heyn, and D. Heller. 1980. "Crassulaceae." In *Conspectus Florae Orientalis*. Jerusalem: Israel Academy of Sciences and Humanities. 1: 71–73.

Zonneveld, B. J. M. 1986. "Another hybrid *Orostachys—Orostachys* 'Noordwijk'." *British Cactus and Succulent Journal* 4(4): 99.

Index

Italic numbers indicate main treatments; boldface indicates plate and figure numbers.

Adromischus, 59, 61, **Fig. 4.7**
    A. roaneanus, **Fig. 4.6**
Aeonium, 68, **Fig. 4.12**
    A. arboreum, 230
    A. tabuliforme, **Fig. 4.11**
Afrovivella, 82
Aichryson, 68, **Fig. 4.12**
    A. punctatum, **Fig. 4.11**
Aithales rubens, see *Sedum rubens*
Aizoon group, 33, 48, 53, 78, 79, 81, *146*, **Figs. 3.10, 4.16**
Aizopsis, 81, 148
Altamiranoa, *73*, 264
    A. calcicola, see *Sedum calcicola*
    A. parva, see *Sedum parvum*
Amerosedum
    A. debile, see *Sedum debile*
    A. divergens, see *Sedum divergens*
    A. lanceolatum, see *Sedum lanceolatum*
    A. leibergii, see *Sedum leibergii*
    A. stenopetalum, see *Sedum stenopetalum*
Anacampseros, 266
Andinum group, 264
Asterosedum
    A. spurium, see *Sedum spurium*
    A. stellatum, see *Sedum stellatum*

Breitungia oregana, see *Sedum oreganum*
Bryophyllum, 60

CAM, 27
Chamaerhodiola group, 77, *295*, **Fig. 4.16**

Chamaerhodiola
    C. algida, see *Sedum alsium*
    C. fastigiata, see *Sedum fastigiatum*
Chenopodium album, 278
Chetyson pulchellum, see *Sedum pulchellum*
Chiastophyllum, 59, 61, 72, **Fig. 4.7**
    C. oppositifolium, 61, **Fig. 4.6**
Clausenellia ternata, see *Sedum ternatum*
Clementsia group, 77, *297*, **Fig. 4.16**
Clementisa
    C. rhodantha, see *Sedum rhodanthum*
    C. semenovii, see *Sedum semenovii*
Cockerellia
    C. cockerellii, see *Sedum cockerellii*
    C. nivea, see *Sedum niveum*
Corynephyllum viride, see *Sedum corynephyllum*
Cotyledon, 58–61, **Fig. 4.7**
    C. aggregeata, see *Sedum aggregeatum*
    C. anomola, see *Sedum spathulifolium*
    C. boehmeri, see *Sedum boehmeri*
    C. brittoniana, see *Sedum laxum*
    C. decussata, **Fig. 4.6**
    C. erubescens, see *Sedum erubescens*
    C. fimbriata, see *Sedum limuloides*
    C. glandulifera, see *Sedum moranii*
    C. malacophylla, see *Sedum aggregeatum*
    C. malacophylla var. *japonica*, see *Sedum iwarenge*
    C. minuta, see *Sedum spinosum*
    C. mucizonia, see *Sedum mucizonia*
    C. obtusata, see *Sedum obtusatum*
    C. oregana, see *Sedum oreganum*
    C. oregonensis, see *Sedum oregonense*
    C. papillosa, see *Sedum adenotrichum*
    C. pubescense, see *Sedum pilosum*
    C. sikokiana, see *Sedum leveilleanum*

Cotyledonoideae, *60*, 61–63, **Figs. 4.2, 4.3, 4.6, 4.7**
Crassipedes group, 77, *298*, **Fig. 4.16**
Crassula, 56, 59
   C. argentea, 230
   C. dasyphylla, 259
   C. globilifolia, see *Sedum andegavense*
   C. grisea, **Fig. 4.4**
   C. indica, see *Sedum indicum*
   C. milfordae, 188
   C. rubens, see *Sedum rubens*
   C. sarcocaulis, 236
Crassuloideae, 58, *59*, **Figs. 4.2, 4.3**
Cremnophila, 72, **Fig. 4.13**
   C. nutans, see *Sedum cremnophila*
Cremnosedum
   C. 'Crocodile', see *Sedum* 'Crocodile'
   C. 'Little Gem', see *Sedum* 'Little Gem'

Dinacria, 59
Dudleya, 59, 63, 66, **Figs. 4.8, 4.10**
   D. caespitosa, **Fig. 4.9**
   D. edulis, **Fig. 4.9**

Echeveria, 51, 58, 59, 63, 66, **Figs. 4.8, 4.9, 4.10**
   E. affinis, 221, **Fig. 4.9**
   E. carnicolor, **Fig. 4.9**
   E. derenbergii, 229, 238
   E. gormania, see *Sedum laxum*
   E. lilacina, **Fig. 4.9**
   E. linguifolia, 222
   E. obtusata, see *Sedum obtusatum*
   E. oregana, see *Sedum oreganum*
   E. secunda, 216
   E. sedoides, **Fig. 4.9**
   E. watsonii, see *Sedum oregonense*
Echeverioideae, 59, *63*, **Figs. 4.2, 4.3, 4.8**
Etiosedum annuum, see *Sedum annuum*

Gormania, 73
   G. anomala, see *Sedum spathulifolium*
   G. debilis, see *Sedum debile*
   G. burnhami, see *Sedum obtusatum*
   G. eastwoodiae, see *Sedum laxum*
   G. glandulifera, see *Sedum moranii*
   G. hallii, see *Sedum obtusatum*
   G. laxa, see *Sedum laxum*
   G. obtusata, see *Sedum obtusatum*
   G. oregana, see *Sedum oreganum*
   G. spathulifolia, see *Sedum spathulifolium*
   G. watsoni, see *Sedum oregonense*
Graptopetalum, 59, 63, *67*, **Figs. 4.8, 4.9**
   G. craigii, see *Sedum craigii*

[*Graptopetalum*]
   G. filiferum, **Fig. 4.9**
   G. goldii, see *Sedum allantoides*
   G. pachyphyllum, **Fig. 4.9**
   G. paraguayense, **Fig. 4.9**
   G. pentandrum, **Fig. 4.9**
   G. saxifragoides, **Fig. 4.9**
   G. suaveolens, see *Sedum suaveolens*
Graptosedum
   G. 'Francesco Baldi', 231
   G. 'Vera Higgins', 231
Greenovia, 68, **Fig. 4.12**
   G. aurea, **Fig. 4.11**

Hjaltalinia villosa, see *Sedum villosum*
Hobsonia group, 77, *301*, **Fig. 4.16**
Hylotelephium group, 77, *267*, **Fig. 4.16**
Hylotelephium subgenus, 33, 41, 43, 48, 53, 76, 77,
    79, 81, *266*, **Figs. 3.10, 11.1, 11.2**

Jovibarba, 68, **Figs. 4.11, 4.12**
   J. hirta, **Fig. 4.11**

Kalanchoe, 60
   K. porohydrocalyx, **Fig. 4.5**
   K. species CB178, **Fig. 4.5**
Kalanchoideae, 60, **Figs. 4.2, 4.3, 4.5**
Kalosanthes, 59
Kitchingia, 60

Lenophyllum, 63, *72*, 247, **Fig. 4.13**
   L. guttatum, **Fig. 4.14**
   L. maculatum, 186

Meterostachys group, 73, 79, 81, *174*, **Fig. 4.16**
Meterostachys, 73, 81, **Fig. 4.13**
   M. sikokianus, see *Sedum leveilleanum*
Monanthes, 68, **Fig. 4.12**
   M. muralis, 73, 81, **Fig. 4.11**
Mucizonia group, 79, 81, *175*, **Fig. 4.16**
Mucizonia, 59, 61, 73, *81*, **Figs. 4.7, 4.13**
   M. hispida, see *Sedum mucizonia*

Oreosedum
   O. album, see *Sedum album*
   O. brevifolium, see *Sedum brevifolium*
   O. caeruleum, see *Sedum caeruleum*
   O. dasyphyllum, see *Sedum dasyphyllum*
   O. farinosum, see *Sedum farinosum*
   O. gypsicola, see *Sedum gypsicola*
   O. hirsutum, see *Sedum hirsutum*
   O. magellense, see *Sedum magellense*

328   Index

[Oreosedum]
    O. monregalense, see Sedum monregalense
    O. serpentini, see Sedum serpentini
    O. subulatum, see Sedum subulatum
    O. tenellum, see Sedum tenellum
    O. villosum, see Sedum villosum
Orostachys group, 73, 78, 79, 81, **Fig. 4.16**
Orostachys, 41, 53, 73, 81, **Fig. 4.13**
    O. aggregeatus, see Sedum aggregeatum
    O. boehmeri, see Sedum boehmeri
    O. chanetii, see Sedum chanetii
    O. erubescens, see Sedum erubescens
    O. fimbriatus, see Sedum limuloides
    O. furusei, see Sedum furusei
    O. iwarenge, see Sedum iwarenge
    O. thrysiflorus, see Sedum spinosum var. thrysiflorum

Pachyphytum, 59, 63, **Fig. 4.8**
    P. hookeri, 236, **Fig. 4.9**
Pachysedum group, 51, 67, 77, 213, **Fig. 4.16**
Pagella, 59
Petrosedum, 93
Pistorinia, 59, 61, **Fig. 4.7**
Populisedum group, 77, 281
Primuloida group, 77, 299, **Fig. 4.16**
Procrassula pallidiflora, see Sedum rubens
Prometheum group, 78, 79, 82, 183, **Fig. 4.16**
Prometheum, 82
    P. pilosum, see Sedum pilosum
    P. sempervivoides, see Sedum sempervivoides
Pseudorosularia, 82
Pseudosedum group, 78, 79, 184, **Fig. 4.16**
Pseudosedum multicaule, see Sedum multicaule

Rhodiola group, 77, 289, **Fig. 4.16**
Rhodiola subgenus, 33, 43, 48, 53, 55, 77, 79, 82, 288,
       Figs, 3.10, 4.16
Rhodiola, 82
    R. alsia, see Sedum alsium
    R. amabilis, see Sedum amabile
    R. arctica, see Sedum rosea
    R. asiatica, see Sedum crassipes
    R. atropurpurea, see Sedum integrifolium
    R. bupleuroides, see Sedum bupleuroides
    R. crassipes, see Sedum crassipes
    R. dumulosa, see Sedum dumulosum
    R. fastigiata, see Sedum fastigiatum
    R. heterodonta, see Sedum heterodontum
    R. hobsonii, see Sedum hobsonii
    R. himalensis, see Sedum himalense
    R. imbricata, see Sedum imbricatum
    R. integrifolia, see Sedum integrifolium

[Rhodiola]
    R. ishidae, see Sedum ishidae
    R. kirilowii, see Sedum kirilowii
    R. pamiroalaica, see Sedum imbricatum
    R. primuloides, see Sedum primuloides
    R. recticaule, see Sedum imbricatum
    R. rhodantha, see Sedum rhodanthum
    R. rosea, see Sedum rosea
    R. semenovii, see Sedum semenovii
    R. stephanii, see Sedum crassipes
    R. wallichiana, see Sedum crassipes
Rhopalota, 59
Rochea, 59
Rosularia, 70, 73, 79, 82, 186, **Fig. 4.13**
    R. adenotricha, see Sedum adenotrichum
    R. alpestris, **Fig. 4.14**
    R. hirsuta, see Sedum hirsutum
    R. pilosa, see Sedum pilosum
    R. sempervivoides, see Sedum sempervivoides

Sedastrum
    S. glabrum, see Sedum glabrum
    S. palmeri, see Sedum glabrum
    S. turgidum, see Sedum grabrum
    S. rupicaule, see Sedum ebracteatum
Sedella atrata, see Sedum atratum
Sedeveria, 51
    S. hummellii, 228, **Plate 67**
    S. 'Harry Butterfield', 238, **Plate 74**
Sedoideae, 60, 63, 70, **Figs. 4.2, 4.3, 4.13**
Sedum subgenus, 48, 53, 77, 79, 83, **Figs. 3.10, 4.16**
Sedum
    S. acre, 25, 26, 28, 95, 255, **Plate 3**
        'Aureum', 95
        'Cristatum', 95
        'Elegans', 95
        subsp. majus, 95
        'Minus', 95, **Fig. 5.1**
        subsp. neglectum, 95
        var. sopianae, 96
        'Yellow Queen', 96
    S. acutifolium, see S. subulatum
    S. adenotrichum, 186
    S. adolphii, 214, **Fig. 10.1**, **Plate 56**
    S. aetnense, 303
    S. aggregeatum, 177, **Fig. 7.5**
    S. aizoon, 43, 148, **Fig. 6.1**, **Plate 30**
        f. angustifolium, 149
        var. aurantiacum, see S. aizoon 'Euphorbioides'
        'Euphorbioides', 148
        f. latifolium, 149
    S. alamosanum, 245, 254, **Fig. 10.19**

[Sedum]

S. *alberti*, see S. *gracile*

S. *albescens*, see S. *rupestre*

S. *albomarginatum*, 304

S. *alboroseum*, see S. *erythrosticum*

S. *album*, 20, 60, 75, *127*

  'Athoum', 127, **Fig. 5.20**

  var. *balticum*, 127, **Fig. 5.20**

  subsp. *clusianum*, 127, **Fig. 5.20**, **Plate 21**

  'Coral Carpet', 74, 127, **Fig. 5.20**

  'Fårö Form', 128, **Fig. 5.20**

  var. *gypsicola*, see S. *gypsicola*

  'Hillebrandtii', 128, **Fig. 5.20**

  'Ibiza', 128, **Fig. 5.20**

  'Laconicum', 128, **Fig. 5.20**

  var. *micranthum* subvar. *chloroticum*, 127, **Fig. 5.20**, **Plate 1**

  f. *murale*, 128

  'Rubrifolium', 128

  subsp. *teretifolium*, 128, **Fig. 5.20**

  var. *turgidum*, 128, **Fig. 5.20**

S. *alfredi*, see S. *nagasakianum*

S. *algidum*, see S. *alsium*

S. *allantoides*, 28, *233*, **Plate 72**

  'Goldii', 233, **Plate 73**

S. *alpestre*, 96, **Figs. 5.1, 5.2**

S. *alsinefolium*, 137, 303

S. *alsium*, 295, **Fig. 12.2**

S. *altissimum*, see S. *sediforme*

S. *amabile*, 298, **Fig. 12.2**, **Plate 108**

S. *ambiguum*, see S. *indicum*

S. ×*amecamecanum*, 215, **Fig. 10.2**

S. *amplexicaule*, 53, *117*, **Fig. 5.15**

  subsp. *ibericum*, 117, **Figs. 5.15, 5.16**

S. *anacampseros*, 281, **Fig. 11.2**, **Plate 97**

  var. *majus*, 281

S. *andegavense*, 129, **Figs. 5.20, 5.21**

S. *anglicum*, 26, *104*, 256, **Figs. 3.10, 5.7, 5.8, Plate 9**

  f. *arenarium*, 105, **Fig. 5.7**, **Plate 10**

  var. *hibernicum*, 105, **Fig. 5.7**

  subsp. *melanantherum*, 92, *105*, **Fig. 5.7**

  var. *microphyllum*, 105

  var. *minus*, 105

  var. *pyrenaicum*, 105, **Fig. 5.7**, **Plate 9**

S. *angustifolium*, see S. *greggii*

S. *angustum*, 305

S. *annuum*, 96, *97*, **Figs. 5.1, 5.3**

S. *anomalum*, see S. *spathulifolium*

S. *anopetalum*, see S. *ochroleucum*

S. *aoikon*, see S. *confusum*

S. *apoleipon*, 98, **Figs. 5.1, 5.4**

[Sedum]

S. 'Arthur Branch', 275

S. *asiaticum*, see S. *crassipes*

S. *assyriacum*, 303

S. *athoum*, see S. *album* 'Athoum'

S. *atlanticum*, 135

S. *atratum*, 106, **Figs. 5.7, 5.9**

S. *atratum* subsp. *carinthiacum*, 106

S. *atropurpureuum*, see S. *integrifolium*

S. *australe*, 305

S. *azureum*, see S. *caeruleum*

S. *backebergii*, 264

S. *baleensis*, 304

S. *batallae*, 216, **Fig. 10.3**, **Plate 56**

S. *batesii*, 305

S. ×*battandieri*, 192

S. *bellum*, 246, **Plate 82**

S. *berillonanum*, 264

S. *beyrichianum*, see S. *glaucophyllum*

S. *bithynicum*, see S. *pallidum*

S. *boehmeri*, 177, **Fig. 7.4**

  'Keiko', 178, **Plate 40**

S. *boloniense*, see S. *sexangulare*

S. *bonnafousi*, 305

S. *borissovae*, 99, **Fig. 5.1**, **Plate 4**

S. *borschii*, 196, **Fig. 9.1**, **Plate 49**

S. *botteri*, 305

S. 'Bountiful', 176, **Fig. 7.2**

S. *bourgaei*, 234

S. *bouvieri*, 306

S. *brevifolium*, *130*, 135, **Figs. 5.20, 5.21**, **Plate 22**

  var. *induratum*, 130, **Fig. 5.22**

  f. *quinquefarium*, 130

S. *brissemoreti*, 189, **Figs. 8.1, 8.2**

S. 'Bronze Queen', see S. *lydium*

S. *bulbiferum*, 166

S. *bupleuroides*, 290, **Figs. 3.10, 12.1**, **Plate 102**

S. *burrito*, 234, **Plate 74**

S. *caducum*, 246, **Fig. 10.20**

S. *caeruleum*, 44, *131*, **Fig. 5.20**, **Plate 23**

S. *caespitosum*, 53, *107*, **Figs. 5.7, 5.10**

S. *calcicola*, 235

S. *calichroum*, 305

S. *californicum*, see S. *spathulifolium*

S. *callianthum*, 306

S. *campanulatum*, 303

S. *candollei*, 303

S. *caricum*, 303

S. *caroli-henrici*, 303

S. *caucasicum*, 268, **Fig. 11.1**

S. *cauticola*, 282, **Figs. 11.2, 11.5**

  'Bertram Anderson', 282

[*Sedum cauticola*]
    · 'Lidakense', 282, **Figs. 11.2, 11.5, Plate 98**
    'Robustum', 282, **Fig. 11.5**
    'Ruby King', 282, **Fig. 11.5**
  S. cepaea, 132, **Figs. 5.20, 5.23**
    var. *gracilescens*, 132
  S. chanetii, 178, **Figs. 4.14, 7.6**
  S. chapalense, see *S. ebracteatum*
  S. chihuahuense, 305
  S. chloropetalum, 305
  S. chontalense, see *S. versadense*
  S. chrysanthemifolium, 306
  S. churchillianum, 304
  S. clavatum, 217, **Plates 56, 57**
  S. clavifolium, 305
  S. clusianum, see *S. album* subsp. *clusianum*
  S. coeruleum, see *S. caeruleum*
  S. cockerellii, 248
  S. commixtum, 217, **Fig. 10.4**
  S. compactum, 248, *253*, **Plate 83**
  S. confertiflorum, 303
  S. confusum, 219, **Plate 58**
  S. compressum, see *S. palmeri*
  S. cormiferum, 305
  S. corsicum, see *S. dasyphyllum* var. *glanduliferum*
  S. corynephyllum, 220, **Fig. 10.5**
  S. craigii, 221, **Fig. 3.3, Plate 59**
  S. crassipes, 298, **Fig. 12.2**
    'Asiaticum', 299
    var. *stephanii*, 299
  S. crassularia, 304
  S. cremnophila, 72, *221*, **Plate 60**
    × *Graptopetalum paraguayense*, 222, **Fig. 10.7**
  S. crenulatum, 306
  S. creticum, 303
  S. cretinii, 306
  S. 'Crocodile', 222, **Fig. 10.6**
  S. cruciatum, see *S. monregalense*
  S. cupressoides, *257*, 305
  S. cuspidatum, 223, **Fig. 10.8, Plate 56**
  S. cyaneum, 282, **Figs. 11.2, 11.6**
  S. cymatopetalum, 264, 305
  S. cyprium, 303
  S. cyrenaicum, 303
  S. dasyphyllum, 25, *133*, **Fig. 5.20**
    var. *adenocladum* f. *oppositifolium*, 133, **Fig. 5.24**
    'Atlas Mountain Form', see *S. dasyphyllum* subsp. *oblongifolium*
    var. *glanduliferum*, 133, **Fig. 5.24**
    'Lilac Mound', 136, **Figs. 5.20, 5.24, Plate 25**
    'Lloyd Praeger', 134, **Fig. 5.20**
    var. *macrophyllum*, 131, *134*, **Figs. 5.20, 5.24**

[*Sedum dasyphyllum*]
    var. *mesatlanticum*, 135, **Figs. 5.20, 5.24**
    f. *monstrosum*, 135
    subsp. *oblongifolium*, 136, **Figs. 5.20, 5.24, Plate 24**
    'Opaline', 136, **Fig. 5.20, Plate 25**
    var. *rifanum*, 134
    var. *suendermannii*, 136, **Figs. 5.20, 5.24**
  S. debile, 196, 197, **Fig. 9.1**
  S. decumbens, 219, **Plate 58**
  S. delicum, 303
  S. dendroideum, 224, **Fig. 10.9**
  S. diffusum, 248, **Plate 88**
    'Potosinum', 249, **Plate 88**
  S. discolor, 306
  S. divaricatum, see *S. leibergii*
  S. divergens, 197, **Figs. 9.1, 9.2**
    'Giant Form', 198
  S. diversifolium, see *S. greggii*
  S. douglassii, see *S. stenopetalum*
  S. drymarioides, 44, *158*, **Fig. 6.9**
  S. dumulosum, 299, **Fig. 12.2**
  S. dyvrandae, 264
  S. 'E. O. Orpet', see *S.* 'Giant Burro's Tail'
  S. ebracteatum, *249*, 252, **Fig. 10.21, Plate 84**
  S. ekimianum, 303
  S. ellacombianum, 142, *149*, **Fig. 6.1, Plate 31**
  S. epidendrum, 304
  S. erubescens, 179, **Fig. 3.4, Plate 41**
    var. *japonicum*, 179
  S. erythrosticum, 268, 272, **Figs. 11.1, 11.3**
    f. *variegatum*, 271
  S. ettyuense, 279, **Fig. 11.2**
  S. eupatorioides, 305
  S. ewersii, 266, *284*, **Figs. 3.4, 11.2, Plate 99**
    var. *cyclophyllum*, 285, **Fig. 11.2**
    var. *homophyllum*, 282, *285*, **Fig. 11.2, Plate 100**; 'Rose Carpet', 285
    'Nanum', 285
  S. fabaria, see *S. telephium* subsp. *fabaria*
  S. farinosum Lowe, 92, *191*, **Fig. 8.1, Plate 47**
  S. farinosum Rose, see *S. bellum*
  S. fastigiatum, 296, **Fig. 12.2**
  S. flaccidum, 305
  S. flexuosum, see *S. grisebachii*
  S. formosanum, 159, **Fig. 6.10**
  S. forreri, 305
  S. forsterianum, 118, **Fig. 5.17**
    var. *minus*, 119
    f. *purpureum*, 119
    'Welsh Stonecrop', 119, **Fig. 5.15, Plate 18**
  S. fragrans, 137, **Fig. 5.20**

[*Sedum*]

S. frutescens, 53, *235*, **Plate 75**

S. furfuraceum, 236, **Plate 76**

S. furusei, 178, *180*, **Plate 42**

'Noordwijk', 180

S. fusiforme, 191, **Figs. 3.2, 8.1, 8.3**

S. gattefossei, 304

S. 'Giant Burro's Tail', 238

S. glabrum, 249, *250*, **Figs. 3.3, 3.10**

S. glandulosum, see *S. villosum*

S. glaucophyllum, 198, **Fig. 9.1, Plate 50**

S. glaucum, see *S. hispanicum* var. *minus*

S. globuliferum, 305

S. glomerifolium, 304

S. 'Golden Carpet', see *S. kamtschaticum*

S. gracile, 108, **Fig. 5.7, Plate 11**

S. grandipetalum, 250, **Fig. 10.22**

S. 'Green Rose', 240, **Fig. 10.14**

S. greggii, 250, *251*, **Plate 85**

subsp. *angustifolium*, 251

S. griffithsii, see *S. cockerellii*

S. grisebachii, 99, **Fig. 5.1, Plate 5**

S. griseum, 236, Plate 77

'Green Form', 236

S. guadalajaranum, 237, **Fig. 10.13**

subsp. *viridifolium*, 237

S. guatemalense, 230

S. gypsicola, 128, *137*, **Fig. 5.20**

S. haematodes, see *S. atratum*

S. hakonense, 159, **Fig. 6.11, Plate 34**

var. *rupifragum*, see *S. rupifragum*

S. handelli, 306

S. 'Harvest Moon', 209

S. havardii, 305

S. heckneri, see *S. laxum*

S. hemsleyanum, 249, *252*, **Fig. 10.21**

S. hernandezii, 237

S. heterodontum, 41, 288, *291*, **Figs. 12.1, 12.3**

S. hewittii, 303

S. 'Hidakense', 283, **Fig. 11.5**

S. hierapetrae, 303

S. hillebrandtii, see *S. urvillei*

S. himalense, 296, **Fig. 12.2**

S. hintonii, 252, **Plate 86**

S. hirsutum, 138, **Fig. 5.20, Plate 26**

subsp. *baeticum*, 138, **Fig. 5.28**

S. hispanicum, 108, **Figs. 5.7, 5.11**

var. *minus*, 108, **Fig. 5.7, Plate 12**; 'Aureum', 109

'Pewter', see *S. rubens*

var. *polypetalum*, 109

S. 'Hispidulum', see *S. dasyphyllum* var. *mesatlanticum* f. *monstrosum*

[*Sedum*]

S. hispidum, see *S. dasyphyllum* var. *mesatlanticum* f. *monstrosum*

S. hobsonii, 41, *301*, **Figs. 3.3, 12.2, Plate 110**

S. horakii, see *S. grisebachii*

S. hultenii, 224, **Fig. 10.10**

S. humifusum, 253, **Plate 87**

S. humile, 306

S. hybridum L., 142, *150*, **Fig. 6.2**

var. *dentatum*, 151

'Immergrünchen', 151

S. hybridum Urville ex Boissier, 114

S. hyperaizoon, see *S. maximowiczii*

S. idaeum, 304

S. imbricatum, 292, **Fig. 12.1**

S. incertum, see *S. ebracteatum*

S. inconspicuum, 303

S. indicum, 184, **Fig. 7.11**

var. *densirosulatum*, 185, **Figs. 4.14, 7.12**

var. *indicum*, 185

var. *yunnanense*, 186, **Plate 45**

S. insulare, see *S. villosum*

S. integrifolium, 293, **Fig. 12.1**

var. *atropurpureum*, 293, **Fig. 12.1**

var. *procerum*, 294, **Plate 103**

S. involucratum, see *S. spurium* var. *involucratum*

S. ishidae, 294, **Fig. 12.1**

S. iwarenge, 180

'Fuji', 180

'Natsu Fuji', 180

S. jaccardianum, 304

S. jahandeizii, 304

S. jaliscanum, 76, 305

subsp. *angustifolium*, 76

S. japonicum, 160, **Fig. 6.12, Plate 34**

S. jepsonii, see *S. laxum*

S. jujuyensis, 264

S. kagamontanum, see *S. ettyuense*

S. kamtschaticum, 151, **Figs. 3.3, 3.10, 6.1, Plate 32**

var. *ellacombianum*, see *S. ellacombianum*

var. *floriferum*, 151; 'Weihenstephaner Gold', 151

'Golden Carpet', 152

var. *middendorffianum*, see *S. middendorffianum*

'Takahira Dake', 152

f. *variegatum*, 152

S. kirilowii, 294, **Fig. 12.1, Plate 104**

'Aureum', 294

var. *rubrum*, 294

S. kiusianum, see *S. polytrichoides*

S. kostovii, see *S. grisebachii*

[Sedum]

S. *krajinae*, see S. *acre*

S. *kurilense*, see S. *kamtschaticum*

S. *laconicum*, 99, **Fig. 5.1**, **Plate 6**

S. *lagascae*, 303

S. *lampusae*, 303

S. *lanceolatum*, 199, **Figs. 9.1, 9.3**

   subsp. *nesioticum*, 200

S. *lancerottense*, 189, **Figs. 8.1, 8.2, Plate 46**

S. *latifilamentum*, 305

S. *laxum*, 200, **Figs. 9.1, 9.4**

   subsp. *eastwoodiae*, 201

   subsp. *heckneri*, 201, **Figs. 9.1, 9.5**

   subsp. *latifolium*, 201

   subsp. *perplexum*, 201

S. *leibergii*, 195, 196, *202*, **Fig. 9.6.**

S. *lenophylloides*, see S. *calcicola*

S. *leveilleanum*, 174, **Figs. 4.14, 7.1**

S. *liciae*, 306

S. *liebmannianum*, 252, **Plate 88**

S. *limuloides*, 180, **Fig. 7.7**

S. *lineare*, 161

   var. *robustum*, 161

   f. *variegatum*, 162, **Fig. 6.13, Plate 34**

S. *linearifolium*, 306

S. *litorale*, 152, **Figs. 6.1, 6.4**

S. *litoreum*, 93, *100*, **Figs. 5.1, 5.5**

S. 'Little Gem', 222, **Plate 61**

S. *longibracteatum*, 303

S. *longipes*, 254

   subsp. *rosulare*, 254

S. *louisii*, 303

S. *lucidum*, 226, **Plate 56**

   'Obesum', 226, **Plate 62**

S. *lumholtzii*, 305

S. ×*luteolum*, 117

S. ×*luteoviride*, 226, **Figs. 10.10, Plate 63**

S. *lydium*, 139, **Figs. 5.20, 5.29**

   'Aureum', see S. *hispanicum* var. *minus*

   'Bronze Queen', 139

   'Glaucum', see S. *hispanicum* var. *minus*

S. *macdougallii*, 226, **Plate 64**

S. *madrense*, 305

S. *magellense*, 140, **Figs. 5.20, 5.30**

   subsp. *olympicum*, 140, **Figs. 5.20, 5.31**

S. *makinoi*, 162, **Plate 34**

   f. *variegatum*, 162, **Plate 36**

S. *maurum*, 304

S. *maweanaum*, see S. *acre* subsp. *majus*

S. *maximowiczii*, 153, **Figs. 6.1, 6.5**

S. *maximum*, see S. *telephium* subsp. *maximum*

S. *mekongense*, see S. *multicaule*

[Sedum]

S. *melanantherum*, see S. *anglicum* subsp. *melanantherum*

S. *mellitulum*, 245, *254*

S. *mexicanum*, 255

S. *meyeri-johannis*, 304

S. *micranthum*, see S. *album* var. *micranthum*

S. *microstachyum*, 304

S. *middendorffianum*, 154, **Fig. 6.1, Plate 33**

   var. *diffusum*, 154

   var. *sichotense*, see S. *sichotense*

   'Striatum', 154

S. *millspaughii*, 305

S. *mingjinianum*, 305

S. *minimum*, 305

S. *mite*, see S. *sexangulare*

S. *modestum*, 304

S. *monregalense*, 141, **Figs. 5.20, 5.32**

S. *montanum*, 120, **Figs. 5.15, 5.18**

S. *montenegrinum*, see S. *sexangulare*

S. *mooneyi*, 304

S. 'Moonglow', 209

S. *moranense*, 54, 236, 253, *255*, 259, **Plate 88**

   subsp. *grandiflorum*, 256

   × *Villadia batesii*, 256

S. *moranii*, 202, **Fig. 9.1, Plate 51**

S. *morganianum*, 238, **Plate 74**

S. *mucizonia*, 175, **Fig. 4.14, Plate 39**

S. *mucronatis*, see S. *dasyphyllum* 'Lilac Mound'

S. *multicaule*, 184, **Fig. 7.10.**

S. *multiceps*, 92, 192, **Fig. 8.1, Plate 48**

S. *multiflorum*, 257

S. 'Munstead Dark Red', 274

S. *muscoideum*, 257, **Fig. 10.23**

S. *nagasakianum*, 162, **Fig. 6.14, Plate 34**

S. *nanifolium*, 256, *258*, 260, **Plate 89**

S. *napiferum*, 305

S. *navicularum*, 305

S. *neglectum*, see S. *acre*

S. *nepalicum*, 306

S. *nevadense*, 304

S. *nevii*, 198

S. *nicaeense*, see S. *sediforme* var. *brevirostratum*, see S. *sediforme*

S. *niveum*, 204, **Figs. 9.1, 9.7**

S. *novakii*, see S. *urvillei*

S. *nudum*, 189, **Figs. 8.1, 8.2**

S. *nussbaumerianum*, 227, **Fig. 10.1, Plates 56, 65**

S. *nutans*, see S. *cremnophila*

S. *nuttallianum*, 204, **Plate 52**

S. *oaxacanum*, 259, **Plate 90**

S. *obcordatum*, 238, **Plate 78**

S. *oblanceolatum*, 304

[*Sedum*]

S. *obtusatum*, 38, *205*, Figs. 3.2, 9.1, Plate 53

S. *obtusifolium* var. *listoniae*, 111, Fig. 5.7, Plate 13

S. *ochroleucum*, 93, *120*, Figs. 5.5, 5.18

   subsp. *montanum*, see S. *montanum*

S. *onychopetalum*, 163, Fig. 6.15, Plate 34

S. *oppositifolium*, see S. *spurium* 'Album'

S. *orbatum*, 227, Fig. 10.11, Plate 56

S. *oreganum*, *205*, 206, Figs. 3.6, 9.1

   'Procumbens', 206

   subsp. *tenue*, 206

S. *oregonense*, 38, *206*, Figs. 3.2, 9.1, Plate 53

S. *oryzifolium*, 163, Fig. 6.16, Plate 34

   'Tiny Form', 165, Fig. 6.17

S. *oteroi*, 305

S. *ovatisepalum*, 306

S. *oxycoccoides*, 239, Plate 79

S. *oxypetalum*, 239, Plate 80

S. *pachucense*, 249, 252, Fig. 10.21

S. *pachyclados*, 43, 288, *299*, Fig. 12.2

S. *pachyphyllum*, 43, *228*, 231, Fig. 10.12, Plate 66

S. *painteri*, see S. *pachucense*

S. *pallescens*, 305

S. *pallidum*, 108, *111*, Figs. 5.7, 5.12

   var. *bithynicum*, 109, *111*, Plate 14

S. *palmeri*, 239, Plate 81

   subsp. *emarginatum*, 240

   subsp. *rubromarginatum*, 240

S. *pamiroalaicum*, see S. *imbricatum*

S. *parvum*, 259

   subsp. *diminutum*, 260

S. *pedicellatum*, 304

S. *pentastamineum*, 305

S. 'Philip Holbrook', *275*

S. *pilosum*, 183, Plate 43

S. *platyphyllum*, 229, 233, 305

S. *pluricaule*, 285, Fig. 11.2, Plate 101

   var. *ezawe*, 286, Fig. 11.2

   'Sakhalin', see S. *pluricaule* var. *ezawe*

   var. *yezoense*, 283, *286*, Fig. 11.2; 'Rebun', 286

S. *polystriatum*, 303

S. *polytrichoides*, 165, Fig. 6.18, Plate 34

   'Yabeanum', 166, Fig. 6.19

S. *populifolium*, 266, 273, *286*, Figs. 3.4, 11.2, 11.7

S. *porphyreum*, 303

S. *potosinum*, see S. *diffusum* 'Potosinum'

S. *praegerianum*, see S. *hobsonii*

S. *praealtum*, 230, Plate 68

   subsp. *monticola*, 215, *230*

   subsp. *parvifolium*, 230

S. *praesidis*, see S. *litoreum*

S. *primuloides*, 300, Fig. 12.2

S. *proponticum*, see S. *obtusifolium*

[*Sedum*]

S. *pruinatum*, 121, Fig. 5.15, Plate 19

S. *pruinosum*, see S. *spathulifolium*

S. *puberulum*, 248

S. *pubescens*, 304

S. *pulchellum*, 44, *207*, Fig. 9.1, Plate 54

S. *pulvinatum*, 241, Fig. 10.15

S. *purdyi*, see S. *spathulifolium*

S. *purpurascens*, see S. *telephium*

S. *purpureum*, see S. *telephium*

S. *purpusi*, see S. *confusum*

S. *pusillum*, 304

S. *pyramidalis*, see S. *chanetii*

S. *quadrifidum*, 306

S. *quevae*, 242

S. *quinquefarium*, see S. *brevifolium*

S. *radiatum*, 304

S. *ramosissimum*, see S. *limuloides*

S. *recticaule*, see S. *imbricatum*

S. *reflexum*, see S. *rupestre*

S. *reptans*, 260, Plate 91

   subsp. *carinatifolium*, 260

S. *retusum*, 242, Fig. 10.16

S. *rhodanthum*, 43, *297*, Fig. 12.2, Plate 106

S. *rhodocarpum* subsp. *edwardsii*, 261, Fig. 10.24

S. *rivasgodayi*, 304

S. *robertsianum*, 305

S. 'Ron Evans', 229

S. *rosea*, 288, 293, *294*, Fig. 12.1, Plate 105

   f. *arcticum*, 295

S. 'Rosenteppich', 286

S. *rosulatobulbosum*, 53, *166*, Fig. 6.20, Plate 34

S. *rosulatum*, 186

S. *rubens*, 104, 108, *112*

   'Pewter', 112, Plate 15

   var. *praegeri*, 112

S. *rubroglaucum*, see S. *obtusatum* and S. *oregonense*

S. *rubromucrinatum*, 170

S. ×*rubrotinctum*, 25, *230*, Plate 69

   'Aurora', 230, Plate 69

S. *rubrum* (L.) Thellung, see S. *caespitosum*

S. *rubrum* hort., see *Graptosedum* 'Vera Higgins'

S. *rupestre*, 26, *122*, Figs. 5.15, 5.18

   f. *cristatum*, 123, Plate 20

   'Sandy's Silver Crest', 123

   'Sea Gold', 123

   × S. *montanum* × S. *ochroleucum*, 117

S. *rupestre* sensu Praeger and Evans, see S. *forsterianum*

S. *rupicolum*, 304

S. *rupifragum*, 169, Plates 34, 37

S. *ruprechtii*, see S. *telephium* subsp. *ruprechtii*

S. *ruwenzoriense*, 192, Figs. 8.1, 8.4

[*Sedum*]

S. *sacrum*, 306
S. *samium*, see S. *litoreum*
S. *sarmentosum*, *169*, 255, **Plates 34, 38**
S. *sartorianum*, see S. *urvillei*
S. *saxifragoides*, 306
S. *schizolepis*, 304
S. *sediforme*, 53, *123*, **Figs. 3.2, 3.3, 5.15, 5.19**
S. *selskianum*, 155, **Figs. 6.1, 6.6**
S. *semenovii*, 297, **Fig. 12.2, Plate 107**
S. *semiteres*, 305
S. *sempervivoides*, 183, **Plate 44**
S. *senanense*, 160, **Plates 34, 35**
S. *serpentini*, 142, **Fig. 5.20**
S. *sexangulare*, *101*, 255, **Fig. 5.1, Plate 7**
  subsp. *elatum*, 101
  'Weisse Tatra', 101
S. *shastense*, see S. *lanceolatum*
S. *sichotense*, 155, **Figs. 6.1, 6.7**
S. *sieboldii*, 273, *279*, 280, **Fig. 11.2, Plate 96**
  f. *variegatum*, 279, **Fig. 11.4**
S. *sikokianum* (Makino) Hamet, see S. *leveilleanum*
S. *sikokianum* Maximowicz, see S. *kamtschaticum*
S. 'Silvermoon', 209
S. *sinuatum*, 306
S. *smithii*, 306
S. *sordidum*, 271, **Fig. 11.1**
S. *sorgerae*, 304
S. *sparsiflorum*, see S. *nuttallianum*
S. *spathulifolium*, 207, **Fig. 9.1**
  'Aureum', 209
  var. *majus*, 208
  subsp. *pruinosum*, 208, **Plate 55**; 'Cape Blanco',
    25, *208*; 'Carnea', 209; 'William Pascoe', 209
  subsp. *purdyi*, 209, **Fig. 9.8**
  var. *purpureum*, 25, *208*
  subsp. *spathulifolium*, 209
  subsp. *yosemitense*, 208
S. sp. from Hidalgo, 256, **Plate 88**
S. sp. from Lahul, see S. *amabile*
S. sp. Lau 081, 260, **Plate 91**
S. sp. R.B.G.F. 763791, 161, *169*, **Fig. 6.21,
    Plate 34**
S. sp. from Tiscalatengo Gorge, see S. *clavatum*
S. *spectabile*, 272, **Figs. 3.10, 11.1, 11.3, Plate 93**
  'Brilliant', 272
  'Carmen', 272
  'Meteor', 272
  'Rosenteller', 272
  'Septemberglut', 272
  'Snow Queen', 272
  'Stardust', 272
S. *spinosum*, 181, **Fig. 7.8**

[*Sedum spinosum*]
  var. *minutum*, 181
  var. *thrysiflorum*, 181, **Fig. 7.8**
S. 'Spiral Staircase', 257, **Plate 88**
S. *spurium*, 20, *142*, **Fig. 5.20, Plate 27**
  'Album', 142
  'Album Superbum', 142
  'Bronze Carpet', 143
  'Coccineum', 143
  'Dragon's Blood', see S. *spurium* 'Schorbuser
    Blut'
  'Erd Blut', 143
  'Fuldaglut', 143
  'Green Mantle', 142
  var. *involucratum*, 143
  'Purple Carpet', 143
  'Purpurteppich', see S. *spurium* 'Purple Carpet'
  'Roseum', 143
  'Ruby Mantle', 143
  'Salmoneum', 143
  'Schorbuser Blut', 143
  'Tricolor', 143
  var. *variegatum*, see S. *spurium* 'Tricolor'
S. *stahlii*, 231, *243*, **Fig. 10.17**
S. *stefco*, 113, **Fig. 5.7**
S. *stellatum*, 116, **Fig. 5.7, Plate 16**
S. *stelliforme*, 261
S. *stenopetalum*, 196, *210*, **Figs. 9.1, 9.9**
  'Douglassii', 210
S. *stephanii*, see S. *crassipes*
S. *steudelii*, 304
S. *stoloniferum*, 114, **Fig. 5.7, Plate 17**
S. *stribrnyi*, see S. *urvillei*
S. *suaveolens*, 231, **Plate 70**
S. *subcapitatum*, 306
S. *subtile*, 170, **Fig. 6.22, Plate 34**
S. *subulatum*, 143, **Figs. 5.20, 5.33**
S. *surculosum*, 304
S. *takesimense*, 156, **Figs. 6.1, 6.8**
S. *taquetii*, see S. *viridescens*
S. *tatarinowii*, 272, **Fig. 11.1, Plate 94**
  'Sunset Cloud', 273
S. *telephioides*, 273, **Fig. 11.1**
S. *telephium*, 25, *276*
  'Autumn Joy', 25, *276*, **Fig. 11.1, Plate 95**
  'Evening Cloud', 274
  subsp. *fabaria*, 273, **Fig. 11.1**; var. *borderi*, 274,
    Fig. 11.1; 'Roseo-variegatum', 274
  'Herbstfreude', see S. *telephium* 'Autumn Joy'
  'Indian Chief', see S. *telephium* 'Autumn Joy'
  subsp. *maximum*, 275, **Fig. 11.1**; var. *atropur-
    pureum*, 275
  'Munstead Red', 274

[*Sedum telephium*]
'Pink Jewel, 274
'Ruby Glow', 274, **Fig. 11.1**
subsp. *ruprechtii*, 275, **Fig. 11.1**
'Vera Jameson', 274, **Fig. 11.1**
S. tenellum, 144, **Fig. 5.20, Plate 28**
S. tenuifolium, see *S. amplexicaule*
S. teretifolium, see *S. album* subsp. *teretifolium*
S. ternatum, 211, **Figs. 9.1, 9.10**
var. *minus*, 211
S. tetractinum, 171, **Fig. 6.23, Plate 34**
S. tetramerum, 304
S. torryi, see *S. nuttallianum*
S. tortuosum, 305
S. torulosum, 244, **Fig. 10.18**
S. tosaense, 172, **Fig. 6.24, Plate 34**
S. treleasei, 232, **Plate 71**
'Haren', 232, **Plate 71**
S. tricarpum, 172
S. trichromum, 262
S. trifidum, 306
S. tristriatum, 304
S. trollii, 300, **Figs 3.10, 12.2, Plate 109**
S. tschernokolevii, see *S. sexangulare*
S. tsugaruense, 280, **Fig. 11.2**
S. tuberculatum, 305
S. tuberiferum, 53, *101*, **Figs. 5.1, 5.6**
S. tuberosum, 304
S. turgidum, see *S. album* var. *turgidum*
S. tymphaeum, 114, **Figs. 5.7, 5.14**
S. uniflorum, 165
S. ursi, 102, **Fig. 5.1**
S. urvillei, 102, **Fig. 5.1, Plate 8**
S. ussuriense, 306
S. verloti, see *S. ochroleucum*
S. versadense, 263
f. *chontalense*, 263, **Plate 92**
subsp. *villadioides*, 263
S. versicolor, 304
S. verticillatum, *277*, 278, **Fig. 11.1**
var. *nipponicum*, 277, **Fig. 11.1**
S. villosum, 144, **Fig. 5.20, Plate 29**
var. *glabratum*, 145, **Fig. 5.34**
S. vinicolor, 305
S. viride Makino, 271, *277*, **Fig. 11.1**
S. viride Rose, see *S. corynephyllum*
S. viridescens, 278, **Fig. 11.1**
S. viviparum, 278, **Fig. 11.1**
S. wallichianum, see *S. crassipes*
S. watsoni, see *S. oregonense*
S. winkleri, see *S. hirsutum*
S. woodii, see *S. spathulifolium*
S. wrightii, 257, *263*

[*Sedum wrightii*]
subsp. *densiflorum*, 264
subsp. *priscum*, 264
S. yabeanum, see *S. polytrichoides*
S. 'Yatsugashira', 176, **Fig. 7.3**
S. yosemitense, see *S. spathulifolium*
S. zentaro-tashiroi, 170
S. zlatiborense, see *S. acre*
S. zollikoferi, 304
Sempervivoideae, 67, **Figs. 4.2, 4.3, 4.11, 4.12**
Sempervivella, *73*, 82, **Fig. 4.13**
S. alba, **Fig. 4.14**
Sempervivum, 25, *68*, **Fig. 4.12**
S. cuspidatum, see *Sedum spinosum*
S. multiflorum, see *Sedum indicum*
S. tectorum, **Fig. 4.11**
Sieboldii group, 77, *279*, **Fig. 4.16**
Sinocrassula group, 73, 78, 79, *83*, **Fig. 4.16**
Sinocrassula, 58, *73*, *83*
S. ambigua, see *Sedum indicum*
S. densirosulata, see *Sedum indicum*
S. indica, see *Sedum indicum*
Spathulata spuria, see *Sedum spurium*
Stylophyllum, 66, **Fig. 4.10**

Tacitus, 59, *63*, **Fig. 4.8**
T. bellus, 232, **Fig. 4.9**
Telephiastrum, 267
Telephium, 266
Thompsonella, 59, *63*, *66*, **Fig. 4.8**
T. minutiflora, **Fig. 4.9**
Tillaea muscosa, **Fig. 4.4**
Tylecodon, 59, *61*, **Fig. 4.7**
T. grandiflora, **Fig. 4.6**
T. shafferiana, **Fig. 4.6**

Umbilicus, 59, *61*, *72*, **Fig. 4.7**
U. erubescens, see *Sedum erubescens*
U. hispidus, see *Sedum mucizonia*
U. multicaulis, see *Sedum multicaule*
U. papillosus, see *Sedum adenotrichum*
U. platyphyllus, see *Sedum sempervivoides*
U. pubescens, see *Sedum pilosum*
U. ramosissimus, see *Sedum limuloides*
U. rupestris, **Fig. 4.6**
U. spinosus, see *Sedum spinosum*

Vauanthes, 59
Villadia, 63, 66, 70, *73*, 264, **Fig. 4.13**
V. batesii, 215, 256
V. parva, 258, 259
V. ramosissima, **Fig. 4.14**